A Pragmatic Approach to Multicultural Counselling and Psychotherapy Skills Acquisition

Mkpoikanke Otu
University of Johannesburg, Johannesburg, South Africa

ELSEVIER

ACADEMIC PRESS
An imprint of Elsevier

Academic Press is an imprint of Elsevier
125 London Wall, London EC2Y 5AS, United Kingdom
50 Hampshire Street, 5th Floor, Cambridge, MA 02139, United States

ISBN: 978-0-443-33939-4

For information on all Academic Press publications visit our website at
https://www.elsevier.com/books-and-journals

Publisher: Megan Ball
Acquisitions Editor: Simonetta Harrison
Editorial Project Manager: Himanshi Yadav
Production Project Manager: Kiruthigadevi
Cover Designer: Vicky Pearson Esser

Typeset by TNQ Tech

A Pragmatic Approach to Multicultural Counselling and Psychotherapy Skills Acquisition

Contents

Preface

Counselling and psychotherapy are increasingly practised within culturally diverse and socially complex environments. Migration, shifting identities and persistent social inequalities continue to shape how psychological distress is experienced and expressed. In this context, effective practice requires more than technical competence; it demands cultural awareness, ethical sensitivity and the capacity to respond thoughtfully to clients whose lives are shaped by multiple cultural influences. *A Pragmatic Approach to Multicultural Counselling and Psychotherapy Skills Acquisition* is written in response to these realities.

This book is grounded in practice and draws extensively on the author's professional experience of working with clients from diverse cultural, social and national backgrounds. The author has lived and practised in multi-cultural environments and has engaged directly with the challenges of counselling across differing value systems, belief structures, communication styles and social contexts. In addition, the author's international professional engagements have provided sustained exposure to the complexities of multi-cultural practice, shaping the applied orientation of this work.

To strengthen its relevance and depth, the book incorporates contributions from counsellors, psychotherapists and helping professionals with extensive multi-cultural experience. Their practice-based reflections and real-life case examples illustrate how multi-cultural issues emerge in everyday clinical work, offering a grounded account of the practice rather than an idealised theoretical presentation.

The primary aim of this volume is to provide a practical guide to multi-cultural counselling and psychotherapy. It focuses on the development and application of core counselling skills within diverse cultural contexts, including assessment and diagnosis, treatment planning and intervention, culturally informed ethical practice, supervision, research and professional development. Throughout the book, emphasis is placed on translating multi-cultural knowledge into effective clinical action while remaining responsive to the context, power and difference.

This book is written for students and trainees in counselling, psychology, psychotherapy, social work and related helping professions, as well as for practising counsellors and psychotherapists, supervisors, educators, researchers and allied professionals working in culturally diverse settings. It is intended as a resource for academic study, professional training, supervision and continuing professional development.

Generally, this volume seeks to bridge the gap between theory and practice through a clear, experience-informed and ethically grounded approach to multi-cultural counselling and -psychotherapy. It is hoped that this book will support practitioners, trainees, educators, curriculum developers and policymakers in advancing culturally responsive practice and in promoting equity, professionalism and ethical integrity within the field.

Acknowledgements

The completion of this book has been made possible through the support, encouragement and contributions of many individuals and institutions. I am deeply grateful to all who, in diverse ways, have contributed to the development of this work.

My sincere appreciation goes to colleagues, mentors and fellow professionals in counselling and psychotherapy whose scholarship, clinical insight and thoughtful conversations have shaped my understanding of multi-cultural practice. Their commitment to ethical, culturally responsive work has continually informed the perspectives presented in this book.

I extend my gratitude to the students and trainees I have worked with over the years. Their questions, reflections and lived experiences have challenged assumptions, enriched classroom and clinical discussions and influenced the practical orientation of this volume. This book is, in many respects, informed by their engagement and learning journeys.

I am thankful to the practitioners and supervisors who shared their professional experiences and reflections, which helped ground the discussions in real practice contexts. Their openness and dedication to culturally responsive care provided significant insights that strengthened the applied focus of the book.

I also acknowledge the support of the academic and professional institutions that provided an enabling environment for teaching, research and professional development. My appreciation is extended to the editorial and production teams for their guidance and professionalism throughout the publication process.

Finally, I express my heartfelt gratitude to my family and close friends for their patience, understanding and encouragement during the writing of this book. Their support made it possible to sustain the commitment required to complete this work.

To all who contributed, directly or indirectly, I offer my sincere thanks.

CHAPTER 1

Understanding multicultural counselling: Conceptualization and experiential perspectives

List of abbreviations

ACA	American Counseling Association
APA	American Psychological Association
CBT	Cognitive Behavioral Therapy
MSJCC	Multicultural and Social Justice Counseling Competencies
NGO	Non-Governmental Organization
REBT	Rational Emotive Behavior Therapy
UNN	University of Nigeria, Nsukka
WHO	World Health Organization

Introduction

I originate from Akwa Ibom State in Nigeria and uphold the cultural traditions of the Ibibio/Efik people. However, for the past 11 years, my professional counselling practice has been situated in Enugu State, a region with a distinctly different set of cultural beliefs, values, and practices. My entry into the counselling profession began in a community secondary school, where I served as a counselor under the Federal Government's 1-year compulsory National Youth Service Corps (NYSC) program. The initial months of my placement were marked by intense cultural learning and adaptation. I encountered several situations in which behaviors and actions were interpreted in ways that diverged significantly from my prior understanding. Consequently, I engaged in systematic observation of the school and community environments to gain insight into their belief systems and cultural logic. It became apparent that many interpretations of human experiences were grounded in indigenous belief systems and culturally inherited explanatory models, which differed considerably from psychological and modern scientific perspectives. Furthermore, religion emerged as a powerful determinant of decision-making and everyday conduct. Interestingly, even among those who identified with the same Christian faith as myself, doctrinal and interpretive differences were evident, resulting in divergent worldviews and approaches to personal and social challenges.

A Pragmatic Approach to Multicultural Counselling and Psychotherapy Skills Acquisition. https://doi.org/10.1016/B978-0-443-33939-4.00011-2

These cultural and religious disparities initially created barriers in the counselling relationship. My clients and I often perceived and interpreted issues through fundamentally different lenses, which complicated the process of meaning-making and intervention. However, as I developed an attitude of cultural humility, marked by respect, openness, and sensitivity to difference, I began to experience more effective counselling outcomes. Gradually, I learned to elicit clients' cultural understandings of life events and to co-construct meanings that honored their cultural perspectives while integrating psychological insights. Subsequent academic and professional experiences further strengthened this course. During my Master's and Doctoral studies at the University of Nigeria, Nsukka, I encountered more diverse counselling contexts that revealed deeper layers of cultural variation in psychological expression and coping strategies. Through practicum engagements and case supervision, I cultivated an appreciation for the critical role of cultural awareness and contextual understanding in counselling practice. Following the completion of my Master's degree in 2016, I assumed a faculty position as a counselor educator at the university and subsequently established a community-based counselling clinic. This initiative exposed me to clients from varied socio-economic, religious, and ethnic backgrounds, thus providing a broader spectrum of multicultural experiences. The clinic highlights both my cultural strengths and limitations, revealing the urgent need to institutionalize multicultural dimensions of counselling within both professional practice and training. Nsukka, being a university town, provided a naturally multicultural setting, attracting individuals from diverse Nigerian cultural groups such as Yoruba, Hausa, Tiv, and Igala, among others. These engagements deepened my conviction that effective counselling in a pluralistic society necessitates cultural awareness, sensitivity, and humility as core professional competencies.

My postdoctoral engagement in University of Johannesburg, South Africa further reinforced this awareness. Although my primary responsibilities centered on research, interactions with psychologists and counselors from multiple countries, races, and religious backgrounds expanded my appreciation for the complexities of multicultural counselling in contemporary contexts. These experiences provided the intellectual and experiential foundation for completing this book, which had been conceptualized several years earlier. The purpose of this introductory chapter is therefore to establish a conceptual and experiential foundation for understanding multicultural counselling. It seeks to integrate personal, professional, and contextual perspectives to illuminate how culture, identity, and worldview interact to shape counselling practice and theory in diverse sociocultural settings.

Conceptual clarifications

counselling is often misconstrued as merely giving advice, but authoritative definitions and practice emphasize a far deeper, collaborative process. For example, the American Counseling Association defines counselling as "a professional relationship that empowers diverse individuals, families, and groups to accomplish mental health, wellness, education, and career goals" (American Counseling Association, 2014; Family Institute at Northwestern University, 2025). In this view, counselors do more than fix immediate problems. They guide clients toward insight, skill development and self-directed solutions. As one counselling definition notes, effective counselling is a facilitated, collaborative process, not something the counselor simply does to a passive client (Moloney, 2016). It involves "collaborative discussions in a supportive and confidential environment" aimed at helping clients reframe or resolve life problems. This client-centered stance implies a relational (not top-down advisory) approach which the counselor listens actively, reflects understanding, and "earns the right" to suggest change only after trust is built (Empowerment and Change: The Purpose of Counselling, 2025, pp. 222–267). In practice, this means counselling goes beyond quick fixes or advice. Instead, it helps clients explore their situations and feelings openly, often leading to new insights. For instance, a counselling textbook notes that the "counselling process itself offers empowerment": early sessions of active listening and emotional ventilation can energize clients and spark self-generated insights into problems that once seemed insurmountable. In short, counselling is a transformative educational partnership, not a mere Q&A or directive lecture.

Definitions of counselling and psychotherapy

Generally, counselling refers to the act of guiding, helping, directing, assisting, or assuming a leading responsibility toward someone in need of support (Nwachukwu, 2009). From this perspective, counselling is broadly understood as a helping service. The help rendered may address gaps arising from ignorance of information, misconceptions about an issue, lack of relevant knowledge, erroneous beliefs, unhealthy thoughts, unwanted feelings, maladaptive behaviors, or the need to make important decisions. Professionally, counselling is recognized as a structured and intentional process grounded in established ethical and theoretical frameworks. counselling is described as a professional intervention that relies on communication skills and relationship-building to support individuals (Fabris et al., 2009, 2010). This definition emphasizes the structured and skill-based nature of counselling. The American Counseling Association (ACA) defines counselling as a therapeutic relationship that empowers individuals, families, schools, churches, mosques, and groups to achieve goals, wellness, purpose, and meaningful tasks (American Counseling Association, 2014). Similarly, the British Association for counselling and Psychotherapy (BACP) views counselling more broadly alongside psychotherapy, describing “counselling and psychotherapy” as umbrella terms for talking therapies delivered by trained practitioners to help individuals achieve effective change or enhance wellbeing (British Association for Counselling and Psychotherapy., 2018). Supporting this, a leading counselling textbook highlights that the “primary purpose of counselling and psychotherapy” is to help clients address psychological issues and to work through decisions and crises that have psychological components (Nelson, 2014).

counselling is further described as a helping process where a counselor dedicates time, attention, and skills to assist clients in exploring their situations, identities, and solutions within their environmental limitations (Thakor & Murthy, 2004). This definition highlights the supportive and exploratory aspects of counselling. In academic literature, counselling has also been defined as a process in which the counselor provides information and education about a situation while helping the client make informed choices. This involves one-to-one communication aimed at meeting the client’s specific needs (Omolayo & Judith, 2014). counselling is also defined as an educative and transformational service administered by counselors to individuals or groups to enhance adjustment, growth, and development (Otusum Counselling Training Manual, 2015). This perspective foregrounded the transformative capacity of counselling, an emphasis that later evolved into what is now known as Transformative counselling, a model that integrates education, personal growth, and psychological change. Furthermore, counselling is a professional relationship that empowers diverse individuals, families, and groups to achieve mental health, wellness, education, and career goals (Kaplan et al., 2014).

On the other hand, psychotherapy is a broad and diverse field aimed at treating mental illnesses, behavioral issues, and emotional problems through a professional relationship between a therapist and a client (Längle, 2018; Pusch et al., 2012). The primary goal is to alleviate symptoms, modify problematic behaviors, and promote personal growth and development. A fundamental element of any psychotherapeutic intervention is the therapeutic relationship, which is essential for achieving positive clinical outcomes (Flückiger et al., 2024; Torres et al., 2023). This relationship is characterized by collaboration and individualized treatment plans tailored to the client’s needs. Furthermore, psychotherapy involves various types and formats, each grounded in different theoretical frameworks and techniques. The two largest families of psychotherapy are Cognitive Behavioral Therapy (CBT) and Psychodynamic Psychotherapy (Makover, 2023). Other notable forms include psychoanalysis, pioneered by Sigmund Freud, and Meaning Therapy, which integrates various schools of psychotherapy to focus on personal meaning and positive psychology (Wong, 2010).

Psychotherapy is broadly understood as a psychological treatment that helps people recognize and change troubling patterns in how they think, feel, and behave. It usually takes the form of structured conversations with a trained professional, either individually or in groups, and aims to promote healthier ways of coping, relating, and understanding oneself. What unites the various definitions in the field is the idea that psychotherapy is intentional, based on established psychological knowledge, and directed toward changes the client finds meaningful. It focuses specifically on emotional and behavioral wellbeing rather than physical or medical intervention.

counselling and psychotherapy are often described as overlapping practices. In many contemporary discussions, the two are treated as variations of the same kind of talking therapy, centered on a supportive and collaborative relationship. Much of the literature shapes the boundary between them, emphasizing that both involve guided reflection, emotional support, and techniques drawn from similar therapeutic traditions. Historically, though, the terms did not always carry the same meaning, counselling was once associated more with everyday life decisions, developmental tasks, stress, or situational crises, while psychotherapy was linked to deeper personal change and work with more severe psychological difficulties (Linden, 2016). Although this distinction has softened over time, it still surfaces occasionally as counselling is sometimes described as more focused, practical, and time-limited, whereas psychotherapy is portrayed as longer-term, more exploratory, and aimed at uncovering underlying patterns. However, differences sometimes appear in training routes and workplace settings as well. Counselors often work in schools, communities, or organisational environments to support adjustment and decision-making. Psychotherapists are more commonly connected with clinical settings where people seek help for diagnosable mental-health concerns. In many places, becoming a psychotherapist requires additional specialized training, while the title "counselor" can involve a broader range of qualifications depending on local regulation. Despite this, the techniques used in both roles frequently overlap, making the practical distinction increasingly narrow. The way the terms are used can also vary by country. Some regions treat "counselling" and "psychotherapy" as interchangeable, while others maintain more formal differences based on professional identity, regulation, and training pathways. Nonetheless, in everyday practice the work often looks quite similar, and the choice of term tends to be influenced as much by local conventions as by differences in the nature of the therapy itself.

People often think of counselling simply as an advice-giving activity. But advice is only a very small part of what counselling truly is. counselling goes much deeper. It has the power to transform a person's life from the inside out. It involves profound teaching, reflection, exploration, and re-ordering of thoughts not just telling someone what to do or what not to do. When a client goes through proper counselling, where the mysteries, principles, and patterns of life are explained in a meaningful way, that client is likely to experience a renewed mind and an increased ability to make healthy, logical, and productive choices. For this reason, it is important to see counselling as more than advice. counselling is a process of deep teaching, guided discovery, unlearning and relearning, intentional training, and constructive change. It is a developmental journey that reshapes people and their situations for the better.

One important truth I always emphasize is that many people already know what is right and what is wrong, yet they still struggle to do the right thing. Knowledge alone does not automatically produce change. If counselling only tells people what to do, those who lack the internal capacity or motivation will still fall back into unhealthy patterns. Beyond information, people often need skills, clarity, self-awareness, or strength to carry out what is right. Sometimes what they need is a deeper understanding of themselves, their experiences, their emotions, or their environment. Therefore, counselors must guide clients into the kind of contextual and topical knowledge that opens their eyes, expands their understanding, and equips them to pursue positive change.

Another helpful way to understand counselling is to see it as an empowerment process. In society, the word empowerment is frequently used to describe giving people money, resources, or materials, especially youths and women. Governments and organizations use the term when distributing financial support, tools, or short-term skill-acquisition opportunities. Those forms of empowerment have their own value. But if we examine the concept more deeply, true empowerment aligns more closely with the work of counselling. Counselors empower people from within. They help clients transform their minds, strengthen their decision-making abilities, develop new ways of thinking, and display behavior that is productive, responsible, and life-enhancing. To me, that is the highest form of empowerment, greater than financial assistance or sponsorship for vocational skills. This is not to belittle material or skill-based empowerment; they are important. Rather, the point is that the counselor's work is to empower clients in the specific areas where they struggle so that real, consistent, and self-sustaining change can occur.

My years of engagement with clients have taught me that every client needs empowerment in one form or another. Some need social empowerment such as help with relationships, communication, or interpersonal skills. Others need psychological empowerment including clarity, emotional regulation, confidence, or self-esteem. Some require spiritual empowerment, while others may need financial or physical empowerment, depending on the nature of their challenge. As the counselor identifies the client's presenting problem, he or she must also identify the type of empowerment that will help the client overcome that challenge. This is important because people do not change by accident. Real transformation requires a motivating force within the individual. In counselling, empowerment functions as that motivating force. It is the internal and external energy that drives a person to overcome obstacles, make healthy decisions, express positive behaviors, maximize their potential, and pursue their goals. Psychology describes motivation as either intrinsic or extrinsic (Mail et al., 2014). Intrinsic motivation comes from within one's passions, values, strengths, and internal desires. Extrinsic motivation comes from outside support, encouragement, resources, accountability, and external guidance. In counselling, the counselor contributes to both forms of motivation. Through guidance, insight, support, and the right techniques, the counselor helps the client gain internal motivation while also providing external structure and encouragement. This dual empowerment enables clients to step out confidently, take positive action, and become active participants in their own growth and transformation.

Multicultural counselling and psychotherapy

Definition and Scope: Multicultural counselling/psychotherapy recognizes that all helping relationships are culturally inflected. Culture can be broadly defined as "the integrated system of learned behavior patterns, including knowledge, belief, art, law, custom, language, and religion, that a person acquires as a member of society or organisation" (Johnson, 2021). In this view, multicultural counselling refers to any therapeutic relationship in which two or more participants differ in culture, including ethnicity, language, religion, socioeconomic class, gender, sexual orientation, and life history (Aluede & Maliki, 2005). Furthermore, multicultural counselling is a specialized field within counselling that addresses the diverse cultural, racial, and ethnic backgrounds of clients (Hotifah & Hamidah, 2019). It emphasizes the need for counselors to be competent in understanding and integrating cultural differences into the counselling process to provide effective and respectful services. Thus, any counselling relationship in which two or more of the participants differ in cultural backgrounds, values and lifestyle is defined as multicultural counselling (Sue, 2017).

However, multicultural counselling goes beyond a set of techniques or interventions. It represents both a conceptual perspective and a professional practice orientation that recognizes the profound influence of culture on human experience. It acknowledges that both the counselor and the client enter the therapeutic relationship with distinct cultural identities, worldviews, and value systems that shape their perceptions of health, distress, communication, and meaning (Amat et al., 2020). Within this framework, the counselling encounter becomes a space for mutual cultural awareness where the counselor actively seeks to understand the client's sociocultural context while remaining conscious of their own cultural assumptions and biases. This understanding promotes an atmosphere of inclusion, acceptance, and reciprocal respect, which is essential for establishing trust and psychological safety within the therapeutic process. When counselors engage clients through a culturally responsive lens, they validate diverse ways of knowing, being, and healing, thereby enhancing the relevance and effectiveness of counselling interventions. Such sensitivity ensures that clients do not feel marginalized or misunderstood but rather experience therapy as a process that honors their identity and lived experience. Ultimately, multicultural counselling strengthens the therapeutic alliance by fostering empathy, authenticity, and shared understanding between counselor and client.

From an ethical standpoint, multicultural counselling extends beyond cultural sensitivity to encompass a commitment to justice, equity, and professional competence. Ethical standards in counselling emphasize that practitioners must not only acknowledge cultural diversity but also actively address systemic and interpersonal barriers that may disadvantage certain groups (Hailes et al., 2020). Principles such as respect for human dignity, nonmaleficence, beneficence, fidelity, and competence acquire deeper meaning in multicultural contexts, where counselors must interpret and apply them through the lens of clients' cultural realities. This demands continuous self-reflection, lifelong learning, and humility, as cultural competence is not a static achievement but an evolving process of awareness, knowledge, and skill development. In Sub-Saharan Africa, where cultural, linguistic, and religious pluralism are integral to everyday life, these ethical considerations take on additional layers of complexity. Counselors must navigate diverse belief systems, indigenous healing traditions, and communal orientations that may differ markedly from individualistic models of therapy (Eriacho, 2019). Therefore, the integration of multicultural principles within counselling practice is both a moral imperative and a professional necessity. It ensures that counselling remains contextually relevant, ethically grounded, and responsive to the lived realities of clients.

Theoretical Foundations: Multicultural counselling theory emerged in the 1970–80s in response to civil rights and globalization. Historically, mainstream psychotherapies were developed in Western cultures and often assumed universal norms. Multicultural theory challenges this by situating all psychological processes in cultural context. Foundational scholars (e.g., Wrenn, Sue, Pedersen) noted that counselors risk cultural encapsulation if they ignore cultural difference (Pedersen, 2001). Pedersen (2001) argued that broad definitions of culture imply that every counselling encounter involves culture and that a multicultural perspective should guide diagnosis and treatment. Likewise, Sue et al. (1992) and colleagues maintained that culture shapes clients' worldviews and that therapists must adapt their models accordingly. Theoretical models of identity formation describe how both minority and majority individuals develop awareness of race and culture. Emic (culture-specific) versus etic (universal) approaches debate how much therapy should be adapted. In sum, the foundation is that culture is a lens on human experience: schemas, symptom expression, coping styles and healing rituals all vary by culture.

Leading models conceptualize counselor competence as integrating awareness, knowledge, and skills (often called attitudes) to work effectively across cultures. Sue et al. (1992) outlined a tripartite competency model that counselors' beliefs and attitudes must include openness to diversity and critical self-examination; knowledge must include understanding of clients' cultural histories and worldviews; and skills must enable culturally appropriate interventions. For example, a culturally skilled counselor "recognizes their own cultural worldview, assumptions, values, and biases" (Awareness); understands "diverse cultural groups' worldviews, histories, and specific experiences" (Knowledge); and can "implement culturally appropriate interventions and advocacy strategies" (Skills). These competencies have been elaborated into lists of behaviors (e.g., seeking client feedback, using interpreters, understanding power dynamics) (Sue et al., 1992). In 2015 the American Counseling Association expanded this model into the Multicultural and Social Justice Counseling Competencies (MSJCC), explicitly adding a social-justice dimension. The MSJCC emphasizes advocacy that counselors must work to dismantle systemic barriers and promote equity at client, community, and policy levels.

Key characteristics of a multicultural counselor

1. ***Cultural Self-Awareness***: They actively reflect on their own cultural background, values, biases, and assumptions. They understand how their personal worldview shapes their perceptions of clients and remain alert to potential blind spots.
2. ***Respect for Difference***: They approach client diversity with genuine curiosity and openness. Rather than assuming sameness, they honor each person's unique cultural identity, traditions, and lived experience.
3. ***Knowledge of Cultural Contexts***: They are informed about the social, historical, and cultural factors that influence clients' wellbeing such as family structures, community norms, migration experiences, religion, discrimination, or socioeconomic challenges.
4. ***Skills in Culturally Responsive Practice***: They adapt their methods and communication style to fit the client's cultural context. This might involve adjusting language, pacing, goal-setting, or preferred ways of expressing emotion.
5. ***Awareness of Power and Privilege***: They recognize the power dynamics inherent in the counselling relationship and understand how societal inequalities can shape a client's experience. They work to create a space where the client feels seen, safe, and respected.
6. ***Ability to Build Culturally Sensitive Rapport***: They know how to form trusting relationships across cultural lines by listening deeply, validating clients' worldviews, and showing humility, especially when they are unfamiliar with the client's background.
7. ***Advocacy Mindset***: They acknowledge the impact of systemic barriers (such as discrimination, marginalization, or lack of access to resources) and, when appropriate, support clients in navigating or challenging these barriers.
8. ***Flexibility and Openness to Learning***: They understand that cultural competence is not a static achievement. They remain committed to lifelong learning, regularly seeking out new knowledge, feedback, and training to better serve their clients.

9. ***Ethical Integrity***: They practice ethically by recognizing when cultural issues fall outside their expertise and by seeking supervision, consultation, or referral when needed.
10. ***Personal Humility***: They do not position themselves as the ultimate authority on culture. Instead, they allow the client to guide them in understanding cultural meanings and practices.
11. ***Non-Discrimination and Cultural Acceptance***: They do not reject, avoid, or withdraw from clients because of cultural differences. Instead, they embrace these differences as part of the therapeutic process and make every effort to create a safe, inclusive environment for all clients.

Components of multicultural counselling and psychotherapy

Cultural self-awareness

A fundamental component of multicultural work is the counselor's ability to examine their own cultural identity, values, and social position. This includes acknowledging personal biases, stereotypes, and learned assumptions that may unintentionally shape the therapeutic process. Self-awareness helps the counselor recognize when their own worldview differs from the client's and allows them to approach the relationship with humility. Rather than assuming neutrality, the counselor actively reflects on how their background influences the questions they ask, the interpretations they make, and the interventions they consider appropriate.

Understanding the client's cultural worldview

Multicultural therapy emphasizes understanding how clients interpret their experiences through the lens of their cultural upbringing. This involves exploring the client's beliefs, traditions, roles, family structures, spiritual practices, and meanings attached to mental health or distress. It also includes awareness of how culture shapes communication styles. For example, whether emotions are expressed openly or quietly, or whether help-seeking carries stigma. By recognizing these cultural frameworks, counselors can tailor their support in ways that feel respectful and relevant to the client.

Culturally sensitive communication

Effective communication requires awareness of both verbal and nonverbal cultural norms. Counselors may need to adjust how they speak, listen, question, or give feedback. In some cultures, direct eye contact signals respect, while in others it may feel confrontational. Some clients may prefer storytelling, metaphors, or indirect communication, while others value directness. The counselor's sensitivity to these differences can greatly influence the client's comfort, trust, and willingness to share freely.

Adaptation of therapeutic approaches

Multicultural counselling avoids imposing a single therapeutic model on all clients. Instead, counselors adapt techniques and goals to reflect the client's cultural expectations and values. For instance, a highly individualistic approach may not resonate with someone who defines wellbeing through family harmony or community belonging. Similarly, exploring childhood experiences may not be culturally appropriate for clients who emphasize practical solutions over historical reflection. Adaptation ensures therapy remains meaningful and culturally congruent.

Addressing power, privilege, and oppression

Many clients have experiences shaped by social inequalities such as racism, classism, sexism, homophobia, or migration-related stress. Multicultural counselling acknowledges that mental health cannot be separated from these broader contexts. Counselors explore how systemic barriers and discrimination affect clients' self-esteem, safety, identity, and opportunities. This component also involves being aware of the inherent power imbalance between therapist and client and working to create a more collaborative and equal therapeutic relationship.

Incorporation of cultural strengths and resources

Rather than viewing cultural differences as barriers, multicultural counselling recognizes them as sources of strength. This may include valuing a client's cultural traditions, family ties, spiritual practices, community networks, or culturally specific coping mechanisms. Incorporating these strengths reinforces the client's identity and empowers them to draw on their cultural heritage as part of the healing process. It also signals respect for the client's background.

Collaborative goal setting

In multicultural practice, therapeutic goals are developed jointly rather than imposed by the counselor. What counts as "progress" can vary across cultures. For some clients, progress may mean emotional expression; for others, maintaining emotional restraint may reflect strength. By involving clients in goal-setting, counselors ensure that therapy respects the client's own values, priorities, and definitions of wellbeing.

Advocacy and systemic awareness

Multicultural counselling extends beyond the therapy room when necessary. Many client challenges stem from external causes such as poverty, discrimination, or limited access to services. In these cases, counselors may support clients in navigating systems, finding resources, or understanding their rights. Advocacy does not mean taking over the client's voice but helping them overcome systemic obstacles that hinder their progress.

Use of culturally appropriate assessment

Psychological assessments and diagnostic tools are often developed within specific cultural contexts and may not apply universally. A behavior seen as problematic in one culture may be perfectly normal in another. Multicultural counselors therefore apply diagnostic impressions cautiously and seek culturally informed interpretations. They ask contextual questions, consult cultural knowledge, and avoid labeling behavior without understanding its cultural meaning.

Building a culturally safe relationship

A culturally safe relationship is one where the client feels seen, respected, and free from judgment. It involves creating an atmosphere where the client can express cultural identity without fear of misunderstanding or prejudice. Safety is enhanced when the counselor shows genuine interest, avoids assumptions, and allows the client to guide cultural discussions. Trust grows when clients feel they do not need to hide or minimize their cultural selves.

Ongoing learning and supervision

Multicultural competence is a continuing journey rather than a fixed achievement. Counselors engage in lifelong learning through training, self-reflection, supervision, and dialog with diverse communities. They remain open to feedback from clients and colleagues, recognizing that mistakes can be learning opportunities. This commitment ensures that their practice evolves alongside the diverse populations they serve.

Reflection on practising as a counselor and counselor educator in a multicultural setting

1. **Practise Cultural Humility**: Cultural humility involves recognizing that you cannot fully understand another person's cultural experience and approaching each interaction with openness and respect. In my experience, I found that being curious and open

allowed clients and students to share their perspectives more freely. By asking questions and listening without judgment, I could learn from them and create a relationship based on trust and mutual respect.

2. **Engage in Continuous Self-Reflection**: Self-reflection means regularly examining your own values, beliefs, and biases to ensure they do not negatively influence your work. I noticed that reflecting on my assumptions helped me remain neutral and responsive. By being aware of how my worldview shaped my perceptions, I was able to avoid projecting my own beliefs onto clients or students, which strengthened the therapeutic and educational relationship.
3. **Use Culturally Sensitive Communication**: Culturally sensitive communication involves adjusting your language, tone, pace, and nonverbal cues to align with the cultural norms of those you are working with. I observed that clients differed in how they expressed emotions—some preferred direct conversation, while others were more reserved. Adjusting my communication style to match these preferences improved understanding and engagement.
4. **Validate the Client's or Student's Cultural Identity**: Validation means acknowledging and respecting the cultural beliefs, values, and traditions of clients or students. I found that when I explicitly recognised a client's or student's cultural background, they felt more accepted and understood. This encouraged them to share openly and participate fully in both counselling sessions and classroom discussions.
5. **Adapt Strategies and Methods**: Adaptation involves modifying counselling or teaching techniques to fit the cultural context, ensuring that interventions are relevant and meaningful.
   I noticed that some clients responded well to structured exercises, while others preferred reflective discussion or storytelling. Similarly, using culturally relevant examples in teaching helped students engage more deeply with the material.
6. **Foster an Inclusive, Non-Judgmental Environment**
   Creating an inclusive environment means ensuring that individuals feel safe to express themselves without fear of judgment or exclusion. I observed that clients and students were more willing to engage when they felt accepted, regardless of differences in language, dress, or worldview. This openness facilitated deeper learning and personal growth.
7. **Avoid Stereotyping and Over-Generalization**: Avoiding stereotypes means seeing each person as a unique individual rather than assuming they fit a cultural norm. I realised that by focusing on individual narratives rather than generalisations, I could tailor my approach effectively. This helped build trust and strengthened my relationships with both clients and students.
8. **Recognize the Role of Family and Community**: Family and community often shape clients' decisions, coping strategies, and support networks. I noticed that involving

these systems, when appropriate, improved engagement and outcomes. Recognizing the influence of social structures helped me provide more culturally responsive guidance.

9. **Uphold Ethical Sensitivity Across Cultures**: Ethical sensitivity involves adapting professional standards to respect cultural variations in confidentiality, boundaries, and autonomy. I became aware that clients' understanding of ethical norms could differ from my own. Adjusting my approach while maintaining professional integrity ensured that individuals felt safe and respected.
10. **Promote Equity and Challenge Discrimination**: Equity requires actively addressing bias and creating fair, inclusive spaces for all participants. I observed that when I addressed discriminatory attitudes and encouraged respectful dialog, clients and students felt more included and valued. This enhanced engagement and participation.
11. **Do Not Reject Clients Because of Cultural Differences**: Counselors and educators must provide support to all individuals regardless of cultural background and seek guidance when unsure. I consciously ensured that I never withdrew from clients due to cultural differences. When challenges arose that exceeded my expertise, I sought supervision rather than avoidance, which reinforced trust and allowed clients to access meaningful support.

Research background

Over 70% of adults in the United States consider religion an important part of their lives, and the majority of clients express a desire to have the opportunity to discuss their religious or spiritual beliefs during therapy sessions (Abrams, 2023; Zara Abrams, 2023). However, surveys indicate that as many as 80% of practicing counselors and psychotherapists report having received minimal or no formal training in addressing spiritual and religious issues within the therapeutic context (Vieten et al., 2016). Multicultural counselling recognizes that a person's cultural identity, including ethnicity, race, language, religion and socioeconomic background, profoundly shapes their mental health and worldview. It is "about appreciating that individuals are not all the same" and ensuring that their cultural background is an essential part of assessment and treatment (Bouvé Communications, 2023). In today's increasingly diverse societies, counselors need to take a holistic approach to understand and address clients' needs. However, it is important to emphasize that the counselor's goal is not to alter clients' cultural beliefs, but rather to help them draw upon their existing cultural resources as sources of strength and resilience during difficult times.

In Nigeria, a nation of over 350 ethnic groups multicultural issues are paramount. Clients span languages (e.g., English, Hausa, Yoruba, Igbo, pidgin) and religions (Islam, Christianity, traditional) and rural-urban divides. Cultural norms (e.g., collectivism, respect for elders, community-oriented problem-solving) differ sharply from Western individualism (Mathew & Azuji, 2025). For instance, decision-making often involves extended family or village elders, and psychological distress may be expressed somatically or spiritually rather than as "talk therapy" complaints. Deeply held beliefs in ancestors or spirits mean that many Nigerians first consult traditional healers for mental distress (Adekunle, 2011). Indeed, an estimated 80% of Nigerians use indigenous healers for health concerns (Ayeni, 2024; Salako et al., 2023). Yoruba Babalawo (Ifa priests) and herbalists, for example, play roles akin to counselors: they create a climate of trust and empathy, then diagnose and address life problems ranging from marital strife to infertility (Adekunle, 2011). Such healers see clients' issues as often rooted in broken taboos, ancestral displeasure, or the influence of gods; their "techniques" include divination, prayers, sacrifices and community rituals. In this context, Western-style talk therapy is often unfamiliar; even those who see a psychologist may expect some integration of prayer or spiritual meaning. However, many counselors and psychologists receive limited training in integrating spirituality and religion into therapy, even though these aspects can serve as powerful sources of resilience and support during difficult periods (Abrams, 2023). This suggests that, rather than criticizing or neglecting the spiritual dimensions of life in therapy or counselling, practitioners should seek to understand and thoughtfully integrate authentic forms of spirituality and religious practice that can enhance the healing process. When genuine spiritual and religious values are not properly identified and embraced by both counselor and client, there is a risk of misapplying or diminishing their true potential. Therefore, counselors and clients must develop a shared cultural understanding that supports the inclusion of practices beneficial to the counselling or therapeutic process. In essence, multicultural counselling entails drawing upon and harmonizing the cultural values, beliefs, and practices of both the counselor and the client to foster effective and culturally meaningful therapeutic outcomes.

Studies in Nigeria reflect these realities. Counselors report that clients' culture strongly shapes help-seeking and treatment acceptance (Anjorin & Hassan Wada, 2022). For example, it is found that traditional belief systems and religion present unique challenges, as many clients seek indigenous or religious remedies before or alongside psychological services (Adekunle, 2011; Salako et al., 2023). Nigerian counselors must therefore blend approaches. This may mean inviting family participation, using metaphors and stories from local folklore, or framing therapy goals in terms of communal values. It also means respecting indigenous therapies. A Nigerian-positive psychotherapy called Meseron Therapy exemplifies this synthesis based on a Urhobo word meaning "I refuse," it teaches clients to vocally reject negative thoughts and affirm positive ones (Awaritefe & Ofovwe, 2007; Bushura Afolabi & Osagiator Joy, 2014; Nwaka & Awaritefe, 2018). Empirical reviews emphasize that African clients benefit when therapy incorporates spirituality, rituals, and community practices (Shaka et al., 2025).

The counselor must therefore remain culturally humble, sensitive, and collaborative in pursuing this goal. In view of the background, the following research questions and objectives guided the research in this chapter.

Research objectives

1. To explore how practising counselors, psychologists, and psychotherapy professionals conceptualize multicultural counselling in their professional contexts.
2. To examine the experiences and perceptions of counselors regarding the challenges and opportunities in delivering multicultural counselling services.
3. To identify strategies and practices that professionals consider effective in promoting culturally responsive counselling and psychotherapy.
4. To gather recommendations from professionals on improving multicultural counselling training and practice in the local context (e.g., Nigeria).

Research questions

1. How do practising counselors and psychotherapists conceptualize multicultural counselling within their professional contexts?
2. What are the lived experiences of counselors in delivering multicultural counselling services, and what challenges and opportunities do they encounter?
3. What strategies and practices do professionals perceive as effective in promoting culturally responsive counselling and psychotherapy?
4. What recommendations do counselors have for improving multicultural counselling training, supervision, and practice, particularly within the local context?

Methodology

Approach

This study adopts a qualitative research approach, which is particularly suited for exploring the subjective experiences, perceptions, and conceptualizations of counselors, psychologists, and psychotherapists engaged in multicultural counselling. Qualitative methods allow for a deep, nuanced exploration of participants' lived experiences, enabling the researcher to capture complex, context-dependent phenomena (Lewis, 2015). This approach provides rich, detailed data that can uncover underlying themes, practices, and challenges faced by professionals in multicultural contexts, facilitating a deeper understanding of how these practitioners navigate and address the unique demands of working with diverse populations (Willig & Rogers, 2017). By focusing on individual narratives, qualitative research can offer insights that are not easily captured through quantitative methods, making it an ideal choice for investigating the intricacies of multicultural counselling practice (Braun & Clarke, 2006).

Research paradigm

This research is situated within the constructivist paradigm, which posits that knowledge is co-constructed through human interaction and interpretation (Schwandt, 2023). The constructivist approach emphasizes that reality is subjective, fluid, and context-dependent, shaped by individual experiences, social contexts, and cultural frameworks (Klymenko, 2014). In this study, the researcher aims to explore how counselors and psychotherapists make sense of their multicultural experiences through their unique perspectives and personal narratives. This paradigm allows the study to capture the complexity of multicultural counselling practices and highlights how professional identity and cultural context influence the way practitioners interpret and navigate their work. The constructivist approach supports the view that understanding is not objective but is constructed through ongoing dialog and engagement with the world around us.

Ontology

The ontological stance of this study is relativist, positing that the reality of multicultural counselling is not fixed or universal but is instead constructed through the lived experiences and interpretations of the participants (Crotty, 1998). This approach recognizes that cultural context, individual experiences, and professional training significantly influence how counselors and psychotherapists perceive and engage with multicultural issues. As such, the study acknowledges that different practitioners may have distinct realities and ways of conceptualizing multicultural counselling, shaped by their unique backgrounds and contexts (Gergen, 2015). Consequently, the research does not aim to define a singular, objective reality, but rather seeks to explore a range of context-dependent understandings, reflecting the diversity of perspectives within the field (Charmaz, 2014).

Epistemology

The epistemological stance of this research is interpretivist, which is focused on understanding how individuals construct meaning within their social world (Schwandt, 2014). This approach emphasizes that knowledge is not objective or universal, but is socially constructed and context-dependent (Gergen, 2015). The goal of this study is to gain deeper insight into the subjective interpretations and experiences of counselors and psychotherapists as they navigate the challenges and practices of multicultural counselling. By focusing on participants' verbal narratives, behaviors, and reflections, the study assumes that meaning is made through human interaction, and that researchers can access these constructions of reality through in-depth engagement with participants (Charmaz, 2014). This epistemological position highlights the importance of understanding individual perspectives and the contextual factors that shape the way practitioners interpret their work.

Axiology

The axiological position of this research acknowledges that the researcher's values, beliefs, and cultural background inevitably influence the research process (Guba & Lincoln, 1994). In the context of a study focused on multicultural counselling, the researcher is mindful of the potential biases that may arise from their own cultural standpoint. This awareness helps ensure that the researcher maintains an approach characterized by fairness, transparency, and respect for the diverse experiences and perspectives of the participants (Finlay, 2002). The researcher's goal is to minimize personal bias while ensuring that the findings genuinely reflect the participants' perspectives, and contribute to advancing multicultural counselling practices within the local context. The researcher remains committed to upholding ethical standards throughout the research, ensuring that the study not only provides valuable insights into the field but also fosters a more inclusive and culturally responsive practice.

Research design

This research follows a qualitative exploratory design, which is well-suited for examining the lived experiences and conceptualizations of counselors and psychotherapists in the context of multicultural counselling. The aim is to delve deeply into how professionals approach multicultural issues, the challenges they encounter, and the strategies they employ to navigate these challenges. The qualitative design is chosen for its flexibility in data collection, allowing for the exploration of complex, context-specific phenomena in rich detail (Creswell & Poth, 2018). This approach provides the necessary depth to understand the subjective experiences and nuanced perspectives of practitioners, which would be difficult to capture through quantitative methods. It is particularly beneficial for gaining insights into how multicultural counselling is conceptualized in practice and how cultural factors influence therapeutic interventions (Braun & Clarke, 2013).

Sampling techniques

This study used purposeful sampling to select participants who had direct experience in multicultural counselling. Purposeful sampling was chosen as it allowed the researcher to select individuals who could provide rich, detailed, and contextually relevant data based on their specific experiences (Palinkas et al., 2015). The sample focused on practising counselors, psychologists, and psychotherapists who were actively involved in multicultural settings.

Participants were selected based on the following inclusion criteria.

- Professional Experience: Participants had at least 2 years of practice in multicultural counselling or psychotherapy. This criterion ensured that participants had sufficient experience to provide meaningful insights into the challenges and practices associated with multicultural counselling.
- Cultural Expertise: Participants had experience working with clients from diverse cultural backgrounds, including but not limited to ethnic, linguistic, or religious diversity. This criterion was crucial for ensuring that participants were directly engaged in the type of counselling practices relevant to the study's focus.
- Active Practitioners: Only those who were actively engaged in counselling or psychotherapy practice were included. This ensured that the participants' perspectives were based on their ongoing professional experiences rather than outdated or theoretical knowledge.

The sample size was determined by data saturation, which was typically reached when no new significant insights emerged from further data collection (Guest et al., 2020). For this study, it was anticipated that 15 to 20 participants would be sufficient to achieve saturation and capture a variety of perspectives and experiences within the field of multicultural counselling.

Data collection

Data collection for this study was conducted using a combination of semi-structured interviews and focus groups, which together allowed for a comprehensive exploration of the experiences, perceptions, and strategies employed by counselors and psychotherapists in multicultural counselling settings.

The semi-structured interviews were the primary method for data collection. These interviews enabled the researcher to engage deeply with participants, encouraging them to share their personal and professional experiences in the field of multicultural counselling. The interview guide was developed based on the study's research questions and included open-ended prompts designed to elicit detailed responses. This approach provided the flexibility to follow up on interesting points or issues that emerged during the conversation. Participants were encouraged to discuss a range of topics, including the challenges they faced in multicultural settings, the strategies they employed to address these challenges, and their recommendations for improving multicultural counselling practices. Each interview lasted between 60 and 90 min, allowing ample time for in-depth discussion. All interviews were audio-recorded with the participants' consent, ensuring that the data could be transcribed accurately for later analysis.

In addition to the semi-structured interviews, focus groups were conducted as a supplementary data collection method. The use of focus groups allowed for the capture of group dynamics and collective perspectives on multicultural counselling. These sessions provided an opportunity for participants to share and discuss their experiences in a more interactive setting, encouraging peer-to-peer dialog that could reveal shared challenges and common strategies in dealing with multicultural issues. The focus groups were structured around the same key themes as the interviews, but with a greater emphasis on collaborative problem-solving and discussion. The researcher facilitated the sessions, ensuring that all participants had the opportunity to contribute their insights. The focus group sessions lasted between 90 min and 2 h, providing sufficient time for participants to engage in rich, meaningful discussions. Like the interviews, the focus groups were audio-recorded with participants' consent, ensuring the accurate capture of their contributions.

To ensure the data was accurately captured and preserved, all interviews and focus group sessions were audio-recorded. With the participants' consent, these recordings were transcribed verbatim by a professional transcription service. The transcription process ensured that every detail of the participants' responses was captured for thorough analysis. Transcriptions provided an exact record of the verbal data, enabling the researcher to analyze the content effectively and with a high degree of accuracy. The verbatim transcripts also allowed the researcher to examine the subtleties of participants' language, tone, and emphasis, which contributed to a deeper understanding of their experiences and perspectives.

Through this multi-method approach, the study gathered rich, diverse data that provided a comprehensive view of the experiences and practices of counselors and psychotherapists working in multicultural counselling contexts. The combination of individual interviews and group discussions ensured that both individual experiences and shared perspectives were captured, leading to a more holistic understanding of the challenges, strategies, and recommendations within the field.

Data analysis

The data were analyzed using thematic analysis, a widely-used qualitative data analysis method that allows for the identification and interpretation of patterns or themes within qualitative data (Braun & Clarke, 2006). The analysis process involved the following steps.

1. Familiarization with the Data: The researcher listened to the audio recordings and read through the transcripts to gain a thorough understanding of the content. During this

stage, the researcher made initial notes and observations, identifying potential themes and areas of interest within the data.

2. Coding: The researcher used open coding to assign initial labels to segments of data that were relevant to the research questions. This process was inductive, meaning that codes emerged naturally from the data without predefined categories. The researcher aimed to capture meaningful patterns or recurring ideas that could inform the research questions.
3. Theme Development: The codes that were related to one another were grouped together into themes. These themes represented key concepts and patterns identified in the data, such as the challenges faced by counselors, strategies they employed, and their perceptions of multicultural counselling. Themes were carefully selected to reflect the core issues discussed by participants.
4. Review and Refinement of Themes: The identified themes were reviewed and refined to ensure they accurately represented the data. This stage involved revisiting the original data to confirm that the themes aligned with the participants' actual experiences and perspectives. The researcher checked for consistency and ensured that the themes were distinct and well-defined.
5. Final Interpretation: In the final stage of analysis, the researcher interpreted the themes in relation to the research questions. The researcher made connections between the themes and drew conclusions about how counselors and psychotherapists conceptualized and practiced multicultural counselling. The interpretation aimed to highlight key insights regarding the ways in which multicultural counselling is navigated by professionals, as well as the challenges and strategies they encounter in their work.

Ethical considerations

Ethical considerations were central to ensuring that the research was conducted responsibly, with respect for the participants and their rights. The following ethical principles guided the study.

Informed consent: Explanation of the study

All participants were provided with an informed consent form before participation. The form clearly outlined the purpose of the study, the research process, the potential risks, and the expected benefits of participating. It explained the voluntary nature of participation, meaning that participants could choose not to participate or withdraw at any time without penalty.

Participant Rights: Participants were informed that their participation was entirely voluntary, and they had the right to withdraw at any point in the study without any consequences. Informed consent was sought for both the interview and the focus group sessions.

Confidentiality and Anonymity: Participants were assured that all information shared would be kept confidential. Pseudonyms were used in all reports, transcripts, and analyses to ensure that participants could not be identified. The recordings were stored securely and were accessible only to the researcher and authorized personnel.

Confidentiality and anonymity

Data Protection: All data, including audio recordings and transcripts, were stored securely and handled with the utmost confidentiality. Data were stored in password-protected files, and any paper records were locked in a secure location.

Pseudonyms: To ensure anonymity, participants were assigned pseudonyms in all written records. Any identifying information such as names, job titles, or specific locations was removed from the analysis and reports.

Confidentiality in Reporting: In reporting the findings, no identifying information about participants or specific details that could trace responses back to individuals was included. The findings focused on the thematic analysis of responses rather than individual identities.

Voluntary participation and right to withdraw

Voluntary Participation: Participation in the study was completely voluntary. Participants were informed that they were under no obligation to take part, and their decision to participate did not affect their professional standing or relationships with colleagues, institutions, or organizations.

Right to Withdraw: Participants were reminded at the start of the study that they had the right to withdraw at any point without any negative consequences. If they chose to withdraw, their data was not used, and they were not further contacted.

Non-coercion

Participants were invited to join the study without any form of coercion. The researcher ensured that all participants fully understood the voluntary nature of the study and that no undue pressure was exerted on them to participate.

Respect for cultural sensitivity

Given the multicultural nature of the study, it was critical to respect the diverse cultural backgrounds of the participants. The researcher ensured that.

- Cultural differences were respected, and assumptions based on stereotypes were avoided.
- Culturally appropriate language and communication styles were used during interviews and focus groups.
- Participants' emotional responses during discussions about their challenges were carefully monitored, ensuring that they felt respected and heard.

Transparency and accountability

Researcher Transparency: The researcher-maintained transparency throughout the research process, informing participants about the study's aims, procedures, and the use of their data.

Research Integrity: The researcher conducted the study with full integrity, adhering to ethical guidelines for qualitative research. This included presenting findings truthfully, acknowledging potential biases, and ensuring that the study's results were not manipulated.

Risk of harm

Psychological Impact: Given the nature of the study, discussing personal experiences and challenges in multicultural counselling could evoke strong emotional responses. Participants were informed of this possibility in advance, and efforts were made to create a safe, supportive space for them to share their thoughts and feelings.

Support for Participants: If a participant experienced distress or discomfort during the interview or focus group, they were given the option to pause or stop the session. In cases where further emotional support was required, participants were provided with referrals to appropriate professional counselling services if needed.

Ethical approval

Institutional Approval: Before data collection began, ethical approval was sought from the relevant Institutional Review Board (IRB) or Ethics Committee at the researcher's institution. This approval ensured that the study adhered to established ethical guidelines for research involving human participants.

Data use and publication

Data Usage: The data collected was used solely for the purposes of this research project. No data was shared or used for commercial purposes.

Publication of Results: The results of the study were published in academic journals, books, or presented at conferences. However, only aggregate findings and anonymized data were presented to ensure that no participant could be identified.

Results

Themes and subthemes

The following sections present the themes and subthemes derived from the data collected through semi-structured interviews and focus groups. These themes capture the core aspects of counselors' and psychotherapists' experiences and conceptualizations of multicultural counselling, as well as the challenges, strategies, and recommendations they identified during the research.

Theme 1: Conceptualizations of multicultural counselling

This theme explores how participants conceptualized and defined multicultural counselling within their professional contexts. Across interviews, counselors, psychologists, and psychotherapists emphasized that multicultural counselling extends beyond simple acknowledgment of diversity. It involves a deep understanding of clients' cultural, social, and historical backgrounds and the integration of this awareness into the counselling process.

Subtheme 1.1: Broad definition of multicultural counselling

Participants broadly defined multicultural counselling as a process that embeds cultural awareness, sensitivity, and responsiveness into the therapeutic relationship. They described it as a holistic approach that recognizes clients' cultural identities and integrates that understanding throughout therapy.

One psychotherapist explained that "*multicultural counseling is all about embedding cultural awareness into the therapeutic process. It means understanding where clients come from, not just ethnically, but from a social and historical context, and using that knowledge to guide our approach. Without it, we risk missing important aspects of the client's life*" (Participant 1, Psychotherapist).

A counselor described multicultural counselling as "*creating a therapeutic environment where clients feel understood on a deeper level, where we not only recognize their cultural background but also integrate that into every aspect of therapy. It is about making the therapy fit the client, not the other way around*" (Participant 2, Counselor).

Another participant expanded the definition by emphasizing intersectionality: "*It is not only about race but also gender, religion, and socio-economic background, and how all of those things shape the way a person interacts with the world. If we do not acknowledge those factors, we cannot provide effective care*" (Participant 3, Psychologist).

Several participants stressed that multicultural counselling requires more than surface-level awareness. It involves applying cultural understanding to specific therapeutic techniques. As one counselor noted, "*It goes beyond just cultural awareness. It is about integrating cultural knowledge with therapeutic techniques. I try to tailor my approach based on the client's cultural values and beliefs, which helps them feel more comfortable and supported in therapy*" (Participant 4, Counselor).

Participants also emphasized mutual respect and the reciprocal nature of multicultural counselling. One counselor explained, "*When I think of multicultural counselling, I think of a two-way process. It is not just about me understanding their culture but also about creating a space where clients can feel safe to share and express their cultural identities. That is what makes therapy effective and meaningful*" (Participant 7, Counselor).

Subtheme 1.2: Individual and cultural differences

Participants highlighted the importance of balancing individual uniqueness with broader cultural influences. They emphasized that effective multicultural counselling requires understanding clients as individuals shaped by both personal experiences and cultural contexts.

One psychotherapist reflected that "*people are shaped by both their personal experiences and their cultural context. It is about seeing the individual, but also recognizing that their identity is influenced by their culture and environment*" (Participant 1, Psychotherapist).

Similarly, a counselor shared, "*It is essential to acknowledge the individual story of each client, but we cannot ignore the role culture plays in shaping their experiences. I always try to balance both, understanding their unique circumstances and the broader cultural factors that may impact their worldview*" (Participant 2, Counselor).

Another participant described the central challenge of achieving this balance: "*The challenge in multicultural counseling is striking that balance between recognizing a person's individuality and considering how culture plays into their life*" (Participant 3, Psychologist).

Participants also cautioned against overgeneralizing cultural characteristics. As one psychologist observed, "*Sometimes, clients' cultural backgrounds may influence the way they view their own personal issues. Acknowledging that is key to providing effective therapy. However, it is also important not to generalize based on culture, because each individual's experience is shaped by both their personal history and their cultural context*" (Participant 6, Psychologist).

Overall, participants agreed that successful multicultural counselling depends on continuous reflection and sensitivity to how personal and cultural narratives intersect within the therapeutic process.

Subtheme 1.3: Professional adaptation to diversity

Participants described the ways they adapt their counselling techniques and engagement styles to meet the needs of clients from diverse cultural backgrounds. Flexibility, openness, and cultural humility were described as essential professional qualities.

A psychotherapist recounted, "*When I began working in diverse cultural settings, I quickly realized that I had to be flexible in my approach. I could not just apply the same therapeutic techniques to everyone*" (Participant 1, Psychotherapist).

Another counselor emphasized, "*Adapting my approach to the cultural context of each client has been key. For example, I learned that in some cultures, the family unit plays a much bigger role in the client's life, so I have to consider family dynamics when planning interventions*" (Participant 2, Counselor).

Participants also described adjusting to clients' expectations and communication styles. One psychologist noted, "*Some cultural groups value a more hierarchical therapeutic relationship, while others prefer a more egalitarian one. I adapt my style accordingly to ensure that the client feels comfortable and respected*" (Participant 4, Counselor).

A psychotherapist added, "*I have learned to constantly adapt. For example, when working with clients from collectivist cultures, I might involve family members in sessions. On the other hand, individualistic cultures may require more focus on the client's personal autonomy and goals*" (Participant 5, Psychotherapist).

Participants viewed this adaptability as a dynamic and ongoing process. As one counselor summarized, "*Multicultural counselling is not a one-size-fits-all approach. My techniques have evolved to ensure that they are culturally relevant and sensitive, based on the client's background. I constantly reassess whether my methods are working for each individual client*" (Participant 7, Counselor).

In summary, this theme reveals that multicultural counselling, as conceptualized by participants, involves an ongoing process of reflection, adaptation, and engagement. It is not static knowledge but a dynamic and relational practice that enables counselors to connect meaningfully with clients from diverse cultural, social, and spiritual contexts.

Theme 2: Challenges in multicultural counselling

This theme examines the challenges participants faced while providing multicultural counselling and the ways these difficulties influenced their practice. Four subthemes emerged: language barriers, cultural misunderstanding and stereotyping, limited training in multicultural competence, and ethical dilemmas.

Subtheme 2.1: Language barriers

Participants consistently identified language barriers as a major obstacle in multicultural counselling. They reported that differences in language or dialect often hindered effective communication and the development of therapeutic rapport.

One psychotherapist shared that "*Language has been one of the biggest barriers in my practice. I work with clients who speak various dialects, and sometimes, I feel like there's a disconnect. Even when we use a translator, it's not always the same. Certain nuances in language get lost, and that affects how we connect*" (Participant 1, Psychotherapist).

Similarly, a counselor noted, "*One challenge I regularly face is when clients speak a language I don't fully understand. Even with interpreters, some words or concepts just don't translate well, and that can lead to miscommunication. It makes me feel like I'm not fully reaching my client*" (Participant 2, Counselor).

Other participants emphasized that communication difficulties extend beyond literal translation. Participant 5, a psychotherapist, remarked that "*Sometimes, the language barrier is more than just understanding words—it's about understanding context. Certain phrases, or even body language, might have different meanings in different cultures, and trying to communicate those subtleties becomes difficult*" (Participant 5, Psychotherapist).

Participants also noted that even when client and counselor shared a common language, cultural differences shaped understanding. One counselor explained, "*With some clients, even though we share a common language, the cultural context of the language makes it difficult to fully communicate. There are phrases or concepts they may understand differently than I do, and it sometimes takes extra effort to bridge that gap*" (Participant 7, Counselor).

Subtheme 2.2: Cultural misunderstanding and stereotyping

Many participants highlighted cultural misunderstandings and stereotyping as obstacles in building trust and rapport with clients. These challenges often stemmed from assumptions about clients' behaviors, values, or family structures based on their cultural background.

One psychotherapist explained, "*One of the biggest challenges I've faced in multicultural counseling is dealing with assumptions. Sometimes, I catch myself assuming something about a client based on their cultural background, and I have to remind myself that not everyone fits into a certain stereotype. These assumptions can hinder trust and make it harder to connect*" (Participant 1, Psychotherapist).

Another counselor shared, "*Stereotyping can be very subtle, but it's still there. For instance, I had a client from a collectivist culture who was assumed to have close-knit family support, but in reality, their family was dysfunctional. I've learned that these assumptions can prevent me from truly understanding the client's situation*" (Participant 2, Counselor).

A psychologist reflected, "*Cultural misunderstandings happen frequently, especially when I'm not fully aware of the cultural practices or values a client holds. I remember a case where a client from an Asian background was perceived as silent or uncooperative, but in their culture, silence was a sign of respect, not disengagement. These misunderstandings definitely affect how we build rapport*" (Participant 3, Psychologist).

Several participants described the subtle nature of unconscious bias. One psychotherapist stated, "*Sometimes, there's an unconscious bias that gets in the way. For example, I had a client who was from a conservative culture, and I initially assumed they would not be open to discussing LGBTQ + issues. But when I asked, they were very open to talking about it. It was a good reminder not to generalize based on cultural background*" (Participant 5, Psychotherapist).

Overall, participants emphasized that awareness of stereotyping and active reflection are crucial to fostering trust and effective therapeutic relationships.

Subtheme 2.3: Limited training in multicultural competence

Several participants reported that their professional training inadequately prepared them for multicultural counselling. While general cultural sensitivity was sometimes covered, most felt that training lacked practical guidance for real-world application.

One psychotherapist remarked, "*I have to be honest, my initial training didn't adequately prepare me for working with clients from diverse cultural backgrounds. We touched on multicultural issues, but there was no deep dive into how to apply that knowledge in real therapy settings. It left me feeling unprepared when I started working with clients from different cultures*" (Participant 1, Psychotherapist).

Similarly, a counselor reflected, "*When I first began practicing, I quickly realized that the basic cultural training I received wasn't enough. It's one thing to read about cultural sensitivity, but it's another to actually navigate these issues in real-world sessions. I had to learn as I went, and sometimes, that wasn't the best way*" (Participant 2, Counselor).

Participants described a gap between theoretical knowledge and practical competence. A psychologist noted, "*My training was focused on general counselling techniques, but there was very little emphasis on multicultural competence. When I started seeing clients from different backgrounds, I felt I didn't have the tools or the language to understand their cultural context. I had to seek out additional training on my own*" (Participant 3, Psychologist).

Several participants emphasized the importance of self-directed learning. One counselor explained, "*In my training, we didn't get enough practical exposure to multicultural counseling. We were introduced to the concept of diversity, but I didn't feel fully prepared to handle the challenges that arise when working with clients from cultures vastly different from my own*" (Participant 7, Counselor).

Subtheme 2.4: Ethical dilemmas

Participants highlighted the ethical challenges of balancing cultural respect with professional obligations. Situations frequently arose in which culturally expected behaviors conflicted with counselling ethics.

A psychotherapist recounted, "*One of the most difficult ethical dilemmas I've faced was when a client from a very traditional cultural background asked me to help them with something that contradicted my professional ethics. They wanted me to support a decision that would harm their well-being, but culturally, it was expected. I had to navigate that very carefully, balancing respect for their culture and my professional obligations*" (Participant 1, Psychotherapist).

A counselor described a similar challenge, "*Ethical dilemmas often arise when clients have deeply ingrained cultural beliefs that conflict with mental health practices. I had a situation where a client's family wanted to make decisions on their behalf, but I knew the client had the right to autonomy in their care. Navigating that conflict was really challenging from both an ethical and cultural perspective*" (Participant 2, Counselor).

Participants also described dilemmas related to family involvement and religious beliefs. One psychologist reflected, "*It's hard when clients have cultural practices that challenge the therapeutic process. I've had clients from cultures where there's a strong belief in healing through family or community, which conflicts with the more individualistic approach we take in therapy. I have to carefully consider how to respect those cultural values while adhering to my ethical responsibility to provide individual care*" (Participant 9, Psychologist).

Across accounts, participants stressed that multicultural counselling often requires navigating these complex ethical tensions thoughtfully, with both cultural humility and professional integrity.

Theme 3: Strategies for effective multicultural counselling

This theme outlines the strategies and approaches participants use to overcome the challenges of multicultural counselling and enhance the effectiveness of their practice. Four subthemes were identified: cultural humility and self-reflection, building cultural competence, collaboration and referral, and a client-centered approach.

Subtheme 3.1: Cultural humility and self-reflection

Participants emphasized cultural humility as a cornerstone of effective multicultural counselling. They highlighted the importance of ongoing self-reflection, acknowledging personal biases, and remaining open to learning about clients' cultural backgrounds.

One psychotherapist noted, "*Cultural humility is at the core of my practice. I'm always aware that I don't know everything about a client's culture, so I approach every session with a willingness to learn. It's about recognizing that my own background shapes how I see the world, and I have to check that to make sure I'm not imposing my values on the client*" (Participant 1, Psychotherapist).

A counselor described cultural humility as transformative, stating, "*Cultural humility has been a game-changer for me. It's not about being an expert in every culture, but about being open to understanding each client's cultural perspective. Self-reflection is key—I constantly check my assumptions and biases, especially when working with clients from cultures different from my own*" (Participant 2, Counselor).

Other participants stressed the iterative nature of cultural humility. A psychologist explained, "*I think cultural humility is the most important strategy in multicultural counseling. I've learned that I don't have all the answers, and that's okay. I need to be open to exploring the client's worldview and be honest with them about my own limitations in understanding their cultural experience*" (Participant 3, Psychologist).

Several participants described self-reflection as essential to improving cultural understanding. One counselor shared, "*In the beginning of my practice, I thought I could learn everything I needed to know about different cultures. But over time, I realized that cultural humility means acknowledging that you'll always have more to learn. I practice self-reflection after each session, thinking about what went well and what I could have done differently in understanding the client's culture*" (Participant 4, Counselor).

Participants consistently emphasized that cultural humility requires introspection and openness, which allows for authentic connections and a deeper understanding of clients' cultural contexts.

Subtheme 3.2: Building cultural competence

Another strategy highlighted by participants was the continuous development of cultural competence. They described attending workshops, training programs, and engaging with relevant literature as essential to maintaining culturally informed practice.

One psychotherapist explained, "*Building cultural competence has been a priority for me throughout my career. I constantly seek out workshops and training programs that focus on multicultural counselling. It's important to stay current with new research and theories, as cultures are always evolving, and so should our approaches*" (Participant 1, Psychotherapist).

A counselor emphasized the ongoing nature of this work, stating, "*Cultural competence isn't something you can just learn once—it's a continuous process. I attend workshops regularly and make sure I'm reading the latest literature on multicultural counselling. This proactive approach has allowed me to be more confident in my practice with clients from different backgrounds*" (Participant 2, Counselor).

Participants highlighted that cultural competence involves both theoretical knowledge and practical application. A psychologist noted, "*Through cultural competence training, I've gained the confidence to engage more deeply with clients from different backgrounds. I now understand that cultural competence is not just about understanding facts about a culture, but about applying that knowledge with sensitivity and flexibility*" (Participant 9, Psychologist).

Continuous professional development was described as critical for effectively addressing cultural differences and improving client outcomes.

Subtheme 3.3: Collaboration and referral

Participants reported that collaboration with other professionals, cultural advisors, or community leaders enhanced their ability to work effectively with culturally diverse clients. They also discussed referring clients to specialists when their cultural knowledge was limited.

One psychotherapist explained, "*One of the strategies I've found most helpful is collaborating with cultural advisors or community leaders. Sometimes, I don't have all the cultural knowledge I need to fully understand my client's situation, so I lean on local experts who can provide insights that I wouldn't have access to otherwise*" (Participant 1, Psychotherapist).

A counselor described the importance of referrals, stating, "*When working with clients from backgrounds that I'm not familiar with, I refer them to specialists who have a deeper understanding of the cultural nuances involved. It's important to know when you need to bring in external expertise to ensure the client receives the best care*" (Participant 3, Counselor).

Participants consistently emphasized that collaboration and referral not only enhance the quality of care but also ensure cultural respect and ethical practice. A psychologist remarked, "*Collaboration and referral are integral to my approach. I've had to refer clients to cultural specialists, particularly in cases where their cultural background involved complex practices or beliefs that I wasn't familiar with. It ensures that clients receive the appropriate care while also respecting their cultural identity*" (Participant 6, Psychologist).

Subtheme 3.4: Client-centered approach

Finally, participants highlighted a client-centered approach, in which clients' cultural values, beliefs, and worldviews are actively integrated into therapy. This strategy promotes a more personalized, respectful, and effective counselling experience.

A psychotherapist shared, "*A client-centered approach is key in multicultural counseling. I focus on understanding the client's unique cultural values and worldview, and I integrate these into the therapeutic process. This helps the client feel valued and understood, and it makes the therapy much more meaningful*" (Participant 1, Psychotherapist).

A counselor explained, "*When I work with clients from diverse cultural backgrounds, I always make sure to adapt my approach to align with their cultural values. A client-centered approach isn't just about listening—it's about actively involving the client's cultural identity in the process and making them feel that their worldview is respected*" (Participant 2, Counselor).

Other participants emphasized that client-centered practice strengthens therapeutic relationships and fosters client engagement. One psychologist noted, "*Adopting a client-centered approach means that I see the client as a person with a unique cultural background and worldview. I don't treat them as just a case; I consider how their cultural influences might shape their experience. This helps build trust and a deeper therapeutic connection*" (Participant 6, Psychologist).

Participants agreed that centering the client's culture in therapy requires flexibility, attentiveness, and a commitment to understanding the client's perspective without imposing external norms or values.

Theme 4: Recommendations for improving multicultural counselling training and practice

This theme presents participants' recommendations for enhancing multicultural counselling in both training and professional practice. Four subthemes emerged: enhanced training programs, ongoing professional development, policy and organizational support, and community and peer support networks.

Subtheme 4.1: Enhanced training programs

Participants recommended that multicultural counselling should be integrated more comprehensively into professional training. They suggested training programs should emphasize cultural competence, cultural humility, and ethical considerations in multicultural contexts.

A psychotherapist emphasized, "*I firmly believe that multicultural counselling should be a core component of training programs. We need to move beyond just a session or two on cultural awareness and really dive deep into cultural competence, cultural humility, and how to apply these concepts in practice. It's not enough to just understand the theory—training needs to be practical and specific to real-world issues*" (Participant 1, Psychotherapist).

A counselor added, "*Multicultural training should be comprehensive. It's not just about learning about different cultures, but understanding the complexities of cultural competence, humility, and ethics in real-world practice. I think it should be integrated into every aspect of training, from theory to practicum, so that new counselors are better prepared for the diversity they'll encounter*" (Participant 2, Counselor).

Other participants highlighted the need for practical, applied training. A psychologist explained, "*Training in multicultural counselling needs to be more rigorous and specific. Counselors and psychotherapists should receive training that not only covers cultural awareness but also addresses the skills and strategies needed to work effectively in multicultural settings. The current training isn't enough to prepare us for the complexities of working with clients from different backgrounds*" (Participant 3, Psychologist).

Participants emphasized that enhanced training should provide both theoretical knowledge and practical experience to prepare practitioners for real-world multicultural contexts.

Subtheme 4.2: Ongoing professional development

Participants stressed the importance of continuous professional development to remain updated on emerging research, techniques, and cultural trends. Frequent workshops and networking with multicultural experts were highlighted as essential.

A psychotherapist stated, "*Ongoing professional development is crucial in the field of multicultural counselling. The world is changing, and cultures are evolving. We need to stay updated on new research, techniques, and cultural trends to ensure we're offering the best possible care to our clients*" (Participant 1, Psychotherapist).

A counselor observed, "*I can't stress enough how important continuous education is in this field. The multicultural landscape changes constantly, and we, as practitioners, need to adapt. That means attending workshops, reading recent research, and engaging with multicultural experts to stay informed and improve our practice*" (Participant 2, Counselor).

Participants highlighted that professional development ensures counselors remain competent, culturally responsive, and prepared to address evolving client needs. A psychologist added, "*Continuous learning is vital, especially in multicultural counselling. Attending more frequent workshops and participating in peer groups allows me to stay current on best practices and hear from experts who can offer fresh perspectives and techniques*" (Participant 6, Psychologist).

Subtheme 4.3: Policy and organizational support

Participants emphasized the need for institutions to create policies that prioritize multicultural competence. They recommended providing resources, establishing culturally sensitive guidelines, and embedding multicultural counselling into organizational practices.

One psychotherapist explained, "*It's essential that institutions prioritize multicultural competence in their policies. Organizations need to create an environment that supports diversity by providing resources like training programs, support groups, and access to cultural consultants. This ensures that multicultural counselling isn't just a concept, but something that is integrated into daily practice*" (Participant 1, Psychotherapist).

A counselor highlighted the role of top-down implementation, "*I think a lot of the work in multicultural counselling starts with institutional policies. It's important for organizations to not just talk about diversity but to implement policies that promote it. Whether it's offering training, ensuring diverse representation in leadership, or having guidelines for culturally sensitive practices, these changes need to come from the top down*" (Participant 2, Counselor).

Participants agreed that policy and organizational support are crucial for making multicultural counselling sustainable and effective. A psychologist noted, "*Policy and organizational support are crucial for making multicultural counselling a reality. I would like to see more institutions develop clear policies around cultural competence that include regular assessments of how well therapists are integrating these practices into their work. The more support we get from our organizations, the better equipped we'll be*" (Participant 6, Psychologist).

Subtheme 4.4: Community and peer support networks

Participants recommended the creation of peer and community support networks to provide guidance, share best practices, and support practitioners in multicultural counselling.

A psychotherapist shared, "*One of the best ways to stay grounded in multicultural counselling is by having strong peer support networks. I've found that connecting with other professionals who are dealing with similar cultural issues helps me stay on track and get fresh ideas for my practice. It's essential to have a community that shares resources and supports one another*" (Participant 1, Psychotherapist).

A counselor added, "*I can't stress enough how important peer support is in multicultural counselling. We all encounter similar challenges when working with clients from different backgrounds, and being able to discuss these with colleagues or a support group has been invaluable. It creates a safe space for sharing and learning from each other's experiences*" (Participant 2, Counselor).

Participants emphasized that community and peer support networks foster continuous learning, collaboration, and professional growth, enhancing both practitioner confidence and client outcomes. A psychologist concluded, "*In my experience, the best way to grow as a multicultural counselor is through ongoing collaboration and support from peers. These networks create opportunities for us to learn together, share our knowledge, and tackle challenges as a team rather than individually*" (Participant 10, Psychologist).

Summary of findings

The study explored the experiences, challenges, strategies, and recommendations of counselors and psychotherapists working in multicultural counselling settings. The findings revealed several key themes that highlight the complexities of multicultural counselling, the challenges faced by practitioners, and the strategies they employ to provide effective therapy.

Conceptualizations of multicultural counselling

Participants defined multicultural counselling as the integration of cultural sensitivity and awareness into therapeutic practice. They emphasized the importance of understanding clients' cultural backgrounds to provide effective care. Many participants described multicultural counselling as a process that goes beyond acknowledging cultural differences; it involves adapting therapeutic techniques to fit the cultural context of each client. Participants recognized that multicultural counselling requires a balance between addressing both individual experiences and broader cultural influences, ensuring that therapy is both personal and culturally relevant. Additionally, counselors and psychotherapists described how their approaches to therapy have adapted to the diverse cultural settings in which they work. This flexibility is essential to building trust and rapport with clients from various cultural backgrounds.

Challenges in multicultural counselling

The participants identified several challenges in providing multicultural counselling, particularly those related to cultural differences and communication barriers. One significant challenge was language barriers, which many participants reported as impeding effective communication. Even when using interpreters, participants found that misunderstandings often arose, especially when nuances of language or cultural expressions were lost in translation. Participants also discussed the difficulties of navigating cultural misunderstandings and stereotyping. These challenges were often related to assumptions made about clients based on their ethnic or cultural background, which created barriers to trust and rapport. Additionally, many participants expressed concerns about the limited training they received in multicultural competence during their professional education. They felt that their formal training did not adequately prepare them for the complexities of multicultural counselling, leaving them to learn and adapt through experience. Ethical dilemmas were also a recurring challenge, particularly when clients' cultural values conflicted with the professional ethical standards. Participants described situations where they had to balance respecting a client's cultural beliefs with their ethical obligation to provide care that met professional standards.

Strategies for effective multicultural counselling

Participants shared various strategies they used to address these challenges and enhance their multicultural counselling practice. A key strategy was the adoption of cultural humility, which involves ongoing self-reflection and a willingness to learn from clients about their cultural backgrounds. This approach helped therapists recognize their own biases and limitations, fostering a more open and respectful therapeutic relationship. Building cultural competence was also highlighted as essential for effective practice. Participants emphasized the need for continuous learning through workshops, training programs, and literature to stay updated on cultural trends and improve their understanding of diverse cultural contexts. Collaboration and referral were other important strategies. Participants often sought guidance from cultural advisors, community leaders, or other professionals with specialized knowledge when they encountered cultural challenges that went beyond their own expertise. They also referred clients to specialists when necessary to ensure they received the appropriate care. Lastly, a client-centered approach was considered crucial. Participants emphasized the need to integrate clients' cultural values and worldviews into the therapeutic process, ensuring that therapy was personalized, respectful, and relevant to each client's unique background.

Recommendations for improving multicultural counselling training and practice

Participants made several recommendations for improving multicultural counselling, focusing on the need for more comprehensive training, ongoing professional development, and institutional support. Many participants advocated for the incorporation of multicultural counselling into professional training programs. They recommended that counselors and psychotherapists be required to undergo specific training that addresses cultural competence, cultural humility, and the ethical considerations of working in multicultural contexts. Ongoing professional development was also seen as critical. Participants suggested that therapists should engage in regular workshops and networking opportunities to stay updated on new research, techniques, and cultural trends. In addition, they emphasized the need for organizations to develop policies that prioritize multicultural competence. These policies could include providing resources, creating culturally sensitive guidelines, and ensuring that multicultural counselling is embedded into institutional practices. Finally, participants recommended the establishment of peer support networks and community-based resources. These networks would allow professionals to share best practices, learn from each other's experiences, and provide ongoing guidance in navigating the challenges of multicultural counselling.

Discussion of findings

The findings from this study provide valuable insights into the complexities and challenges faced by counselors and psychotherapists in multicultural counselling settings. Participants emphasized the importance of cultural competence, humility, and self-reflection, along with the need for more comprehensive training and institutional support. This discussion synthesizes the key findings from the study and places them within the context of the existing literature, offering reflections on how these findings contribute to our understanding of multicultural counselling and its practices.

Conceptualizations of multicultural counselling

The participants in this study conceptualized multicultural counselling as a dynamic and context-dependent practice that integrates cultural sensitivity and awareness into therapeutic interventions. This aligns with previous research that emphasizes the necessity of cultural competence in therapy (Sue et al., 2019). The findings reflect an understanding of multicultural counselling that goes beyond simply acknowledging cultural differences to actively integrating clients' cultural contexts into every aspect of therapy. This approach allows for a deeper, more respectful understanding of the client's experiences, ultimately enhancing the therapeutic relationship. The participants' emphasis on balancing individual and cultural factors is consistent with the notion that multicultural counselling requires flexibility and adaptation (Pedersen et al., 2008). By recognizing both individual differences and cultural influences, therapists can create more personalized and relevant therapeutic experiences for their clients.

In practice, Nigerian counselors have adapted Western therapeutic methods by incorporating local idioms, expressions of faith, and group or family-oriented formats where appropriate. However, there is a growing need for the formal inclusion of prayer and scriptural reflection in counselling, particularly when both counselor and client share the same faith and worship practices. For example, if both identify as Christians and hold faith in Jesus Christ, there should be no reason to exclude prayer or reference to the Word of God during or after counselling sessions. In cases where the counselor and client are uncertain about each other's faith, private prayer may be appropriate without the need for explicit disclosure. Conversely, when the counselor and client differ in faith or worship patterns, it is advisable to refrain from formal prayers or religious references to uphold professional boundaries and ethical standards. Nevertheless, counselors may encourage clients to engage in faith-based or cultural practices consistent with the client's belief system if such practices are essential to healing. Thus, multicultural counselling may require either integration or the respectful omission of certain cultural or spiritual elements to enhance the counselling process. Ultimately, the goal of counselling is to promote healing and resolution of the client's concerns, not to endorse or criticize any particular culture or religion.

Challenges in multicultural counselling

The challenges identified by the participants are language barriers, cultural misunderstandings, limited training, and ethical dilemmas, reflecting common obstacles in multicultural counselling, as highlighted in the literature. Language barriers were particularly salient, with participants acknowledging that even with the use of interpreters, communication can still be compromised, leading to misunderstandings and a potential breakdown in the therapeutic process. This highlights the need for counselors to develop skills in working with interpreters and navigating language complexities, as well as understanding how language influences emotional expression. If this raises the issue of involving a third party in the counselling process, then ethical considerations would have to be applied where the counselor would need to inform the client about the need for an interpreter and ensure that the client consent to it. If the client rejects or if the counselor perceives ineffectiveness in the counselling process due to a third part's involvement, there might be need for referral to another counselor who complies with the client's language. On the other hand, this finding suggests the need for counselors to learn the language of their host community to be able to attend to multiple clients effectively. Another implication is the need for counselors to work in a team of multicultural counselors to have experts that may blend with clients from differs cultural contexts.

The issue of cultural misunderstanding and stereotyping was also a recurring theme. Participants recognized that assumptions based on clients' ethnic or cultural background can hinder trust and rapport-building. This is consistent with previous findings that highlight the importance of avoiding stereotyping in multicultural settings and instead focusing on the uniqueness of each client's experiences (Tummala-Narra, 2015). The participants' concerns about limited training in multicultural competence resonate with the broader call in the literature for more robust and inclusive training in counselling programmes. This finding suggests that while awareness of cultural diversity is often introduced in training, more specialized and practical approaches are needed to equip counselors with the skills to navigate the complexities of working with diverse populations.

Lastly, the ethical dilemmas faced by participants in balancing cultural values with professional ethical standards highlight a significant challenge in multicultural counselling. Therapists are often faced with the difficult task of respecting a client's cultural beliefs while upholding ethical standards of care. This finding aligns with previous studies that emphasize the tension between cultural respect and professional ethics (Sue et al., 2019). The fact that participants had to navigate these dilemmas on a case-by-case basis reinforces the need for clearer ethical guidelines that account for cultural differences in therapeutic contexts.

Strategies for effective multicultural counselling

Participants described four interrelated strategies for working effectively across cultural difference: cultural humility, ongoing development of cultural competence, collaboration with cultural experts and other professionals, and a client-centered approach. These strategies map directly onto contemporary debates and guidance in the multicultural counselling literature, which emphasizes that technical knowledge alone is insufficient; effective practice also requires self-awareness, flexibility and attention to sociopolitical context.

Cultural humility and ongoing self-reflection: Participants foregrounded cultural humility as a stance of continual learning, self-examination, and openness to correction. This mirrors the conceptual shift in health and mental-health education away from a static "competence as mastery" model toward humility as an ethical, reflective practice. Tervalon and Murray-García's influential formulation argues that clinicians should practise lifelong self-reflection, recognize power imbalances, and approach clients as partners in learning rather than objects of study. Cultural humility therefore supports responsiveness to culturally specific meanings, reduces reification of stereotypes, and promotes trust in therapeutic relationships (Tervalon & Murray-García, 1998).

Building cultural competence as an ongoing process: Respondents emphasized professional development, workshops and applied training to build the knowledge, skills and attitudes needed for culturally responsive work. This aligns with foundational competency models that describe awareness, knowledge and skill domains, and with more recent updates that explicitly integrate social justice and advocacy into clinical competence. The current mainstream guidance frames competence not as a one-off checklist but as iterative learning that combines theory, reflective practice and supervised application (Sue et al., 2019).

Collaboration, referral and working with community experts: Participants' reports that they routinely collaborate with cultural advisors, community leaders, interpreters and specialists reflects evidence that cross-sector partnerships improve assessment accuracy and therapeutic fit. In many African settings a large proportion of people initially consult traditional and religious healers for mental and social problems; mental health clinicians who liaise respectfully with these providers or local cultural authorities can shorten care pathways, reduce conflict about treatment goals, and co-design culturally credible interventions. Empirical studies from sub-Saharan Africa document widespread use of traditional healers and show that integrating or coordinating with community healing resources can improve accessibility and acceptability of care (Abbo, 2011).

Client-centered adaptation and therapeutic flexibility: Finally, participants' emphasis on adapting therapy to clients' cultural values and worldviews echoes culture-centered counselling theories that recommend adapting modalities, formats and goals to local meanings. Pedersen and others have argued for a culture-centered orientation that treats culture as central to diagnosis, formulation and intervention rather than peripheral. In practice this means varying modality (e.g. individual versus family or group therapy), integrating local metaphors or faith practices when appropriate, and negotiating goals collaboratively so interventions are both effective and legitimate within the client's sociocultural world (Pedersen, 2001).

Taken together, the strategies reported by participants align with an evidence-based consensus: effective multicultural counselling combines reflexive practice (cultural humility), documented frameworks and training (competence models and MSJCC), and pragmatic partnerships with community resources to produce culturally relevant care. For training programs and services this implies three actionable priorities: incorporate reflective training and supervised practice in cultural humility, require continuing education linked to concrete skills and casework, and encourage institutional mechanisms for community collaboration and culturally informed referral pathways. These steps are consistent with best practice recommendations in the literature and with studies that document improved client engagement and outcomes when culturally congruent approaches are used (Ayeni, 2024).

Recommendations for improving multicultural counselling training and practice

The recommendations made by participants, enhanced training programs, ongoing professional development, and greater institutional support, mirror the calls for reform in the literature. Participants stressed the need for comprehensive multicultural training programmes that go beyond theoretical knowledge and include practical, culturally relevant skills. This aligns with the consensus in the field that multicultural counselling requires not just awareness but also concrete skills that can be applied in practice (Sue et al., 2019). The call for ongoing professional development reflects an understanding that cultural competence is not static but requires continuous growth. Given the rapidly changing nature of cultural dynamics, therapists must remain adaptable and open to learning. The establishment of peer support networks and community-based resources was another key recommendation. Such networks foster a sense of community among multicultural therapists and provide opportunities for sharing best practices and learning from one another, which can enhance the overall quality of care provided to clients.

Finally, the importance of institutional support was highlighted. Participants suggested that organizations should develop policies that prioritize multicultural competence, providing resources and creating culturally sensitive guidelines for therapists. This organizational commitment would not only support therapists but also ensure that multicultural counselling becomes a central part of the institution's practices.

Conclusion

This chapter scientifically highlights the complexity of multicultural counselling and the challenges faced by therapists in providing culturally competent care. While many challenges exist, the chapter demonstrated that employing strategies such as cultural humility, continuous learning, and collaboration with other professionals can enhance multicultural counselling. The recommendations for improving training and practice emphasize the need for ongoing professional development, institutional support, and the creation of peer networks. These chapter contribute to the broader discourse on multicultural counselling and highlight the importance of both personal and systemic changes in improving the effectiveness of therapy for diverse populations.

Implications

The findings of this study have significant implications for the practice, training, and development of multicultural counselling. The study highlights key areas where improvements are needed, as well as strategies that can enhance the effectiveness of therapeutic interventions with diverse populations. Below, the implications are discussed in terms of professional practice, training, and organizational support.

Implications for professional practice

The study emphasizes the need for cultural humility and self-reflection in multicultural counselling. These findings suggest that counselors and psychotherapists should approach each therapeutic relationship with a mindset of learning, recognizing their own biases, and being open to clients' cultural perspectives. This shift toward humility and self-awareness can lead to more effective and empathetic therapeutic interventions.

Additionally, the study highlights the importance of building cultural competence through ongoing learning. It is clear that therapists need to engage in continuous professional development to stay informed about new research, techniques, and cultural trends. This finding suggests that therapists who do not prioritize ongoing learning may risk becoming disconnected from the diverse populations they serve, potentially diminishing the quality of care they provide.

Furthermore, the chapter highlights the need for collaboration and referral to specialists when required. This highlights that multicultural competence is not solely the responsibility of the individual therapist but requires a broader, more collaborative approach. By working with cultural consultants, community leaders, or specialists, therapists can ensure that clients receive culturally appropriate care. This implies that therapists must be proactive in recognizing when they need support and should not hesitate to refer clients to those with specialized expertise.

Implications for training programs

One of the most prominent implications of the study is the need for enhanced training in multicultural counselling. Participants consistently indicated that their initial training in multicultural competence was insufficient, which led to challenges in effectively serving clients from diverse cultural backgrounds. The findings suggest that counselling programs should incorporate comprehensive and practical multicultural training that goes beyond theoretical knowledge to include culturally relevant skills and strategies. This training should address not only cultural awareness but also how to apply cultural competence in real-world therapeutic settings, equipping therapists with the tools necessary to navigate complex cultural dynamics.

Moreover, training programs should place a greater emphasis on cultural humility and ethical considerations in multicultural contexts. Given the ethical dilemmas participants faced when balancing clients' cultural values with professional standards, it is crucial that training programs equip therapists with the skills to navigate these situations effectively. The integration of ethical decision-making frameworks that account for cultural differences would be essential in preparing future therapists for the challenges they may face in diverse cultural contexts.

Implications for ongoing professional development

The study clearly indicates that ongoing professional development is essential for counselors and psychotherapists working in multicultural settings. Participants emphasized the importance of attending workshops, conferences, and networking with experts in the field to stay updated on new cultural trends, research, and therapeutic techniques. This suggests that professional development in multicultural counselling should be an ongoing commitment throughout a therapist's career, not a one-time event during training. Therapists who engage in continuous learning will be better equipped to meet the evolving needs of diverse clients.

To support ongoing development, professional associations and organizations should provide regular opportunities for networking and peer support. This could include creating spaces where therapists can share experiences, discuss challenges, and learn from each other. Such opportunities will help build a community of professionals who are dedicated to improving their multicultural competence and who can rely on each other for guidance and support.

Implications for institutional and organizational support

The study also emphasizes the critical role of institutional support in promoting multicultural competence. Participants recommended that organizations supporting therapists develop policies that prioritize multicultural competence, offering resources and support for therapists to better serve diverse clients. Institutions should create an environment where multicultural counselling is not only encouraged but actively supported through comprehensive policies, training, and access to cultural resources.

Organizational support should include the development of culturally sensitive policies, guidelines for therapeutic practice, and systems for ensuring that multicultural counselling is integrated into every aspect of the institution's operations. Institutions that fail to prioritize multicultural competence risk perpetuating a lack of cultural awareness and competency in their therapeutic services. Therefore, organizations must take a proactive stance by ensuring that cultural competence is embedded into both their professional standards and everyday practices.

Broader implications for multicultural counselling practice

Finally, the findings underscore the importance of fostering a culture of respect and inclusivity within the broader field of mental health. Multicultural competence is a dynamic and evolving process that requires the collective effort of individual therapists, training programs, and institutional frameworks. The integration of multicultural competence into all aspects of professional practice, through ongoing development, policy support, and peer networks, will ensure that therapists are equipped to address the complex needs of increasingly diverse populations.

Therapists who embrace cultural humility and engage in ongoing learning will be better able to serve their clients effectively, ensuring that multicultural counselling becomes a core component of their professional practice. The study highlights that multicultural counselling is not an isolated skill but an integral part of effective therapy that benefits from continuous engagement, collaboration, and institutional support.

References

Abbo, C. (2011). Profiles and outcome of traditional healing practices for severe mental illnesses in two districts of Eastern Uganda. *Global Health Action, 4*. https://doi.org/10.3402/gha.v4i0.7117

Abrams, Z. (2023). *Can religion and spirituality have a place in therapy? Experts say yes.* American Psychological Association.

Adekunle, S. A. (2011). *Yoruba traditional beliefs and the treatment of mental illness in Ile-Ife, Osun state.*

Aluede, O., & Maliki, A. (2005). The imperativeness of multiculturalism to counselling practice in Nigeria. *Studies of Tribes and Tribals, 3*(2). https://doi.org/10.1080/0972639x.2005.11886527

Amat, S., Bakar, A. Y. A., Sahid, S., Mahmud, M. I., Shah, K. M., & Karim, D. N. F. M. (2020). Validation of multicultural counselling competencies scale among malaysian counsellor trainees: A confirmatory factor analysis. *Journal of Education and E-Learning Research, 7*(4). https://doi.org/10.20448/journal.509.2020.74.373.379

American Counseling Association. (2014). 2014 ACA code of ethics. In *American counseling association code of ethics*. https://doi.org/10.1111/j.1559-3584.2008.ethics.x

Anjorin, O., & Hassan Wada, Y. (2022). Impact of traditional healers in the provision of mental health services in Nigeria. In *Annals of medicine and surgery* (Vol 82). https://doi.org/10.1016/j.amsu.2022.104755

Awaritefe, A., & Ofovwe, C. E. (2007). Meseron therapy: An African approach to psychological treatment. *IFE PsychologIA, 15*(2). https://doi.org/10.4314/ifep.v15i2.23745

Ayeni, V. (2024). Nigerians turn to traditional healers as prices of drugs go out of reach. *Punch*. https://punchng.com/nigerians-turn-to-traditional-healers-as-prices-of-drugs-go-out-of-reach/

Bouvé Communications. (2023). *What is multicultural counseling and why is it important?*.

Braun, V., & Clarke, V. (2006). Using thematic analysis in psychology. *Qualitative Research in Psychology, 3* (2). https://doi.org/10.1191/1478088706qp063oa

Braun, V., & Clarke, V. (2013). *Successful qualitative research: A practical guide for beginners*. Sage.

British Association for Counselling and Psychotherapy. (2018). *Ethical framework for the counselling professions 2 BACP ethical framework for the counselling professions*. www.bacp.co.uk

Bushura Afolabi, A., & Osagiator Joy, A. (2014). Confronting negative thoughts using meseron therapy: A clinician approach. *IFE PsychologIA, 22*(2).

2025 Empowerment and change: The purpose of counselling (pp. 222–267). (2025).

Charmaz, K. (2014). *Constructing grounded theory* (2nd ed.). Sage.

Creswell, J. W., & Poth, C. N. (2018). *Qualitative inquiry and research design: Choosing among five approaches* (4th ed.). Sage.

Crotty, M. (1998). *The foundations of social research: Meaning and perspective in the research process*. Sage.

Eriacho, B. (2019). Considerations for psychedelic therapists when working with Native American people and communities. *Journal of Psychedelic Studies, 4*(1). https://doi.org/10.1556/2054.2019.030

Fabris, C., Coscia, A., Bertino, E., Prete, M., Occhi, L., Giuliani, F., & Quadrino, S. (2009). Counselling in neonatal intensive care unit (NICU). *Early Human Development, 85*(10 Suppl. L.). https://doi.org/10.1016/j.earlhumdev.2009.08.014

Fabris, C., Coscia, A., Tonetto, P., Bertino, E., & Quadrino, S. (2010). Counselling in neonatal intensive care unit. *Minerva Pediatrica, 62*(3 Suppl. 1).

Finlay, L. (2002). Negotiating the swamp: The opportunity and challenge of reflexivity in research practice. *Qualitative Research, 2*(2), 209–230. https://doi.org/10.1177/146879410200200205

Flückiger, C., Willutzki, U., grosse Holtforth, M., & Wampold, B. E. (2024). Psychotherapy works: Outlook into the future of a modern, collaborative treatment. *Psychotherapie, 69*(1). https://doi.org/10.1007/s00278-023-00703-4

Gergen, K. J. (2015). *An invitation to social construction* (3rd ed.). Sage.

Guba, E. G., & Lincoln, Y. S. (1994). Competing paradigms in qualitative research. In Denzin N.K., & Lincoln Y.S. (Eds.), *Handbook of qualitative research* (pp. 105–117). Sage.

Guest, G., Namey, E., & Chen, M. (2020). A simple method to assess and report thematic saturation in qualitative research. *PLoS One, 15*(5). https://doi.org/10.1371/journal.pone.0232076

Hailes, H. P., Ceccolini, C. J., Gutowski, E., & Liang, B. (2020). Ethical guidelines for social justice in psychology. *Professional Psychology: Research and Practice, 52*(1), 1–11. https://doi.org/10.1037/pro0000291

Hotifah, Y., & Hamidah. (2019). Systematic literature review: Concept, dimension, and antecedent multicultural counselling competence. *International Journal of Innovation, Creativity and Change, 5*(5).

Johnson, K. (2021). African indigenous healers and counseling : A case study of Babalawo. *OSP Journal of Health Care and Medicine, 2*(2), 2–5.

Kaplan, D. M., Tarvydas, V. M., & Gladding, S. T. (2014). 20/20: A vision for the future of counseling: The new consensus definition of counseling. *Journal of Counseling and Development, 92*(3). https://doi.org/10.1002/j.1556-6676.2014.00164.x

Klymenko, L. (2014). "Involve me, and I will understand": How to engage students in political science classes. *Osterreichische Zeitschrift Fur Politikwissenschaft, 43*(3).

Längle, A. (2018). Spirituality in psychotherapy? The relationship of immanence and transcendence in existential analysis. In *Living your own life: Existential analysis in action*. https://doi.org/10.4324/9780429476792-3

Lewis, S. (2015). Qualitative inquiry and research design: Choosing among five approaches. *Health Promotion Practice, 16*(4). https://doi.org/10.1177/1524839915580941

Linden, M. (2016). Counselling as distinguished from psychotherapy: Tasks, interaction, methods, problems and responsibilities. *Psychotherapeut, 61*(4). https://doi.org/10.1007/s00278-016-0116-1

Mail, F. B., Wan Mamat, W. H. B., Vengadasalam, C., Zin, I. B. M., Zakaria, Z., & Yaacob, S. E. (2014). Relationship between intrinsic and extrinsic factors with patriotism of the student athletes. *Research Journal of Applied Sciences, 9*(3). https://doi.org/10.3923/rjasci.2014.160.168

Makover, R. B. (2023). General principles of psychotherapy. In *Annotated psychotherapy*. https://doi.org/10.4324/9781003353003-2

Mathew, I., & Azuji, B. (2025). *Approaches to resolving client problems in counselling in a multiethnic society as perceived by guidance counsellors in Anambra state*.

Moloney, L. (2016). *Defining and delivering effective counselling and psychotherapy*. https://aifs.gov.au/sites/default/files/cfca38-effective-counselling_0.pdf

Nelson, J. (2014). *Nelson-Jones' theory and practice of counselling and psychotherapy*. https://uk.sagepub.com/sites/default/files/upm-binaries/65524_Nelson_Jones.pdf?utm

Nwachukwu, D. (2009). *Guidance and counseling practicum in pre-primary, primary and secondary schools. A guide to guidance counselors: Methods, skills, techniques and competencies*. University of Calabar Press.

Nwaka, P. E., & Awaritefe, A. (2018). Meseron therapy as a motivation theory. *International Journal for Psychotherapy in Africa, 3*(1).

Omolayo, B., & Judith, O. (2014). Counselling and psychotherapy : Is there any difference? *IFE PsychologIA, 22*(2).

Otusum Counselling Training Manual. (2015). *Definition of counselling*.

Pedersen, P. B., Draguns, J. G., Lonner, W. J., & Trimble, J. E. (2008). Counseling across cultures. In *Counseling across cultures*. https://doi.org/10.4135/9781483329314

Palinkas, L. A., Horwitz, S. M., Green, C. A., Wisdom, J. P., Duan, N., & Hoagwood, K. (2015). Purposeful sampling for qualitative data collection and analysis in mixed method implementation research. *Administration and Policy in Mental Health and Mental Health Services Research, 42*(5), 533–544. https://doi.org/10.1007/s10488-013-0528-y

Pedersen, P. B. (2001). Multiculturalism and the paradigm shift in counselling: Controversies and alternative futures. *Canadian Journal of Counselling, 35*(1).

Pusch, D., Dobson, K. S., & O'Brien, P. J. (2012). Psychotherapy. In *Encyclopedia of human behavior* (2nd ed.). https://doi.org/10.1016/B978-0-12-375000-6.00298-6

Salako, L. O., Oyekola Ibrahim, N., & Maroh Great, I. (2023). *Indigenous/cultural/spiritual healing practices: A report of interaction with traditional healers in Ogun state south west Nigeria*.

Schwandt, T. A. (2014). *The Sage dictionary of qualitative inquiry* (4th ed.). Sage.

Schwandt, T. A. (2023). The SAGE dictionary of qualitative inquiry. In *The SAGE dictionary of qualitative inquiry*. https://doi.org/10.4135/9781483398969

Shaka, N., Zewdie, T., & Wubih, T. (2025). Afro-centric mental health counseling practices, challenges and future directions: A literature review. In *Journal of cultural cognitive science*. Springer. https://doi.org/10.1007/s41809-025-00188-4

Sue, D. W., Arredondo, P., & McDavis, R. J. (1992). Multicultural counseling competencies and standards: A call to the profession. *Journal of Counseling and Development, 70*(4). https://doi.org/10.1002/j.1556-6676.1992.tb01642.x

Sue, D. W., Sue, D., Neville, H. A., & Smith, L. (2019). *Counseling the culturally diverse: Theory and practice* (8th ed.). NJ: Wiley.

Sue, S. (2017). In search of cultural competence in psychotherapy and counseling. In *Counseling psychology*. https://doi.org/10.4324/9781315259178-36

Tervalon, M., & Murray-García, J. (1998). Cultural humility versus cultural competence: A critical distinction in defining physician training outcomes in multicultural education. *Journal of Health Care for the Poor and Underserved, 9*(2), 117–125. https://doi.org/10.1353/hpu.2010.0233

Thakor, H. G., & Murthy, P. S. (2004). Counselling of leprosy affected persons and the community. *Journal of the Indian Medical Association, 102*(Issue 12).

The Family Institute at Northwestern University. (2025). *What is counseling?*.

Torres, R. H., Lappin, L. P., Calvo, P. H., & Díaz, C. V. (2023). Basic principles of psychotherapy. *Medicine (Spain), 13*(84). https://doi.org/10.1016/j.med.2023.08.008

Tummala-Narra, P. (2015). Cultural competence as a core emphasis of psychoanalytic psychotherapy. *Psychoanalytic Psychology, 32*(2). https://doi.org/10.1037/a0034041

Vieten, C., Scammell, S., Pierce, A., Pilato, R., Ammondson, I., Pargament, K. I., & Lukoff, D. (2016). Competencies for psychologists in the domains of religion and spirituality. *Spirituality in Clinical Practice, 3*(2). https://doi.org/10.1037/scp0000078

Willig, C., & Rogers, W. S. (2017). The SAGE handbook of qualitative research in psychology. In *The SAGE handbook of qualitative research in psychology*. https://doi.org/10.4135/9781526405555

Wong, P. T. P. (2010). Meaning therapy: An integrative and positive existential psychotherapy. *Journal of Contemporary Psychotherapy, 40*(2). https://doi.org/10.1007/s10879-009-9132-6

CHAPTER 2

Core principles and ethical standards in multicultural counselling

Introduction

The counselling profession is founded upon a commitment to ethical conduct, cultural competence, and the promotion of human dignity. In an increasingly interconnected and multicultural world, the ethical foundations of counselling require both universal consistency and contextual sensitivity. Counselors are called not only to adhere to established codes of professional ethics but also to interpret these standards in light of the diverse cultural, spiritual, and social contexts in which they practice. Consequently, an understanding of core ethical principles within multicultural counselling is indispensable for sustaining professional integrity and ensuring client welfare across cultural boundaries. This chapter examines the core principles and ethical standards that underpin multicultural counselling, emphasizing their relevance, interpretation, and adaptation within diverse sociocultural contexts, particularly in Sub-Saharan Africa. While ethical frameworks such as those articulated by the American Counseling Association (ACA), the British Association for Counseling and Psychotherapy (BACP), and the Canadian Counseling and Psychotherapy Association (CCPA) offer globally accepted benchmarks, their practical application in African contexts often encounters cultural complexities. In regions where communalism, spirituality, and kinship structures define social life, ethical concepts such as autonomy, confidentiality, and justice may assume meanings distinct from those found in Western professional paradigms.

In Sub-Saharan Africa, counselling practice often operates at the intersection of modern professional ethics and indigenous moral systems. Traditional African societies emphasize interdependence, communal wellbeing, and moral responsibility to others, values encapsulated in the African philosophy of Ubuntu, which foregrounds shared humanity and mutual care. These perspectives challenge counselors to re-examine conventional Western ethical assumptions rooted in individualism and secular rationalism. For example, the principle of autonomy may need to be balanced with communal decision-making, and confidentiality reinterpreted in light of collective approaches to healing and conflict resolution. The emergence of multicultural counselling as both a theoretical and practical discipline has thus prompted critical reflection on how global ethical standards can be

A Pragmatic Approach to Multicultural Counselling and Psychotherapy Skills Acquisition. https://doi.org/10.1016/B978-0-443-33939-4.00005-7

harmonized with local cultural realities. This chapter situates that reflection within a cross-sectional study of counselors, psychologists, and educators, exploring how ethical dilemmas are experienced, interpreted, and resolved in multicultural practice. The study investigates not only how counselors uphold professional standards but also how they navigate tensions between universal ethical codes and culturally embedded expectations.

Furthermore, the chapter highlights the urgent need to contextualize ethical frameworks through culturally responsive adaptations rather than wholesale adoption. Drawing on comparative insights from global and African perspectives, it underscores the view that ethical competence extends beyond compliance with professional codes to encompass cultural humility, moral reflexivity, and situational discernment. This form of ethical awareness enables counselors to make contextually appropriate decisions that uphold both the dignity of the client and the moral values of the community. Ultimately, this chapter aims to advance a nuanced understanding of ethics in multicultural counselling by identifying core principles that can serve as universal anchors while allowing flexibility for cultural adaptation. Through empirical analysis and conceptual discussion, it seeks to demonstrate that ethical counselling in pluralistic societies depends on a dynamic interaction between professional standards and cultural legitimacy, a balance that safeguards both ethical integrity and cultural relevance in counselling practice.

Research background

In an increasingly globalized and diverse world, the practice of counselling is evolving to accommodate the complexities of multiculturalism. One of the foundational pillars of effective multicultural counselling is the adherence to ethical standards and professional principles that promote equity, justice, and respect for all individuals. Without a strong ethical foundation, counselling in multicultural contexts risks perpetuating cultural misunderstandings, biases, and systemic inequalities (Sue et al., 1992). Ethical standards in counselling are codified sets of principles designed to guide practitioners in maintaining professionalism, ensuring client safety, and upholding human dignity. These standards include core values such as confidentiality, informed consent, cultural sensitivity, respect for autonomy, and non-maleficence (British Association for Counseling and Psychotherapy (BACP), 2018; American Counseling Association (ACA), 2014). In multicultural contexts, ethics take on additional significance because counselors must navigate the intersecting layers of cultural norms, traditions, language, power dynamics, and value systems. The inability to apply ethical principles in a culturally responsive manner can result in miscommunication, cultural offense, and reduced effectiveness in therapeutic outcomes (Arredondo et al., 1996).

International professional bodies such as the ACA in the United States and the BACP in the United Kingdom have recognized the centrality of multiculturalism in ethical counselling practice. For example, the ACA Code of Ethics (2014) emphasizes the need for counselors to develop cultural competence, engage in self-reflection, and avoid imposing their own values on clients. Similarly, the BACP Ethical Framework (2018) calls on practitioners to demonstrate cultural humility and adapt their interventions to fit the context of each client. Despite these efforts, implementing multicultural ethical standards remains a challenge in many parts of the world, especially in countries where counselling is still emerging as a professional field. In the African context, and specifically Nigeria, counselling has undergone a gradual transformation from informal guidance practices to a more structured and formalized profession. Counselling in Nigeria began in the late 1950s, primarily as career guidance provided by school administrators and missionaries (Makinde, 1983). The initial stages lacked professional training or ethical frameworks. Over time, counselling gained national recognition, culminating in its inclusion in the National Policy on Education in 1981 (Federal Ministry of Education, 2004). Despite this progress, Nigeria still faces significant challenges in developing and institutionalizing ethical guidelines that are reflective of its socio-cultural realities.

One key concern is the over-reliance on Western models of ethics, which, while comprehensive, are not always congruent with African communal values, belief systems, and indigenous modes of healing. For instance, the concept of individual autonomy, a central ethical principle in Western counselling, may conflict with the communal orientation prevalent in many African societies, where family or community input is integral to decision-making (Akpa-Inyang & Chima, 2021). Additionally, concepts such as respect for elders, spiritual perspectives on mental health, and traditional roles of authority often influence clients' expectations and experiences of counselling in Nigeria. The enactment of the Counseling Practitioners Council of Nigeria (CPCN) Act in 2022 marked a major milestone in the formal regulation of counselling practice in the country. However, the adaptation and domestication of ethical standards remain a pressing issue. While many Nigerian counselors are trained using ethical codes developed by international bodies, there is limited emphasis on how these principles should be contextualized to fit Nigerian cultural settings. As a result, counselling practices may appear disconnected from the cultural realities of the clients they are meant to serve, contributing to low public confidence and underutilization of counselling services (Sani & Kulumbu, 2018). Moreover, empirical evidence suggests that some practitioners in Nigeria lack sufficient training in ethics and multicultural competence, further complicating the quality and relevance of counselling services offered (Jr et al., 2018; Odeleye et al., 2024). This highlights the urgent need for culturally grounded ethical education in counselor training programmes, as well as the development of national ethical codes that reflect the diversity and values of Nigerian society.

Statement of the problem

Multicultural counselling continues to face significant challenges due to inadequate adherence to core ethical principles and the limited integration of culturally relevant standards into professional counselling practice, especially in developing countries like Nigeria. While global ethical codes, such as those of the American Counseling Association (ACA) and the British Association for Counseling and Psychotherapy (BACP), offer structured guidance for ethical practice, their principles are often rooted in Western values and worldviews. This has resulted in ethical frameworks that may not fully address the socio-cultural dynamics in non-Western settings.

In Nigeria, the counselling profession has historically drawn from these foreign models without sufficient contextual adaptation. Many practitioners operate without a deep understanding of how to apply ethical standards within Nigeria's diverse cultural landscape. Despite the recent establishment of the Counseling Practitioners Council of Nigeria (CPCN) and the inclusion of counselling in the National Policy on Education, ethical challenges remain, including lack of cultural competence, inconsistent professional conduct, and public skepticism about the relevance of counselling services. Thus, there is a pressing need to assess how well counselors understand and implement ethical standards in multicultural contexts and to identify gaps between global ethical norms and the local cultural realities of counselling practice in Nigeria. Addressing these gaps is essential for ensuring effective, culturally sensitive counselling services that resonate with clients' lived experiences.

Research objectives

The main objective of this study is to examine the core principles and ethical standards guiding multicultural counselling practice and to assess their application within culturally diverse contexts, with a focus on Nigeria.

Specific objectives

1. To identify the core ethical principles that underpin multicultural counselling globally.
2. To examine the extent to which Nigerian counselors are aware of and apply these ethical standards in their practice.
3. To find out the frequency of the ethical practice by the counselors in Nigeria.
4. To explore the challenges faced by Nigerian counselors in implementing ethical standards in multicultural settings.
5. To assess the cultural relevance of existing ethical frameworks used in Nigeria.

Research questions

1. What are the core ethical principles that guide multicultural counselling globally?
2. To what extent are Nigerian counselors aware of and compliant with these ethical principles?
3. What is the frequency of the ethical practice by the counselors in Nigeria?
4. What are the major challenges Nigerian counselors face in applying ethical principles within multicultural contexts?
5. How culturally relevant are the existing ethical frameworks used in Nigerian counselling practice?
6. What culturally contextualized strategies can be recommended to enhance ethical practice in multicultural counselling in Nigeria?

Literature review

This literature review explores existing scholarship on ethical principles in counselling, with a specific emphasis on multicultural contexts. It critically examines global perspectives on ethical standards, the application and adaptation of these standards in non-Western settings, and the particular challenges faced in the Nigerian context. Key themes include multicultural counselling competence, ethical dilemmas in diverse cultural settings, indigenization of ethical frameworks, and efforts toward professionalization in Nigeria.

Global ethical standards in counselling

Globally, professional counselling bodies such as the American Counseling Association (ACA) and the British Association for Counseling and Psychotherapy (BACP) have developed extensive ethical codes to guide counselors. The ACA Code of Ethics (2014) emphasizes autonomy, beneficence, non-maleficence, justice, and fidelity, while urging counselors to be sensitive to multicultural issues through awareness, knowledge, and skills (American Counseling Association, 2014). The BACP (2018) Ethical Framework similarly underlines cultural awareness, fairness, and commitment to clients' rights and values. These frameworks advocate cultural competence as a cornerstone of ethical counselling. Sue et al. (2019) assert that the failure to recognize cultural differences in values, communication styles, and healing processes can lead to cultural imposition and harm. Thus, ethical principles in multicultural counselling are not merely procedural but must be responsive to the cultural and social realities of clients.

Multicultural competence and ethical practice

Multicultural competence refers to a counselor's ability to work effectively with individuals from diverse backgrounds. Arredondo et al. (1996) developed the Multicultural Competency Model, which includes three domains: counselor self-awareness, knowledge of client's cultural worldview, and culturally appropriate intervention strategies. Research shows that ethical dilemmas often arise when counselors lack cultural competence. For example, Chao et al. (2011) found that counselors with lower multicultural training were more likely to unintentionally impose their values, leading to breaches of ethical principles such as respect and non-maleficence. Cultural competence, therefore, is essential to ethical practice, especially in pluralistic societies where misinterpretation of cultural norms can result in ethical violations.

Counselling ethics in African and Nigerian contexts

In Africa, counselling practices have traditionally existed in indigenous forms, including community dialog, spiritual consultation, and oral storytelling. However, the formal professionalization of counselling is relatively recent, particularly in a country like Nigeria. The development of counselling in Nigeria began in the late 1950s and gained state-level recognition with its inclusion in the National Policy on Education in 1981 (Federal Ministry of Education, 2004). Despite growth in academic training and government recognition, Nigerian counselling still relies heavily on Western ethical frameworks, which may not fully reflect local cultural norms. One may argue that ethical codes need to be contextualized. For instance, the principle of individual autonomy, a cornerstone of Western ethics, may not align with Nigerian communal values where family or elders often influence personal decisions. The enactment of the Counseling Practitioners Council of Nigeria (CPCN) Act in 2022 marked a turning point, offering regulatory oversight for ethical conduct. However, one may observe that this legal framework has not yet translated into widespread ethical awareness or culturally adapted practice among professionals.

Ethical challenges in multicultural counselling

Ethical challenges in multicultural counselling often stem from value conflicts, miscommunication, power imbalances, and a lack of cultural awareness. In Nigeria, these challenges are compounded by factors such as inconsistent training standards, limited supervision, and lack of public awareness about the counselling profession. Counselors may also face dilemmas when navigating sensitive cultural issues such as gender roles, religious practices, or family hierarchies (Egbo, 2015). Thus, in such situations, adherence to imported ethical codes without local adaptation may create more confusion than clarity. Moreover, the integration of indigenous belief systems, such as spirituality, ancestor reverence, and communal decision-making, requires counselors to apply ethical principles with flexibility and respect. This calls for an expansion of ethical education in counselor training programmes to include African worldviews and culturally grounded approaches to ethics (Onyilofor, 2013).

Emerging trends and the way forward

Recent trends in multicultural counselling advocate for ethical pluralism, the idea that different ethical systems can coexist and should be adapted contextually. Scholars (Pedersen et al., 2008; Tanaka-Matsumi, 2022; Zea & Echeverry, 1998) argue that the universal application of a single ethical code is both impractical and ethically questionable in multicultural settings. In Nigeria, there is increasing advocacy for the development of indigenous ethical frameworks, informed by African philosophies such as Ubuntu, which emphasizes interconnectedness, respect, and community welfare. Integrating these values into counselling ethics could make ethical practice more authentic and culturally resonant. Furthermore, ongoing collaboration between counselling regulatory bodies, universities, and cultural institutions can help promote ethical awareness, improve professional standards, and increase public trust in counselling services.

Methodology

Research design

This study utilized a cross-sectional descriptive survey design. This design was selected because it allows for the collection of data from a large number of participants at a single point in time, enabling the researcher to describe current practices, perceptions, and challenges related to ethical standards in multicultural counselling. A mixed-methods approach—combining both quantitative (survey) and qualitative (interviews and focus groups)—was adopted to capture the breadth and depth of participants' experiences.

Population of the study

The population of the study comprises all professional counselors practicing in Nigeria, particularly those working in schools, hospitals, private clinics, and community-based organisations. Emphasis was placed on practitioners operating in multicultural settings or regions with ethnically and linguistically diverse populations (e.g., Enugu State, Lagos, Akwa Ibom, and Abuja).

Sample and sampling technique

A purposive sampling technique was used to select participants who are actively engaged in multicultural counselling practice. To ensure representation, the sample included.

- 150 practising counselors for the quantitative survey
- 15 counselors for in-depth interviews
- 3 focus group discussions with 6–8 participants each

The selection criteria included.

- Minimum of a bachelor's degree in guidance and counselling or related field
- At least 2 years of counselling experience
- Experience working with culturally diverse clients

This sampling strategy ensured that the perspectives collected were relevant and reflective of real-world multicultural counselling practice.

Instruments for data collection

Quantitative Tool: A structured questionnaire titled "*Multicultural Counseling Ethics Questionnaire (MCEQ)*" was developed by the researcher and validated by experts in counselling psychology and multicultural studies. It contained closed-ended items on Likert scales designed to measure.

- Awareness of core ethical principles
- Frequency of ethical practice
- Perceived challenges in applying ethical standards
- Cultural relevance of current ethical codes

Qualitative tools

- **Semi-structured interview guide:** Used to explore counselors' in-depth experiences and perceptions regarding ethical dilemmas and culturally relevant practices.
- **Focus group discussion guide:** Designed to stimulate dialog among counselors regarding common ethical challenges in multicultural settings and recommendations for improvement.

Validity and reliability of instruments

To ensure content and face validity, instruments were reviewed by three experts in counselling and research methodology. A pilot study was conducted with 10 counselors not included in the final sample. The Cronbach's alpha reliability coefficient for the questionnaire was calculated at 0.81, indicating good internal consistency.

Procedure for data collection

Data collection was conducted over a 6-week period. The researcher distributed questionnaires to participants via professional counselling associations, conferences, and institutions. In-depth interviews and focus group discussions were conducted in-person and virtually, depending on participants' availability and location. All interviews were recorded with participant consent and later transcribed for analysis.

Ethical approval was obtained from the relevant university ethics committee. Informed consent was secured from all participants, and confidentiality was maintained throughout the study.

Methods of data analysis

Quantitative Data: Data from the questionnaires were analyzed using descriptive statistics (mean, frequency, and percentage) and inferential statistics (chi-square tests and correlation analysis) with the aid of SPSS software (Version 26).

Qualitative Data: Interview and focus group transcripts were analyzed thematically using NVivo software. Thematic analysis followed (Braun & Clarke, 2006) six-step process.

1. Familiarization with the data
2. Generating initial codes
3. Searching for themes
4. Reviewing themes
5. Defining and naming themes
6. Producing the report

This dual approach to analysis enabled triangulation of findings for greater validity and depth.

Ethical considerations

The study adhered strictly to ethical standards for research involving human subjects. Ethical clearance was obtained from the university's Research Ethics Committee. Participation was voluntary, and informed consent was obtained. Anonymity and confidentiality were ensured. Participants were given the right to withdraw from the study at any time without consequences.

Results

Demographic characteristics of participants

The study involved a demographically diverse sample of mental health counselors across Enugu State and surrounding regions.

Participants' ages ranged from 22 to 64 years, indicating representation across early, mid, and late career stages (Fig. 2.1). Noticeable peaks were observed around ages 36, 44, and 60, each with a frequency of 6–7 respondents, suggesting common age brackets for practising counselors. The overall age distribution was multimodal and non-symmetrical, reflecting a rich intergenerational composition of the sample.

The bar chart in Fig. 2.2 shows an equal distribution of gender among the participants, with 75 male and 75 female respondents. This balance ensures that gender-based comparisons in the analysis are valid and unbiased, as neither group is overrepresented.

As depicted in Fig. 2.3, respondents had between 2 and 38 years of professional counselling experience. The distribution shows significant variation, with experience peaks around 12, 20, 27, and 30 years. This suggests that both early-career and seasoned professionals were well represented, offering diverse insights into the adoption of mobile therapy systems in depression treatment.

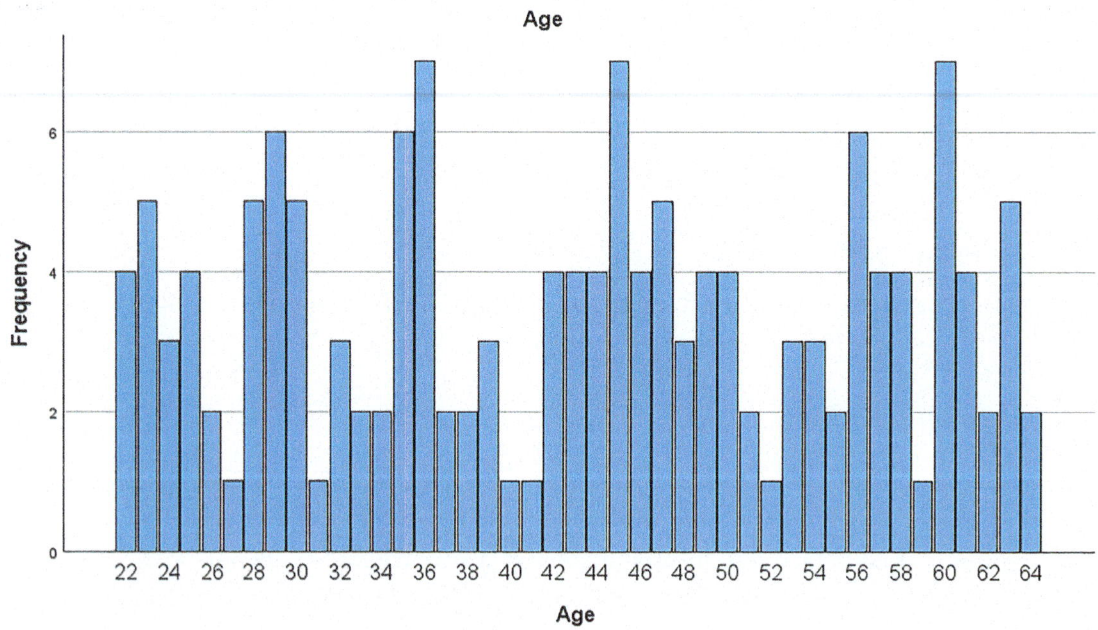

Figure 2.1
Age distribution.

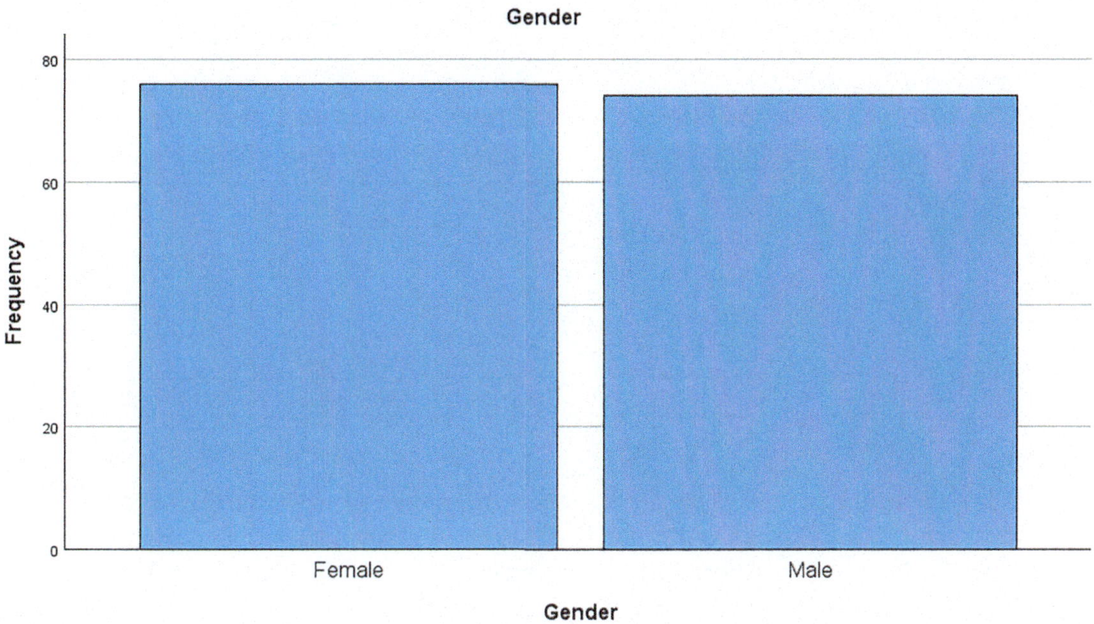

Figure 2.2
Gender distribution.

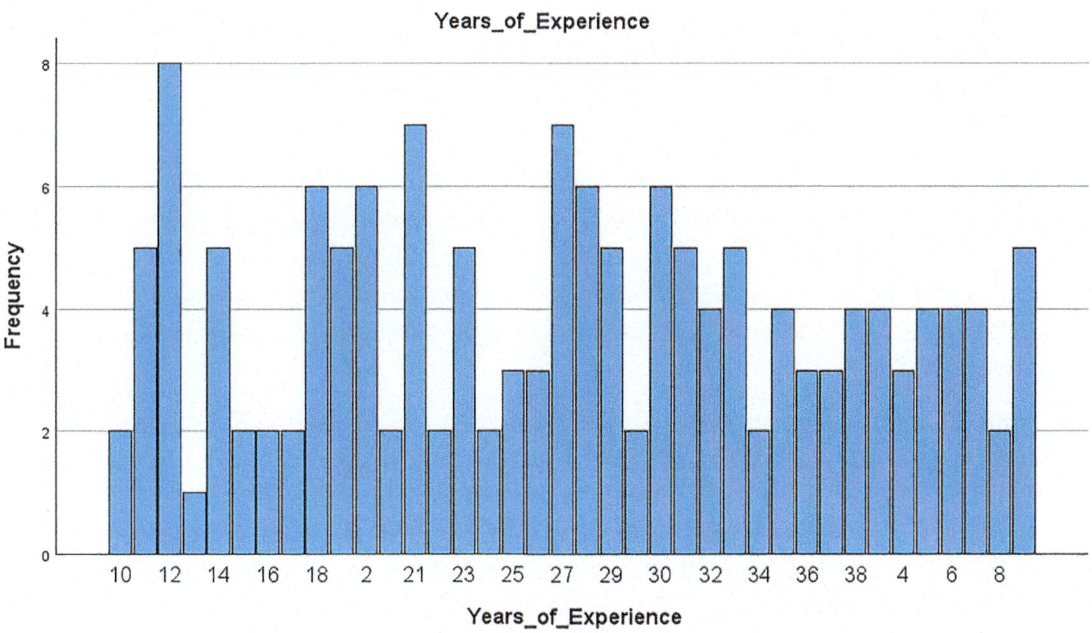

Figure 2.3
Years of experience.

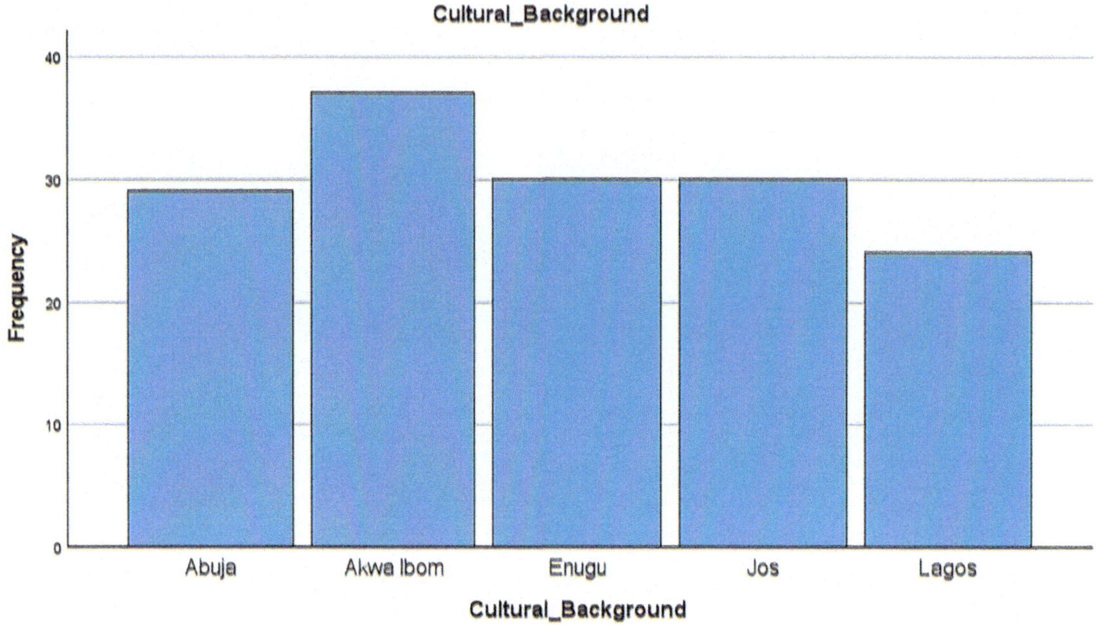

Figure 2.4
Cultural background.

Figure 2.4 presents the cultural distribution of participants based on their state of origin. The sample included counselors from Akwa Ibom (n ≈ 36), Enugu (n ≈ 30), Jos (n ≈ 30), Abuja (n ≈ 29), and Lagos (n ≈ 26). This spread across different geo-cultural regions of Nigeria enhances the contextual validity of the findings, particularly in evaluating culturally responsive approaches to mobile mental health interventions.

Table 2.1 presents the descriptive statistics of 26 ethical principles that underpin multicultural counselling globally. The analysis reflects respondents' self-reported adherence to core ethical values, grouped into five overarching domains: *Respect and Cultural Sensitivity, Competence and Professional Responsibility, Ethical Practice and Confidentiality, Client Autonomy and Social Justice*, and *Relational and Spiritual Considerations*.

Across all 26 items, the mean scores ranged between 2.85 and 3.27 on a 5-point scale, indicating a generally positive orientation toward the ethical standards measured. Notably, Item 9, which assesses the use of culturally validated assessment tools to avoid misdiagnosis, recorded the highest mean value of 3.273. This suggests strong awareness among practitioners of the importance of culturally appropriate diagnostic practices. Conversely, Item 8, relating to seeking consultation on cultural matters, received the lowest mean score (2.853), pointing to a potential gap in help-seeking or collaborative practices when addressing cultural complexities in counselling.

Table 2.1: Descriptive Statistics of the core ethical principles that guide multicultural counselling globally.

		95% confidence interval mean					
	Mean	Upper	Lower	Std. deviation	Coefficient of variation	Shapiro–Wilk	*P*-value of Shapiro–Wilk
Item 1	2.940	3.159	2.721	1.357	0.462	0.898	<0.001
Item 2	2.973	3.203	2.744	1.423	0.479	0.885	<0.001
Item 3	3.160	3.398	2.922	1.475	0.467	0.869	<0.001
Item 4	3.127	3.357	2.897	1.425	0.456	0.884	<0.001
Item 5	3.000	3.218	2.782	1.351	0.450	0.898	<0.001
Item 6	3.107	3.340	2.873	1.448	0.466	0.876	<0.001
Item 7	3.093	3.316	2.871	1.377	0.445	0.895	<0.001
Item 8	2.853	3.079	2.627	1.402	0.491	0.889	<0.001
Item 9	3.273	3.505	3.041	1.437	0.439	0.873	<0.001
Item 10	3.027	3.273	2.780	1.528	0.505	0.859	<0.001
Item 11	3.027	3.261	2.792	1.451	0.480	0.880	<0.001
Item 12	2.973	3.213	2.734	1.483	0.499	0.872	<0.001
Item 13	2.967	3.203	2.731	1.463	0.493	0.873	<0.001
Item 14	3.007	3.243	2.771	1.463	0.487	0.876	<0.001
Item 15	3.013	3.238	2.788	1.395	0.463	0.891	<0.001
Item 16	2.927	3.165	2.688	1.480	0.506	0.870	<0.001
Item 17	2.980	3.205	2.755	1.397	0.469	0.891	<0.001
Item 18	2.973	3.194	2.752	1.371	0.461	0.895	<0.001
Item 19	2.873	3.099	2.648	1.397	0.486	0.890	<0.001
Item 20	3.020	3.238	2.802	1.353	0.448	0.899	<0.001
Item 21	2.880	3.110	2.650	1.423	0.494	0.883	<0.001
Item 22	3.067	3.294	2.840	1.408	0.459	0.888	<0.001
Item 23	3.000	3.239	2.761	1.479	0.493	0.871	<0.001
Item 24	3.020	3.251	2.789	1.431	0.474	0.884	<0.001
Item 25	2.920	3.166	2.674	1.526	0.523	0.859	<0.001
Item 26	3.040	3.261	2.819	1.370	0.451	0.895	<0.001
Respect and cultural sensitivity	18.307	18.860	17.754	3.427	0.187	0.988	0.241
Competence and professional responsibility	18.247	18.826	17.667	3.593	0.197	0.988	0.224
Ethical practice and confidentiality	14.893	15.430	14.356	3.328	0.223	0.985	0.103
Client autonomy and social justice	14.813	15.276	14.351	2.865	0.193	0.970	0.003
Relational and spiritual considerations	11.980	12.461	11.499	2.980	0.249	0.970	0.002

Despite individual item variability, response consistency was fairly stable, with coefficients of variation remaining between 0.439 and 0.523. However, the results of the Shapiro–Wilk test for all individual items were statistically significant ($P < 0.001$), indicating non-normal distribution of responses, which is common in attitudinal and self-assessment data in social sciences.

When grouped by thematic domains, the analysis revealed strong support for principles under *Respect and Cultural Sensitivity* (mean = 18.31, SD = 3.427), as well as *Competence and Professional Responsibility* (mean = 18.25, SD = 3.593). These domains were also found to be normally distributed, as indicated by non-significant Shapiro–Wilk test results ($P = 0.241$ and $P = 0.224$, respectively). Similarly, the domain of *Ethical Practice and Confidentiality* received a moderately high endorsement (mean = 14.89, SD = 3.328) with near-normal distribution ($P = 0.103$), reflecting a commitment to confidentiality and ethical behavior in culturally diverse settings.

However, some domains were less strongly endorsed. *Client Autonomy and Social Justice*, though valued (mean = 14.81, SD = 2.865), exhibited significant non-normality ($P = 0.003$), suggesting greater variability in how practitioners engage with these principles. Likewise, *Relational and Spiritual Considerations* had the lowest overall mean (11.98, SD = 2.980) and also showed significant deviation from normal distribution ($P = 0.002$), potentially indicating divergent views on the integration of spirituality and relational dynamics in multicultural contexts (Table 2.2).

To assess the extent to which Nigerian counselors are aware of and compliant with ethical principles guiding multicultural counselling, descriptive statistics were computed for four

Table 2.2: Descriptive Statistics showing the extent Nigerian counselors are aware of and compliant with the ethical principles.

	Mean	Std. deviation	Shapiro–Wilk	*P*-value of Shapiro–Wilk
I am familiar with the main ethical principles that guide multicultural counselling practice (MCEQ1)	2.920	1.383	0.894	<0.001
I understand the importance of confidentiality in multicultural counselling settings (MCEQ2)	3.193	1.422	0.881	<0.001
I recognize the need to obtain informed consent in multicultural counselling contexts (MCEQ3)	3.113	1.473	0.873	<0.001
I am aware of the ethical principle of cultural competence in counselling (MCEQ4)	3.187	1.397	0.888	<0.001
Total awareness score	12.413	3.163	0.978	0.016

core items measuring ethical awareness and compliance (MCEQ1–MCEQ4). Each item was measured on a 5-point Likert scale, where higher scores indicate stronger agreement.

The mean scores for individual items ranged from 2.920 to 3.193, indicating moderate to moderately high awareness and compliance across the measured principles. Specifically, respondents reported the highest awareness with respect to the importance of confidentiality in multicultural counselling settings (MCEQ2; $M = 3.193$, $SD = 1.422$), followed closely by awareness of the ethical principle of cultural competence (MCEQ4; $M = 3.187$, $SD = 1.397$). The lowest mean score was recorded for general familiarity with ethical principles (MCEQ1; $M = 2.920$, $SD = 1.383$), suggesting some variability in baseline knowledge.

An aggregate awareness/compliance score was computed (labeled "Awareness"), with a mean of 12.413 (SD = 3.163) out of a possible 20. This reflects a moderately high level of ethical awareness and compliance among the counselors sampled. The Shapiro–Wilk test was conducted to assess the normality of the distribution. Results for each individual item (MCEQ1–MCEQ4) were statistically significant ($P < 0.001$), indicating a deviation from normal distribution. However, the aggregate awareness score showed only a mild violation of normality ($W = 0.978$, $P = 0.016$), suggesting that the total score approximates normality more closely than the individual items and can be cautiously used in parametric tests if needed.

Table 2.3 presents a combined analysis of counselors' awareness of ethical principles across three demographic variables: gender, cultural background, and highest qualification.

Table 2.3: Summary of awareness of ethical principles by gender, cultural background, and highest qualification.

Category	Group	N	Mean	Std. deviation	F-value	Sig. (p)	Eta	Eta^2
Gender	Female	76	12.87	3.13				
	Male	74	11.95	3.15	3.238	0.074	0.146	0.021
	Total	150	12.41	3.16				
Cultural background	Abuja	29	12.62	2.61				
	Akwa Ibom	37	12.89	3.38				
	Enugu	30	12.63	3.25				
	Jos	30	11.67	3.81				
	Lagos	24	12.08	2.38	0.758	0.555	0.143	0.020
	Total	150	12.41	3.16				
Highest qualification	Bachelor	82	12.60	3.06				
	Master	45	12.49	3.22				
	PhD	13	12.00	3.19				
	Prof. Certificate	10	11.10	3.81	0.746	0.526	0.123	0.015
	Total	150	12.41	3.16				

It includes descriptive statistics (mean and standard deviation), ANOVA results, and measures of association. In terms of gender, female counselors had a higher mean awareness score (12.87) compared to male counselors (11.95). Although the difference appears noticeable, it was not statistically significant ($F = 3.238$, $P = 0.074$). However, the Eta value of 0.146 and Eta squared of 0.021 indicate a small effect size, meaning gender accounts for about 2.1% of the variance in awareness scores. For cultural background, Akwa Ibom counselors reported the highest awareness (mean = 12.89), while those from Jos had the lowest (mean = 11.67). Despite these differences, the ANOVA result ($F = 0.758$, $P = 0.555$) shows that the variation in awareness across the different cultural groups is not statistically significant. The Eta squared value (0.020) also suggests a small effect size, with cultural background explaining only 2% of the variance.

Regarding highest qualification, counselors with a bachelor's degree had the highest awareness (mean = 12.60), closely followed by master's degree holders (12.49) and Ph.D. holders (12.00). Those with professional certificates reported the lowest awareness (mean = 11.10). Again, the differences were not statistically significant ($F = 0.746$, $P = 0.526$), and the Eta squared value of 0.015 shows a very small effect size.

The descriptive statistics in Table 2.4 provide insights into the frequency with which Nigerian counselors engage in key ethical practices within multicultural counselling contexts. Overall, the total frequency mean score is 11.740 (out of a possible 20, assuming a 5-point scale for each of the four items), indicating a moderate level of ethical practice among the counselors sampled. Looking at individual practices, the highest mean score (3.073) was recorded for the item "*I update my knowledge about ethical standards*

Table 2.4: Descriptive Statistics for the frequency of ethical practice by the Nigerian counselors.

	Mean	Std. deviation	Shapiro-Wilk	*P*-value of Shapiro-Wilk
I regularly apply ethical principles in my multicultural counselling sessions.	2.900	1.432	0.881	<0.001
I seek supervision or consultation when faced with ethical dilemmas in multicultural counselling.	2.900	1.446	0.879	<0.001
I consistently respect clients' cultural values and beliefs during counselling.	2.867	1.403	0.888	<0.001
I update my knowledge about ethical standards relevant to multicultural counselling	3.073	1.429	0.882	<0.001
Total frequency	11.740	2.666	0.983	0.068

relevant to multicultural counselling", suggesting that among the practices listed, counselors most frequently engage in efforts to stay informed about ethical standards. This reflects a positive attitude toward ongoing professional development.

Two practices, "*I regularly apply ethical principles in my multicultural counselling sessions*" and "*I seek supervision or consultation when faced with ethical dilemmas in multicultural counselling*", both had mean scores of 2.900, reflecting a moderate but not consistent level of engagement. This suggests that while many counselors apply ethical principles and seek guidance, these practices may not be fully integrated into their routine behavior.

The lowest mean score (2.867) was reported for "*I consistently respect clients' cultural values and beliefs during counselling.*" Although still moderate, this score is somewhat concerning, as cultural respect is a foundational element of ethical multicultural counselling. The slight drop may indicate a need for stronger emphasis on cultural competence in training and practice.

The standard deviations for all four items range from 1.403 to 1.446, indicating moderate variability in responses. This suggests that while some counselors frequently engage in these practices, others report doing so infrequently. The Shapiro–Wilk tests for the individual items all yielded P-values less than 0.001, indicating significant deviations from normality in the data distribution. However, the total frequency score has a Shapiro–Wilk P-value of 0.068, which is above the 0.05 threshold, suggesting that the overall frequency distribution is approximately normal and suitable for parametric analysis.

Table 2.5 summarizes the frequency of ethical practice among Nigerian counselors across three demographic variables: gender, cultural background, and highest qualification, along with the results of statistical tests examining differences between groups.

Regarding gender, male counselors reported a higher mean frequency of ethical practice (12.24) compared to female counselors (11.25). This difference was statistically significant ($F = 5.357$, $P = 0.022$), indicating that gender has a meaningful influence on how often counselors engage in ethical practices. The effect size (Eta squared = 0.035) suggests this influence is small but notable.

In terms of cultural background, counselors from Akwa Ibom showed the highest frequency of ethical practice (mean = 12.73), whereas those from Abuja reported the lowest (mean = 11.00). However, these differences were not statistically significant ($F = 2.062$, $P = 0.089$). The effect size (Eta squared = 0.054) indicates a small to moderate amount of variance in ethical practice frequency might be explained by cultural background, but the evidence is not strong enough to confirm this definitively.

Table 2.5: Summary of frequency of ethical practice by gender, cultural background, and highest qualification.

Category	Group	N	Mean	Std. deviation	F-value	Sig. (p)	Eta	Eta^2
Gender	Female	76	11.25	2.71				
	Male	74	12.24	2.54	5.357	0.022	0.187	0.035
	Total	150	11.74	2.67				
Cultural background	Abuja	29	11.00	2.60				
	Akwa Ibom	37	12.73	2.93				
	Enugu	30	11.57	2.30				
	Jos	30	11.73	2.64				
	Lagos	24	11.33	2.53	2.062	0.089	0.232	0.054
	Total	150	11.74	2.67				
Highest qualification	Bachelor	82	11.72	2.55				
	Master	45	11.64	3.04				
	PhD	13	12.31	2.32				
	Prof. Certificate	10	11.60	2.46	0.223	0.880	0.068	0.005
	Total	150	11.74	2.67				

Looking at highest qualification, counselors with PhDs reported the highest mean frequency of ethical practice (12.31), followed by those with bachelor's degrees (11.72), master's degrees (11.64), and professional certificates (11.60). The differences among these groups were not statistically significant ($F = 0.223$, $P = 0.880$), and the very small effect size (Eta squared = 0.005) suggests that educational level has minimal impact on ethical practice frequency in this sample.

Overall, the analysis suggests that while gender significantly affects the frequency of ethical practice, with males reporting higher engagement, cultural background and educational qualifications do not have statistically significant effects. Other factors beyond these demographics may play a larger role in influencing ethical behavior among Nigerian counselors.

The results presented in Table 2.6 indicate that Nigerian counselors face several notable challenges when applying ethical principles within multicultural contexts. Among the identified difficulties, the most prominent is the challenge of balancing ethical standards with cultural differences in counselling, which recorded the highest mean score of 3.093. This suggests that counselors often find it difficult to reconcile universal ethical expectations with the diverse cultural values of their clients.

Closely following this, many counselors reported that conflicting cultural values sometimes challenge their ethical decision-making, with a mean score of 3.047. This

Table 2.6: Descriptive Statistics for the major challenges Nigerian counselors face in applying ethical principles within multicultural context.

	Mean	Std. deviation	Shapiro–Wilk	*P*-value of Shapiro–Wilk
I find it difficult to balance ethical standards with cultural differences in counselling.	3.093	1.444	0.881	<0.001
Conflicting cultural values sometimes challenge my ethical decision-making.	3.047	1.297	0.905	<0.001
I experience challenges when clients' cultural beliefs contradict standard ethical codes.	2.960	1.330	0.901	<0.001
Lack of culturally specific ethical guidelines limits my counselling practice.	2.953	1.416	0.887	<0.001
Total challenges	12.053	2.731	0.977	0.012

reflects the tension that arises when cultural norms or practices are at odds with professional ethical codes, creating dilemmas that counselors must navigate with care.

Counselors also acknowledged experiencing difficulties when clients' cultural beliefs directly contradict established ethical standards, as indicated by a mean score of 2.960. This highlights situations where counselors may feel constrained or uncertain about how to proceed ethically without disregarding a client's cultural background.

Lastly, the lack of culturally specific ethical guidelines was identified as a challenge, with a mean score of 2.953. This suggests that many counselors feel the general ethical codes available do not adequately address the complexities of working within Nigeria's culturally diverse environment.

Overall, the total mean score across all items was 12.053, reflecting a moderate level of perceived challenge. Although not extreme, these consistent reports indicate a real need for clearer, culturally informed ethical frameworks and more support for counselors working in multicultural settings. The Shapiro–Wilk test showed that individual responses were not normally distributed ($P < 0.001$ for all items), which may suggest varying individual experiences; however, the composite challenge score approached normality ($P = 0.012$), supporting the reliability of the overall trend.

The results on Table 2.7 reveal that Nigerian counselors, regardless of gender, cultural background, or academic qualification, reported a generally consistent level of challenges in applying ethical principles within multicultural contexts. On average, female counselors had a mean challenge score of 12.04 (SD = 2.77), while male counselors scored slightly higher at 12.07 (SD = 2.71). However, the difference between the two groups was not

Table 2.7: Summary of challenges by gender, cultural background, and highest qualification.

Category	Group	N	Mean	Std. deviation	F	Sig.	Eta	Eta^2
Gender	Female	76	12.04	2.77	0.004	0.950	0.005	0.000
	Male	74	12.07	2.71				
Cultural background	Abuja	29	12.17	2.98	0.496	0.739	0.116	0.013
	Akwa Ibom	37	12.22	2.52				
	Enugu	30	11.53	2.61				
	Jos	30	12.43	3.13				
	Lagos	24	11.83	2.46				
Highest qualification	Bachelor	82	12.21	2.61	1.437	0.234	0.169	0.029
	Master	45	11.42	2.90				
	PhD	13	12.54	3.02				
	Professional Cert.	10	13.00	2.36				
Total		150	12.05	2.73				

statistically significant, as indicated by an ANOVA result of F(1, 148) = 0.004, $P = 0.950$. The effect size was extremely small ($Eta^2 = 0.000$), showing that gender had virtually no influence on the reported challenges.

When considering cultural background, mean scores varied slightly across locations. Counselors from Jos reported the highest average challenge score (M = 12.43), followed by those from Akwa Ibom (M = 12.22), Abuja (M = 12.17), Lagos (M = 11.83), and Enugu (M = 11.53). Despite these differences, the ANOVA revealed no statistically significant effect of cultural background on the challenges faced, F(4, 145) = 0.496, $P = 0.739$. The effect size was small ($Eta^2 = 0.013$), indicating that cultural background accounted for only a minimal proportion of the variance in the scores.

In terms of highest academic qualification, professional certificate holders reported the greatest challenges (M = 13.00), followed by Ph.D. holders (M = 12.54), bachelor's degree holders (M = 12.21), and master's degree holders (M = 11.42). Yet again, these differences were not statistically significant, as shown by F(3, 146) = 1.437, $P = 0.234$. The effect size ($Eta^2 = 0.029$) suggested a small influence of qualification on perceived challenges.

Overall, the data indicate that counselors across all categories experience similar levels of difficulty in navigating ethical principles in multicultural settings, and none of the demographic variables examined—gender, cultural background, or qualification—had a significant impact on these challenges.

The results in Table 2.8 provide insight into the perceived cultural relevance of existing ethical frameworks in Nigerian counselling practice. Overall, counselors expressed

Table 2.8: Descriptive Statistics for the cultural relevant of the existing ethical frameworks used in Nigerian counselling practice.

	Mean	Std. deviation	Shapiro–Wilk	*P*-value of Shapiro–Wilk
Existing ethical codes adequately address cultural diversity issues in counselling.	3.033	1.368	0.897	<0.001
Ethical guidelines should be adapted to better reflect multicultural realities.	2.720	1.327	0.892	<0.001
I believe culturally relevant ethical codes improve counselling outcomes.	3.100	1.527	0.859	<0.001
I am confident in my ability to apply ethical codes in culturally diverse counselling situations	2.620	1.491	0.844	<0.001
Total relevance	11.473	2.923	0.987	0.177

moderate agreement that the current ethical codes are culturally responsive, though their views also highlight areas needing improvement.

On average, respondents somewhat agreed that existing ethical codes adequately address cultural diversity issues in counselling, with a mean score of 3.03 (SD = 1.37). A slightly higher average score was recorded for the belief that culturally relevant ethical codes improve counselling outcomes (M = 3.10, SD = 1.53), suggesting counselors acknowledge the importance of cultural relevance in promoting effective counselling.

However, when asked whether current ethical guidelines should be adapted to better reflect multicultural realities, the mean score was slightly lower at 2.72 (SD = 1.33), indicating a mild level of agreement and a potential perception that the current frameworks may not fully capture Nigeria's cultural complexity. Furthermore, confidence in applying ethical codes in diverse cultural settings received the lowest mean score of 2.62 (SD = 1.49), suggesting that many counselors feel underprepared or uncertain about navigating ethical issues across cultural lines.

The total mean score for cultural relevance was 11.47 (SD = 2.92), and the Shapiro–Wilk test for normality showed that the total score distribution was approximately normal (W = 0.987, $P = .177$), which validates the use of parametric statistics for further analysis.

In summary, while Nigerian counselors recognize the importance of culturally relevant ethical frameworks and generally agree that such frameworks contribute positively to counselling outcomes, there is also a notable concern that existing codes may not fully align with multicultural realities, and that practitioners may lack the confidence to apply these codes effectively in culturally diverse settings.

The analysis in Table 2.9 examined whether perceptions of the cultural relevance of existing ethical frameworks in Nigerian counselling vary by gender, cultural background, and highest qualification. Regarding gender, female counselors had a slightly higher mean score (11.63) than males (11.31), suggesting a marginally greater perception of cultural relevance among females. However, the difference was not statistically significant ($F(1,148) = 0.45$, $P = .504$), with a very small effect size (Eta squared = 0.003). This indicates gender does not meaningfully influence perceptions of cultural relevance.

Among cultural backgrounds, mean scores ranged from 10.97 (Abuja) to 11.83 (Enugu), showing some variation in perceptions across regions. Still, the differences were not statistically significant ($F(4,145) = 0.35$, $P = .844$), and the effect size was small (Eta squared = 0.010). This suggests cultural background does not have a significant impact on how counselors view the cultural relevance of ethical frameworks.

For highest qualification, Master's degree holders reported the highest mean relevance score (12.00), while Bachelor's degree holders scored lowest (11.17). Yet, this variation

Table 2.9: Combining the descriptive statistics, ANOVA results, and measures of association for the cultural relevance of existing ethical frameworks by Gender, Cultural Background, and Highest Qualification.

Category	Group	N	Mean	Std. deviation	ANOVA: F	Sig. (*P*-value)	Eta	Eta squared
Gender	Female	76	11.63	3.01	0.45	0.504	0.055	0.003
	Male	74	11.31	2.84				
	Total	150	11.47	2.92				
Cultural background	Abuja	29	10.97	3.64	0.35	0.844	0.098	0.010
	Akwa Ibom	37	11.57	2.83				
	Enugu	30	11.83	2.77				
	Jos	30	11.40	2.81				
	Lagos	24	11.58	2.55				
	Total	150	11.47	2.92				
Highest qualification	Bachelor	82	11.17	2.93	0.83	0.478	0.130	0.017
	Master	45	12.00	3.16				
	PhD	13	11.31	2.66				
	Professional Certification	10	11.80	1.81				
	Total	150	11.47	2.92				

was not statistically significant ($F(3,146) = 0.83$, $P = .478$), with a small effect size (Eta squared = 0.017). Therefore, educational attainment does not appear to influence perceptions of cultural relevance significantly.

Overall, these findings suggest that Nigerian counselors, regardless of gender, cultural background, or highest qualification, share a relatively similar view of the cultural relevance of existing ethical frameworks, with no statistically significant differences between groups.

Qualitative results

In response to the question, "*What culturally contextualized strategies can be recommended to enhance ethical practice in multicultural counselling in Nigeria?*", the analysis of data from 15 in-depth interviews and 3 focus group discussions revealed five overarching themes and 11 sub-themes. These reflect the voices of Nigerian counselors grounded in their diverse cultural, religious, and professional realities.

Theme 1: Integration of indigenous knowledge systems

Sub-theme 1.1: Recognition of traditional healing practices

Participants expressed that ethical multicultural counselling in Nigeria must acknowledge and, where appropriate, interface with indigenous healing traditions. Counselors reported that clients often perceive traditional healers as their first line of care.

> *Ignoring traditional beliefs in therapy can make the client feel misunderstood. Many of them grew up with these systems before hearing of Western counselling.* (Counsellor 4)

Sub-theme 1.2: Collaboration with cultural custodians

Counselors recommended strategic collaboration with traditional rulers, elders, and custodians of cultural values to ensure ethical congruence between counselling and the client's community expectations.

> *An elder from the community can help explain our role to clients. This prevents ethical clashes and promotes acceptance.* (Counsellor 2)

Theme 2: Faith-based ethical engagement

Sub-theme 2.1: Inclusion of spiritual worldviews in counselling

Given the high level of religiosity in Nigerian society, participants stressed that ethical counselling must accommodate the spiritual beliefs of clients—be they Christian, Muslim, or traditionalist.

> *For many clients, prayer, fasting, or talking to their pastor is part of healing. We must respect that and ethically weave it into therapy.* (Counsellor 10)

Sub-theme 2.2: Collaboration with faith leaders

Respondents noted that pastors, imams, and other spiritual leaders often act as informal counselors and could serve as cultural bridges.

> *We don't work in isolation. Sometimes the pastor or imam can help guide the client's values, especially in family cases. We must ethically partner with them.* (Counsellor 10)

Theme 3: Language and culturally aligned communication

Sub-theme 3.1: Use of indigenous languages for ethical clarity

Participants observed that ethical concepts like informed consent and confidentiality should be explained in clients' native languages to ensure true understanding.

> *Many rural clients nod in agreement even when they don't understand the English explanation. Ethical practice requires we speak their language, literally and culturally.* (Counsellor 6)

Sub-theme 3.2: Reframing ethical concepts to fit communal worldviews

Respondents emphasized that concepts such as autonomy and confidentiality, traditionally individualistic, need to be interpreted in the light of communal values.

> *In our culture, decisions are not made alone. We must explain confidentiality in a way that respects the family's role without breaching ethics.* (Counsellor 3)

Theme 4: Contextualized ethical training and supervision

Sub-theme 4.1: Localized case studies in ethics training

Counselors argued that ethical training should draw on local dilemmas and culturally relevant case studies, rather than relying on Western ethics frameworks.

> *Ethics courses should include scenarios from our schools, churches, and villages. That's how we learn to respond ethically in our context.* (Counsellor 2)

Sub-theme 4.2: Continuous professional development in cultural competence

Participants recommended ongoing workshops and seminars that include cultural humility, anti-bias training, and ethical decision-making in multicultural scenarios.

We are dealing with ethnic diversity, religion, and class every day. Our ethics workshops must reflect that complexity. (Counsellor 1)

Theme 5: Systemic and Institutional Support for multicultural ethics

Sub-theme 5.1: Policy inclusion of multicultural ethics

Respondents advocated for national ethical codes and counselling regulations to explicitly address multicultural and faith-based ethical considerations.

Our ethics code is silent on cultural issues. It needs updating to reflect who we really are as a people. (Counsellor 12)

Sub-theme 5.2: Institutional collaboration with cultural and religious structures

Participants proposed that counselling institutions, regulatory bodies, and ministries should build structured relationships with traditional and faith-based institutions.

When the counselling body partners with the traditional council or church associations, our ethics become part of the community. (Counsellor 4)

Interpretive summary

The findings from the qualitative strand of this study highlight the deep interconnection between culture, religion, and ethics in Nigerian counselling practice. Counselors emphasized that culturally contextualized ethical practice is not merely about avoiding violations but about building trust, understanding, and relevance in the therapeutic process. Strategies such as engaging faith leaders, speaking indigenous languages, drawing on local ethics case studies, and reframing Western ethical norms through communal lenses were widely endorsed. Participants called for systemic changes in policy and training that embed multicultural and spiritual realities into ethical guidelines. Ultimately, ethical multicultural counselling in Nigeria must be community-embedded, spiritually sensitive, and culturally fluent to be truly effective.

Discussion of findings

The study identified 26 core ethical principles that guide multicultural counselling practice globally and assessed their perceived relevance and application among Nigerian counselors. These principles encompass critical domains such as cultural respect, identity, communication, humility, confidentiality, informed consent, advocacy, and spiritual integration.

Respect for cultural beliefs and identity

The highest-rated items reflect foundational principles such as respecting clients' cultural beliefs, honoring their cultural identity throughout counselling, and adapting communication styles to align with cultural norms. These findings align with existing multicultural counselling competencies which underscore the need for culturally responsive attitudes, knowledge, and skills. Participants' strong endorsement of cultural respect and identity confirms that these values are well recognized among Nigerian counselors (Arredondo & Tovar-Blank, 2013; Berger et al., 2014; Tomlinson-Clarke, 2013), likely due to the country's ethnolinguistic diversity and collective social orientation. However, the moderate standard deviations suggest variability in how consistently these principles are applied. For example, while the mean for "I respect and Honor clients' cultural beliefs, values, and customs without judgment" is 2.94, the standard deviation of 1.36 indicates differences in interpretation or practice. This highlights the need for clearer ethical guidance and training on navigating cultural sensitivity within professional limits.

Cultural humility and competence

The principles related to cultural humility, such as acknowledging the limits of one's cultural knowledge and seeking supervision when necessary, were also positively endorsed. These align with best practices in multicultural counselling which prioritize ongoing self-reflection and supervision to guard against cultural bias (Ioakeimidou, 2025; Mosher et al., 2017; Zhang et al., 2022). The endorsement of "I actively pursue ongoing training to improve my multicultural counselling competence" further suggests an openness among Nigerian counselors to continuous learning. However, the variation in responses may reflect unequal access to such training, particularly for rural or under-resourced practitioners.

Culturally appropriate assessment and intervention

The mid-level endorsement of culturally validated assessment tools and interventions raises a concern. While respondents agreed with the principles, the relatively lower mean scores for items like "I use culturally validated assessment tools to avoid misdiagnosis" and "I ensure that counselling interventions are adapted to be culturally appropriate" suggest implementation challenges. This could be attributed to a lack of locally validated instruments, a problem widely reported in African mental health research (Betancourt et al., 2009; Greene et al., 2023). Without culturally appropriate tools, even ethically aware counselors may inadvertently misdiagnose or mismanage culturally complex cases.

Confidentiality, consent, and ethical boundaries

The ethical principles on confidentiality, informed consent, and dual relationships received high agreement, especially in terms of explicitly clarifying confidentiality and ensuring consent processes are culturally sensitive. Nonetheless, qualitative reports indicated ethical tension between respecting client confidentiality and meeting communal expectations—such as family involvement in therapy. This tension reflects a broader ethical dilemma noted in African contexts, where individual rights often coexist with communal obligations (Nwoye, 2015). For instance, the challenge of explaining confidentiality within extended family systems necessitates reframing Western principles to suit local cultural logics.

Advocacy, empowerment, and social justice

Principles such as advocating for social justice, challenging systemic barriers, and supporting culturally defined autonomy received moderate endorsement. These findings are significant, as they reflect the ethical call to not only respond to individual clients but also address structural inequalities that marginalize diverse populations (Sue et al., 2019). However, lower scores on these items may indicate that while counselors conceptually agree with advocacy-based ethics, practical enactment remains limited. This is consistent with literature suggesting that advocacy and social justice work is often underemphasized in both counselling training and professional development in sub-Saharan Africa (Sinclair et al., 2024).

Intersectionality and spiritual integration

Two of the more nuanced principles—considering intersectionality and incorporating spiritual beliefs—received lower mean scores relative to the others. Intersectionality is essential to understanding how clients experience multiple layers of identity-related stress or privilege. Its underrepresentation may signal limited exposure among Nigerian counselors to contemporary diversity theories. Similarly, spiritual integration—although culturally essential—was endorsed less frequently than expected, given Nigeria's deeply religious context. This may reflect ethical uncertainty about how to incorporate faith without overstepping professional boundaries, especially when clients' beliefs differ from those of the counselor. Interestingly, the principle "I incorporate clients' spiritual and religious beliefs into counselling as appropriate" had a mean below 3.0, suggesting that despite the cultural centrality of religion, formal integration of spirituality into counselling remains uneven. This disconnect could be resolved by developing ethical guidelines that specifically address faith-based counselling practices within multicultural contexts, as advocated by Moodley and West (2005).

In addition, this study investigated the awareness, application, and cultural relevance of ethical principles guiding multicultural counselling among Nigerian counselors, using a mixed-methods approach. The findings reveal a complex but insightful picture of the ethical landscape in Nigerian multicultural counselling, reflecting both global standards and local contextual dynamics. The results are discussed across four major areas: counselors' awareness and compliance, frequency of ethical practices, perceived cultural challenges, and recommendations for culturally responsive strategies.

Awareness and compliance with ethical principles

The findings reveal that Nigerian counselors exhibit a moderate to moderately high level of awareness regarding multicultural ethical principles, with mean scores ranging between 2.85 and 3.27 across specific items. Items related to cultural competence, informed consent, and confidentiality scored highest, indicating that these principles have become relatively well integrated into the ethical consciousness of practitioners. This finding supports existing literature which identifies these domains as foundational pillars in multicultural counselling ethics (Pedersen et al., 2008).

Nevertheless, the relatively lower mean scores on items addressing the recognition of cultural autonomy and intersectionality suggest that awareness is still uneven. Cultural autonomy—particularly the client's right to make informed decisions within their sociocultural context—was not as strongly endorsed, which may reflect the continuing tension between individualistic Western ethics and communal African values (Nwoye, 2015). The modest mean for intersectionality awareness also indicates a need to expand counselors' understanding of how ethnicity, religion, gender, and socioeconomic status intersect in shaping ethical concerns.

Frequency of ethical practice

The frequency of ethical practice among counselors mirrored the awareness scores, with moderate consistency observed. The practice of updating one's ethical knowledge was the most frequently reported, indicating a willingness among counselors to stay current with professional standards. However, practices directly tied to cultural sensitivity—such as respecting culturally based healing systems, reframing confidentiality to reflect communal values, and integrating spiritual beliefs—were less frequently reported. This disconnect may stem from ethical codes that prioritize individual autonomy and confidentiality, which may not fully align with African communal structures where decision-making often involves family and spiritual leaders (Eze, 2015).

Gender-based differences were noted, with female counselors reporting slightly higher awareness but slightly lower frequency of practice compared to their male counterparts.

Although this difference was not statistically significant, it may reflect differences in ethical training, practice exposure, or role negotiation in culturally patriarchal contexts. Academic qualification and cultural background did not significantly influence awareness or frequency scores, suggesting that ethical competency may be more tied to individual orientation and professional development than to demographics alone.

Cultural relevance and ethical tensions

A critical finding of this study lies in counselors' perception of ethical principles as only moderately culturally relevant. Although most respondents agreed that ethical codes are essential to client wellbeing, a significant number expressed concerns about the applicability of these codes in the Nigerian context. This confirms critiques in the literature that current global ethical frameworks are often rooted in Euro-American individualism and fail to account for collectivist orientations in African societies (Gyekye, 2011). For instance, the concept of client autonomy is often challenged by cultural expectations of family involvement and elder authority, especially in rural communities.

Moreover, participants in the qualitative phase identified practical dilemmas arising from efforts to apply Western ethical norms without adaptation. For example, confidentiality—a cornerstone of ethical counselling—was described as difficult to enforce when community norms demand information sharing with parents, elders, or religious leaders. These observations echo the findings of (Gerstein et al., 2012), who emphasize the importance of ethical pluralism and cultural reflexivity.

Qualitative insights: Culturally responsive ethical strategies

The qualitative analysis further illuminated how Nigerian counselors navigate these tensions and what culturally contextualized strategies they recommend. Five major themes emerged: integration of indigenous knowledge systems, faith-based ethical engagement, culturally aligned communication, contextualized ethics training, and systemic support.

Integration of Indigenous Knowledge Systems involved collaboration with traditional healers and elders. Participants emphasized that indigenous systems are still trusted by many clients, and ethical counselling must respectfully acknowledge and, where appropriate, collaborate with these traditional institutions. This reflects Nwoye's (2015) African communal healing model and supports the call by Fadele et al. (2024) for culturally embedded counselling systems.

Faith-Based Ethical Engagement was seen as crucial, particularly because religious institutions serve as the primary support systems for many Nigerians. Participants reported that clients often consult pastors, imams, or spiritualists before seeking professional counselling. Ethical frameworks that ignore this reality risk appearing irrelevant or even antagonistic. This insight affirms the importance of spiritual integration in counselling, as noted by Moodley and West (2005), who argue for the ethical incorporation of clients' spiritual worldviews in multicultural practice.

Culturally Aligned Communication emphasized the importance of language and framing. Participants noted that ethical principles like informed consent must be explained in indigenous languages and framed in a way that aligns with communal logic. For example, the idea of confidentiality was more acceptable when explained as a form of respect for the family's honor, rather than as an individualistic right. This practice is consistent with the narrative counselling models that emphasize co-constructing meaning within the client's cultural worldview (Peltier et al., 2024).

Contextualized Ethics Training was identified as a core need. Many participants criticized ethics education in Nigeria for relying too heavily on foreign case studies that are irrelevant to local realities. They advocated for training grounded in Nigerian cultural contexts, including case-based learning and exposure to indigenous ethical dilemmas. Authors argue, ethical competence requires culturally relevant pedagogy, not merely the transplantation of Western standards (Nwikina, 2013).

Systemic and Institutional Support was another prominent theme. Participants emphasized the importance of revising national ethical codes to reflect multicultural considerations and advocated for formal partnerships between counselling institutions and cultural/religious authorities. This systemic approach aligns with global recommendations for ethics codes to be both universal and adaptable (Mirza et al., 2023).

Implications and contribution to knowledge

Collectively, these findings underscore the need for a hybrid ethical framework that harmonizes global professional standards with Nigeria's socio-cultural realities. Rather than discarding Western ethical norms, the study supports a contextual adaptation—an indigenized model of ethics that reflects communalism, spirituality, and cultural fluidity. The insights from this research also contribute to the global discourse on ethical counselling by demonstrating that ethical practice is not culturally neutral. As such, the Nigerian case can inform other multicultural settings where Western norms may clash with local values.

Appendix A

Multicultural counselling ethics questionnaire (MCEQ)

Developed Dr. Mkpoikanke Otu and validated by experts in counselling psychology and multicultural studies.

Instructions

Please respond to each statement below by selecting the option that best represents your level of agreement or frequency of occurrence. Your responses will be kept confidential and used for research purposes only.

Section A: Awareness of core ethical principles

Statements	1. Strongly disagree	2. Disagree	3. Neutral	4. Agree	5. Strongly agree
1. I am familiar with the main ethical principles that guide multicultural counselling practice. 2. I understand the importance of confidentiality in multicultural counselling settings. 3. I recognize the need to obtain informed consent in multicultural counselling contexts. 4. I am aware of the ethical principle of cultural competence in counselling.					

Section B: Frequency of ethical practice

Statements	1. Never	2. Rarely	3. Sometimes	4. Often	5. Always
1. I regularly apply ethical principles in my multicultural counselling sessions. 2. I seek supervision or consultation when faced with ethical dilemmas in multicultural counselling. 3. I consistently respect clients' cultural values and beliefs during counselling. 4. I update my knowledge about ethical standards relevant to multicultural counselling.					

Section C: Perceived challenges in applying ethical standards

Statements	1. Strongly disagree	2. Disagree	3. Neutral	4. Agree	5. Strongly agree
1. I find it difficult to balance ethical standards with cultural differences in counselling. 2. Conflicting cultural values sometimes challenge my ethical decision-making. 3. I experience challenges when clients' cultural beliefs contradict standard ethical codes. 4. Lack of culturally specific ethical guidelines limits my counselling practice.					

Section D: Cultural relevance of current ethical codes

Statements	1. Strongly disagree	2. Disagree	3. Neutral	4. Agree	5. Strongly agree
1. Existing ethical codes adequately address cultural diversity issues in counselling. 2. Ethical guidelines should be adapted to better reflect multicultural realities. 3. I believe culturally relevant ethical codes improve counselling outcomes. 4. I am confident in my ability to apply ethical codes in culturally diverse counselling situations.					

Demographic information (optional)

Age: __________

Gender: __________

Years of counselling experience: __________

Cultural background: __________

Highest qualification in counselling: _________

Appendix B

Questionnaire on core ethical principles guiding multicultural counselling globally

Dear Participant,

This questionnaire is designed to assess your agreement with core ethical principles that guide multicultural counselling globally. Please read each statement carefully and indicate your level of agreement using the scale below:

1 = Strongly Disagree | 2 = Disagree | 3 = Neutral | 4 = Agree | 5 = Strongly Agree.

Thank you for your participation.

Cluster 1: Respect and cultural sensitivity

1. I respect and honor clients' cultural beliefs, values, and customs without judgment. □1 □2 □3 □4 □5
2. I acknowledge the importance of clients' cultural identity in all stages of counselling. □1 □2 □3 □4 □5
3. I maintain cultural humility by acknowledging what I do not know about clients' cultures. □1 □2 □3 □4 □5
4. I adapt communication styles to align with clients' cultural preferences and norms. □1 □2 □3 □4 □5
5. I recognize and respect culturally-based coping mechanisms and healing practices. □1 □2 □3 □4 □5
6. I ensure counselling environments are welcoming and inclusive of diverse cultural backgrounds. □1 □2 □3 □4 □5

Cluster 2: Competence and professional responsibility

7. I actively pursue ongoing training to improve my multicultural counselling competence. □1 □2 □3 □4 □5
8. I recognize the limits of my expertise and seek consultation or supervision on cultural issues. □1 □2 □3 □4 □5
9. I use culturally validated assessment tools to avoid misdiagnosis. □1 □2 □3 □4 □5
10. I ensure that counselling interventions are adapted to be culturally appropriate. □1 □2 □3 □4 □5
11. I provide services in the client's preferred language or arrange qualified interpreters when needed. □1 □2 □3 □4 □5
12. I maintain professional integrity by addressing ethical dilemmas through appropriate channels. □1 □2 □3 □4 □5

Cluster 3: Ethical practice and confidentiality

13. I ensure informed consent processes are culturally sensitive and clearly understood by clients. □1 □2 □3 □4 □5
14. I respect confidentiality while balancing cultural norms about sharing information with families. □1 □2 □3 □4 □5
15. I clarify limits of confidentiality explicitly and in a culturally appropriate manner. □1 □2 □3 □4 □5
16. I avoid dual relationships that may exploit or harm clients, especially in cultural contexts. □1 □2 □3 □4 □5
17. I prevent harm and avoid stereotyping or cultural bias in counselling practice. □1 □2 □3 □4 □5

Cluster 4: Client autonomy and social justice

18. I respect clients' right to make informed decisions within their cultural context. □1 □2 □3 □4 □5
19. I support clients' empowerment, recognizing cultural definitions of autonomy and family roles. □1 □2 □3 □4 □5
20. I actively advocate for clients' social justice and equity in access to resources and services. □1 □2 □3 □4 □5
21. I challenge systemic barriers that negatively impact culturally diverse populations. □1 □2 □3 □4 □5
22. I include considerations of intersectionality in understanding client challenges and strengths. □1 □2 □3 □4 □5

Cluster 5: Relational and spiritual considerations

23. I build culturally respectful rapport and trust with clients. □1 □2 □3 □4 □5
24. I acknowledge the role of family, community, and cultural systems in clients' well-being. □1 □2 □3 □4 □5
25. I incorporate clients' spiritual and religious beliefs into counselling as appropriate. □1 □2 □3 □4 □5
26. I am sensitive to cultural rituals or practices that influence healing and therapy outcomes. □1 □2 □3 □4 □5

References

Akpa-Inyang, F., & Chima, S. C. (2021). South African traditional values and beliefs regarding informed consent and limitations of the principle of respect for autonomy in African communities: A cross-cultural qualitative study. *BMC Medical Ethics, 22*(1). https://doi.org/10.1186/s12910-021-00678-4

Arredondo, P., Toporek, R., Brown, S. P., Jones, J., Locke, D. C., Sanchez, J., & Stadler, H. (1996). Operationalization of the multicultural counseling competencies. *Journal of Multicultural Counseling and Development, 24*(1). https://doi.org/10.1002/j.2161-1912.1996.tb00288.x

Arredondo, P., & Tovar-Blank, Z. G. (2013). Multicultural competencies: A dynamic paradigm for the 21st century. In *APA handbook of multicultural psychology* (Vol. 2) Applications and training. https://doi.org/10.1037/14187-002

Berger, L. K., Zane, N., & Hwang, W. C. (2014). Therapist ethnicity and treatment orientation differences in multicultural counseling competencies. *Asian American Journal of Psychology, 5*(1). https://doi.org/10.1037/a0036178

Betancourt, T. S., Bass, J., Borisova, I., Neugebauer, R., Speelman, L., Onyango, G., & Bolton, P. (2009). Assessing local instrument reliability and validity: A field-based example from northern Uganda. *Social Psychiatry and Psychiatric Epidemiology, 44*(8). https://doi.org/10.1007/s00127-008-0475-1

Braun, V., & Clarke, V. (2006). Using thematic analysis in psychology. *Qualitative Research in Psychology, 3* (2). https://doi.org/10.1191/1478088706qp063oa

British Association for Counselling and Psychotherapy. (2018). Ethical framework for the counselling professions 2 BACP ethical framework for the counselling professions. www.bacp.co.uk.

Chao, R. C. L., Wei, M., Good, G. E., & Flores, L. Y. (2011). Race/ethnicity, color-blind racial attitudes, and multicultural counseling competence: The moderating effects of multicultural counseling training. *Journal of Counseling Psychology, 58*(1). https://doi.org/10.1037/a0022091

Counseling Association, A. (2014). *ACA code of ethics as approved by the ACA governing council mission.*

Egbo, A. C. (2015). The challenges of guidance and counselling practices as perceived by secondary school counsellors in Enugu State Nigeria. *International Journal of Educational Research, 3*(5).

Eze, C. (2015). Indigenizing counselling valuing the afterlife with the Igbo of south eastern Nigeria: A case for ino-uwa based intervention. *Journal of Psychology in Africa, 25*(2). https://doi.org/10.1080/14330237.2015.1021508

Fadele, K. P., Igwe, S. C., Toluwalogo, N.-O., Udokang, E. I., Ogaya, J. B., & Lucero-Prisno, D. E. (2024). Mental health challenges in Nigeria: Bridging the gap between demand and resources. *Cambridge Prisms: Global Mental Health, 11*. https://doi.org/10.1017/gmh.2024.19

Federal Ministry of Education. (2004). *National policy on education* (4th ed.). NERDC Press.

Gerstein, L. H., Paul Heppner, P., Ægisdóttir, S., Leung, S. M. A., & Norsworthy, K. L. (2012). Cross-cultural counseling: History, challenges, and rationale. In *Essentials of cross-cultural counseling*. https://doi.org/10.4135/9781452275505.n1

Greene, M. C., Ventevogel, P., Likindikoki, S. L., Bonz, A. G., Turner, R., Rees, S., Misinzo, L., Njau, T., Mbwambo, J. K. K., & Tol, W. A. (2023). Why local concepts matter: Using cultural expressions of distress to explore the construct validity of research instruments to measure mental health problems among Congolese women in Nyarugusu refugee camp. *Transcultural Psychiatry, 60*(3). https://doi.org/10.1177/13634615221122626

Gyekye, K. (2011). Tradition and modernity: Philosophical reflections on the African experience. In *Tradition and modernity: Philosophical reflections on the African experience*. https://doi.org/10.1093/acprof:oso/9780195112252.001.0001

Ioakeimidou, A. (2025). Cultural humility as a mechanism for building working alliance cultural humility as a mechanism for building working alliance with international counseling supervisees with international counseling supervisees part of the counseling commons, education commons, and the international and intercultural communication commons. https://digitalcommons.montclair.edu/etd.

Jr, W., Å-, ç, Brock, B., Member Moss Breen, C. J., & Gail Jensen, D. M. (2018). *Dissertation approved by r ˆ4 committee member.*

Makinde, O. (1983). *Fundamentals of guidance and counselling*. Macmillan.

Mirza, H., Bellalem, F., & Mirza, C. (2023). Ethical considerations in qualitative research: Summary guidelines for novice social science researchers. *Social Studies and Research Journal, 11*(1).

Moodley, R., & West, W. (2005). Integrating traditional healing practices into counseling and psychotherapy. In *Integrating traditional healing practices into counseling and psychotherapy.* https://doi.org/10.4135/9781452231648

Mosher, D. K., Hook, J. N., Captari, L. E., Davis, D. E., DeBlaere, C., & Owen, J. (2017). Cultural humility: A therapeutic framework for engaging diverse clients. *Practice Innovations, 2*(4). https://doi.org/10.1037/pri0000055

Nwikina, L. (2013). Fostering ethical behavior and culture in Nigeria schools. *International Journal of Learning and Development, 3*(6). https://doi.org/10.5296/ijld.v3i6.4706

Nwoye, A. (2015). What is African psychology the psychology of? *Theory and Psychology, 25*(1). https://doi.org/10.1177/0959354314565116

Odeleye, D. A., Ola Afolaranmi, A., & Obaloluwa Ojo, S. (2024). Training and education of pastoral care and counselling professionals in Africa. *In International Journal of Contemporary Research in Humanities, 2* (1). https://orcid.org/0000-0002-0917-2883.

Onyilofor, F. N. C. (2013). Repositioning guidance and counselling and curriculum innovation in higher education in Nigeria. *Journal of International Education Research, 9*(2). https://doi.org/10.19030/jier.v9i2.7720

Pedersen, P. B., Draguns, J. G., Lonner, W. J., & Trimble, J. E. (2008). Counseling across cultures. In *Counseling across cultures.* https://doi.org/10.4135/9781483329314

Peltier, C., Dickson, S., Grandpierre, V., Oltean, I., McGregor, L., Hageltorn, E., & Young, N. L. (2024). Culturally appropriate consent processes for community-driven indigenous child health research: A scoping review. *BMC Medical Ethics, 25*(1). https://doi.org/10.1186/s12910-023-00996-9

Sani, M., & Kulumbu, U. (2018). Ethical issues in professional counselling practice in Nigeria. *Prestige Journal of Education, 1*(1).

Sinclair, V. M., La Guardia, A. C., Saunders, R. M., & Tichavakunda, A. A. (2024). Counselors as social justice advocates: Experiences addressing systemic marginalization. *Journal for Social Action in Counseling and Psychology, 16*(1), 19–42. https://doi.org/10.33043/y6594b8924

Sue, D. W., Arredondo, P., & McDavis, R. J. (1992). Multicultural counseling competencies and standards: A call to the profession. *Journal of Counseling and Development, 70*(4). https://doi.org/10.1002/j.1556-6676.1992.tb01642.x

Sue, D. W., Sue, D., Neville, H. A., & Smith, L. (2019). *Counseling the culturally diverse: Theory and practice* (8th ed.). NJ: Wiley.

Tanaka-Matsumi, J. (2022). Counseling across cultures: A half-century assessment. *Journal of Cross-Cultural Psychology, 53*(7–8). https://doi.org/10.1177/00220221221111810

Tomlinson-Clarke, S. (2013). Multicultural counseling competencies: Extending multicultural training paradigms toward globalization. *Ideas and Research You Can Use: VISTAS 2013, 3.*

Zea, M. C., & Echeverry, J. J. (1998). Review of counseling across cultures. *Cultural Diversity and Mental Health, 4*(1). https://doi.org/10.1037/1099-9809.4.1.72

Zhang, H., Watkins, C. E., Hook, J. N., Hodge, A. S., Davis, C. W., Norton, J., Wilcox, M. M., Davis, D. E., DeBlaere, C., & Owen, J. (2022). Cultural humility in psychotherapy and clinical supervision: A research review. In *Counselling and psychotherapy research* (Vol 22). https://doi.org/10.1002/capr.12481. Issue 3.

CHAPTER 3

Essential counselling skills for multicultural counselling practice

Introduction

The increasing cultural diversity in contemporary societies has intensified the need for counsellors to possess skills that are not only foundational to effective therapeutic practice but also adaptable across varied cultural contexts. Multicultural counselling extends beyond the traditional application of counselling microskills. It requires practitioners to integrate cultural knowledge, cultural humility, and self-awareness into their helping relationships. As Sue et al. (1992) argue in their foundational model, effective multicultural counselling is grounded in the integration of awareness, knowledge, and skills, enabling counsellors to respond appropriately to the worldviews and lived realities of culturally diverse clients. This chapter therefore focuses on identifying and examining the counselling skills essential for competent and ethical multicultural practice.

Core counselling skills such as active listening, empathy, reflection, attending behaviours, and appropriate questioning remain central in therapeutic encounters. However, their application is greatly influenced by the cultural backgrounds, communication patterns, and relational norms of clients (Hill, 2019). Counsellors must therefore not only master these skills but also develop the competence to modify them sensitively across cultures. Research shows that cultural competence enhances a counsellor's ability to build trust, avoid misinterpretation, and strengthen therapeutic alliances with clients from diverse groups (Sue & Sue, 2017). Consequently, understanding how counsellors adapt fundamental skills in response to cultural expectations is crucial for ensuring inclusive and effective practice. Equally important is the role of cultural humility and self-awareness, which have emerged as indispensable components of multicultural counselling. Cultural humility emphasises an ongoing commitment to self-reflection, recognition of personal biases, and openness to learning from clients' cultural perspectives (Hook et al., 2013). This orientation enables counsellors to approach clients without assumptions, thereby improving empathy, reducing cultural misunderstandings, and promoting collaborative meaning-making.

Despite the recognised importance of these competencies, counsellors often encounter significant challenges in multicultural practice. Barriers such as language differences,

A Pragmatic Approach to Multicultural Counselling and Psychotherapy Skills Acquisition. https://doi.org/10.1016/B978-0-443-33939-4.00006-9

conflicting cultural norms, stereotyping, and limited formal training in multicultural counselling hinder the effective use of essential skills (Jones-Smith, 2020; Sue et al., 2019). These challenges highlight the need for continued inquiry into how counsellors navigate complex cultural dynamics and what support systems can strengthen their professional capabilities. Against this backdrop, this chapter investigates the counselling skills required for effective multicultural practice and examines how cultural competence, cultural humility, and self-awareness shape the delivery of these skills. It further explores the challenges counsellors face when working with culturally diverse clients and proposes practical strategies for enhancing multicultural counselling competence. The insights generated are intended to inform both counselling practice and training, particularly within contexts such as Africa, where culturally relevant scholarship remains comparatively limited.

Conceptual framework of essential counselling skills for multicultural counselling

Essential counselling skills have been conceptualised in the literature from multiple theoretical and practical perspectives. Generally, skills refer to the learned abilities that enable individuals to perform specific tasks effectively within a given professional context (Ridley et al., 2021). In counselling, these skills constitute the observable behaviours, interpersonal techniques, and cognitive capacities that enable practitioners to respond appropriately to clients' needs. Scholars commonly define counselling skills as the foundational micro-skills, relational competencies, and process-oriented abilities that counsellors apply to facilitate client growth, understanding, and problem resolution (Ivey et al., 2025; Yibeltal Yedemie, 2021). Thus, essential counselling skills encompass the range of capabilities required to initiate, sustain, and conclude therapeutic conversations in a manner that supports psychological well-being. According to Yaumas et al. (2018), essential counselling skills represent the minimum proficiency that counsellors or counsellors-in-training must demonstrate to competently manage counselling sessions. These include both technical skills, such as listening, questioning, reflecting, and interpreting, and personal attributes such as empathy, cultural sensitivity, and professional self-awareness (Knox & Hill, 2021). In multicultural counselling, essential counselling skills must also incorporate culturally responsive competencies, defined as the counsellor's ability to adapt communication, assessment, and intervention strategies to align with clients' cultural worldviews, identities, and sociocultural contexts (Hays, 2016; Sue, 2017). This integrated view positions essential counselling skills not merely as abilities but as dynamic, culturally situated capacities that support ethical and effective therapeutic engagement across diverse client populations.

From my point of view, essential counselling skills constitute the foundational requirements for carrying out counselling duties and performing counselling roles effectively. They represent the core expertise that enables counsellors to execute their responsibilities accurately, ethically, and with professional adequacy. In practice, counsellors require a combination of expertise, skills, and personal qualities to function optimally. Consequently, counselling skills can also be understood as personal characteristics or attributes that counsellors embody. When counselling skills are viewed as abilities, emphasis is placed on the capacities and competencies counsellors must develop to function effectively in diverse situations. When conceptualised as expertise, attention shifts to the professional knowledge and mastery acquired through structured training and supervised practice. Conversely, when counselling skills are regarded as personal characteristics, the focus is on the personality structure and dispositions that are shaped and refined through counsellor education to align with counselling roles and expectations. Based on my experience as a counsellor and counsellor educator, individuals often move through these definitional layers as they progress in their professional journey. Counsellors-in-training begin by acquiring basic counselling skills. With practice and mastery, these skills evolve into professional expertise. Ultimately, the highest goal is for these skills to mature into enduring personal attributes. At this stage, counsellors demonstrate a level of integration where their professional skills are naturally reflected in their character and interpersonal presence. They become seasoned practitioners whose demeanour and conduct readily signal their identity as counsellors, as personal attributes tend to be consistently observable.

From a multicultural counselling perspective, these skills gain even deeper significance. Effective multicultural practice requires counsellors not only to possess technical abilities but also to apply them with cultural sensitivity, humility, and responsiveness. Core skills such as empathy, active listening, questioning, and assessment must be adapted to clients' cultural meanings, communication styles, worldviews, and value systems. For example, demonstrating empathy may require understanding culturally specific expressions of emotion; building rapport may depend on honouring cultural protocols; and accurate assessment often necessitates awareness of cultural norms that shape behaviour, help-seeking patterns, and interpretations of wellbeing. Therefore, in multicultural contexts, counsellors must integrate cultural competence into their skillset by demonstrating awareness of their own cultural assumptions, knowledge of clients' sociocultural backgrounds, and the ability to apply culturally appropriate interventions. Skills therefore extend beyond technique to include cultural curiosity, openness, non-judgement, and respect for cultural identities and lived experiences. These dimensions ensure that counselling interactions are not only effective but also culturally affirming and empowering.

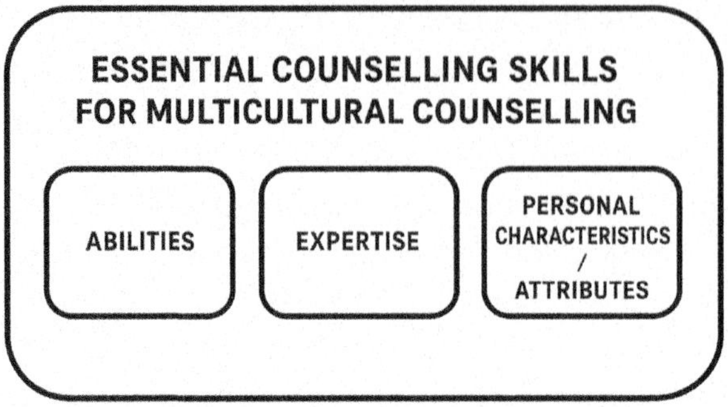

Figure 3.1

Fig. 3.1 presents the conceptual framework of essential counselling skills for multicultural counselling, illustrating how counselling skills operate at three interrelated levels: abilities, expertise, and personal characteristics/attributes. The framework shows that effective multicultural counselling requires counsellors to develop foundational abilities, advance these into professional expertise through training and supervised practice, and ultimately embody them as personal characteristics. Together, these three domains interact to support culturally responsive and competent counselling practice. The following table summarises the key areas of skills that enable counsellors to be effective in their roles.

Table 3.1 outlines the essential counselling skills required for effective multicultural counselling practice, presented through six interrelated modules that collectively address the technical, interpersonal, and contextual dimensions of culturally responsive helping. Although these modules are conceptually distinct, they function as an integrated framework that supports counsellors in navigating the complex cultural dynamics that shape client experiences. The interdependence of the modules allows practitioners to move fluidly between concrete skills, attitudinal qualities, and broader professional competencies as they build therapeutic relationships with clients from diverse cultural backgrounds (Hays, 2016; Sue et al., 2019).

The first module in Table 3.1 focuses on action response skills, which include probing, questioning, exploring, silence, confronting, interpreting, assurance, and guiding clients towards catharsis. These skills direct the therapeutic process by helping clients articulate concerns, clarify their thoughts, and arrive at new insights (Corey, 2013). Probing and questioning refer to prompts that encourage deeper elaboration, allowing clients to expand on issues that may be communicated indirectly in certain cultures. For example, when working with clients who express distress through metaphors or proverbs, gentle probing helps clarify meaning without imposing an external interpretation. Exploring involves assisting clients to examine thoughts, emotions, and behaviours in relation to their cultural expectations. The use of silence allows space for reflection or emotional processing,

Table 3.1: Essential counselling skills for multicultural counselling.

Module	Skill set	Specific skills
Action response skills	Skills that help counsellors guide clients' emotional and cognitive processing	Probing, questioning, exploring, silence, confronting, interpreting, assurance, catharsis
Process skills	Skills that regulate the counselling process and maintain therapeutic conditions	Confidentiality, empathetic understanding, rapport building, genuineness
Attending skills	Skills for demonstrating presence, interest, and contextual attunement	Assuring, attending physically, minimal prompts, attending personally, attending contextually, responding to context, responding to feelings, responding to meaning, establishing rapport
Listening skills	Skills for receiving, processing, and communicating understanding	Reflection, clarification, paraphrasing, patience, information relay, eye contact
Personal and interpersonal competencies	Intrapersonal and interpersonal attributes that underpin effective multicultural counselling	Cultural humility, emotional intelligence, social intelligence, self-awareness
Counselling support skills (21st-century skills)	Higher-order abilities that enhance problem-solving and collaborative engagement	Critical thinking, problem-solving, flexibility, networking/collaboration, communication, leadership

although its meaning varies across cultures; in some contexts, silence is a sign of respect, while in others it may signal discomfort. Confronting involves sensitively addressing inconsistencies in clients' narratives, though this must be moderated according to cultural norms surrounding directness. Interpreting allows counsellors to suggest possible meanings or patterns behind a client's experiences, but this requires cultural contextualisation to avoid misinterpretation. Skills such as assurance and catharsis support emotional safety and expression, and their effectiveness depends heavily on cultural norms regarding emotional display.

The second module concerns process skills, which include confidentiality, empathetic understanding, rapport building, and genuineness. These skills shape the relational climate of counselling and help establish trust. Confidentiality, though a universal ethical principle, may require explanation for clients from collectivist cultures where sharing personal information within extended family networks is normative. Empathetic understanding involves perceiving the client's subjective world and communicating that understanding in culturally sensitive ways. This may include recognising that certain emotions are communicated through behaviour or silence rather than direct statements. Rapport building is essential for forming a trusting therapeutic alliance, and in many cultural contexts, counsellors may need to invest more time in relational warm-up before addressing clinical issues. Genuineness allows counsellors to interact authentically, though this authenticity must be expressed in ways that respect cultural norms around hierarchy, formality, or professional boundaries (Pedersen, 2001).

The third module presented in Table 3.1 addresses attending skills, which include assuring, physical attending, the use of minimal prompts, attending personally, attending contextually, and responding to context, feelings, and meaning. These skills demonstrate the counsellor's presence, attention, and respect, and they are particularly important during the early stages of counselling (Chan, 2010). Physical attending relates to posture, eye contact, and spatial orientation, all of which carry cultural meanings. For instance, while direct eye contact may signal engagement in some Western contexts, it may be interpreted as disrespectful in cultures where modesty is valued. Minimal prompts such as nodding or brief verbal cues encourage continued sharing, but excessive prompting may overwhelm clients from cultures that prefer slower, more contemplative communication. 'Attending personally' refers to acknowledging the client's cultural identity, social roles, and lived experiences, while 'attending contextually' involves sensitivity to broader sociopolitical realities such as migration pressures or systemic discrimination. Responding to context, feelings, and meaning allows counsellors to interpret what clients communicate through both verbal and culturally patterned non-verbal cues.

The fourth module centres on listening skills, reflection, clarification, paraphrasing, patience, information relay, and attention to culturally patterned eye contact. Listening is foundational to effective counselling, yet it requires adaptation in multicultural contexts. Reflection involves mirroring the client's feelings and is especially important when emotional expression is subtle or encoded within culturally specific narratives. Clarification allows counsellors to check their understanding of culturally loaded expressions or metaphors. Paraphrasing restates clients' messages in the counsellor's words, but it must be done carefully to avoid distorting meaning, particularly when clients communicate indirectly. Patience is essential when clients express themselves through storytelling, pauses, or extended silence. Information relay helps clients summarise complex experiences, such as negotiating between personal goals and communal expectations, while attention to eye contact ensures that the counsellor responds appropriately to cultural norms regarding visual engagement.

The fifth module consists of personal and interpersonal competencies, cultural humility, emotional intelligence, social intelligence, and self-awareness. These competencies provide the attitudinal foundation for effective multicultural practice. Cultural humility emphasises the counsellor's recognition of their own cultural limitations and the need for ongoing learning, encouraging a stance of openness towards clients' worldviews (Tervalon & Murray-García, 1998). Emotional intelligence supports accurate reading of clients' emotional expressions, which may be shaped by cultural norms and therefore not aligned with Western assumptions about affect. Social intelligence enables counsellors to navigate culturally patterned interpersonal dynamics, such as power distance or gendered communication roles. Self-awareness requires counsellors to reflect on their own biases, assumptions, and cultural positioning to avoid imposing personal perspectives on clients' experiences (Hays, 2016).

The final module, counselling support skills, reflects the broader professional competencies needed for contemporary multicultural counselling practice. These include critical thinking, problem-solving, flexibility, communication, collaboration, and leadership. Critical thinking enables counsellors to analyse culturally complex situations from multiple perspectives. Problem-solving supports clients whose challenges may involve interactions across family systems, schools, workplaces, or community structures. Flexibility is essential for adapting Western-derived counselling models to fit locally grounded cultural values, worldviews, and healing traditions. Effective communication ensures that counsellors convey information clearly while respecting linguistic and cultural preferences. Collaboration and networking help counsellors work across institutional and community boundaries, while leadership involves advocacy for clients who may face structural barriers or cultural marginalisation (Sue et al., 2019).

How I teach essential counselling skills for multicultural counselling practice

In teaching essential counselling skills over the years, especially in multicultural settings like ours, I have come to appreciate that these skills are not merely professional tools; they gradually become part of who we are as counsellors. In my classes, I always tell students that counselling skills begin with abilities, develop into expertise through practice, and eventually mature into personal attributes that shape their professional identity. This understanding guides the way I structure my course modules and how I help them see each skill not just as something to learn, but as something they must grow into.

When I teach action response skills, for instance, I emphasise that probing, questioning, and exploring are more than skills. They are part of how we enter the client's world. I often demonstrate probing by showing students how a simple invitation, such as 'Tell me more about how that situation affects you', can open a culturally safe space for clients who might normally withhold personal feelings. In multicultural counselling, I remind students that questions must be culturally sensitive. A question that honours family values in collectivist cultures, such as 'How does your family usually engage with decisions like this?' shows respect and avoids imposing individualistic assumptions. I explain how silence, something many new counsellors fear, becomes a powerful ally when used intentionally. Students learn that silence may communicate thoughtfulness, respect, or emotional restraint for some clients, and that they must allow silence to speak its cultural meaning. Even confrontation, which is often misunderstood, must be shaped by cultural awareness. I usually demonstrate this in class by offering soft, respectful confrontations that acknowledge discrepancies without threatening the client's sense of harmony or face. Skills such as assurance and facilitating catharsis are also deeply shaped by culture; I encourage students to recognise when a client needs reassurance that their emotions are valid, or when they need space to release feelings often suppressed in their cultural environment.

As students move to process skills, I highlight that confidentiality is one of the strongest pillars of trust in counselling. Many clients from cultures that value honour, reputation, and family cohesion fear disclosure. I frequently share examples from practice, explaining how clearly communicating the limits and protections of confidentiality helps clients feel safe. Empathic understanding is another skill I urge students to cultivate, not just intellectually but also emotionally. I tell them, 'You may not share your client's cultural background, but you can share their human feelings', and this perspective helps them bridge cultural gaps with sincerity. Rapport building becomes easier when students learn to adapt to culturally familiar greetings, tones, and relational expectations. Genuineness, I teach them, is not simply showing authenticity but doing so in ways that honour cultural norms around emotional expression.

My lecture on attending skills is often one of the most practical and interactive. I demonstrate how physical attending (posture, distance, seating) changes depending on cultural expectations about personal space. Students practice minimal prompts and contextual attending in role plays, learning that a simple nod or 'Hmm' can encourage clients who value indirect communication. I encourage them to observe context deeply: socioeconomic realities, gender expectations, religious influences, and cultural narratives all shape the client's meaning-making process. When teaching how to respond to feelings and meaning, I demonstrate with common culturally embedded expressions. For instance, when a client says, 'I do not want to bring shame to my family', the meaning goes beyond personal fear; it connects to cultural honour, communal identity, and obligation. Students learn to listen for hidden cultural layers beneath emotional expressions.

Listening skills, though central, must be culturally adapted as well. In my class, I remind students that reflection, clarification, and paraphrasing must always honour the client's language and worldview. I often model how to paraphrase without distorting cultural meaning. Patience is another skill I emphasise repeatedly; some cultures encourage thoughtful reflection before speaking, and I teach students to embrace silence and slow pacing rather than rushing the process. Eye contact also requires careful adaptation. I share examples demonstrating how direct eye contact may signal confidence in one culture but disrespect in another, and students practice adjusting their gaze accordingly.

Personal and interpersonal competencies are, in my view, the heart of multicultural counselling. I tell my students that cultural humility is not a skill they learn once. It is a posture they carry throughout their career. It involves openness, respect, and the willingness to learn from clients. I encourage them to reflect on their biases, values, and assumptions as part of developing self-awareness. Emotional intelligence helps them regulate their own reactions and understand those of clients. Social intelligence enables them to read social cues within cultural contexts. I share personal reflections from my own counselling experiences to show how these competencies develop over time and through intentional practice.

Finally, I integrate 21st-century counselling support skills into the course because today's multicultural counselling demands advanced cognitive and relational abilities. Skills like critical thinking, problem-solving, and flexibility help counsellors navigate complex cultural and systemic issues. I often guide students through real-life scenarios requiring adaptive communication, creativity, and ethical reasoning. Networking and collaboration become especially important when working with clients whose cultures rely on extended family systems, community elders, or faith-based structures. Communication and leadership skills empower counsellors to advocate for equitable treatment and culturally inclusive environments. Across all these modules, I consistently tell my students that the ultimate goal is not just to perform counselling skills but to become counsellors whose attitudes, behaviours, and presence reflect these skills naturally. In multicultural counselling, competence grows from the continuous blending of ability, expertise, and personal attributes. Thus, the more counsellors integrate these skills into their daily interactions, the more they become the kind of professionals whose work is culturally attuned, relationally grounded, and personally authentic.

Empirical perspective

Research objectives and questions

This study aims to examine the essential counselling skills required for effective multicultural counselling. Specifically, it seeks to identify and explore the key counselling skills and how they can be applied in multicultural settings. It also examines how cultural competence enhances the use of these core skills, enabling counsellors to establish trust and build strong therapeutic relationships with clients from diverse backgrounds. In addition, the study assesses the role of cultural humility and self-awareness in counselling practice, focusing on how counsellors' recognition of their own biases affects their ability to provide culturally sensitive care. The study further evaluates the challenges and barriers counsellors face in applying essential skills with clients from different cultural contexts, including issues such as language barriers, cultural misunderstandings, and limited training. Finally, it aims to provide practical recommendations for developing and enhancing multicultural counselling skills.

Based on these objectives, the study is guided by four research questions: What are the key counselling skills essential for effective multicultural counselling practice? How does cultural competence influence the application of core counselling skills in multicultural settings? What challenges and barriers do counsellors face in applying these skills with clients from diverse cultural backgrounds? And what strategies and resources can help counsellors enhance their multicultural counselling skills and competencies?

Methodology

Approach

This study adopted a mixed-methods approach, combining both quantitative and qualitative methods. The mixed-methods approach enabled a wide-ranging exploration of the essential counselling skills required for effective multicultural counselling, where the quantitative component provided measurable data on the competencies, barriers, and practices of counsellors, while the qualitative component offered in-depth insights into the experiences and perceptions of counsellors in multicultural settings (Kuo et al., 2020).

Research paradigm

This study utilised a combination of two paradigms: the positivist paradigm for the quantitative approach and the interpretivist paradigm for the qualitative approach. The choice of these paradigms was driven by the need to explore both the measurable, objective elements of multicultural counselling skills and the nuanced, subjective experiences of counsellors working in diverse cultural contexts.

Positivist paradigm

The positivist paradigm guided the quantitative component of the study, which focused on the objective measurement of counsellors' competencies, perceived barriers, and practices in multicultural counselling. In this paradigm, reality is assumed to be objective, measurable, and independent of the researcher. This approach focuses on gathering quantifiable data and testing relationships between variables to draw generalisable conclusions (Park et al., 2020).

The positivist approach is particularly suited to the study's aim of identifying key counselling skills that can be quantified and assessed across a large sample of counsellors. The use of structured instruments, such as surveys and questionnaires, allowed for the collection of data on specific, observable factors such as the frequency of use of core counselling skills (e.g., empathy, active listening) and the prevalence of barriers in multicultural settings (e.g., language barriers, cultural misunderstandings). The ability to test relationships between cultural competence and counselling outcomes provided a basis for generalising findings across different contexts, which is essential for understanding broad trends in multicultural counselling practice. This paradigm enabled the research to focus on measurable variables, such as the level of cultural competence and the frequency of challenges faced by counsellors, and test hypotheses about the relationships between these variables (Goh et al., 2015). Thus, the study provided objective evidence that contributed to the general understanding of multicultural counselling skills by using statistical methods to analyse large standardised datasets.

Interpretivist paradigm

In contrast, the interpretivist paradigm guided the qualitative component of the study, which explored the subjective experiences of counsellors working with clients from diverse cultural backgrounds. This paradigm recognises that knowledge is socially constructed and that individuals' meanings and understandings are influenced by their cultural context, experiences, and personal interactions (The Interpretive Paradigm, 2024; Vitale, 2023).

The interpretivist approach is particularly suited to the study's goal of exploring the lived experiences and perceptions of counsellors regarding multicultural practice. While the quantitative data provides a broad overview, the qualitative phase seeks to uncover the deeper, more personal insights that counsellors have about their practices, challenges, and the impact of cultural competence on their work. Semi-structured interviews and focus groups allowed the researcher to engage with participants on a more personal level, exploring how they interpret and respond to cultural differences in counselling contexts.

The interpretivist paradigm focused on understanding how counsellors' cultural humility, self-awareness, and interpersonal dynamics influenced their practices in multicultural settings (Mehra et al., 2025). The qualitative approach enabled the researcher to delve deeper into the meanings counsellors attached to their experiences with diverse clients, how they adapted their counselling skills, and how cultural understanding shaped their approach to establishing trust and building therapeutic relationships. Moreover, this paradigm provided rich, context-specific insights that could not be captured through quantitative methods alone. It also acknowledged the complexity of multicultural counselling, where a range of subjective factors, including personal values, cultural biases, and emotional responses, play a significant role in shaping a counsellor's practice.

Combined justification for the use of both paradigms

The combination of positivist and interpretivist paradigms in this study reflects the need for an inclusive understanding of essential multicultural counselling skills. While the positivist paradigm provided an objective measure of competencies and barriers, the interpretivist paradigm explored the underlying experiences, attitudes, and contextual factors that shaped counsellors' practices. Thus, the study allowed for a richer, more nuanced exploration of multicultural counselling skills – quantifying the core competencies and barriers faced by counsellors while also capturing the personal and cultural dimensions of their work.

The integration of these two paradigms ensured that the research could address both the broad trends in essential multicultural counselling skills (through quantitative analysis) and the context-specific, subjective experiences of counsellors (through qualitative analysis). This approach provided a more holistic view of the complexities of essential multicultural counselling skills and helped to better understand the challenges and competencies involved in working with clients from diverse cultural backgrounds.

Ontology

Ontology in research refers to the nature of reality and how it is understood or perceived by researchers (Poli & Obrst, 2010). In this study, the ontology aligns with both realism and relativism, which reflects the dual nature of the study's approach: the quantitative phase being grounded in realism and the qualitative phase adopting relativism. This combination of ontological perspectives is essential for exploring both the objective realities of multicultural counselling practices and the subjective experiences shaped by cultural contexts.

Realism (in the quantitative phase)

In the quantitative phase of the study, the ontology aligns with realism, which assumes that objective realities exist and can be measured independently of the researcher's perspective. This approach views the constructs under investigation, such as counsellors' essential multicultural counselling skills, perceived barriers, and practices in multicultural counselling, as real and observable phenomena. These elements can be quantified using structured instruments such as surveys or questionnaires, which collect data on aspects of multicultural counselling that are tangible and measurable.

The use of a realist ontology is appropriate for the quantitative phase because the study seeks to measure specific variables, such as the frequency of challenges faced by counsellors in multicultural settings (e.g., language barriers, cultural misunderstandings) and the perceived level of competence in applying multicultural counselling skills. These aspects are considered real and objective because they can be observed, categorised, and quantified through standardised measurement tools. The assumption in realism is that the data derived from these measurements are not subject to individual interpretations. This approach supports the notion that the realities of multicultural counselling practices, as experienced by practitioners, can be understood through objective, empirical evidence that applies broadly across different settings (McPhail & Lourie, 2017; Wynn & Williams, 2012).

Relativism (in the qualitative phase)

In the qualitative phase, the study adopts a relativist ontology, which acknowledges that multiple realities exist, shaped by individuals' unique experiences, perceptions, and cultural contexts (Ballinger, 2004; Kasperek, 2023). This approach recognises that reality is not singular but constructed through interactions and experiences within specific social and cultural environments. It assumes that each counsellor's understanding of multicultural counselling may be different, depending on their cultural background, personal experiences, and professional training.

The relativist ontology is well-suited for the qualitative phase because it allows for the exploration of counsellors' subjective experiences and personal interpretations of their work with clients from diverse cultural backgrounds. Counsellors' perceptions of their multicultural competencies, challenges, and practices are influenced by their individual cultural lenses and worldviews. Therefore, these experiences cannot be generalised or measured objectively, as they differ from person to person and are shaped by cultural, social, and personal factors (Collins & Arthur, 2010).

For instance, the way a counsellor from a collectivist culture understands and practices empathy may differ significantly from the approach of a counsellor from an individualist culture. These variations cannot be captured through standardised instruments alone but require in-depth exploration through methods like semi-structured interviews or focus groups. The relativist approach emphasises that these culturally shaped perspectives are real and valid and must be understood within the context of each counsellor's background and experiences. Furthermore, relativism recognises the fluidity of meaning, acknowledging that counsellors' perceptions of cultural competence, empathy, and the challenges they face are not fixed but evolve over time and through experience. This perspective enables the researcher to explore the rich diversity of counsellors' subjective understandings and responses to multicultural counselling, providing insight into how cultural context influences therapeutic practices (McAuliffe et al., 2012).

Epistemology

The epistemology for this study combines both empiricism (quantitative phase) and interpretivism (qualitative phase).

- Empiricism (quantitative) values observable and measurable phenomena (Felgner, 2023; Lipton, 2015). The study gathers data through structured questionnaires and surveys, relying on empirical evidence to assess the competencies, barriers, and practices of counsellors.
- Interpretivism (qualitative) values subjective understanding and emphasises the importance of interpreting participants' experiences and the meanings they attach to their work (Babones, 2016). In-depth interviews and focus groups serve to co-construct knowledge with the participants and gain insight into their lived experiences in multicultural counselling settings.

Axiology

The axiology of this study emphasises the value-laden nature of the research process. It acknowledges that the researcher's values and assumptions can influence data collection, analysis, and interpretation, especially in a multicultural context (Goundar, 2025; Richards et al., 2022). The study values cultural sensitivity, respect, and understanding, ensuring that the voices of participants from diverse backgrounds are heard and respected. This is particularly important in the qualitative phase, where the researcher's cultural understanding shapes the interpretation of the data.

Research design

This study adopted a sequential explanatory mixed-methods design, where quantitative data were collected first, followed by qualitative data collection to provide further explanations or insights into the initial findings.

- Quantitative Phase: A structured questionnaire was used to collect data on counsellors' self-reported competencies, barriers, and practices related to multicultural counselling.
- Qualitative Phase: Semi-structured interviews or focus groups were conducted to explore the experiences, challenges, and perceptions of counsellors in multicultural settings.

The combination of these two approaches allowed for triangulation, providing a more comprehensive understanding of multicultural counselling practices.

Sampling techniques

Quantitative sampling

The participants for this study were recruited through a stratified random sampling technique to ensure a diverse and representative sample of practising counsellors. Initially, over 2000 counsellors were contacted via email and invited to participate in the study. The email included an introduction to the research, its objectives, and a request for participation. Within two weeks of sending the email, 750 counsellors responded expressing their interest in participating. These respondents were then assessed for eligibility based on specific criteria. From this group, 300 counsellors met the necessary criteria to participate in the study.

To ensure diversity in the sample, the 300 participants were stratified to include counsellors from different cultural backgrounds, various professional settings (such as schools, private practice, healthcare, and other settings), and different geographic locations. This stratification ensured that the sample accurately reflected the diverse professional and cultural contexts in which the counsellors worked, thus providing a comprehensive view of multicultural counselling practices.

By reaching out to a wide network and utilising a stratified random sampling approach, the study successfully recruited a representative group of practising counsellors from across different settings and backgrounds, providing robust data for analysis.

Qualitative sampling

A purposive sampling technique was employed to select counsellors who had experience working in multicultural settings and were willing to participate. A total of 20 counsellors were selected for the semi-structured interviews. These counsellors were chosen based on their expertise in multicultural counselling and their willingness to share their experiences.

Inclusion criteria

To ensure that the sample was representative and relevant to the research objectives, the following inclusion criteria were applied:

1. Professional Status: Participants must be practising counsellors with a valid certification or license to practice in their respective countries or regions.
2. Experience: Participants must have a minimum of 1 year of professional experience in counselling, ensuring they have sufficient exposure to multicultural counselling settings.
3. Multicultural Experience: Participants must have had direct experience working with clients from diverse cultural, ethnic, or linguistic backgrounds in their counselling practice.

4. Language Proficiency: Participants must be proficient in the language of the survey (English), ensuring they can understand and respond accurately to the questionnaire.
5. Consent: Participants must voluntarily agree to participate in the study and provide informed consent, acknowledging their understanding of the study's purpose, procedures, and confidentiality agreements.

Exclusion criteria

The following criteria were used to exclude potential participants who did not meet the study's requirements:

1. Non-professional Status: Individuals who are not practising counsellors or are in academic or training roles without active client counselling experience were excluded.
2. Limited Experience: Participants with fewer than 1 year of professional counselling experience were excluded to ensure that all participants had sufficient practical experience in multicultural counselling.
3. Lack of Multicultural Experience: Counsellors who have no experience working with clients from diverse cultural backgrounds were excluded, as this study specifically focuses on multicultural counselling practices.
4. Non-proficiency in Language: Individuals who were not proficient in the language of the survey (English) were excluded, as the study materials were only available in English.
5. Withdrawal of Consent: Any participant who withdrew their consent or did not wish to participate after initial contact was excluded from the study.

Instrument for data collection

The Multicultural Counselling Competencies and Barriers Questionnaire was designed to assess the competencies, practices, and challenges faced by counsellors in multicultural counselling settings. This instrument combines both quantitative and qualitative measures to provide a wide-ranging evaluation of the counsellors' skills, cultural competence, and the barriers they encounter when working with clients from diverse cultural backgrounds.

The questionnaire is divided into six sections, each targeting different aspects of multicultural counselling:

Demographic Information: This section collects basic information about the participants, including age, gender, years of professional experience, primary setting, ethnic/cultural background, and languages spoken. These data help contextualise the responses and provide insights into how demographic variables might influence counsellors' multicultural practices.

Counselling Skills for Multicultural Practice: This section evaluates the counsellors' perceived competencies in core skills essential for effective multicultural counselling. Participants rate their agreement with statements related to essential skills such as empathy, active listening, communication, trustworthiness, congruence, questioning techniques, and self-awareness. Responses are measured using a 5-point Likert scale (1 = strongly disagree, 5 = strongly agree), enabling quantitative analysis of the participants' self-reported skills.

Cultural Competence: This section assesses the counsellors' understanding and application of cultural competence in their practice. Participants respond to statements related to their knowledge of cultural differences, their ability to handle cultural issues, and their engagement with ongoing cultural competence training. Again, a 5-point Likert scale is used to quantify responses.

Perceived Barriers to Effective Multicultural Counselling: This section explores the obstacles that counsellors face when applying their multicultural skills. Barriers such as language differences, limited cultural understanding, and lack of training are addressed. Responses are measured on a 1-5 Likert scale (1 = never, 5 = always), providing data on the frequency with which these barriers are encountered in practice.

Self-reported Practices in Multicultural Counselling: In this section, counsellors are asked how often they engage in various practices aimed at enhancing multicultural competence, such as seeking feedback, engaging in professional development, and reflecting on cultural biases. A 5-point Likert scale is again used to measure the frequency of these practices (1 = never, 5 = always).

Open-ended Questions: This section includes qualitative questions to capture the counsellors' personal experiences and strategies. Participants are asked to describe the most significant challenges they face, strategies they use to overcome cultural barriers, resources they find helpful, and how they incorporate cultural humility into their practice. This section allows counsellors to provide rich, detailed insights into their multicultural counselling experiences.

The instrument is designed to be easy to administer and understand while capturing both quantitative data on multicultural competencies and barriers, as well as qualitative insights into counsellors' experiences and challenges. It combines Likert scale items for standardised data and open-ended questions for in-depth responses, offering a comprehensive view of counsellors' multicultural counselling practices.

This instrument was developed based on established frameworks in multicultural counselling and reviewed by experts in the field to ensure content validity (Guindon, 2019; Hafina et al., 2023; Johnston & Smith, 2005; Loughran, 2018; Shwetha et al., 2022). It is intended to provide useful information for identifying areas of strength and improvement in counsellors' multicultural competencies, guiding professional development and training in diverse settings. The items of the questionnaire were selected from multicultural counselling literature and counsellors' competencies.

Validity of the instrument

The Multicultural Counselling Competencies and Barriers Questionnaire was designed to assess counsellors' competencies, challenges, and strategies in multicultural counselling settings. The validity of this instrument referred to its ability to accurately measure what it was intended to measure: multicultural counselling skills, cultural competence, and barriers in multicultural practice. To ensure the instrument was valid, several forms of validity were considered.

Content validity

Content validity refers to the extent to which the instrument covered the full range of skills, competencies, and challenges involved in multicultural counselling. The questionnaire was developed based on established theories and frameworks in multicultural counselling (Aga Mohd Jaladin et al., 2020; Goh et al., 2015). These frameworks highlighted the essential skills needed to work effectively with clients from diverse backgrounds, such as empathy, active listening, cultural humility, and communication. The questionnaire included both Likert-scale items and open-ended questions to comprehensively assess these competencies, barriers, and practices in multicultural settings. Experts in multicultural counselling (such as university professors, experienced practitioners, and scholars) reviewed the instrument for its content and inclusiveness and ensured that all major aspects of multicultural counselling were adequately covered.

Construct validity

Construct validity refers to the extent to which the instrument measures the theoretical constructs it was intended to assess, such as multicultural competence, cultural humility, and counsellors' self-reported practices (Vespia et al., 2010). Multicultural competence was operationalised through the inclusion of questions related to counsellors' knowledge, adaptability, and self-awareness when working with clients from diverse cultural backgrounds. Also, cultural humility was assessed through questions related to counsellors' ability to recognise their biases and remain open to learning from clients. Furthermore, self-reported practices and barriers in multicultural settings were measured to provide insight into the practical application of the skills and challenges faced in real-world settings. The questionnaire was designed with these constructs in mind and was validated through feedback from professionals who specialised in multicultural counselling, ensuring that the items corresponded with the theoretical constructs of the field.

Criterion-related validity

Criterion-related validity refers to the extent to which the instrument's results correlated with other established measures of the same constructs. The instrument was validated by comparing the responses to established and well-tested tools, such as the Cultural Competence Assessment Tool (CCAT) or the Multicultural Counselling Inventory (MCI), which measured similar constructs related to cultural competence and counselling skills (Campbell et al., 2018; Dunaway et al., 2012; Harris-Haywood et al., 2014; Truong et al., 2017). A correlation analysis was conducted to compare the results from this questionnaire with the results from other validated instruments in multicultural counselling, providing evidence for its criterion-related validity.

Face validity

Face validity refers to the degree to which the instrument appeared to measure what it was supposed to measure, based on the judgement of laypersons or experts in the field. The questionnaire was reviewed by a panel of experts in multicultural counselling, including faculty members, practising counsellors, and researchers in the field. The feedback from the panel indicated that the questions were relevant to multicultural counselling, and the instrument appeared to measure the skills and barriers it was designed to assess. Additionally, practising counsellors and students in multicultural counselling programmes were asked to review the questionnaire. Their feedback confirmed that the questions were clear, relevant, and aligned with their experiences in multicultural counselling.

Reliability of the instrument

The reliability of the Multicultural Counselling Competencies and Barriers Questionnaire was assessed using Cronbach's alpha, a measure of internal consistency that indicates how closely related the items are within the instrument. A high Cronbach's alpha value suggests that the items are consistently measuring the same underlying construct (Aga Mohd Jaladin et al., 2020; Merino-Soto, 2016). The Cronbach's alpha for the instrument was calculated to be 0.728, based on a total of 33 items. This value indicates acceptable internal consistency. Generally, a Cronbach's alpha value above 0.7 is considered good, suggesting that the instrument's items are reliably measuring the same construct. In this case, the alpha value of 0.728 falls within the acceptable range, indicating that the instrument is sufficiently reliable for assessing multicultural counselling competencies and barriers. This reliability statistic suggests that the questionnaire is well-aligned in measuring the intended constructs, such as cultural competence, counselling skills, and the barriers faced by counsellors in multicultural settings.

Data analysis

- **Quantitative Data Analysis**:
  The quantitative data were analysed using SPSS. Descriptive statistics (means, frequencies) were used to summarise the counsellors' competencies and practices, while inferential statistics were used to test the relationships between cultural competence and counselling skills, as well as to identify barriers. The statistical significance was set at $P < .05$.
- **Qualitative Data Analysis**:
  The qualitative data were analysed using thematic analysis, following the approach outlined by Braun and Clarke (2006). This involved the following:
  1. Transcribing the interviews and focus group discussions verbatim
  2. Familiarising with the data through repeated reading
  3. Generating initial codes based on significant patterns or insights
  4. Searching for and reviewing themes
  5. Defining and refining the themes
  6. Writing up the analysis, integrating the themes into a coherent narrative

The qualitative data were analysed using software such as NVivo, which assisted in organising and coding the data.

Ethical considerations

This study adhered to ethical guidelines to ensure the protection of participants' rights and confidentiality.

- **Informed Consent**: All participants were provided with clear and concise information about the study, including their voluntary participation, the purpose of the study, and their right to withdraw at any time without penalty.
- **Confidentiality**: All personal information and responses were kept confidential, with data stored securely and anonymised in any reports or publications.
- **Participant Welfare**: Participants were informed of any potential risks or discomforts, and support services were made available if needed.

Results

The demographic analysis of the participants in this study presented in Table 3.2 reveals a diverse group across several variables. In terms of age, there is a broad distribution, with the largest groups represented in the age ranges of 36–37 years, accounting for 11 and 12 participants, respectively. Other significant age groups include those in their 30s and 40s, with participants fairly spread across these age ranges. The statistical significance of the

Table 3.2: Analysis of the demographic variables.

Variable	Level	Counts	Total	Proportion	*P*
Age	25	9	300	0.030	<0.001
	26	7	300	0.023	<0.001
	27	7	300	0.023	<0.001
	28	8	300	0.027	<0.001
	29	10	300	0.033	<0.001
	30	10	300	0.033	<0.001
	31	10	300	0.033	<0.001
	32	8	300	0.027	<0.001
	33	6	300	0.020	<0.001
	34	7	300	0.023	<0.001
	35	5	300	0.017	<0.001
	36	11	300	0.037	<0.001
	37	12	300	0.040	<0.001
	38	6	300	0.020	<0.001
	39	5	300	0.017	<0.001
	40	10	300	0.033	<0.001
	41	9	300	0.030	<0.001
	42	13	300	0.043	<0.001
	43	7	300	0.023	<0.001
	44	9	300	0.030	<0.001
	45	7	300	0.023	<0.001
	46	10	300	0.033	<0.001
	47	12	300	0.040	<0.001
	48	10	300	0.033	<0.001
	49	11	300	0.037	<0.001
	50	8	300	0.027	<0.001
	51	7	300	0.023	<0.001
	52	4	300	0.013	<0.001
	53	11	300	0.037	<0.001
	54	5	300	0.017	<0.001
	55	8	300	0.027	<0.001
	56	9	300	0.030	<0.001
	57	10	300	0.033	<0.001
	58	4	300	0.013	<0.001
	59	7	300	0.023	<0.001
	60	8	300	0.027	<0.001
Gender	Male	146	300	0.487	0.686
	Female	154	300	0.513	0.686
Years of professional experience	0–5 years	84	300	0.280	<0.001
	6–10 years	69	300	0.230	<0.001
	11–15 years	66	300	0.220	<0.001
	16+ years	81	300	0.270	<0.001
Primary setting	Other	82	300	0.273	<0.001
	Private practice	75	300	0.250	<0.001
	School	72	300	0.240	<0.001

Continued

Table 3.2: Analysis of the demographic variables.—cont'd

Variable	Level	Counts	Total	Proportion	*P*
	Healthcare	71	300	0.237	<0.001
Ethnic cultural background	Caucasian	54	300	0.180	<0.001
	Other	50	300	0.167	<0.001
	Hispanic	57	300	0.190	<0.001
	Asian	69	300	0.230	<0.001
	African	70	300	0.233	<0.001
Languages spoken	Other	65	300	0.217	<0.001
	French	67	300	0.223	<0.001
	Spanish	50	300	0.167	<0.001
	English	59	300	0.197	<0.001
	Arabic	59	300	0.197	<0.001

Proportions tested against value: 0.5.

age distribution was confirmed by a *P*-value of less than 0.001, indicating that the age distribution significantly deviates from an equal distribution, as expected given the varied age groups in the sample.

In terms of gender, the sample was nearly balanced, with 146 male participants (48.7%) and 154 female participants (51.3%). The *P*-value of 0.686 suggests that there was no significant difference in the gender distribution, demonstrating an equal representation of male and female participants.

When examining professional experience, the data shows that 28% of participants had 0–5 years of professional experience, 23% had 6–10 years, 22% had 11–15 years, and 27% had 16+ years of experience. The *P*-value for this variable was less than 0.001, which indicates that the distribution of professional experience was significantly different from a 50–50 split, reflecting the diversity in experience among participants. This highlights that the sample included both relatively new and more experienced professionals.

Looking at the primary setting in which the participants work, the largest group (27.3%) was categorised as 'Other', followed by participants in private practice (25%), schools (24%), and healthcare (23.7%). The *P*-value for this variable was less than 0.001, suggesting that the distribution was significantly different from an equal distribution. This indicates that the participants were fairly evenly distributed across various settings, though the 'Other' category had the highest proportion.

Regarding ethnic and cultural background, the sample was also quite diverse. The largest groups were participants of Asian (23%) and African (23.3%) descent, followed by Hispanic (19%) and Caucasian (18%) participants. The *P*-value for this variable was also less than 0.001, indicating a significant difference from an equal distribution, and demonstrating that the sample represented a broad range of ethnic and cultural backgrounds.

Finally, the analysis of languages spoken revealed that the participants were also diverse in terms of linguistic background. French was spoken by 22.3% of the participants, Arabic and English were each spoken by 19.7%, and Spanish was spoken by 16.7%. The *P*-value for this variable was less than 0.001, indicating a significant difference from an equal distribution. This highlights the multilingual nature of the sample, with a strong representation of French and Arabic speakers.

Analysing the research questions

1. What are the key counselling skills that are essential for effective multicultural counselling practice?
   The descriptive statistics for the key counselling skills essential for effective multicultural counselling practice presented in Table 3.3 reveal important insights into the responses of the participants. The mean scores for these skills vary, reflecting the relative importance and perceived effectiveness of each skill in multicultural contexts. For instance, Encouraging Emotional Expression had the highest mean score of 3.193, suggesting that participants view this skill as crucial in fostering an environment where clients can express their emotions freely. Non-judgemental attitude also scored

Table 3.3: Descriptive statistics showing key counselling skills that are essential for effective multicultural counselling practice.

Counselling skills	Mean	Std. deviation	Shapiro–Wilk	*P*-value of Shapiro–Wilk
1. Culturally competent counselling	3.067	1.415	0.884	<0.001
2. Rapport building	2.997	1.370	0.897	<0.001
3. Understanding cultural context	3.000	1.421	0.886	<0.001
4. Adaptability in techniques	3.107	1.369	0.896	<0.001
5. Empathy	2.987	1.435	0.879	<0.001
6. Active listening	3.030	1.424	0.884	<0.001
7. Effective communication	2.887	1.344	0.899	<0.001
8. Trust building	2.957	1.412	0.887	<0.001
9. Congruence	2.973	1.397	0.891	<0.001
10. Questioning skills	2.920	1.486	0.869	<0.001
11. Catharsis	3.103	1.437	0.881	<0.001
12. Reflection	2.977	1.399	0.890	<0.001
13. Non-judgemental attitude	3.137	1.394	0.887	<0.001
14. Cultural self-awareness	3.080	1.431	0.884	<0.001
15. Cultural humility	3.000	1.431	0.882	<0.001
16. Client-centred approach	2.980	1.376	0.895	<0.001
17. Encouraging emotional expression	3.193	1.357	0.894	<0.001
18. Support for self-exploration	2.957	1.443	0.881	<0.001

relatively high, with a mean of 3.137, indicating its importance in ensuring that clients feel accepted and understood regardless of cultural differences.

Other skills, such as adaptability in techniques and cultural self-awareness, had mean scores of 3.107 and 3.080, respectively, emphasising the need for flexibility in counselling approaches and the counsellor's ability to recognise and manage their own cultural biases. On the lower end, Effective Communication and Support for Self-exploration had the lowest mean scores of 2.887 and 2.957, suggesting that, while these skills are still considered important, they are not seen as critical as some of the other skills in multicultural settings.

The standard deviation values for all skills range from 1.344 to 1.486, indicating a moderate level of variation in how participants rated the importance of these skills. This suggests that there is some diversity in how counsellors perceive the importance of these competencies. Additionally, the Shapiro–Wilk test for normality was performed on each skill, with the results showing *P*-values consistently less than 0.001, indicating that the data for each skill is not normally distributed. This suggests that while these skills are generally seen as important, there may be varying degrees of agreement among participants about their significance.

2. How does cultural competence influence the application of core counselling skills in multicultural settings?

   The results of Pearson's correlation analysis in Table 3.4 indicate that the relationship between cultural competence and the application of core counselling skills in multicultural settings is very weak. The Pearson's r value for this relationship is −0.007, suggesting a negligible negative correlation between cultural competence and counselling skills. This means that, according to the data, there is no significant linear relationship between a counsellor's cultural competence and their ability to apply core counselling skills in a multicultural setting.

   The *P*-value of 0.905 is much higher than the typical threshold of 0.05 for statistical significance, indicating that the relationship between cultural competence and core

Table 3.4: Pearson's correlations showing how cultural competence influences the application of core counselling skills in multicultural settings.

Variable		Key counselling skills	Cultural competence
1. Key counselling skills	Pearson's r	–	
	P-value	–	
	VS-MPR[a]	–	
2, Cultural competence	Pearson's r	−0.007	–
	P-value	0.905	–
	VS-MPR[a]	1.000	–

[a]Vovk-Sellke Maximum *p*-Ratio: Based on the *P*-value, the maximum possible odds in favour of H_1 over H_0 equals $1/(-e\ P \log(P))$ for $P \leq .37$ (Sellke et al., 2001).

counselling skills is not statistically significant. In other words, the data suggest that cultural competence does not significantly influence the application of key counselling skills, such as active listening, empathy, or effective communication, in multicultural settings.

The Vovk-Sellke Maximum *p*-Ratio (VS-MPR) of 1.000 further supports this finding, as it shows that the odds in favour of the alternative hypothesis (H_1) over the null hypothesis (H_0) are essentially equal, indicating no substantial evidence to suggest that cultural competence has a meaningful effect on the application of counselling skills. In summary, the results do not support a significant relationship between cultural competence and the effective application of core counselling skills in multicultural settings. This suggests that other factors, beyond cultural competence, may play a more important role in influencing the counsellor's ability to apply essential counselling skills effectively in diverse cultural contexts.

3. What challenges and barriers do counsellors face when applying essential counselling skills with clients from diverse cultural backgrounds?

   The descriptive statistics for the challenges and barriers faced by counsellors when applying essential counselling skills with clients from diverse cultural backgrounds are presented in Table 3.5. The table provides the mean, standard deviation, and Shapiro–Wilk test results for each challenge, highlighting the level of difficulty that counsellors experience in different aspects of multicultural counselling.

   The mean scores for all the challenges are relatively high, ranging from 3.033 to 3.147, indicating that counsellors generally consider these barriers to be moderately significant in their practice. For example, language barriers when communicating with clients had the highest mean score of 3.147, suggesting that language differences are a prominent challenge for counsellors working with clients from diverse backgrounds. Similarly,

Table 3.5: Descriptive statistics showing the challenges and barriers counsellors face when applying essential counselling skills.

	Mean	Std. deviation	Shapiro–Wilk	*P*-value of Shapiro–Wilk
Language barriers when communicating with clients.	3.147	1.444	0.877	<0.001
Limited understanding of clients' cultural backgrounds.	3.097	1.374	0.894	<0.001
Lack of formal multicultural competence training.	3.033	1.380	0.892	<0.001
Cultural misunderstandings between the counsellor and client.	3.113	1.339	0.900	<0.001
Challenges in adapting counselling methods to fit cultural norms and values	3.123	1.381	0.873	<0.001

cultural misunderstandings between the counsellor and client had a mean of 3.113, emphasising the difficulty in bridging cultural gaps during counselling sessions.

Other notable challenges include limited understanding of clients' cultural backgrounds, with a mean of 3.097, indicating that counsellors often struggle to fully comprehend the cultural context of their clients' issues. The lack of formal multicultural competence training was also identified as a barrier, with a mean score of 3.033, showing that many counsellors feel unprepared due to insufficient training in multicultural practices.

Finally, challenges in adapting counselling methods to fit cultural norms and values had a mean of 3.123, highlighting that counsellors face difficulties when attempting to adjust their techniques to align with the diverse cultural values and norms of their clients.

The standard deviations for all barriers range from 1.339 to 1.444, indicating that while there is some variability in the responses, most participants generally agree on the significance of these barriers. The relatively moderate spread suggests that, though the barriers are widely recognised, some variation exists in how strongly participants feel about each challenge.

The Shapiro–Wilk test results show P-values less than 0.001 for all barriers, indicating that the distribution of responses for each challenge is not normally distributed. This suggests that the perceptions of these challenges differ across participants, with some counsellors perhaps facing more intense difficulties than others, depending on their individual experiences.

In conclusion, the results highlight that language barriers, cultural misunderstandings, and a lack of formal multicultural training are seen as significant challenges by counsellors in multicultural counselling settings. These barriers are perceived to moderately hinder the effective application of counselling skills, and the variability in responses suggests that these challenges may be more pronounced for some counsellors than others.

Results from the qualitative analysis

To analyse the qualitative data, we'll focus on the responses provided by the 30 participants in the open-ended questions. Specifically, we'll explore the following:

1. Challenges faced in multicultural counselling.
2. Strategies used to overcome challenges.
3. Resources found helpful in enhancing multicultural counselling skills.
4. How cultural humility is incorporated into practice.
5. The most important skill for effective multicultural counselling.

For each of these categories, I will provide a summary and identify common themes and frequently mentioned responses. Let me start by reviewing and analysing the qualitative data. The qualitative data contains responses to four key categories related to multicultural counselling, as outlined earlier. I will now summarise and analyse the common themes for each category.

Challenges faced in multicultural counselling

Here are the most frequently reported challenges based on the responses:

- Language Barriers: A common challenge, with many counsellors reporting difficulties in communication due to clients speaking different languages.
- Lack of Training: A number of participants mentioned that they had not received enough training in multicultural counselling, making it harder to understand and address cultural differences effectively.
- Miscommunication: Participants highlighted miscommunication arising from cultural misunderstandings, which often leads to difficulties in building rapport and understanding client needs.
- Cultural Misunderstandings: Issues stemming from not fully understanding the cultural background and values of clients were frequently mentioned.

Themes: The most common challenges mentioned were language barriers, lack of training, and cultural misunderstandings. These reflect a need for increased training and cultural competence to better support clients from diverse backgrounds.

Strategies used to overcome challenges

Here are the most frequently mentioned strategies used by counsellors to overcome the challenges they face:

- Language Support Services: Many participants reported using language support services, such as interpreters or translation tools, to help overcome language barriers.
- Cultural Competence Workshops: Participants indicated that they attended cultural competence workshops to improve their understanding and ability to work effectively with clients from diverse cultural backgrounds.
- Peer Feedback: Several counsellors mentioned seeking peer feedback to gain insights into handling multicultural challenges.
- Self-reflection: A few counsellors stated they engaged in self-reflection to understand their own biases and improve their cultural humility.

Themes: The most common strategies included using language support services, attending cultural competence workshops, and seeking peer feedback. These strategies reflect a strong focus on learning and adaptation to handle multicultural challenges.

Resources found most helpful

The resources that participants found most helpful in enhancing their multicultural counselling skills include the following:

- Peer Support: Many counsellors found peer support to be invaluable for discussing challenges and sharing strategies.
- Literature: Participants often referred to literature (books, articles, and research papers) as a source of knowledge to enhance their understanding of multicultural issues.
- Cultural Competence Workshops: As mentioned in the strategies, workshops were cited as an essential resource for improving cultural competence.
- Online Resources: Some participants found online resources, including websites and webinars, to be helpful for gaining new perspectives and strategies.

Themes: Peer support and literature were the most frequently cited resources. These indicate a reliance on collaborative learning and self-directed learning to develop multicultural competence.

Incorporating cultural humility

In terms of how counsellors incorporate cultural humility into their practice, the following approaches were most commonly mentioned:

- Self-reflection: Many participants emphasised self-reflection as a key strategy for recognising and addressing personal biases.
- Attending Training: A significant number of counsellors mentioned attending training programmes specifically designed to improve cultural humility and awareness.
- Learning from Clients: Some participants highlighted their approach of learning from clients, understanding that each client's cultural background brings a unique perspective.
- Seeking Feedback: A few counsellors indicated that they actively seek feedback from clients or peers on how they can improve their cultural sensitivity.

Themes: Self-reflection and learning from clients were the most prominent methods for incorporating cultural humility, showcasing the counsellors' focus on continuous personal growth and client-centred learning.

Most important skill for effective multicultural counselling

The most important skills for effective multicultural counselling, as identified by the participants, include the following:

- Active Listening: Many counsellors emphasised the importance of active listening in understanding clients' needs and perspectives.

- Adaptability: A significant number of participants mentioned adaptability, stressing the need to tailor approaches to fit the diverse needs of clients.
- Cultural Competence: Several counsellors cited cultural competence as a crucial skill for effectively working with clients from different cultural backgrounds.
- Empathy: Some participants mentioned empathy as essential for building trust and understanding in a multicultural context.

Themes: Active listening, adaptability, and cultural competence were the top skills identified by the participants, underscoring the need for flexibility and understanding in multicultural counselling.

Discussion of findings

The findings from both the quantitative and qualitative data provide valuable insights into the key aspects of multicultural counselling practice, shedding light on the challenges faced by counsellors, the skills required, and the strategies they employ to enhance their effectiveness in working with diverse populations.

Key counselling skills

The descriptive statistics revealed that participants considered skills such as culturally competent counselling, rapport building, understanding cultural context, and empathy as essential for effective multicultural counselling. Among these, encouraging emotional expression was rated the most important skill, highlighting the significance of creating a safe environment for clients to openly express their emotions. This finding aligns with previous literature, which emphasises the importance of empathy and active listening as foundational skills in building therapeutic relationships, especially in multicultural contexts (Sue et al., 2019).

Interestingly, effective communication and support for self-exploration were rated lower in importance, suggesting that while these skills are still seen as crucial, they might not be as immediately pressing as emotional expression and cultural competence. This distinction could point to the specific challenges multicultural counsellors face, where the need to understand and connect with clients' cultural contexts may outweigh other counselling skills.

Cultural competence and application of counselling skills

The Pearson's correlation analysis indicated that cultural competence does not significantly influence the application of core counselling skills in multicultural settings. The correlation between cultural competence and skills such as empathy, active listening, and communication was found to be negligible, with a very weak negative correlation

(−0.007) and a *P*-value of 0.905, suggesting no statistically significant relationship. This finding challenges the assumption that cultural competence directly enhances the application of these skills. It suggests that other factors, such as individual counsellor characteristics, training, and experiences, may play a more pivotal role in determining how effectively counsellors apply these skills in multicultural contexts.

One possible explanation for this finding could be the complex nature of multicultural counselling, where cultural competence alone may not be sufficient to bridge the gap between counsellors and clients from diverse backgrounds. The diverse experiences, backgrounds, and perceptions of both clients and counsellors likely influence how these core skills are applied. It could also suggest that counsellors may require more specific, adapted training and ongoing practice beyond general cultural competence to fully engage in the application of these skills effectively.

Challenges and barriers in multicultural counselling

The qualitative findings revealed that language barriers were one of the most frequently cited challenges faced by counsellors. Participants reported difficulties in effectively communicating with clients who spoke different languages, which often impeded the establishment of trust and understanding. This finding is consistent with previous research, which has shown that language barriers can create significant obstacles in the counselling process, especially when interpreters or translation services are not available (Ling et al., 2021).

Another major challenge highlighted was the lack of formal multicultural competence training. Many counsellors felt unprepared to handle the complexities of multicultural counselling due to insufficient training, which often limited their ability to address cultural differences effectively. This finding underscores the importance of cultural competence training and the need for continuous professional development in this area. This aligns with the broader literature, which calls for more focused training and workshops to help counsellors develop the skills necessary for working with diverse populations (Sue et al., 2019).

Strategies for overcoming challenges

In terms of strategies to overcome these challenges, counsellors frequently cited the use of language support services and peer feedback as effective means to navigate multicultural difficulties. The use of interpreters and translation tools was particularly noted as a helpful approach in overcoming language barriers. Furthermore, attending cultural competence workshops and engaging in self-reflection were key strategies that counsellors employed to increase their understanding of cultural issues and improve their practice. This reflects a strong commitment to learning and adapting, both individually and through collaborative support systems like peer feedback.

These strategies emphasise the importance of collaborative learning and self-awareness in developing multicultural counselling skills. However, they also highlight the need for systemic changes, such as better access to training and more support from peers and mentors, to ensure that counsellors are well-equipped to handle the challenges they face in multicultural settings.

Incorporation of cultural humility

The qualitative findings also indicated that self-reflection and learning from clients were key ways in which counsellors incorporated cultural humility into their practice. Many participants emphasised that cultural humility is an ongoing process, where they must continually reflect on their biases, engage in training, and learn from clients' experiences. This finding aligns with the literature on cultural humility, which emphasises the importance of counsellors adopting a mindset of lifelong learning and openness to the perspectives and cultural knowledge of their clients (Tervalon & Murray-García, 1998).

Important counselling skills

In terms of the most important skills for multicultural counselling, participants identified active listening, adaptability, and cultural competence as the top skills necessary for working effectively with clients from diverse backgrounds. This reflects the growing recognition of the need for counsellors to be flexible and attuned to the specific cultural needs of their clients. While empathy was also seen as important, it was ranked lower in comparison to skills related to understanding and adapting to cultural differences, which may suggest that cultural competence and adaptability are viewed as more immediate needs in multicultural counselling.

Conclusion

The findings suggest that while cultural competence is important, it is not a sufficient factor in ensuring the effective application of core counselling skills in multicultural settings. Language barriers, misunderstandings, and lack of training are significant challenges that hinder effective practice, underscoring the need for tailored training programmes and continuous professional development. Furthermore, the strategies employed by counsellors, such as peer feedback and self-reflection, highlight the importance of ongoing learning and adaptation. Finally, active listening, adaptability, and cultural competence are critical skills that counsellors must develop and apply to provide effective multicultural counselling. The findings reinforce the need for systemic changes in training and support to improve the effectiveness of multicultural counselling practices.

Implications

The findings of this study have several important implications for the field of multicultural counselling, especially in terms of training, practice, and ongoing professional development for counsellors. These implications are particularly relevant for enhancing the effectiveness of counsellors working with clients from diverse cultural backgrounds.

Need for comprehensive multicultural competence training

The study revealed that a lack of formal multicultural competence training is one of the major barriers to effective multicultural counselling. As many counsellors reported feeling unprepared due to insufficient training, this finding highlights the critical need for more robust and comprehensive training programmes. Training should go beyond the basics of cultural awareness and address specific, actionable skills such as adapting counselling techniques to fit cultural norms, effectively using language support services, and overcoming cultural misunderstandings.

Training institutions, professional associations, and counselling organisations should invest in developing and providing specialised multicultural counselling programmes. These programmes should be integrated into counsellor education and professional development to ensure counsellors are equipped with the necessary tools to navigate cultural complexities in practice.

Ongoing professional development and self-reflection

Counsellors who engaged in self-reflection and sought peer feedback were able to better understand and address the challenges of multicultural counselling. The study also highlighted the importance of cultural humility, where counsellors must continually reflect on their biases, seek feedback, and learn from their clients. This underscores that multicultural competence is not a one-time achievement but a continuous process that requires lifelong learning.

Professional development opportunities such as peer supervision, cultural competence workshops, and self-reflection practices should be promoted and made accessible to all practising counsellors. Ongoing support systems that encourage reflection and feedback are essential for counsellors to keep improving their multicultural counselling skills.

Addressing language barriers

Language barriers were identified as a major challenge for counsellors when working with clients from different cultural backgrounds. While many counsellors utilised language support services like interpreters, the findings point to a gap in the availability of such services or the counsellors' ability to utilise them effectively. This limitation can hinder effective communication and the overall therapeutic process.

Counselling organisations and institutions should prioritise providing language support resources, such as trained interpreters or translation tools, to facilitate communication between counsellors and clients from diverse linguistic backgrounds. Additionally, counsellors should be trained to effectively use these resources and integrate them into their practice to ensure better understanding and rapport-building with clients.

Importance of adaptability and flexibility

The study found that adaptability and cultural competence were identified as critical skills for working effectively in multicultural settings. Counsellors need to be able to tailor their approaches based on the unique cultural needs and values of their clients. However, counsellors also faced challenges in adapting their techniques to align with cultural norms, which indicates a gap in practical application.

Counselling training programmes should emphasise the importance of flexible, client-centred approaches that allow for adaptation to various cultural contexts. Counsellors should be trained not only in theoretical cultural knowledge but also in the practical skills needed to implement this knowledge in diverse situations.

Collaborative learning and resource sharing

The study highlighted the significant role of peer support and literature in enhancing counsellors' multicultural competence. This suggests that learning from colleagues and using literature as a resource are key strategies for overcoming challenges and improving practice.

Professional networks, mentoring programmes, and collaborative platforms should be developed where counsellors can share resources, experiences, and insights. Additionally, more research-based and practical resources focused on multicultural issues in counselling should be made accessible to all practitioners.

Emphasising the role of empathy and client-centred approaches

Empathy, although important, was considered less significant compared to other skills like active listening and cultural competence. This finding suggests that while empathy is essential, counsellors may prioritise skills that allow them to understand and adapt to their clients' cultural contexts more immediately.

While empathy should remain a core counselling skill, training programmes should place a stronger emphasis on developing cultural competence and active listening skills, which are crucial for understanding and relating to clients from diverse cultural backgrounds. Counsellors should be taught how to apply empathy within the context of cultural differences, ensuring that clients feel both understood and respected.

References

Aga Mohd Jaladin, R., Amit, N., Anuar, A. A., Fernandez, J. A., Salleh, S., Rais, H., & Lim, H. S. (2020). Development of a continuous professional development training module based on multicultural counselling competency for professional counsellors in Malaysia. *Journal of Adult and Continuing Education, 26*(2), 242–261. https://doi.org/10.1177/1477971419896375

Babones, S. (2016). Interpretive quantitative methods for the social sciences. *Sociology, 50*(3), 453–469. https://doi.org/10.1177/0038038515583637

Ballinger, C. (2004). Writing up rigour: Representing and evaluating good scholarship in qualitative research. *British Journal of Occupational Therapy, 67*(12), 540–546. https://doi.org/10.1177/030802260406701204

Braun, V., & Clarke, V. (2006). Using thematic analysis in psychology. *Qualitative Research in Psychology, 3* (2), 77–101. https://doi.org/10.1191/1478088706qp063oa

Campbell, A., Vance, S. R., & Dong, S. (2018). Examining the relationship between mindfulness and multicultural counseling competencies in counselor trainees. *Mindfulness, 9*(1), 79–87. https://doi.org/10.1007/s12671-017-0746-6

Chan, L. (2010). Intentional interviewing and counseling: Facilitating client development in a multicultural society, by Allen E. Ivey, Mary B. Ivey and Carlos P. Zalaquett. *Asia Pacific Journal of Counselling and Psychotherapy, 1*(2). https://doi.org/10.1080/21507686.2010.493204

Collins, S., & Arthur, N. (2010). Culture-infused counselling: A model for developing multicultural competence. *Counselling Psychology Quarterly, 23*(2), 217–233. https://doi.org/10.1080/09515071003798212

Corey, G. (2013). *Theory and practice and psychotherapy of counseling* (9th ed.).

Dunaway, K. E., Morrow, J. A., & Porter, B. E. (2012). Development and validation of the cultural competence of program evaluators (CCPE) self-report scale. *American Journal of Evaluation, 33*(4), 496–514. https://doi.org/10.1177/1098214012445280

Felgner, U. (2023). Empiricism in mathematics. In *Science networks historical studies* (Vol 62). https://doi.org/10.1007/978-3-031-27304-9_11

Goh, M., Koch, J. M., & Sanger, S. (2015). Cultural intelligence in counseling psychology: Applications for multicultural counseling competence. In *Handbook of cultural intelligence theory measurement and applications*. https://doi.org/10.4324/9781315703855-21

Goundar, P. R. (2025). Researcher positionality: Ways to include it in a qualitative research design. *International Journal of Qualitative Methods, 24*. https://doi.org/10.1177/16094069251321251

Guindon, M. H. (2019). Questioning skills and systematic inquiry. In *A counseling primer an orientation to the profession*. https://doi.org/10.4324/9780429436031-21

Hafina, A., Rusmana, N., Ramdhani, R. N., & Guntara, R. G. (2023). Application of evaluation and supervision model of counselling skills: Implementation, testing, and integration. *Journal of Engineering Science & Technology, 18*, 106–117.

Harris-Haywood, S., Goode, T., Gao, Y., Smith, K., Bronheim, S., Flocke, S. A., & Zyzanski, S. (2014). Psychometric evaluation of a cultural competency assessment instrument for health professionals. *Medical Care, 52*(2), e7–e15. https://doi.org/10.1097/MLR.0b013e31824df149

Hays, P. A. (2016). Addressing cultural complexities in practice: Assessment, diagnosis, and therapy (3rd ed.). In *Addressing cultural complexities in practice: Assessment, diagnosis, and therapy* (3rd ed.). https://doi.org/10.1037/14801-000

Hill, C. E. (2019). Helping skills: Facilitating exploration, insight, and action (5th ed.). In *Helping skills: Facilitating exploration, insight, and action* (5th ed.). https://doi.org/10.1037/0000147-000

Hook, J. N., Davis, D. E., Owen, J., Worthington, E. L., & Utsey, S. O. (2013). Cultural humility: Measuring openness to culturally diverse clients. *Journal of Counseling Psychology, 60*(3). https://doi.org/10.1037/a0032595

Ivey, A. E., Ivey, M. B., & Zalaquett, C. P. (2025). *Essentials of intentional interviewing: Counseling in a multicultural world.*

Johnston, B., & Smith, V. (2005). Exploring students' experience of training for counselling skills and the impact on practice. *International Journal of Palliative Nursing, 11*(8), 410–418. https://doi.org/10.12968/ijpn.2005.11.8.19608

Jones-Smith, E. (2020). Culturally diverse counseling: Theory and practice. In *Culturally diverse counseling: Theory and practice.* https://doi.org/10.4135/9781071800744

Kasperek, A. (2023). The multiplicity of realities in selected works by Emmanuel Carrère: Around the literary inspirations of sociology | Wielość rzeczywistości w wybranych utworach Emmanuela Carrère'a. Wokół literackich inspiracji socjologii. *Przeglad Socjologii Jakosciowej, 19*(1), 22–39. https://doi.org/10.18778/1733-8069.19.1.02

Knox, S., & Hill, C. E. (2021). Training and supervision in psychotherapy: What we know and where we need to go. In M. Barkham, W. Lutz, & L. G. Castonguay (Eds.), *Bergin and Garfield's handbook of psychotherapy and behavior change* (7th ed., pp. 327–349). John Wiley & Sons, Inc.

Kuo, B. C. H., Soucie, K., & Huang, S. (2020). Developing clinical trainees' multicultural counseling competencies through working with refugees in a multicultural psychotherapy practicum: A mixed-methods investigation. *International Journal for the Advancement of Counselling, 42*(3), 249–268. https://doi.org/10.1007/s10447-019-09392-8

Ling, K. T. K., Hassan, S. A., & Jailani, O. (2021). The impact of language barriers faced by counsellors and refugee clients in counselling: A systematic review. *International Journal of Academic Research in Business and Social Sciences, 11*(12). https://doi.org/10.6007/ijarbss/v11-i12/11904

Lipton, P. (2015). Empiricism, history of. In *International encyclopedia of the social behavioral sciences* (2nd ed.). https://doi.org/10.1016/B978-0-08-097086-8.85047-3

Loughran, H. (2018). Counselling skills for social workers. In *Counselling skills for social workers.* https://doi.org/10.4324/9781315145853

McAuliffe, G. J., Grothaus, T., Jensen, M., & Michel, R. (2012). Assessing and promoting cultural relativism in students of counseling. *International Journal for the Advancement of Counselling, 34*(2), 118–135. https://doi.org/10.1007/s10447-011-9142-4

McPhail, G., & Lourie, M. (2017). Getting real: Is realism a blind spot in research methodology? *New Zealand Journal of Educational Studies, 52*(2), 285–299. https://doi.org/10.1007/s40841-017-0087-y

Mehra, L. M., Kallen, A. M., Potter, M., Udupa, N. S., Bryen, C. P., Kemper, T. S., Sachs-Ericsson, N. J., & Joiner, T. E. (2025). Therapist cultural humility in early psychotherapy: A catalyst for improved client functioning at treatment termination. *Psychotherapy Research, 36*(2), 287–307. https://doi.org/10.1080/10503307.2025.2481268

Merino-Soto, C. (2016). Differences between Cronbach's alpha coefficients, with small samples and parts: A VB program | Diferencias entre coeficientes alfa de Cronbach, con muestras y partes pequeñas: Un programa VB. *Anales de Psicología, 32*(2), 587–588. https://doi.org/10.6018/analesps.32.2.203841

Park, Y. S., Konge, L., & Artino, A. R. (2020). The positivism paradigm of research. *Academic Medicine, 95*(5), 690–694. https://doi.org/10.1097/ACM.0000000000003093

Pedersen, P. B. (2001). Multiculturalism and the paradigm shift in counselling: Controversies and alternative futures. *Canadian Journal of Counselling, 35*(1).

Poli, R., & Obrst, L. (2010). The interplay between ontology as categorial analysis and ontology as technology. In *Theory and applications of ontology computer applications*. https://doi.org/10.1007/978-90-481-8847-5_1

Richards, J. C., Batastini, A., Chen, H., Angelo-Rocha, M., & Fung, K. (2022). Incorporating the arts to evoke qualitative students' axiological values that influence all phases of interpretive inquiry. In *Engaging students in socially constructed qualitative research pedagogies*. https://doi.org/10.1163/9789004518438_008

Ridley, C. R., Sahu, A., Console, K., Surya, S., Tran, V., Xie, S., & Yin, C. (2021). The process model of multicultural counseling competenceψ. *The Counseling Psychologist, 49*(4). https://doi.org/10.1177/0011000021992339

Sellke, T., Bayarri, M. J., & Berger, J. O. (2001). Calibration of p values for testing precise null hypotheses. *The American Statistician, 55*(1), 62–71. https://doi.org/10.1198/000313001300339950.

Shwetha, N., Megha, M., & Sudhin, K. (2022). Determining counseling self-efficacy of Indian students of speech language pathology. *Clinical Practice and Epidemiology in Mental Health, 18*(1). https://doi.org/10.2174/17450179-V18-E2209290

Sue, S. (2017). In search of cultural competence in psychotherapy and counseling. *Counseling Psychology.* https://doi.org/10.4324/9781315259178-36

Sue, D. W., Arredondo, P., & McDavis, R. J. (1992). Multicultural counseling competencies and standards: A call to the profession. *Journal of Counseling and Development, 70*(4). https://doi.org/10.1002/j.1556-6676.1992.tb01642.x

Sue, D. W., & Sue, D. (2017). *Counseling the culturally diverse: Theory and practice* (7th ed.). John Wiley & Sons.

Sue, D. W., Sue, D., Neville, H. A., & Smith, L. (2019). *Counseling the culturally diverse: Theory and practice, 8th edition*. NJ: Wiley.

Tervalon, M., & Murray-García, J. (1998). Cultural humility versus cultural competence: A critical distinction in defining physician training outcomes in multicultural education. *Journal of Health Care for the Poor and Underserved, 9*(2), 117–125. https://doi.org/10.1353/hpu.2010.0233

The Interpretive Paradigm. (2024). In *Understanding communication research methods: A theoretical and practical approach* (4th ed.). https://doi.org/10.4324/9781003432173-4

Truong, M., Gibbs, L., Pradel, V., Morris, M., Gwatirisa, P., Tadic, M., de Silva, A., Hall, M., Young, D., Riggs, E., Gondal, I., & Waters, E. (2017). A cultural competence organizational review for community health services: Insights from a participatory approach. *Health Promotion Practice, 18*(3), 466–475. https://doi.org/10.1177/1524839916689546

Vespia, K. M., Fitzpatrick, M. E., Fouad, N. A., Kantamneni, N., & Chen, Y.-L. (2010). Multicultural career counseling: A national survey of competencies and practices. *The Career Development Quarterly, 59*(1), 54–71. https://doi.org/10.1002/j.2161-0045.2010.tb00130.x

Vitale, G. (2023). Research methodology. In *Sidrea series in accounting and business administration: Vol. Part F205*. https://doi.org/10.1007/978-3-031-30988-5_3

Wynn, D., & Williams, C. K. (2012). Principles for conducting critical realist case study research in information systems. *MIS Quarterly Management Information Systems, 36*(3), 787–810. https://doi.org/10.2307/41703481

Yaumas, N. E., Syafimen, S., Mohd, N. N., Mahmud, Z., Jusnimar, U., Ismail, W., & Rahayu, T. (2018). The importance of counselling basic skills for the counsellors. *International Journal of Pure and Applied Mathematics, 119*(18).

Yibeltal Yedemie, Y. (2021). In R. Nelson-Jones (Ed.) (3rd ed.)*International quarterly of community health education: Vol 41. A book review on basic counseling skills: A helper's manual*. https://doi.org/10.1177/0272684x20933514 3.

CHAPTER 4

Critical counselling techniques used in multicultural counselling and psychotherapy

Introduction

In an increasingly globalised and culturally plural world, counselling and psychotherapy must respond to the diversity of clients' cultural backgrounds, including ethnicity, religion, language, values, socioeconomic status, and other identity markers. Culture profoundly shapes how clients understand psychological distress, express emotions, seek help, and engage with therapeutic processes. Consequently, mainstream counselling techniques, often developed within Western, monocultural contexts, may be ineffective, or even harmful, if applied 'as is' to clients from different cultural worlds (e.g., minority, migrant, or non-Western populations). This recognition has spurred growing interest in culturally responsive counselling that adapts therapeutic methods to align with clients' cultural realities, worldviews, and healing practices (Skoli et al., 2025).

Given this background, the central aim of this chapter is to examine critically the counselling techniques used in multicultural counselling and psychotherapy to identify which techniques are commonly employed; how mainstream therapies are adapted to address cultural differences; what barriers counsellors face in doing so; and how culturally adapted techniques can be systematically integrated into professional practice to improve outcomes. A strong impetus for this inquiry comes from evidence that culturally adapted psychotherapies yield better outcomes for clients from diverse backgrounds than unadapted treatments. For example, meta-analytic evidence demonstrates that culturally adapted psychological treatments for depressive disorders significantly outperform usual care or no-treatment controls (Chowdhary et al., 2014). Meanwhile, other analyses show that when therapists demonstrate multicultural competence, including cultural awareness, knowledge, and culturally sensitive skills, clients rate their therapeutic experience more positively, correlating with improved treatment outcomes (Soto et al., 2019). However, 'cultural adaptation' is not a single, simple process. It involves deliberate and systematic modification of both content and delivery of therapy. Scholars have developed multiple models and frameworks to guide such adaptations. For instance, adaptations may involve

A Pragmatic Approach to Multicultural Counselling and Psychotherapy Skills Acquisition. https://doi.org/10.1016/B978-0-443-33939-4.00001-X

changes in language, metaphors, cultural values underpinning the therapy, communication style, involvement of family or community, and therapist–client relationship dynamics (Böttche et al., 2021; Nagayama Hall et al., 2019).

Moreover, culturally responsive counselling demands that therapists cultivate what many scholars call 'multicultural competence', encompassing self-awareness of their own cultural biases, deep knowledge of diverse cultural contexts, and the skills to intervene appropriately and sensitively (Sue et al., 2009). Without such competence, and without systematic adaptation, evidence-based psychotherapies risk being mismatched to clients' cultural realities, reducing efficacy or even causing harm (Lee et al., 2021). In the context of counselling practice in culturally diverse settings, these concerns are particularly salient. As one study of cross-cultural counselling practice in Africa observes, differences in cultural values, beliefs, languages and norms between counsellor and client can significantly influence therapeutic relationships and outcomes (Mamud, 2015).

Thus, this chapter offers a comprehensive and critical exploration of the following research objectives.

1. To identify key counselling techniques used with clients from diverse cultural backgrounds.
2. To explore how mainstream counselling techniques are adapted to address cultural differences, aligning interventions with clients' cultural values, beliefs, and practices.
3. To examine the challenges and barriers counsellors encounter when applying culturally adapted techniques.
4. To provide evidence-based recommendations for integrating culturally adapted counselling techniques into professional practice.

Counselling techniques: A conceptual clarification

Defining counselling techniques

In the professional literature on counselling and psychotherapy, 'counselling techniques' (also called interventions or methods) are typically defined as the structured therapeutic interventions or procedures that a counsellor employs, grounded in a theoretical framework, to assist clients in achieving change, growth or relief from psychological distress. As one authoritative text on psychotherapy explains, counselling is 'not only a relationship characterized by core conditions, but also a repertoire of interventions derived from different theoretical positions' (e.g., psychoanalytic, cognitive-behavioural, humanistic) (Nelson, 2025).

Thus, counselling techniques are the concrete 'what' of therapy: the deliberate, theory-based actions or procedures (rather than the underlying theory itself or the interpersonal style or 'skills'). This distinction between techniques (the 'what') and skills/conditions (the 'how') is recognised in counselling training curricula. For instance, in a standard course outline for guidance and counselling, 'techniques' are distinguished from 'skills', indicating that techniques refer to the structured methods used in counselling, while skills refer to interpersonal abilities (Augustine & Aminu, 2022). A comprehensive textbook that maps psychotherapy interventions describes 'techniques' as methods drawn from major therapeutic models (e.g., psychoanalysis, cognitive-behavioural, Gestalt, narrative, etc.), each linked to its theoretical assumptions. Thus, counselling techniques are the structured, theory-based therapeutic interventions and methods that trained counsellors deploy to facilitate clients' insight, emotional processing, behaviour change or personal growth within a therapeutic process.

Theoretical foundations of counselling techniques

No counselling technique stands alone in a vacuum. Each is embedded in a broader theoretical orientation that provides the conceptual rationale for why that intervention should facilitate change. Theories of psychotherapy act as a map linking a client's difficulties (e.g., maladaptive thoughts, unresolved conflicts, emotional distress) to specific mechanisms of change and thereby guiding which techniques are logical, coherent, and potentially effective (Nelson, 2010). For instance, when a therapist adopts a cognitive-behavioural orientation, the underlying assumption is that a client's emotional distress and dysfunctional behaviour are maintained by maladaptive cognitions and learned maladaptive responses. Accordingly, the therapist employs structured, goal-directed techniques such as cognitive restructuring (to challenge and change distorted thinking), behavioural experiments, or exposure exercises (to modify learned avoidance or fear responses) in order to help the client correct dysfunctional patterns and reduce symptoms. The theoretical logic is grounded in cognitive theory and behavioural learning principles: by changing thought patterns and behavioural responses, emotional distress follows (McManus, 2022).

By contrast, a psychodynamic (or psychoanalytic) orientation conceptualises psychological difficulties quite differently. Here, current symptoms are often understood to stem from unconscious conflicts, early life experiences, and intrapsychic dynamics. In this framework, techniques such as free association, dream analysis, or interpretation of transference and defence mechanisms are appropriate, because they aim to bring unconscious material to conscious awareness, allowing the client to work through deep-rooted conflicts, gain insight, and achieve psychological integration (Nelson, 2014). Meanwhile, therapists rooted in the humanistic–existential orientation draw from philosophies emphasising personal growth, agency, self-actualisation, and subjective meaning. Their techniques are otherwise discussed as skills, counsellors' attributes or conditions for effective counselling. They arise from core conditions such as empathy, genuineness, and unconditional positive regard and are implemented in an environment of acceptance and support. The therapeutic interventions are not heavily directive or symptom-focused; instead, they aim to foster self-exploration, personal growth, and actualisation of the client's potential. What counts in this orientation is less a structured protocol than the facilitation of an enabling relational and experiential context (Nelson, 2010).

Thus, in all these theoretical cases – cognitive-behavioural, psychodynamic, humanistic/existential – the techniques used are not arbitrary. They are theoretically determined. A therapist's theoretical orientation supplies the conceptual foundation and defines 'what is problematic', 'why it is problematic', and 'how change can happen'. In turn, this theoretical foundation shapes what interventions (techniques) make sense, how they are delivered, and what goals they target. Moreover, theoretical orientation influences not only what techniques are selected, but also how therapy is structured overall, the therapy's goals (symptom relief vs. insight vs. growth), timeframe (short-term vs. long-term), and relationship dynamics. In short, theoretical orientation provides the roadmap; techniques constitute the interventions along that map. Without theory, techniques become disconnected, potentially ineffective or incoherent. With theory, techniques gain meaning, purpose, and direction. A sound theoretical foundation ensures that counselling interventions are not an eclectic mishmash but deliberate, rational, and aligned with a coherent understanding of human distress and change.

Techniques of guidance and counselling

History: Modern guidance and counselling originated in the early 20th century. In 1908, Frank Parsons founded the first vocational guidance bureau in Boston, pioneering career counselling by matching people's skills and interests to occupations (Aviles et al., 2015). As psychological theories emerged, counselling expanded beyond vocational advice. Freud's psychoanalysis (early 1900s) introduced talk therapy for unconscious conflicts, and Carl Rogers' humanistic approach (1940s) emphasised non-directive support (Yao & Kabir, 2023). Similarly, mid-century developments included Ellis's rational emotive behaviour therapy (REBT) and Frankl's logotherapy. Pastoral counselling (integrating faith and therapy) emerged around the same time – for example, the Blanton-Peale Institute in the 1930s–40s – blending religion and psychotherapy. In recent decades, these techniques have spread worldwide but are adapted to local contexts. For example, African counselling practice stresses cultural relevance: young clients often defer to elders, so techniques must respect local norms.

Freudian and Neo-Freudian techniques

Psychoanalytic (Freudian) approaches use psychodynamic methods to explore unconscious drives. In therapy, the counsellor helps the client uncover hidden conflicts from early life and repressed desires (Opland & Torrico, 2024). Key Freudian techniques include the following:

- **Free association**: Clients say whatever comes to mind without censorship, allowing hidden thoughts and feelings to surface.
- **Dream analysis**: Interpreting dreams as symbolic manifestations of unconscious wishes (Freud's 'royal road' to the unconscious).
- **Defence mechanism analysis**: Identifying unconscious defences (e.g., repression, projection, denial) that protect the ego from anxiety.
- **Transference interpretation**: Exploring feelings the client projects onto the therapist (and vice versa) to reveal unresolved interpersonal dynamics.

Neo-Freudians (e.g., Adler, Jung, Horney) built on Freud's methods but shifted focus. For example, Adlerian techniques involve lifestyle (style-of-life) analysis – examining family birth order, social context and personal goals to reinterpret feelings of inferiority – and using encouragement to replace self-defeating beliefs (Cedeno & Torrico, 2024). Jungian therapy retains dream and free-association work but emphasises interpreting archetypal symbols and the collective unconscious. Overall, these psychodynamic techniques remain talk-based and exploratory, adapted by each theorist to social and cultural themes.

Rational emotive behaviour therapy (Ellis)

REBT is an active, cognitive-behavioural approach (1950s) that focuses on how beliefs about events cause emotional distress. The therapist teaches clients to identify and dispute irrational beliefs using structured models (King et al., 2024). Techniques include.

- **ABC (Activating event–Belief–Consequence) framework**: Mapping how an activating event (A) triggers an irrational belief (B), leading to emotional/behavioural consequences (C).
- **Disputation of irrational beliefs**: Actively challenging 'must' and 'should' statements and catastrophic thinking. The counsellor and client collaboratively dispute irrational ideas so that new, rational beliefs replace them.
- **Cognitive restructuring**: Teaching clients to reframe negative self-talk and rehearse logical, self-affirming thoughts (often through rational emotive imagery or role-play).
- **Homework and practice**: Assigning exercises (e.g., thought records, relaxation or breathing techniques) for the client to reinforce rational thinking outside sessions.

Most REBT interventions explicitly strengthen rational beliefs and set homework. In practice, therapists use a direct, teaching style – for example, continually disputing irrational thoughts until the client adopts healthier ideas.

Logotherapy (Frankl) techniques

Logotherapy (Viktor Frankl, 1950s) is an existential therapy centred on finding meaning. Its techniques are designed to help clients discover purpose even in suffering. Three hallmark techniques are as follows (Devoe, 2012; Längle, 2015):

- **Socratic (meaning) dialogue**: The therapist uses guided questioning (à la Socrates) to lead clients to articulate their own life values and purposes, helping them realise that meaning comes from the individual.
- **Paradoxical intention**: Clients are encouraged to deliberately confront or exaggerate their fears/symptoms. For example, a client with insomnia might purposefully try to stay awake – this often breaks the anxiety cycle and diminishes the symptom. Humour is sometimes used to 'distract' anxiety.
- **Dereflection**: This involves redirecting attention away from the symptom or self-focus towards others or a meaningful goal. For instance, someone obsessively worried about public speaking might be asked to focus on how their talk could help the audience, rather than on their own fear.

By these methods, Frankl's goal is to shift the client from rumination to responsibility and to highlight that they are free to choose their attitude towards any situation. (Frankl also spoke of 'attitude modification', urging clients to change their perspective on unchangeable events.)

Pastoral counselling techniques

Pastoral counselling (often in Christian contexts) blends psychotherapy with spiritual care. Counsellors who are clergy or spiritual leaders use many standard counselling techniques in a faith context, adding explicitly religious methods (Welton, 2014). Common pastoral techniques include the following:

- **Prayer and Scripture**: Therapists may pray with or for the client and encourage the client to pray on their own. Reading and reflecting on sacred texts (e.g., Bible passages) is used to provide guidance, comfort, or insight.
- **Spiritual narrative and values exploration**: Discussion focuses on the client's faith, purpose, values and spiritual struggles. Counsellors address questions like 'Where is God in this?' or use religious metaphors to help clients find meaning and hope.

- **Faith-based coping exercises**: Techniques such as meditation on faith-based affirmations or the use of rituals (e.g., lighting candles, confession/practice of forgiveness) are sometimes incorporated.
- **Pastoral presence**: Like a shepherd, the counsellor provides an accepting, compassionate presence (similar to Rogerian acceptance) but explicitly rooted in theological understanding (O'Callaghan et al., 2020).

In pastoral counselling, the goal is not only psychological relief but also spiritual growth. By integrating prayer, scripture, and theology into talk therapy, pastoral counsellors help clients apply their beliefs to life problems and find solace in faith.

My lecture approach

Over the past century, a wide array of counselling approaches have emerged, each with its own set of techniques aligned to its core principles. These approaches are often grouped into broad theoretical schools, such as cognitive-behavioural, psychodynamic, humanistic, and others, which encompass specific modalities. Below, we examine key classifications of counselling techniques, illustrating their purposes, principles, and examples of techniques in each category.

Psychodynamic techniques

Whenever I introduce psychodynamic work to my students, I remind them that this is one of the oldest traditions in counselling, yet it remains deeply relevant today. Psychodynamic thinking begins with the idea that human beings carry within them layers of experience that are not always fully conscious. Early relationships, unresolved emotions, and buried memories often continue to shape a person's present behaviour in ways they may not immediately recognise. Because of this, psychodynamic techniques are designed to help clients uncover the deeper roots of their struggles, bringing into the light what has silently influenced them for years.

In psychodynamic practice, the counselling room becomes a space where the client's inner world is allowed to speak. Clients are encouraged to explore their thoughts freely, and as they do so, patterns slowly emerge. Techniques such as free expression of thoughts, exploration of childhood relationships, and the gentle interpretation of recurring themes help the client gradually make sense of feelings that may once have been too overwhelming or confusing. For instance, the simple act of inviting a client to share whatever comes to mind is not just a conversation. It gives the unconscious an opportunity to surface, and often, important emotional truths appear in these spontaneous reflections.

One of the most distinctive aspects of psychodynamic work is the therapeutic relationship itself. As the client and counsellor interact over time, old relational patterns often reappear in the relationship. This is what we describe as transference. When approached with patience and sensitivity, these moments are not disruptions; they are opportunities for insight. They allow the client to re-experience deeply rooted emotions in a safe, supportive environment and gradually work through them in healthier ways.

In more contemporary forms of psychodynamic therapy, the approach tends to be more flexible and conversational. Rather than spending years in analysis, many clients work on focused concerns within a shorter timeframe. Still, what remains constant is the heart of the psychodynamic tradition: helping the client understand the meaning of their emotional life. Through exploring past experiences, noticing present relational patterns, and making unconscious feelings conscious, clients often discover a sense of clarity and relief that allows them to move forward with renewed self-understanding. The essence of psychodynamic techniques is this: when people understand the emotional roots of their difficulties, they regain the freedom to respond, rather than remain trapped in old patterns. This renewed awareness becomes the foundation for change.

Cognitive-behavioural techniques

Cognitive-behavioural approaches are grounded in the understanding that thoughts, emotions, and behaviours operate as an interconnected system. When thinking becomes distorted or overly negative, emotional responses tend to follow the same pattern, and behaviour often shifts in ways that reinforce distress. In this model of understanding human functioning, problematic patterns are maintained through cycles of maladaptive thoughts and avoidance-based behaviours that gradually become habitual.

Cognitive-behavioural techniques are designed to interrupt these cycles by helping clients observe, question, and modify the thoughts and behaviours that contribute to their difficulties. One of the foundational methods in this tradition is thought monitoring. This technique encourages clients to pay attention to the flow of their internal dialogue, particularly in moments of heightened emotion. By recording these thoughts and examining the situations in which they arise, clients begin to recognise common cognitive patterns such as automatic negative thoughts or exaggerated interpretations of events. The ability to identify these patterns marks an important step towards change.

Cognitive restructuring builds upon this awareness by guiding clients to examine the accuracy and usefulness of their thoughts. Instead of accepting internal statements at face value, clients are encouraged to consider alternative interpretations, evaluate evidence, and develop more balanced perspectives. The aim is to replace habitual distortions with realistic and constructive ways of thinking. Over time, shifts in thinking produce corresponding changes in emotional responses.

Behavioural methods complement these cognitive strategies by addressing the learned habits that contribute to ongoing distress. Behavioural activation is frequently used when clients experience withdrawal, low energy, or reduced engagement in meaningful activities. The technique involves a gradual reintroduction of purposeful actions, organised in small and manageable steps. As clients begin to resume valued activities, improvements in mood and motivation often follow, creating a positive cycle of reinforcement.

For clients dealing with anxiety, exposure techniques are central. These techniques involve systematic and supportive contact with situations or experiences that have been avoided due to fear. Exposure is introduced gradually, allowing clients to confront feared stimuli in a controlled way while learning that anxiety diminishes with repeated experience. Through this process, clients develop greater confidence in their ability to manage discomfort, and the intensity of their anxiety typically decreases over time.

A consistent feature across all cognitive-behavioural techniques is the emphasis on practice and repetition. Change is not expected to occur solely within the counselling session. Instead, clients are encouraged to apply the techniques between sessions so that new patterns become integrated into daily life. Homework assignments, self-monitoring exercises, and behavioural practice tasks serve this purpose by reinforcing learning outside the therapeutic environment.

Humanistic and person-centred techniques

When I teach humanistic and person-centred counselling, I like to begin by reminding my students that this approach is built on a deep respect for the individual. At its core is the belief that every person possesses an innate capacity for growth, authenticity, and self-direction. Psychological difficulties often arise when this natural movement towards growth becomes blocked, sometimes by criticism, fear, trauma, or environments that do not allow a person to express who they truly are. Humanistic techniques are therefore designed to create a therapeutic atmosphere where clients feel safe enough to explore themselves honestly, without fear of judgement or pressure.

In the person-centred tradition, the technique is not something the counsellor does to the client; rather, it is the quality of the relationship they build together. I often describe this approach as creating a warm emotional climate where the client can hear themselves more clearly. The counsellor listens with deep attentiveness, reflects feelings, and responds with openness. Through this kind of genuine presence, clients begin to reconnect with their inner experiences, many of which they may have ignored, suppressed, or never fully understood.

Students sometimes ask me whether person-centred therapy has 'techniques' in the traditional sense. I explain that while this approach does not rely on structured procedures, it does rely on intentional therapeutic attitudes that function as techniques in their own right. When a counsellor offers authenticity, accurate empathy, and unconditional respect, these conditions work together as powerful therapeutic tools. They help clients reduce defensiveness, access deeper feelings, and gain the confidence to explore their thoughts honestly. As clients begin to sense that their experiences are valid and accepted, they naturally move towards greater clarity and self-understanding.

In broader humanistic work, such as Gestalt therapy or experiential therapies, the techniques become more structured. Here, the emphasis is on increasing present–moment awareness so that clients can fully experience their thoughts, emotions, and bodily sensations. For example, a therapist may guide a client to stay with a feeling instead of analysing it, allowing the emotion to unfold and express its meaning. Exercises like role-playing, guided imagery, or the well-known empty-chair dialogue help clients express unfinished emotional business or explore parts of themselves that have been neglected.

Even when these experiential exercises are used, the humanistic approach remains grounded in authenticity and personal meaning. The intention is not to push the client towards a particular insight, but to help them encounter their inner experiences directly and honestly. The counsellor remains a companion rather than an authority figure – someone who honours the client's autonomy and trusts in their ability to grow when given the right emotional environment.

Ultimately, humanistic and person-centred techniques aim to reconnect the client with the truth of who they are. By creating conditions of acceptance and encouraging genuine self-exploration, these approaches help clients rediscover strengths, clarify their values, and move towards a more integrated and authentic life. In this way, change arises not through instruction, but through the client's own expanding awareness of themselves.

Gestalt techniques

When I introduce Gestalt techniques to my students, I emphasise that this approach is deeply experiential. It does not simply invite clients to talk about their lives; it encourages them to experience their emotions, thoughts, and bodily sensations in the present moment. Gestalt counselling grew out of the belief that people often fragment their experiences, pushing away uncomfortable feelings, avoiding unfinished conflicts, or living more in the past or future than in the 'here and now'. Gestalt techniques are therefore designed to help clients reclaim these lost or disowned parts of themselves.

A central idea I highlight in class is that awareness itself is curative. When clients become fully aware of what they feel, need, or fear in the present, they start to integrate parts of themselves that were once disconnected. Gestalt techniques give this awareness a structure and a voice. Unlike the relatively non-directive person-centred approach, Gestalt work can be quite active, creative, and expressive. It often invites clients to enact rather than merely describe experiences.

One of the most recognisable Gestalt techniques is the empty-chair dialogue. In my teaching, I explain that this technique provides clients with a safe way to externalise an internal conflict or converse with someone who is not physically present. A client might speak to an imagined parent, partner, or even to a part of themselves, perhaps the fearful self or the angry self. By voicing each side of the dialogue, clients often uncover emotions, beliefs, or unmet needs that have been sitting beneath the surface. The purpose is not to dramatise the experience but to give expression to what has been left unsaid or unresolved.

Another important Gestalt technique involves focusing on body awareness. In class, I encourage students to appreciate that the body often reveals what the mind tries to avoid. A counsellor may gently ask a client to pay attention to a tightness in the chest or a trembling in the hands, exploring what emotion or message the body is communicating. This can lead to powerful insights, because clients learn to listen to themselves in a more holistic way.

Gestalt work also makes use of guided imagery and role-playing, where clients enact scenes from their lives or revisit past situations as if they were happening now. These exercises can help clients identify patterns, perhaps a tendency to stay silent, to apologise, to avoid conflict, or to suppress anger. When these patterns are brought into the present moment through action rather than analysis, clients can begin experimenting with new ways of responding.

Throughout all these techniques, the counsellor plays the role of an active facilitator. I often tell students that the counsellor's presence in Gestalt therapy is authentic, spontaneous, and sometimes even confrontational, but always in a supportive and constructive manner. The goal is to help clients recognise how they interrupt their own growth or hide from their own feelings, and then guide them towards integrating those parts into a fuller sense of self.

In essence, Gestalt techniques are about awakening the client to who they are in the present moment. By encouraging expression, embodiment, and direct experience, these techniques help clients confront unfinished emotional business and move towards greater wholeness. What emerges is a deeper sense of responsibility, authenticity, and personal empowerment – qualities that grow naturally as awareness expands.

Existential and logotherapy techniques

When teaching existential and logotherapy approaches, I emphasise that these techniques are rooted in the search for meaning and the acknowledgement of fundamental human concerns. Existential counselling begins with the understanding that each person must navigate issues such as freedom, responsibility, isolation, mortality, and the search for purpose. Psychological difficulties often arise when individuals feel disconnected from their own values, struggle with choices, or experience a sense of meaninglessness. Techniques in this tradition are designed to help clients confront these realities, clarify their values, and take responsibility for shaping their lives.

In existential counselling, techniques are less about structured exercises and more about the process of deep, reflective dialogue. Counsellors use open-ended questions, guided reflection, and Socratic exploration to encourage clients to examine the assumptions that guide their lives. Clients are invited to explore questions such as 'What gives your life meaning?' or 'How do your choices align with the person you want to become?' These discussions help clients confront fears or avoidance patterns and make conscious decisions aligned with their authentic selves. The emphasis is on awareness and responsibility, fostering the recognition that while we cannot control all circumstances, we can choose our response to them.

Logotherapy, developed by Viktor Frankl, is a specific existential approach that places meaning at the centre of therapy. The primary goal of logotherapy techniques is to help clients discover purpose even in the face of suffering. Techniques often include Socratic dialogue, where clients are guided to reflect on the sources of meaning in their lives, and dereflection, which shifts focus from problems and preoccupations to values, goals, or responsibilities. Another technique, paradoxical intention, encourages clients to approach feared or anxiety-provoking situations with humour or intentional exaggeration, helping them break the cycle of anticipatory anxiety.

A key feature of existential and logotherapy techniques is that they are highly personalised and client-centred. Unlike highly structured interventions, the counsellor's role is to facilitate self-exploration, helping clients identify personal meaning, confront existential anxiety, and make authentic choices. The focus is not on symptom reduction alone but on cultivating a life that the client experiences as purposeful and aligned with their core values.

These techniques are particularly powerful when working with clients who feel stuck in life transitions or face chronic illness, grief, or existential despair. By helping clients recognise their freedom to choose, understand the meaning inherent in their experiences, and take responsibility for their actions, existential and logotherapy techniques foster resilience, clarity, and a renewed sense of purpose.

Pastoral counselling techniques

Pastoral counselling integrates psychological principles with spiritual and religious perspectives, recognising that many clients draw strength, guidance, and meaning from their faith or spiritual beliefs. In this approach, counselling techniques are designed not only to address emotional and behavioural concerns but also to nurture spiritual well-being. Pastoral counselling assumes that spiritual values, religious practices, and faith communities can play a central role in the healing process and in helping clients cope with life challenges.

The techniques used in pastoral counselling are diverse, but all are grounded in creating a safe, compassionate space where clients can explore both personal and spiritual dimensions of their lives. Listening remains central, but the pastoral counsellor often incorporates reflective practices that encourage clients to examine their relationship with God, their sense of purpose, or their moral and ethical beliefs. Prayer, meditation, scripture reflection, and guided spiritual exercises are often used to help clients gain perspective, find comfort, and cultivate inner resources for coping.

Another important pastoral technique is spiritual reframing, where the counsellor helps the client interpret challenges and experiences through the lens of faith or spiritual understanding. For example, a client struggling with grief might explore the experience as a spiritual journey or consider how personal loss fits within a larger sense of purpose or divine plan. Similarly, pastoral counsellors often use narrative techniques that encourage clients to tell their life stories, highlighting moments of resilience, spiritual insight, or growth in character.

Pastoral counselling also emphasises moral and ethical reflection. Clients are guided to examine how their choices align with their values and spiritual beliefs. This process often involves exploring responsibility, forgiveness, and reconciliation, both with others and with oneself. Techniques may include journaling, reflective dialogue, or structured exercises that encourage self-examination and the integration of spiritual principles into daily life.

A distinctive feature of pastoral counselling is its holistic perspective. It recognises that emotional, psychological, and spiritual dimensions of life are intertwined, and it seeks to promote well-being across all these areas. By addressing both inner psychological needs and spiritual concerns, pastoral counselling techniques offer clients a comprehensive framework for coping with challenges, finding meaning, and achieving personal growth.

In practice, pastoral counselling does not impose belief but rather respects the client's spiritual framework, using techniques that resonate with the individual's values and faith orientation. This personalised approach often strengthens engagement, deepens insight, and fosters resilience, enabling clients to navigate life's difficulties with both practical strategies and spiritual support.

Integrative and eclectic techniques

Integrative and eclectic approaches recognise that no single theoretical model can fully address the complexity of human experience. Counsellors who work from this perspective draw on multiple theories and techniques, selecting those that best fit the needs, preferences, and context of each client. The emphasis is on flexibility and responsiveness rather than rigid adherence to one school of thought, allowing the counsellor to tailor interventions in a way that maximises effectiveness.

In practice, integrative techniques may combine cognitive-behavioural strategies with humanistic presence, psychodynamic exploration, or spiritual guidance, depending on the client's presenting concerns. For example, a counsellor may use thought records and cognitive restructuring to help a client with anxiety while simultaneously exploring underlying relational patterns using psychodynamic techniques. At the same time, the therapist might incorporate person-centred empathy to provide a supportive and accepting environment. The eclectic approach allows the counsellor to blend these methods seamlessly, addressing both immediate symptoms and deeper developmental or existential issues.

The core principle of integrative work is that theory informs practice but does not constrain it. Counsellors consider the evidence base for different interventions, the client's cultural and personal context, and the therapeutic goals established collaboratively. Techniques are selected based on their appropriateness for the client's unique situation rather than the counsellor's personal preference or allegiance to a single orientation.

One common integrative method is technical eclecticism, where the counsellor intentionally mixes techniques from different approaches without attempting to create a new theoretical framework. This allows for flexibility in session planning and responsiveness to client feedback. Another approach is theoretical integration, in which the counsellor consciously combines elements of two or more theories into a coherent, unified framework. For instance, some therapists blend cognitive-behavioural strategies with psychodynamic insights to address both conscious thought patterns and unconscious emotional drivers.

Integrative and eclectic techniques are particularly valuable in culturally diverse contexts, where clients' values, beliefs, and lived experiences may not align neatly with a single therapeutic model. By drawing on a range of interventions, counsellors can adapt techniques to respect cultural norms, address specific needs, and foster engagement and trust.

Ultimately, the strength of integrative and eclectic approaches lies in their adaptability and responsiveness. They encourage counsellors to be creative and reflective, to draw on the full spectrum of available methods, and to remain attuned to the client's evolving needs. By combining techniques thoughtfully, counsellors can provide comprehensive and personalised care that addresses the complexity of human problems while supporting growth, resilience, and well-being.

Research methodology

The methodology of this research is designed to provide an all-inclusive understanding of the critical counselling techniques used in multicultural settings. As multicultural counselling is inherently complex, the research employs a mixed-methods approach to offer both in-depth qualitative insights and measurable quantitative data. This methodological approach allows for a multifaceted exploration of the following:

- The techniques that are employed in multicultural counselling and psychotherapy
- The adaptations made to mainstream techniques to cater to cultural differences
- The challenges and barriers that practitioners face when applying these adapted techniques
- Evidence-based recommendations for integrating these culturally adapted techniques into professional practice

Approach

The study adopts an exploratory and descriptive approach. The exploratory approach is vital for uncovering under-researched aspects of multicultural counselling, particularly regarding how mainstream counselling techniques are adapted for different cultural contexts. This allows the study to identify new perspectives on counselling techniques that may not be thoroughly understood or documented in existing literature.

Research paradigm

The research is conducted within a pragmatic paradigm, which is particularly suited for mixed-methods research as it allows for the use of multiple research strategies to address complex real-world problems. Pragmatism focuses on finding practical solutions and understanding what works in specific contexts, making it ideal for examining how counselling techniques can be adapted to meet the needs of clients from diverse cultural backgrounds (Shen et al., 2017).

A pragmatic paradigm does not commit to a specific philosophical stance, making it flexible in accommodating both qualitative and quantitative approaches. This paradigm emphasises outcomes and solutions, which align with the goal of providing evidence-based recommendations for integrating culturally adapted techniques into professional practice (Feilzer, 2010). Pragmatism also acknowledges that the nature of knowledge is influenced by context, which is significant when considering how cultural factors shape counselling practices (Shaw et al., 2010). Thus, pragmatism supports the use of mixed methods, combining qualitative and quantitative approaches to provide a comprehensive understanding of research problems (Gobo, 2023).

Ontology

The ontological stance of this research aligns with interpretivism, which suggests that reality is socially constructed and that the meanings people attach to their experiences can differ widely (McAuliffe et al., 2012). This aligns with the nature of multicultural counselling, where practitioners' and clients' realities are shaped by their cultural backgrounds, worldviews, and personal experiences (Collins & Arthur, 2010).

From an interpretivist perspective, the study acknowledges that different individuals may have unique perspectives on the application and adaptation of counselling techniques based on their cultural beliefs, values, and practices. As such, the research does not seek a single, objective truth but rather aims to understand how diverse cultural perspectives shape the use and adaptation of counselling techniques. This approach allows for an exploration of the subjective experiences of counsellors and clients and how these experiences inform their practice.

Epistemology

The epistemological framework for this study is constructivist. Constructivism asserts that knowledge is constructed through social interactions and is deeply influenced by individuals' experiences and contexts. In the case of multicultural counselling, knowledge about the adaptation of techniques is shaped by the lived experiences of both counsellors and clients (Becerra & Castorina, 2018; Llanas, 2018).

Constructivism is relevant to this study as it emphasises the importance of understanding how individuals co-create meaning in their interactions. Counsellors and clients, through their conversations, interactions, and shared experiences, construct their understanding of what counselling techniques work or do not work in particular cultural settings. Knowledge in this study is not seen as an absolute truth, but as something that is co-constructed through the perspectives and insights of the participants involved. The researcher will gather knowledge through the subjective accounts of the participants and will interpret this knowledge in a manner that reflects their cultural and personal experiences.

Axiology

In terms of axiology, this study acknowledges the role of values in the research process, both in how the researcher approaches the study and in how participants' experiences are interpreted. As multicultural counselling is deeply embedded in cultural contexts, the values of both the researcher and participants will inevitably shape the findings (Robitschek & Hardin, 2017).

The researcher will approach the study with cultural humility, acknowledging that their own cultural beliefs and values may influence their interpretation of the data. This means the researcher will actively reflect on their biases throughout the research process, taking steps to ensure that they remain open to the perspectives of participants from diverse cultural backgrounds. The study will also respect the values and worldviews of the participants, ensuring that the voices and experiences of both counsellors and clients are given equal weight in the analysis.

The goal is to produce research that is culturally sensitive and that contributes to the ongoing development of inclusive and effective counselling practices that respect diverse cultural values and perspectives.

Research design

This study uses a mixed-methods design, combining both qualitative and quantitative research approaches. This design allows for a holistic exploration of multicultural counselling techniques. This study uses a mixed-methods design, combining both qualitative and quantitative research approaches. This design allows for a holistic exploration of multicultural counselling techniques (Aramo-Immonen, 2013; He, 2024). This is crucial in multicultural counselling, where both statistical trends and personal experiences are important. Additionally, researchers can cross-verify data by employing a variety of techniques, which improves the validity and dependability of the results. This triangulation aids in confirming findings and offering a more sophisticated comprehension of multicultural counselling approaches (Porcino & Verhoef, 2010).

Sample and sampling techniques

The study involved a total of 400 professional counsellors and psychotherapists who were all based in Nigeria. Although the participants were geographically located within Nigeria, they had extensive experience providing counselling services to clients from a wide range of cultural backgrounds, both within and outside the country. These counselling interactions occurred through both onsite (in-person) sessions and online platforms, giving participants a unique multicultural counselling exposure. Their clients included individuals from African, Asian, European, Middle Eastern, Indigenous, and other cultural groups, making them well suited to respond to issues relating to multicultural counselling techniques.

A purposive sampling technique was adopted to select participants who met specific inclusion criteria. To be eligible for the study, participants were required to be currently practicing as counsellors in Nigeria, possess at least a bachelor's degree in counselling, psychology, or a related field, and have at least 2 years of active counselling experience. Furthermore, they must have counselled clients from culturally diverse backgrounds, whether through direct face-to-face interactions within Nigeria or via virtual counselling platforms with clients across borders.

Participants were drawn from various states in Nigeria that have well-established and functional counselling associations. These states included Akwa Ibom, the Federal Capital Territory (FCT), Lagos, Jos (Plateau State), Sokoto, Enugu, and Anambra. The selection of these locations was deliberate, aimed at reaching a broad spectrum of experienced professionals who are actively engaged in the counselling profession.

Recruitment was carried out through collaboration with counselling outlets, heads of counselling units in educational institutions, and organisers of counsellors' training workshops and seminars. Additionally, invitations were circulated via email, WhatsApp, and other professional platforms where practising counsellors are known to engage. All participants were provided with detailed information about the study, and only those who gave informed consent were included in the final sample.

The demographic data obtained from the respondents – such as age, gender, years of experience, highest level of education attained, and the primary cultural backgrounds of their clients – confirmed that the sample comprised a diverse and professionally credible group. This made the study's findings relevant and applicable to understanding the dynamics of multicultural counselling in the Nigerian context.

Data collection

Data was collected using a combination of qualitative and quantitative methods to gain an inclusive understanding of the counselling techniques used in multicultural settings, the adaptations made to those techniques, and the challenges faced by counsellors. This mixed-methods approach enabled the researcher to capture both the depth and breadth of experiences in multicultural counselling. The data collection methods included.

Multicultural counselling techniques questionnaire (MCTQ)

The instrument used in this study is an MCTQ designed to explore multicultural counselling techniques, how these techniques are adapted to meet the diverse cultural needs of clients, and the challenges faced by counsellors when working in multicultural contexts. The questionnaire is structured to capture both quantitative data through Likert-scale responses and qualitative data through open-ended questions, offering a balanced approach to gather both numerical insights and in-depth descriptive feedback.

The first section of the questionnaire collects basic demographic information about the participants, such as their age, gender, years of experience in counselling, and the cultural backgrounds of the clients they work with. This demographic data provides important context for analysing the responses and helps the researcher understand how factors like age or professional background might influence the counsellor's approach to multicultural counselling.

The following sections focus on the practical aspects of multicultural counselling. Participants are asked to identify the types of counselling techniques they use when working with clients from diverse cultural backgrounds. The techniques listed include widely used approaches such as cognitive-behavioural therapy (CBT), person-centred therapy, narrative therapy, purpose-based career coaching and others. Respondents are asked to rate how frequently they use each technique on a 1- to 5-point Likert scale, where 1 represents 'never' and 5 represents 'always'. This section provides valuable insight into which techniques are most commonly used by multicultural counsellors.

Another key section of the questionnaire examines how often participants adapt their counselling techniques to address the cultural differences of their clients. Participants are asked to rate the frequency of these adaptations, again using the 1 to 5 Likert scale. This section is essential for understanding how flexible and responsive counsellors are to the cultural needs of their clients and whether they modify traditional therapeutic approaches to make them culturally appropriate.

The next section explores the challenges and barriers counsellors face when using multicultural counselling techniques. Participants are asked to rate the level of difficulty they encounter in various areas, such as language barriers, misunderstanding of cultural values, resistance to certain techniques, and difficulty in building rapport with clients. The challenges are rated on a scale from 1 (no challenge) to 5 (extreme challenge). This section helps identify the primary obstacles that practitioners encounter when applying culturally adapted techniques and provides a clearer understanding of the difficulties faced in multicultural counselling practice.

Structured open-ended questions

The final section, MCTQ, includes four open-ended questions designed to capture more nuanced qualitative data. These questions allow participants to elaborate on their experiences with multicultural counselling techniques, providing detailed examples and personal reflections. Respondents are asked to describe the techniques they have found most effective, how they adapt these techniques to meet cultural needs, and what challenges they face in doing so. This section also provides an opportunity for counsellors to offer recommendations for improving multicultural competence in counselling, contributing to the broader discussion on best practices in the field.

Participants were provided with a set of four structured open-ended questions designed to address the key objectives of the study. These questions allowed the researcher to explore the counsellors' experiences in depth and gather detailed information about the techniques they used with clients from diverse cultural backgrounds. The questions focused on the following areas.

a. The specific counselling techniques employed by the counsellors.
b. How these techniques were adapted to address cultural differences.
c. The challenges faced by counsellors when applying these adapted techniques in practice.
d. Recommendations for improving multicultural competence in counselling.

This approach enabled participants to respond thoughtfully, providing rich qualitative data on their practices and reflections. The open-ended format ensured flexibility, allowing participants to elaborate on their responses, share personal experiences, and highlight any challenges or successes in adapting techniques to meet the cultural needs of clients.

Case studies

Case studies were used to capture real-world examples of how counselling techniques were adapted to meet the cultural needs of clients. Counsellors were asked to provide detailed descriptions of specific instances where they successfully adapted techniques in practice. Each case study included the following key aspects:

- The context of the counselling session, including the cultural background of the client.
- The techniques used by the counsellor and how they were modified to suit the client's cultural context.
- The outcomes of the session, including the effectiveness of the adaptations.
- Any challenges encountered by the counsellor in applying these culturally sensitive approaches.

The case studies provided a practical illustration of how counselling techniques were applied and adapted in real-world settings, offering valuable insights into the dynamic process of multicultural counselling.

Validation and reliability of the instrument

To ensure the quality, accuracy, and appropriateness of the MCTQ, the instrument underwent a multi-step validation process involving various forms of validity.

Face validity

Face validity refers to the degree to which the instrument appears effective in terms of its stated aims. The items in the questionnaire were reviewed by a panel of five experts in counselling psychology and multicultural education (Khazaee-Pool et al., 2024; Setia, 2017). Their feedback confirmed that the instrument items were clear, appropriate, and relevant to the constructs under investigation. Minor adjustments in wording and structure were made based on their suggestions to improve clarity and respondent engagement.

Content validity

Content validity assesses the extent to which the items adequately represent the domain of interest – in this case, multicultural counselling techniques, adaptations, challenges, and barriers (Almanasreh et al., 2022; Spoto et al., 2023).

- A panel of three experienced multicultural counsellors and two academic researchers evaluated the initial pool of items.
- Each item was rated for relevance, clarity, and representativeness using a 4-point scale.
- The Content Validity Index (CVI) was calculated for each item. Items with a CVI below 0.80 were revised or removed.
- Overall, the scale-level CVI (S-CVI) was found to be 0.89, indicating strong content validity.

Reliability of the instrument

To establish the reliability of the MCTQ, a pilot study was conducted among licensed and practicing counsellors in Enugu State, Nigeria. A total of 30 participants were purposively selected from secondary schools, tertiary institutions, and private practice settings. These participants were considered appropriate due to their direct involvement in multicultural counselling practices and interventions.

Table 4.1: Reliability results.

Section	Number of items	Cronbach's alpha (α)	Interpretation
Section A: Counselling techniques used	9	0.73	Good
Section B: Adaptation of techniques	9	0.80	Good
Section C: Challenges and barriers in multicultural counselling	8	0.72	Good

The reliability of the instrument was assessed using Cronbach's alpha coefficient to determine the internal consistency of each section of the questionnaire. The results are presented in Table 4.1.

The reliability of the questionnaire was evaluated using Cronbach's alpha (α), a statistical measure of internal consistency. This measure indicates how well the items in each section of the instrument work together to assess the same underlying construct. Reliability analysis was conducted for each of the three core sections of the instrument: Counselling Techniques Used, Adaptation of Techniques, and Challenges and Barriers in Multicultural Counselling.

For Section A, which assessed the frequency of use of various counselling techniques with clients from diverse cultural backgrounds, the Cronbach's alpha value was 0.73. This indicates a good level of internal consistency, suggesting that the nine items in this section reliably measure the construct of counselling technique usage.

In Section B, which explored how often participants adapt counselling techniques to suit the cultural contexts of their clients, the Cronbach's alpha was 0.80. This score represents a high level of reliability, indicating that the items in this section are strongly related and consistently measure the construct of cultural adaptation in counselling practices.

For Section C, which examined the challenges and barriers encountered in multicultural counselling, the reliability coefficient was 0.72. This also reflects a good level of internal consistency, demonstrating that the items in this section effectively capture the various challenges counsellors face when working with culturally diverse clients.

Overall, the Cronbach's alpha values across all three sections exceed the commonly accepted threshold of 0.70, affirming that the instrument is statistically reliable for assessing multicultural counselling techniques, adaptations, and perceived challenges among counsellors and psychotherapists in Nigeria.

Data analysis

Qualitative data analysis

The qualitative data collected from interviews, focus groups, and case studies were analysed using thematic analysis, a method that allowed for a detailed exploration of the key patterns, themes, and categories within the data. The process of thematic analysis is designed to identify both explicit and underlying meanings in the responses provided by participants, offering a rich understanding of their experiences with multicultural counselling techniques. Below is an expanded description of the procedures followed in this analysis.

1. **Familiarisation with the Data**: The first step in the analysis process involved thoroughly familiarising the researcher with the data. This entailed reading through the interview transcripts, focus group notes, and case study descriptions multiple times to gain an overall understanding of the content. During this stage, initial ideas about the possible themes and patterns began to emerge. The researcher took notes to highlight recurring terms, phrases, and concepts, which helped in identifying early indicators of key themes.
2. **Open Coding**: The next step involved open coding, where the data was broken down into manageable segments. During open coding, each interview, focus group, and case study response was read line by line, and significant elements were labelled with short descriptive codes. These codes captured important aspects of the participants' experiences, such as specific counselling techniques mentioned, cultural considerations, and any challenges or barriers identified. Open coding was performed manually or using qualitative analysis software, allowing the researcher to create an initial set of codes that reflected the diversity of the data.
3. **Axial Coding**: After open coding, the researcher proceeded with axial coding, where codes identified in the previous step were grouped and categorised based on their relationships. This phase aimed to connect various codes into more significant themes and subthemes. e.g., codes related to specific multicultural counselling techniques might have been grouped together, while those related to challenges faced by counsellors were clustered in another category. During axial coding, the researcher looked for patterns of association between the codes, helping to understand how different aspects of the data were related to each other.
4. **Selective Coding**: The final stage of coding, selective coding, focused on identifying the central themes that emerged from the data. This process involved selecting the most salient and relevant codes from the axial coding phase and developing these into broader categories. These categories were then analysed to form key themes that represented the core findings of the study. Selective coding helped refine the data into clear, coherent themes that captured the essence of the participants' experiences, such as the

adaptation of mainstream counselling techniques and the challenges faced in multicultural contexts.

5. **Constant Comparative Method**: To ensure an all-encompassing and nuanced understanding of the data, the constant comparative method was employed. This method involved continuously comparing data from different sources (e.g., between individual interviews, focus groups, and case studies) to identify similarities and differences in the experiences of participants. For instance, the researcher compared how different counsellors described their use of culturally adapted techniques or how various participants reported challenges specific to certain cultural groups. This comparative approach helped to highlight both shared experiences and unique perspectives, providing a deeper understanding of the factors influencing multicultural counselling practices.
6. **Theme Development and Refinement**:
Once the coding process was complete, the researcher engaged in theme development and refinement. This step involved organising the identified themes into a coherent narrative, connecting them back to the research objectives. The themes were analysed in relation to the broader research questions, specifically examining the types of counselling techniques used, how these techniques were adapted to cultural contexts, and the challenges faced by counsellors. Through this iterative process, themes were further refined to ensure they accurately reflected the data and provided meaningful insights into the multicultural counselling process.
7. **Interpretation and Reporting**:
The final step in the thematic analysis was the interpretation and reporting of the findings. The identified themes were discussed in relation to the literature and theoretical frameworks of multicultural counselling. The researcher carefully interpreted the meaning of each theme, highlighting key insights such as the effectiveness of certain counselling techniques in diverse cultural contexts and the ways in which counsellors adapted their approaches to address cultural differences. The findings were presented in a clear, structured report, illustrating the connections between themes and answering the research questions.

Quantitative data analysis

The method of data analysis for this study primarily involved the use of descriptive statistics to summarise and interpret the collected data. This approach was employed to examine the frequency and distribution of responses regarding the use and adaptation of counselling techniques, as well as the challenges faced by counsellors in multicultural settings.

Descriptive statistics were utilised to calculate key measures such as the mean, standard deviation, and confidence intervals. The mean scores were used to determine the average frequency with which specific counselling techniques were employed and adapted, and the level of challenges that participants reported facing. The standard error of the mean and standard deviation helped assess the precision and variability in the responses, providing insight into how consistently techniques were used and how challenges were perceived by different counsellors.

The 95% confidence intervals were also calculated for the mean scores, offering a range within which the true population mean is likely to fall. This measure of precision allowed for a more reliable understanding of the data and indicated the degree of uncertainty around the mean values for each variable.

To assess the normality of the data, the Shapiro–Wilk test was conducted. The *P*-values for all variables were found to be less than 0.001, suggesting that the data did not follow a normal distribution. While this indicates that the data significantly deviated from normality, the descriptive statistics still provided meaningful insights into the practices of the participants. The results are reliable in terms of summarising the general patterns of use and challenges in multicultural counselling, although the non-normality of the data should be kept in mind when interpreting these findings.

Ethical considerations

Ethical considerations were central to ensuring the integrity and quality of this research. The study was reviewed and approved by the Research Ethics Committee of the Department of Counselling and Human Development Studies at the University of Nigeria, Nsukka. The approval ensured that the research adhered to the highest standards of ethical conduct. The following ethical principles guided the study, ensuring that the rights and welfare of all participants were protected throughout the research process.

1. **Informed Consent**: All participants were fully informed about the purpose, procedures, and potential risks associated with the study before their involvement. Informed consent forms were provided to each participant, detailing the study's goals, expected duration, and any possible discomfort or risks. Participants were given ample time to review the information and ask questions before deciding to participate. Written informed consent was obtained from all participants prior to their involvement in the study, ensuring that they voluntarily agreed to take part. Additionally, participants were made aware of their right to withdraw from the study at any time without penalty, and this right was emphasised throughout the process.
2. **Confidentiality**: The study upheld strict confidentiality to protect participants' privacy and personal information. All data collected, including interview transcripts, focus group discussions, and survey responses, were anonymised to ensure that no identifying information could be linked to individual participants. Any personal identifiers, such as

names, addresses, and contact information, were removed from the data before analysis. All records, including digital files and paper documents, were securely stored in compliance with data protection standards. Access to the data was restricted to the research team, ensuring that only authorised personnel handled the sensitive information.

3. **Cultural Sensitivity**: The researcher maintained a high level of cultural sensitivity throughout the study. Given the multicultural nature of the research, it was essential to respect and honour the diverse cultural backgrounds of the participants. The study recognised that each participant's cultural context could influence their experiences and perspectives, and as such, the researcher ensured that these cultural differences were acknowledged and respected. Efforts were made to ensure that participants felt comfortable sharing their views, and the research was conducted in a manner that was culturally appropriate. The researcher also ensured that the findings accurately reflected the diverse viewpoints and experiences of the participants, without bias or misrepresentation.
4. **Right to Withdraw**: Participants were explicitly informed of their right to withdraw from the study at any point without facing any negative consequences. This right was clearly communicated at the start of the study and reiterated at different stages of data collection. If a participant chose to withdraw, all data collected up to that point was discarded upon their request, and they were assured that their decision would have no adverse impact on their participation or relationships with the researchers. This provision ensured that participants had full control over their involvement in the study and were not pressured to continue if they no longer wished to participate.

Quantitative results

The results presented in Table 4.2 provide a detailed breakdown of the demographic characteristics of the participants in the study. These demographics were analysed in relation to their participation in multicultural counselling and psychotherapy. The variables included in the analysis were age, gender, years of experience, level of education, and primary background of clients.

The participants' ages ranged widely, with the highest proportions of participants being in the 29–41 age range. Specifically, participants aged 39 (0.045) and 41 (0.055) made up the largest groups, showing that the majority of respondents were experienced professionals likely with a good understanding of multicultural counselling practices. The age range of 20–24 had smaller proportions, with individual groups in this range contributing less than 0.02 of the total sample, indicating that younger counsellors were under-represented. The analysis revealed that age was a significant variable, with a P-value of < 0.001, suggesting

Table 4.2: Descriptive statistics of the participants' demographics.

Variable	Level	Counts	Total	Proportion	P
Age	20	6	400	0.015	<0.001
	21	7	400	0.018	<0.001
	22	6	400	0.015	<0.001
	23	5	400	0.013	<0.001
	24	5	400	0.013	<0.001
	25	2	400	0.005	<0.001
	27	6	400	0.015	<0.001
	28	6	400	0.015	<0.001
	29	7	400	0.018	<0.001
	30	8	400	0.020	<0.001
	31	14	400	0.035	<0.001
	32	13	400	0.033	<0.001
	33	17	400	0.043	<0.001
	34	17	400	0.043	<0.001
	35	13	400	0.033	<0.001
	36	12	400	0.030	<0.001
	37	11	400	0.028	<0.001
	38	12	400	0.030	<0.001
	39	18	400	0.045	<0.001
	40	11	400	0.028	<0.001
	41	22	400	0.055	<0.001
	42	16	400	0.040	<0.001
	43	7	400	0.018	<0.001
	44	15	400	0.037	<0.001
	45	14	400	0.035	<0.001
	46	19	400	0.048	<0.001
	47	15	400	0.037	<0.001
	48	12	400	0.030	<0.001
	49	8	400	0.020	<0.001
	50	7	400	0.018	<0.001
	51	8	400	0.020	<0.001
	52	3	400	0.007	<0.001
	53	4	400	0.010	<0.001
	54	5	400	0.013	<0.001
	55	7	400	0.018	<0.001
	56	5	400	0.013	<0.001
	57	7	400	0.018	<0.001
	58	4	400	0.010	<0.001
	59	4	400	0.010	<0.001
	60	4	400	0.010	<0.001
	61	3	400	0.007	<0.001
	62	1	400	0.003	<0.001
	63	1	400	0.003	<0.001
	64	2	400	0.005	<0.001
	65	2	400	0.005	<0.001

Continued

Table 4.2: Descriptive statistics of the participants' demographics.—cont'd

Variable	Level	Counts	Total	Proportion	P
	67	1	400	0.003	<0.001
	68	3	400	0.007	<0.001
	69	2	400	0.005	<0.001
	70	3	400	0.007	<0.001
Gender	Female	215	400	0.537	0.147
	Male	185	400	0.463	0.147
Years of experience	1	27	400	0.068	<0.001
	2	19	400	0.048	<0.001
	3	22	400	0.055	<0.001
	4	22	400	0.055	<0.001
	5	22	400	0.055	<0.001
	6	29	400	0.072	<0.001
	7	20	400	0.050	<0.001
	8	24	400	0.060	<0.001
	9	32	400	0.080	<0.001
	10	38	400	0.095	<0.001
	11	16	400	0.040	<0.001
	12	22	400	0.055	<0.001
	13	12	400	0.030	<0.001
	14	12	400	0.030	<0.001
	15	20	400	0.050	<0.001
	16	6	400	0.015	<0.001
	17	11	400	0.028	<0.001
	18	10	400	0.025	<0.001
	19	9	400	0.022	<0.001
	20	7	400	0.018	<0.001
	21	3	400	0.007	<0.001
	22	1	400	0.003	<0.001
	23	3	400	0.007	<0.001
	24	2	400	0.005	<0.001
	25	4	400	0.010	<0.001
	26	2	400	0.005	<0.001
	27	2	400	0.005	<0.001
	28	2	400	0.005	<0.001
	30	1	400	0.003	<0.001
Higher level of education	Master's degree	231	400	0.578	0.002
	Bachelor's degree	105	400	0.263	<0.001
	Doctoral degree	47	400	0.117	<0.001
	Other	17	400	0.043	<0.001
Primary background of client	European	13	400	0.033	<0.001
	Indigenous	13	400	0.033	<0.001
	African	333	400	0.833	<0.001
	Asian	24	400	0.060	<0.001
	Other	9	400	0.022	<0.001
	Middle Eastern	8	400	0.020	<0.001

Proportions tested against value: 0.5.

that age played an important role in the diversity of counselling experience across the sample.

The gender distribution of the participants was relatively balanced, with 215 female participants (0.537) and 185 male participants (0.463). The small differences in gender proportions were statistically insignificant, as indicated by the *P*-value of 0.147, suggesting that gender did not significantly influence the results or the representation of counselling techniques and challenges.

The majority of participants had between 1 and 10 years of experience, with 38 participants reporting 10 years of experience (0.095) as the highest number in this range. Experience levels were statistically significant with a *P*-value of <0.001, indicating that experience in the field influenced the types of techniques used and the challenges faced. There was a notable decrease in participants with more than 15 years of experience, with a large portion reporting 1–9 years of professional practice, demonstrating a younger group of counsellors in the study.

Participants reported varying levels of education, with 231 participants holding a Master's Degree (0.578), representing the largest proportion of the sample. The *P*-value of 0.002 suggests that educational level had an impact on the representation in the study, with those holding a master's degree being the most prevalent group. Bachelor's degree holders (0.263) and doctoral degree holders (0.117) were fewer in number, with a small proportion (0.043) having other levels of education.

The primary background of clients served by the counsellors was overwhelmingly African (0.833), reflecting the significant prevalence of African clients in multicultural counselling settings. The European, Indigenous, Asian, Middle Eastern, and Other backgrounds were far less represented. The *P*-value of < 0.001 for these results confirms the statistical significance of the ethnic background of the clients, suggesting that African clients are most commonly encountered in the multicultural settings of the study sample.

The proportions of the demographic variables were tested against the value 0.5 (a commonly used threshold to examine balanced versus unbalanced distributions). The results showed a significant difference from this threshold in most categories, particularly in age, education, and the ethnic background of the clients. The large proportion of African clients and the predominance of master's degree holders suggest that the sample was skewed towards more experienced counsellors working predominantly with African populations.

The significant *P*-values (<0.001) across all variables confirm that the differences observed in the demographic characteristics were statistically significant, underscoring the relevance of age, education, years of experience, and client background in shaping the study's findings.

Research Question 1: What are the key counselling techniques used with clients from diverse cultural backgrounds?

The results presented in Table 4.3 provide descriptive statistics for the key counselling techniques used with clients from diverse cultural backgrounds. The participants were asked to rate the frequency with which they use various counselling techniques, using a 5-point scale, where 1 represents 'never', 2 represents 'rarely', 3 represents 'sometimes', 4 represents 'often', and 5 represents 'always'.

The mean scores for the different counselling techniques range from 2.91 (for person-centred therapy) to 3.015 (CBT) and 3.04 (for psychodynamic therapy), suggesting that these techniques are generally used with moderate frequency by the participants. All techniques fall between the ratings of 'sometimes' and 'often', with mean scores above 3, indicating that participants commonly use these counselling techniques in their practice.

The standard error of the mean for all techniques is relatively small (ranging from 0.069 to 0.072), which suggests that the estimates of the means are precise, and there is low variability in the sample's ratings. The 95% confidence intervals for the means, ranging from the lower to the upper values, show that the true mean for each technique falls within a narrow range, further reinforcing the precision of the data.

Table 4.3: Descriptive statistics showing the key counselling techniques used with clients from diverse cultural backgrounds.

			95% confidence interval mean				
	Mean	Std. error of mean	Upper	Lower	Std. deviation	Shapiro–Wilk	P-value of Shapiro–Wilk
Cognitive-behavioural therapy	3.015	0.071	3.156	2.874	1.430	0.882	<0.001
Person-centred therapy	2.910	0.071	3.049	2.771	1.413	0.885	<0.001
Narrative therapy	2.962	0.070	3.101	2.824	1.406	0.890	<0.001
Psychodynamic therapy	3.042	0.070	3.180	2.905	1.397	0.891	<0.001
Solution-focused therapy	3.018	0.069	3.154	2.881	1.386	0.889	<0.001
Family therapy	3.020	0.072	3.161	2.879	1.439	0.883	<0.001
Purpose-based career coaching	2.935	0.072	3.077	2.793	1.444	0.881	<0.001
Mindfulness-based therapy	3.007	0.070	3.144	2.871	1.392	0.890	<0.001
Art or play therapy	2.947	0.069	3.083	2.812	1.378	0.892	<0.001

The standard deviation values, ranging from 1.36 to 1.44, indicate that there is some variability in how often different participants use each technique. A higher standard deviation suggests more variability in the frequency of use of that technique among the participants.

The Shapiro–Wilk test was used to assess the normality of the data for each counselling technique. The *P*-values for the Shapiro–Wilk test are all less than 0.001, indicating that the data for each technique significantly deviates from a normal distribution. This suggests that the distribution of responses for the frequency of use of each technique is not perfectly normal, although it does not necessarily invalidate the results.

Overall, these results suggest that participants report using a variety of counselling techniques with moderate frequency in multicultural contexts. The techniques with the highest mean scores (such as psychodynamic therapy and solution-focused therapy [SFT]) are slightly more likely to be used often, while others (like person-centred therapy and art or play therapy) are rated slightly lower, indicating that they may be used less frequently, but still on a regular basis. The variability in responses points to the fact that while many counsellors use these techniques regularly, others may use them less frequently or not at all, highlighting the diverse approaches to multicultural counselling in practice.

Research Question 2: How are mainstream counselling techniques adapted to address cultural differences and meet the specific needs of clients from various cultural backgrounds?

The results presented in Table 4.4 provide descriptive statistics for how mainstream counselling techniques are adapted to address cultural differences and meet the specific needs of clients from various cultural backgrounds. Participants were asked to rate the frequency with which they adapt the listed counselling techniques, using a 5-point scale where 1 = never, 2 = rarely, 3 = sometimes, 4 = often, and 5 = always.

The mean scores for the various techniques ranged from 2.85 (for narrative therapy) to 3.00 (CBT) and 3.05 (for mindfulness-based therapy), indicating that the participants generally adapt these techniques with moderate frequency, between 'sometimes' and 'often'. This suggests that most counsellors reported occasionally modifying their approaches to suit the cultural backgrounds and needs of their clients, with some techniques being adapted more frequently than others.

The standard errors of the mean for all techniques were relatively small, ranging from 0.069 to 0.073, indicating that the estimates of the means were precise. This suggests that the data is consistent, and there is little variation in how participants rated the adaptation of these techniques.

The 95% confidence intervals for the mean scores, which range from the lower to the upper limits, confirm the precision of the estimates. For instance, the confidence interval

Table 4.4: Descriptive statistics showing the mainstream counselling techniques are adapted to address cultural differences and meet the specific needs of clients from various cultural backgrounds.

	Mean	Std. error of mean	95% confidence interval mean Upper	95% confidence interval mean Lower	Std. deviation	Shapiro–Wilk	*P*-value of Shapiro–Wilk
Cognitive-behavioural therapy	3.005	0.072	3.147	2.863	1.444	0.881	<0.001
Person-centred therapy	2.893	0.069	3.028	2.757	1.377	0.894	<0.001
Narrative therapy	2.850	0.071	2.989	2.711	1.419	0.884	<0.001
Psychodynamic therapy	2.945	0.070	3.082	2.808	1.395	0.891	<0.001
Solution-focused therapy	2.893	0.070	3.030	2.755	1.404	0.889	<0.001
Family therapy	3.015	0.073	3.158	2.872	1.458	0.877	<0.001
Purpose-based career coaching	3.020	0.071	3.161	2.879	1.430	0.885	<0.001
Mindfulness-based therapy	3.045	0.070	3.182	2.908	1.392	0.892	<0.001
Art or play therapy	2.962	0.069	3.098	2.827	1.375	0.895	<0.001

for mindfulness-based therapy ranges from 2.908 to 3.182, showing that the true mean for this technique falls within this range, reinforcing the reliability of the data.

The standard deviation values, ranging from 1.375 to 1.458, reflect some variability in the frequency with which the techniques are adapted. Although there is a general trend towards moderate adaptation, the variability indicates that some participants adapt these techniques more frequently, while others do so less often. This suggests a diverse range of practices among counsellors regarding the cultural adaptation of techniques.

The Shapiro–Wilk test was used to assess the normality of the data, and the *P*-values for all techniques were less than 0.001, indicating that the distribution of the data significantly deviates from a normal distribution. Despite this, the results are still meaningful and provide valuable insight into the adaptation of counselling techniques, although the non-normality of the data should be considered in further analyses.

In summary, the results suggest that mainstream counselling techniques are generally adapted with moderate frequency to meet the cultural needs of clients. Techniques such as mindfulness-based therapy, CBT and family therapy were adapted more often, while others like narrative therapy and person-centred therapy were adapted less frequently, although still on a regular basis. The variability in the responses highlights differences in the practices of individual counsellors and their approach to cultural adaptation. The statistical significance of the results, indicated by the Shapiro–Wilk *P*-values, suggests that these findings provide a reliable representation of how counselling techniques are adapted in multicultural counselling settings.

Research Question 3: What challenges and barriers do counsellors face when applying culturally adapted counselling techniques?

The results presented in Table 4.5 provide descriptive statistics regarding the challenges and barriers that counsellors face when applying culturally adapted counselling techniques. Participants were asked to rate the level of challenge they encountered in various areas related to multicultural counselling using a 5-point scale where 1 = no challenge, 2 = slight, 3 = moderate, 4 = significant, and 5 = extreme.

The mean scores for the different challenges ranged from 2.89 (for ethical dilemmas) to 3.11 (for language barriers). These values indicate that, on average, counsellors experience moderate to significant challenges in applying culturally adapted techniques. The mean values being above 2.9 but below 3.5 suggest that these challenges are regularly

Table 4.5: Descriptive statistics showing the challenges and barriers counsellors face when applying culturally adapted counselling techniques.

			95% confidence interval mean				
	Mean	Std. error of mean	Upper	Lower	Std. deviation	Shapiro–Wilk	*P*-value of Shapiro–Wilk
Language barriers	3.110	0.069	3.246	2.974	1.383	0.891	<0.001
Misunderstanding	3.087	0.068	3.221	2.954	1.360	0.897	<0.001
Lack of cultural competence	2.940	0.069	3.076	2.804	1.388	0.890	<0.001
Resistance to certain techniques	3.065	0.071	3.204	2.926	1.418	0.887	<0.001
Difficulty in building rapport	2.980	0.070	3.117	2.843	1.396	0.889	<0.001
Clients' discomfort	2.947	0.068	3.081	2.814	1.356	0.899	<0.001
Ethical dilemmas	2.895	0.071	3.034	2.756	1.412	0.887	<0.001
Lack of cultural resources	3.067	0.072	3.208	2.927	1.433	0.883	<0.001

encountered, but not overwhelmingly so. Most challenges fall between the ratings of 'moderate' and 'significant'.

The standard errors of the mean for all challenges are relatively small (ranging from 0.068 to 0.072), indicating that the means are precise and reliable. This small variability in the means further suggests that most counsellors rated the challenges consistently, indicating a common understanding of the barriers they face.

The 95% confidence intervals for the means, which range from the lower to the upper values for each challenge, also demonstrate the reliability of the findings. For example, the confidence interval for language barriers is from 2.974 to 3.246, meaning that the true mean for this challenge would likely fall within this range. This adds confidence to the interpretation that language barriers are one of the more significant challenges faced by counsellors.

The standard deviation values, ranging from 1.356 to 1.433, show that there is some variability in how participants rated the severity of the challenges. Although the mean scores indicate moderate to significant challenges, the spread in responses indicates that some counsellors may face these issues more frequently or more intensely than others.

The Shapiro–Wilk test for normality was applied to each challenge, and the P-values for all challenges were less than 0.001, indicating that the data significantly deviates from a normal distribution. While this suggests that the data is not normally distributed, the results still provide valuable insights into the experiences of counsellors, though this non-normality should be taken into account when drawing conclusions.

Overall, the results indicate that the most frequently reported challenges for counsellors applying culturally adapted techniques are language barriers, misunderstanding of cultural values, and lack of cultural resources, all of which have mean scores approaching or above 3.0. This suggests that these factors are commonly experienced by counsellors working in multicultural settings. Ethical dilemmas (mean = 2.895) and clients' discomfort (mean = 2.947) were reported as slightly less challenging but still represent notable barriers to effective multicultural counselling. The variability in responses, as indicated by the standard deviations, suggests that while these challenges are commonly faced, the intensity of the challenges varies across different counsellors and their contexts.

Qualitative results

Research Question 1: What specific counselling techniques have you found to be most effective when working with clients from diverse cultural backgrounds?

To address this research question, six counsellors and six psychotherapists were asked to describe the specific counselling techniques they had found most effective when working with clients from diverse cultural backgrounds. The responses were analysed qualitatively to identify the techniques that emerged as most commonly used and considered effective in multicultural contexts.

The data were initially coded using open coding, where key terms and phrases mentioned in the responses were identified. Several themes emerged, with counsellors and psychotherapists mentioning a variety of therapeutic techniques they had employed in multicultural settings. After coding the data, the following primary themes were identified as effective counselling techniques.

- **Culturally Adapted CBT**: Many participants reported that CBT was particularly effective when adapted to accommodate cultural differences. The adaptation of CBT techniques to align with cultural beliefs about mental health and coping strategies was noted as crucial in ensuring that the therapy resonated with clients from diverse cultural backgrounds. One participant mentioned, 'When clients from different cultures face distress, using CBT tailored to their cultural values helps them understand and manage their emotions in a way that feels meaningful to them'.
- **Narrative Therapy**: It was frequently mentioned by participants as an effective approach in multicultural settings. Counsellors and psychotherapists emphasised the power of allowing clients to tell their stories, especially when their cultural identities were central to their experiences. One therapist explained, 'Narrative therapy is effective because it allows clients to share their stories, which often include important cultural elements. It's a way of empowering them to reframe and reinterpret their experiences through the lens of their own culture'. This technique helped clients feel seen and heard, particularly when they were dealing with cultural tensions or conflicts.
- **Person-Centred Therapy**: The person-centred therapy approach also emerged as highly effective, particularly due to its emphasis on building a strong therapeutic alliance. Several respondents highlighted the importance of creating a non-judgemental, empathetic relationship with clients, which transcends cultural boundaries. One counsellor stated, 'The relationship is key. When clients feel truly understood and accepted, regardless of their cultural background, they engage more deeply in the therapeutic process'.
- **Holistic Approaches**: Another significant theme that emerged was the use of holistic approaches, which were noted for being particularly effective with clients from cultures where emotional, spiritual, and physical well-being are viewed as interconnected. A psychotherapist commented, 'When working with clients from holistic cultures, integrating practices that honour their spiritual beliefs and address their emotional and physical health helps them feel more comfortable and supported'.

The analysis also revealed that many counsellors and psychotherapists employed a blended approach, combining elements from different therapeutic techniques. For example, some integrated CBT with narrative therapy to both address clients' cognitive patterns and help them reframe their cultural narratives. One participant noted, 'By blending techniques, we can address the mental health concerns while also honouring the cultural experiences that shape how clients perceive and interact with the world'.

Research Question 2: How do you adapt your counselling techniques to accommodate the cultural beliefs, values, and practices of your clients?

To address the second research question, six counsellors and six psychotherapists were asked how they adapt their counselling techniques to accommodate the cultural beliefs, values, and practices of their clients. The responses were analysed qualitatively to identify common themes and strategies used by practitioners to ensure cultural sensitivity in their therapeutic practices.

The data revealed several key approaches that counsellors and psychotherapists employ to adapt their techniques in multicultural settings:

One of the most frequently mentioned strategies was the personalisation of therapeutic techniques to align with the client's cultural context. Participants reported that they often made adjustments to mainstream techniques to reflect the cultural values, beliefs, and practices of their clients. For instance, a counsellor shared, 'I always ask about the client's cultural background and how their beliefs shape their views on therapy. If a client values family over individual concerns, I might incorporate family dynamics into the sessions more actively, adjusting my approach to fit their worldview'. This personalised approach was found to be essential in building trust and creating a therapeutic environment where clients felt understood and respected.

Another common adaptation strategy was the use of culturally relevant examples and language during therapy. Several participants noted that using examples, metaphors, and language that were familiar to clients from their cultural backgrounds helped make the counselling process more relatable. One psychotherapist explained, 'When working with clients from diverse backgrounds, I make an effort to understand their cultural metaphors or even use stories and examples that are more relevant to their experiences. For example, in a collectivist culture, I might focus on family dynamics or community support as part of the therapy'. By incorporating culturally familiar references, therapists made their interventions feel more meaningful and accessible to clients.

Building cultural awareness and learning from clients was another key theme in the responses. Counsellors and psychotherapists emphasised the importance of engaging in ongoing learning about the cultural backgrounds of their clients and being open to adapting techniques based on the information shared during therapy. One counsellor mentioned, 'I ask questions that help me learn about my client's culture, traditions, and values. It's important for me to adapt my approach based on what I learn during our sessions. It's a process of mutual respect, where I learn and grow alongside my clients'.

This approach of continuous cultural learning helped practitioners adjust their methods based on the evolving needs of each client.

Some participants also highlighted the use of culturally appropriate interventions, such as incorporating spiritual practices or rituals that are important to the client. A psychotherapist noted, 'In some cases, clients may request to incorporate cultural practices like prayer or ritual into the therapy session. I see this as an important aspect of the healing process, and I'm open to integrating those practices if they feel they are helpful'. This flexibility was particularly important when working with clients from cultures where spiritual or religious practices play a central role in health and well-being.

Lastly, respect for cultural differences in communication styles was emphasised. Counsellors and psychotherapists acknowledged that different cultures have varying communication patterns and that adjusting their own style to align with the client's expectations was crucial. One participant shared, 'In some cultures, direct eye contact might be seen as confrontational, so I make an effort to adjust my body language and communication style accordingly to make the client feel more comfortable'. This sensitivity to non-verbal cues and communication preferences helped therapists maintain rapport and foster an open dialogue.

Research Question 3: What challenges have you faced when adapting counselling techniques to meet the cultural needs of your clients?

To address the third research question, six counsellors and six psychotherapists were asked about the challenges they face when adapting counselling techniques to meet the cultural needs of their clients. The qualitative responses were analysed to identify recurring themes and obstacles that practitioners encounter in multicultural counselling settings.

The most commonly reported challenge was language barriers. Many participants highlighted how language differences can hinder effective communication and make it difficult to ensure that the client fully understands the therapeutic process. One counsellor explained, 'Language barriers are a constant challenge. Even if the client speaks the same language as me, there may be cultural nuances or dialects that we don't share, which can affect the depth of our communication'. Some therapists mentioned that relying on interpreters can add complexity to the process, leading to potential misinterpretations or loss of meaning. This difficulty in communication can also affect the client's comfort level in discussing personal issues.

Another significant challenge mentioned by participants was the misunderstanding of cultural values. Counsellors and psychotherapists noted that their own cultural biases or lack of knowledge about the client's background could sometimes result in misunderstandings or misinterpretations of the client's needs. One psychotherapist stated, 'I've had clients from collectivist cultures where the importance of family relationships might be central to their well-being. At times, I may have to adjust my focus from individual well-being to family dynamics, but understanding how deeply these values impact the client can be a challenge'. In some cases, participants shared that they struggled to navigate the difference between their professional framework and the cultural practices of their clients, leading to potential misalignment in treatment goals.

Resistance to certain therapeutic techniques also emerged as a common barrier. Some counsellors found that clients from different cultural backgrounds might be resistant to mainstream therapeutic techniques, especially if they perceive them as incompatible with their cultural beliefs or values. A counsellor explained, 'In some cultures, mental health might be seen as a taboo subject. When I introduce Western therapeutic techniques like CBT, clients sometimes resist or express discomfort with the idea of talking openly about their problems'. This resistance can create a barrier to effective therapy and requires the counsellor to be flexible and creative in how they adapt their methods to make clients feel more comfortable.

Ethical dilemmas also presented challenges in adapting counselling techniques. Some therapists struggled to balance respect for cultural practices with their professional ethical guidelines. One psychotherapist remarked, 'I've encountered ethical dilemmas when clients have cultural practices that contradict what is typically acceptable in therapy. For example, some clients may want to involve family members in all sessions, but as a therapist, I might have concerns about confidentiality or the family dynamics involved'. Navigating these dilemmas often required careful consideration and negotiation with clients to ensure that both cultural practices and ethical standards were respected.

Additionally, a lack of cultural competence and resources was frequently mentioned as a barrier. Several counsellors expressed that they felt ill-equipped to deal with the specific cultural challenges that arose in their practice. One participant stated, 'I sometimes feel like I lack the cultural competence or knowledge to effectively address all the issues my clients bring to therapy. It can be overwhelming to try and keep up with the vast diversity in cultural needs without sufficient training or resources'. This lack of preparedness can lead to feelings of frustration and uncertainty, which, in turn, may affect the therapeutic relationship.

Finally, difficulties in building rapport were noted by some therapists as a challenge. Establishing trust with clients from different cultural backgrounds, particularly when cultural norms regarding communication or relationships differ, was a common concern. A counsellor shared, 'In some cultures, eye contact or direct confrontation may be seen as disrespectful. Adjusting my communication style to respect these cultural norms can be tricky, and sometimes, it takes longer to build the rapport needed for effective therapy'.

In summary, the responses from the counsellors and psychotherapists highlighted several significant challenges in adapting counselling techniques to meet the cultural needs of clients. These challenges included language barriers, misunderstandings of cultural values, resistance to certain techniques, ethical dilemmas, lack of cultural competence and resources, and difficulties in building rapport. Addressing these challenges requires cultural awareness, flexibility, and ongoing professional development to ensure that therapeutic techniques are appropriately adapted to fit the cultural context of the client. These obstacles underscore the importance of cultural competence in ensuring that multicultural counselling is both effective and respectful of the client's background and needs.

Research Question 4: What recommendations do you have for improving multicultural competence in counselling?

To address the fourth research question, six counsellors and six psychotherapists were asked for their recommendations on improving multicultural competence in counselling. The qualitative responses were analysed to identify common strategies and suggestions for enhancing practitioners' ability to work effectively with clients from diverse cultural backgrounds.

The most frequent recommendation was the need for ongoing cultural competence training. Participants emphasised that counsellors should continually develop their understanding of different cultural values, practices, and communication styles. One counsellor stated, 'Cultural competence isn't something you acquire once; it's an ongoing process. I recommend regular training to keep up with the evolving cultural issues and ensure that we don't remain stagnant in our practices'. Many participants suggested that training should go beyond the basics of cultural awareness and delve deeper into specific cultural practices and how they intersect with mental health.

Another common recommendation was the integration of cultural perspectives into supervision and peer support networks. Several therapists pointed out the value of discussing multicultural issues with supervisors and peers who have experience working in similar settings. One psychotherapist explained, 'Having a supervisor who understands the challenges of working with multicultural populations and can provide feedback on how to handle cultural concerns is invaluable. Peer support groups also provide a space to share experiences and strategies for managing cultural differences in therapy'. This underscores the importance of not only training but also providing a network of support for counsellors to exchange insights and best practices.

Building self-awareness and addressing personal biases was also frequently mentioned as a crucial component in improving multicultural competence. Respondents emphasised that counsellors must be aware of their own cultural biases and how these may impact their work with clients. One participant shared, 'I recommend that counsellors regularly engage in self-reflection to examine their own biases and assumptions. Understanding how my cultural background influences my practice helps me approach clients with a more open and empathetic mindset'. This recommendation suggests that developing multicultural competence requires counsellors to work on their own personal growth and openness to learning.

Access to culturally diverse resources was another important suggestion. Participants recommended that counsellors have access to a wide range of culturally specific resources, such as literature, training materials, and community-based organisations that can provide insight into the needs and values of different cultural groups. A psychotherapist mentioned, 'It's important to have access to resources that help me understand the cultural context of the clients I'm working with. Whether it's through books, community events, or collaborating with cultural experts, having those resources readily available is key to improving my practice'. This highlights the need for counsellors to stay informed and continuously integrate new resources into their therapeutic approaches.

Additionally, many participants suggested that counselling programmes and training curricula should place a greater emphasis on multicultural competence from the outset of a therapist's education. One counsellor noted, 'Multicultural competence should be integrated into every aspect of counselling training, not as an add-on, but as a core component of what it means to be a good therapist'. This recommendation points to the importance of embedding cultural sensitivity into the foundational education and professional development of counsellors, ensuring that future practitioners are well-prepared to navigate the diverse cultural dynamics they will encounter in their work.

Finally, some participants highlighted the importance of community engagement and cultural immersion. Counsellors and psychotherapists suggested that spending time in diverse cultural communities could enhance a therapist's understanding and connection to their clients. One participant explained, 'Volunteering or engaging in community activities in culturally diverse settings can give therapists first-hand experience of the challenges and values of different groups. This engagement allows for greater empathy and more meaningful interactions with clients'. This recommendation advocates for immersive learning opportunities to complement formal training and provide practical exposure to cultural diversity.

Case studies

A 35-year-old female client from Nigeria sought therapy for anxiety and depression. She was struggling with familial pressure to marry within her cultural group, which conflicted with her personal aspirations and career goals. The counsellor, residing in Nigeria, conducted the sessions online due to the client's location in the United States. The client expressed feeling overwhelmed by the expectations placed upon her by her family, who viewed marriage as a critical component of personal success and cultural identity. The client felt disconnected from her cultural values but feared disappointing her family. The counsellor initially considered using CBT to address the client's anxiety. However, recognising the importance of the client's cultural context, the counsellor adapted the approach by integrating family therapy principles. This adjustment emphasised the importance of involving her family in the process, aligning with her cultural background, where family relationships were central to well-being. The counsellor worked with the client to explore how her cultural values could coexist with her personal desires, encouraging family discussions to mediate expectations. The client reported feeling more understood and empowered in balancing her personal and cultural needs. The online therapy sessions were effective in facilitating dialogue, and the client's family became more understanding of her individual goals.

A 28-year-old male client, originally from China, sought therapy for feelings of isolation and depression. He had been living in Nigeria for 5 years and struggled with adjusting to the new environment while maintaining ties to his traditional family values. Due to the client's location, the therapy sessions were conducted online. The client's main challenge was the language barrier, as his English proficiency was limited, and he felt misunderstood in many social situations. Additionally, there was a cultural gap between his family's traditional values and the values of Nigeria, causing a sense of alienation. The counsellor, through online sessions, used person-centred therapy, focusing on building a trusting and empathetic relationship. The counsellor also adapted the approach by incorporating culturally relevant metaphors and examples that helped the client relate to the process. The counsellor used phrases and examples familiar to Chinese culture, which allowed the client to feel more connected and understood. The client began to feel more comfortable discussing his feelings and concerns. His understanding of his identity improved, and he was able to better navigate the cultural tension between his family and his social life, as well as gain confidence in expressing himself in therapy and in his daily life.

A 42-year-old Latina woman, residing in the United States, sought therapy online with a psychotherapist based in Nigeria for post-traumatic stress disorder (PTSD) related to domestic violence. She had been struggling with feelings of shame and guilt, deeply rooted in her cultural upbringing. The challenge for the psychotherapist was integrating the client's cultural context into the therapy, particularly the cultural stigma surrounding abuse. The psychotherapist initially considered using traditional therapies but realised the need to adapt the approach to address the client's cultural context. The psychotherapist used narrative therapy, encouraging the client to 're-author' her story. This approach allowed the client to see her trauma as an external influence rather than a reflection of her self-worth. The psychotherapist worked with the client to explore her cultural beliefs about family and how these beliefs impacted her sense of shame. The psychotherapist also acknowledged the client's cultural background, using culturally familiar storytelling techniques. Over time, the client began to view her trauma from a different lens, no longer blaming herself for the abuse. She reported feeling empowered to confront her past and was able to make peace with her cultural beliefs while rejecting those that reinforced her shame.

A 50-year-old Indigenous woman, located in Canada, sought therapy online for anxiety and depression following the loss of a family member. She was deeply connected to her community's spiritual and cultural practices but felt disconnected from her roots due to her Westernised upbringing. The psychotherapist in Nigeria adapted the approach by integrating the client's cultural practices into the therapeutic process. The psychotherapist used a holistic approach, encouraging the client to incorporate traditional healing rituals, such as prayer, smudging, and spending time in nature. These rituals helped the client connect with her spiritual beliefs and family traditions, which were crucial for her emotional healing. The psychotherapist also engaged in spiritual discussions, respecting the client's need for cultural rituals as part of her therapy. The client found comfort in re-engaging with her cultural practices and reported feeling spiritually rejuvenated. Her symptoms of anxiety and depression began to decrease, and she felt more connected to her identity and cultural roots. The integration of these cultural practices into the online therapy sessions was central to her healing process.

A 29-year-old male client of Middle Eastern descent, residing in the United Kingdom, sought therapy online with a Nigerian-based counsellor to address career-related stress and self-esteem issues. The client was struggling with balancing his professional aspirations and his family's expectations regarding his career choices, which often created a sense of internal conflict. The challenge was integrating the client's cultural expectations with his personal goals, especially given the cultural importance of family approval. The counsellor used SFT to help the client set practical, goal-oriented solutions that aligned with his values while also addressing his family's expectations. The counsellor helped the client identify small, actionable steps towards his goals, encouraging him to define success on his own terms. At the same time, the counsellor respected the client's cultural beliefs, discussing ways to navigate family dynamics without disregarding his personal values. The client reported feeling more confident in making decisions that reflected his personal desires while maintaining respect for his family's traditions. The online therapy sessions allowed the client to reconcile his professional aspirations with his cultural identity, reducing his stress and improving his self-esteem.

A counsellor based in Jos, Nigeria, shared a case involving a 19-year-old female client from a conservative Hausa Muslim background who was experiencing symptoms of anxiety and depression following pressure from her family to enter into an arranged marriage. The client felt torn between her personal aspirations to pursue higher education and her family's expectations, which were rooted in long-held cultural traditions. In the initial sessions, the counsellor employed standard CBT techniques, including thought-challenging and goal setting. However, it became clear that the direct questioning and emphasis on individual autonomy made the client uncomfortable and guarded. Recognising the cultural mismatch, the counsellor modified the approach by integrating elements of narrative therapy, which allowed the client to express her story within the context of her cultural values. Rather than challenging the family structure directly, the counsellor encouraged the client to explore her life as a narrative in which she was both a participant and a decision-maker. This allowed space for the client to reflect on her choices without feeling like she was betraying her culture or family.

The outcome of this culturally adapted session was significantly positive. The client gained greater emotional clarity and was able to communicate with her parents more confidently about her desire to postpone marriage while pursuing her education. The counsellor noted improved rapport and trust in subsequent sessions. A key challenge, however, was navigating the tension between advocating for the client's autonomy while remaining respectful of deeply rooted cultural norms. The counsellor had to strike a delicate balance, demonstrating cultural sensitivity while still fostering personal growth. In another case, a male counsellor in Lagos worked with a middle-aged client from an Igbo background who had recently relocated back to Nigeria after living abroad for many years. The client presented with symptoms of isolation, identity confusion, and a sense of reverse culture shock. Initially, the counsellor utilised person-centred therapy techniques, encouraging open dialogue and reflection. However, the client expressed difficulty connecting to the approach, viewing it as 'too abstract' and disconnected from the practical realities he faced.

In response, the counsellor adapted the sessions to include SFT techniques, combined with culturally relevant proverbs and storytelling methods familiar within the client's cultural upbringing. By framing solutions within traditional Igbo wisdom and using familiar metaphors, the counsellor was able to foster a greater sense of comfort and understanding. This culturally grounded approach made the client more engaged and reflective, and eventually helped him reconnect with his values and community involvement. The adapted techniques led to meaningful progress, with the client resuming active participation in a local cultural association and reporting improved emotional stability. One of the challenges the counsellor noted was the need for flexibility in combining Western therapeutic models with indigenous communication styles without diluting the therapeutic goals. This case illustrated the importance of cultural fluency and the counsellor's willingness to listen and adapt in real time.

A 24-year-old Igbo woman in southeastern Nigeria had recently completed a degree in English literature. Employed in a customer service role at a logistics firm, she presented with dissatisfaction and a sense of purposelessness. Her cultural background emphasised stability and respectability in careers such as banking, teaching, or civil service. As such, her interest in storytelling, writing, and youth engagement was often dismissed within her family and community. She approached coaching confused and emotionally conflicted.

In response, the counsellor applied the Psycho-Spiritual Purpose-Based Career Coaching Model (Otu, 2024; Otu & Eseadi, 2024; Otu et al., 2023) and adapted the framework to her cultural context. During the Reimagining phase, the client was guided to visualise her ideal future without cultural or financial constraints. She imagined herself speaking to youth in communities and writing stories that shaped minds. Recognising that imaginative visualisation alone might feel indulgent in her culture, the counsellor grounded the exercise using storytelling methods common in Igbo traditions, helping her connect her career dreams to ancestral wisdom.

The Spiritualising phase encouraged reflection on her faith and how storytelling had been a tool of moral instruction in her culture. In this context, purpose was not merely about career but about spiritual service. Through Self-Discovery, she identified narrative intelligence, empathy, and mentorship as core strengths. The counsellor validated her values within a communal and cultural frame, linking her gifts to the traditional role of women as storytellers and nurturers of wisdom. In the Career-Exploration phase, she researched roles that combined writing, youth engagement, and social impact. She explored possibilities such as literacy outreach, educational radio programming, and content creation. In Identifying, she developed a culturally and spiritually resonant purpose statement: 'To inspire and guide young minds in underserved communities through culturally rooted storytelling'. During Matching, she mapped a realistic path, beginning with a community-based storytelling project in partnership with a local library.

The outcome was highly positive. Within months, she launched a youth storytelling club, received an invitation to facilitate a local literacy event, and began work on a children's book written in Pidgin and Igbo. However, the counselling process was not without challenges. Family members initially dismissed her activities as 'side hobbies'. The counsellor had to continuously affirm the value of her calling using culturally acceptable metaphors – such as comparing her work to that of griots and wise elders who preserve community values. By integrating cultural pride and spirituality, the coach successfully adapted the purpose-based model to her context.

A 38-year-old Yoruba man living in Lagos sought counselling after over a decade in a government IT role. Though financially secure, he reported growing restlessness and spiritual emptiness. A devout Christian and father of three, he expressed a strong desire to 'do something more meaningful' but was unsure how to proceed without destabilising his family's economic foundation. His culture valued economic provision and stability, particularly for male breadwinners, which added pressure and internal conflict.

The counsellor applied the psycho-spiritual purpose-based coaching model (Otu & Eseadi, 2024), carefully adapting it to respect the client's cultural and religious context. In the Reimagining phase, the client described a recurring vision of mentoring young boys in his church on digital skills and character development. Rather than dismiss this as a dream, the counsellor validated it by referencing respected Yoruba elders who combined trade and mentorship.

During the Spiritualising phase, the client was guided to reflect on how his faith called him to serve beyond the workplace. Scripture and prayer were integrated into the session, making the process spiritually familiar and culturally rooted. In the Self-Discovery phase, he identified leadership, empathy, and teaching as core gifts, traits his peers often acknowledged but he had not considered career-relevant. Through Career-Exploration, he investigated practical roles such as tech mentorship, digital discipleship, and establishing a youth tech boot camp. These roles aligned with his Christian values and Yoruba cultural emphasis on mentoring the younger generation. His purpose statement emerged in the Identifying phase as: 'To mentor and empower young men through faith and technology for community transformation'.

The Matching phase led to practical steps. He started a weekend initiative called 'Code & Character' at his church and piloted a mentorship circle for five secondary school boys. The adaptations proved effective: he reported emotional renewal, increased engagement in his church community, and even a stronger sense of purpose at work. One challenge was managing community expectations – some questioned his decision to commit weekends to unpaid work. The counsellor helped him reframe the effort as a 'spiritual investment', using Proverbs and culturally rooted idioms to reinforce purpose as a legacy, not just a profession.

Summary of findings and triangulation

The quantitative data, derived from a structured questionnaire, revealed that mainstream counselling techniques such as CBT, person-centred therapy, narrative therapy, and SFT were most frequently used by counsellors and psychotherapists. The results showed that these techniques were adapted to fit the cultural contexts of clients, with mean scores indicating moderate to high frequency of use and adaptation. Family therapy and mindfulness-based therapy emerged as the techniques most commonly adapted to meet the cultural needs of clients, highlighting the importance of considering family dynamics and holistic healing practices in multicultural settings. The challenges faced by practitioners, such as language barriers, misunderstandings of cultural values, and a lack of cultural competence, were also quantified, revealing that counsellors frequently encountered these barriers, which were rated as significant to extreme in some cases.

Also, the qualitative analysis of open-ended responses provided deeper insights into how counsellors and psychotherapists adapt their techniques to meet cultural needs. Key adaptation strategies included personalising therapy to align with the client's cultural context, using culturally relevant examples and metaphors, incorporating cultural rituals, and adjusting communication styles. A recurring theme was the importance of building cultural awareness and engaging in continuous learning to stay sensitive to diverse cultural values and practices. Participants also emphasised the significance of self-awareness in addressing personal biases, suggesting that ongoing self-reflection was crucial for providing culturally competent care. Several therapists highlighted the challenge of balancing respect for cultural practices with ethical guidelines, particularly when cultural practices conflict with professional ethical standards.

Furthermore, the case studies illustrated real-life applications of culturally adapted counselling techniques. A Nigerian-based therapist working online with clients from various cultural backgrounds, ranging from African to Latina, Chinese, Indigenous, and Middle Eastern backgrounds, demonstrated how online therapy could be effectively adapted to meet the cultural needs of clients. The case studies revealed the use of holistic approaches, narrative therapy, and family involvement, particularly when dealing with clients struggling with family expectations or cultural tensions. These real-world examples provided concrete evidence of how cultural adaptation improves client engagement and therapeutic outcomes. For example, integrating family therapy in a case with a Nigerian client helped resolve family-related anxiety, while narrative therapy empowered a Latina client to reframe her trauma in a culturally relevant way.

Finally, the triangulation of the quantitative, qualitative, and case study findings reveals a cohesive picture of multicultural counselling in practice. Quantitative data highlighted the frequency and effectiveness of adapted counselling techniques, while qualitative responses provided rich, context-specific insights into the challenges and strategies employed by practitioners. The case studies brought these theoretical findings to life, demonstrating how the adaptation of techniques can be successfully implemented in real-world settings with clients from various cultural backgrounds. Overall, the findings suggest that culturally adapted therapies are not only necessary but also highly effective when tailored to the specific needs of diverse populations. The combination of personal reflection, cultural awareness, and the integration of cultural practices was identified as a key factor in enhancing therapeutic outcomes in multicultural counselling contexts.

Implications of the findings

The implications of the findings from this study are far-reaching for both the practice and development of multicultural counselling. These implications can inform how counselling professionals approach therapy with clients from diverse cultural backgrounds, enhance training programmes for future practitioners, and contribute to the evolution of therapeutic models that are sensitive to cultural differences. Below are the key implications of the findings.

Importance of cultural adaptation in counselling techniques

The study emphasises the need for therapists to adapt mainstream counselling techniques, such as CBT, person-centred therapy, and narrative therapy, to meet the cultural needs of clients. This finding highlights the necessity of moving beyond standardised therapeutic models and encourages counsellors to integrate culturally relevant elements into their practice. The implication for practice shows that cultural adaptation is not a supplementary feature but a core component of effective therapy. This suggests that counsellors must continuously develop their understanding of different cultural frameworks to ensure that their methods resonate with clients' values, beliefs, and social contexts.

Furthermore, the increased use of SFT in multicultural settings suggests a potential shift towards more practical, solution-oriented therapies. This could have implications for how therapists are trained to address issues in a more goal-directed manner that is culturally appropriate, particularly for clients in African or similar cultural contexts, where quick resolutions to problems may be more highly valued than long-term introspective therapies.

Cultural competence training and continuous professional development

A major implication of the study is the critical need for ongoing cultural competence training for all counselling professionals. The findings emphasise that multicultural competence is an evolving skill that requires continuous learning, self-reflection, and peer support. This calls for integrating cultural competence training as a continuous process in both initial training programmes and throughout a therapist's career. In practical terms, this means that training curricula should be designed not just to raise awareness of cultural differences but to provide therapists with the tools to effectively integrate these differences into their therapeutic practice.

Moreover, the study highlights the importance of supervision and peer support networks, especially when addressing complex cultural issues in therapy. By establishing stronger support systems for counsellors, these networks can help professionals navigate cultural barriers, reduce isolation, and provide opportunities for mutual learning. Therefore, training and development programmes should integrate supervision practices and opportunities for peer collaboration that focus on cultural issues.

Addressing language barriers and misunderstandings

The findings underscore the persistent challenge of language barriers in multicultural counselling, particularly in online therapy settings. This has significant implications for the delivery of therapy in increasingly globalised and digital contexts. Therapists working with international clients must be equipped with the skills and tools necessary to manage these language differences effectively. This could involve the use of interpreters, translation tools, or culturally competent communication strategies to ensure that both the verbal and non-verbal aspects of therapy are clear and accessible.

Furthermore, the study points to the importance of counsellors' understanding cultural values and how these may influence a client's engagement with therapy. Therapists need to go beyond language barriers and strive to understand the cultural nuances that affect how clients perceive their issues and therapy. This calls for culturally sensitive communication skills that help bridge the gap between the therapist's approach and the client's worldview.

Reducing resistance to mainstream therapeutic models

The study also highlighted resistance to certain therapeutic techniques, particularly when clients from non-Western cultural backgrounds perceive these models as incompatible with their cultural values. This has important implications for therapy, as it suggests that client resistance can hinder the effectiveness of mainstream therapeutic models. The implication for practice is that therapists should be more adaptive and flexible in their approaches. They need to be willing to modify techniques or blend different therapeutic approaches to ensure they meet the client's cultural needs.

In cases where Western techniques like CBT are resisted, therapists might need to explore culturally appropriate interventions or hybrid models that incorporate familiar cultural frameworks into the therapeutic process. For example, integrating family-oriented interventions or spiritual practices into therapy could help build trust and increase engagement. This suggests that counsellors must be trained to recognise and address cultural resistance as part of their practice.

Standardising the integration of cultural practices in therapy

The study suggests that there is a gap in how to systematically integrate cultural practices, such as spirituality and family dynamics, into therapeutic models. The implication for future research is that therapists need to develop frameworks that standardise the integration of cultural elements into therapy, ensuring that these practices are not only culturally respectful but also enhance therapeutic outcomes. The study's findings suggest that cultural rituals and family involvement can play an essential role in therapeutic success, particularly in collectivist cultures.

To address this, professional guidelines or resources could be developed that help therapists determine when and how to incorporate culturally specific practices into their sessions, making it easier for them to adjust techniques without compromising the therapeutic process.

Enhancing online therapy for multicultural clients

As the study also focused on online therapy, it revealed that digital platforms can create barriers, particularly in terms of language and cultural misunderstandings. This has major implications for the future of online therapy in multicultural contexts. The implication is that more attention should be given to how online counselling platforms are designed to ensure they are accessible and effective for clients from diverse cultural backgrounds. This could include features such as language translation tools, culturally sensitive prompts, and virtual resources that support cultural competence.

The rapid increase in telehealth services calls for the development of best practices for multicultural competence in the digital space. Future research should explore how online counselling can be adapted to better address cultural differences, and whether virtual supervision or online peer support networks could be integrated into teletherapy to mitigate challenges faced in this setting.

On the whole, the study's findings have significant implications for the field of multicultural counselling, emphasising the importance of cultural adaptation, cultural competence training, and flexibility in therapeutic practices. The integration of culturally relevant techniques such as family therapy and spiritual practices can enhance therapeutic outcomes for clients from diverse backgrounds. At the same time, barriers such as language differences, misunderstandings of cultural values, and resistance to mainstream techniques remain challenges that need to be addressed through ongoing training, cultural humility, and peer support networks. The study also highlights the increasing role of online therapy, which requires new approaches to ensure effective and culturally competent practice in a digital world. The findings point to both opportunities and challenges in multicultural counselling and call for further research and development of practical guidelines to overcome these barriers.

References

Almanasreh, E., Moles, R. J., & Chen, T. F. (2022). A practical approach to the assessment and quantification of content validity. In *Contemporary research methods in pharmacy and health services*. https://doi.org/10.1016/B978-0-323-91888-6.00013-2

Aramo-Immonen, H. (2013). Mixed methods research design. In *Communications in computer and information science* (Vol 278). https://doi.org/10.1007/978-3-642-35879-1_5

Augustine, C., & Aminu, K. I. (2022). *Techniques of counselling—EGC 804*. National Open University of Nigeria—NOUN. www.nou.edu.ng.

Aviles, B. D., Russell-Chapin, L., & Rybak, C. J. (2015). Role of counselors in multidisciplinary interactions in special education. In *Advances in special education* (Vol 30A). https://doi.org/10.1108/S0270-40132015000030A004

Böttche, M., Kampisiou, C., Stammel, N., El-Haj-Mohamad, R., Heeke, C., Burchert, S., Heim, E., Wagner, B., Renneberg, B., Böttcher, J., Glaesmer, H., Gouzoulis-Mayfrank, E., Zielasek, J., Konnopka, A., Murray, L., & Knaevelsrud, C. (2021). From formative research to cultural adaptation of a face-to-face and internet-based cognitive-behavioural intervention for Arabic-speaking refugees in Germany. *Clinical Psychology in Europe, 3*. https://doi.org/10.32872/cpe.4623

Becerra, G., & Castorina, J. A. (2018). Towards a dialogue among constructivist research programs. *Constructivist Foundations, 13*(2), 191–198.

Cedeno, R., & Torrico, T. (2024). *Adlerian therapy*. Treasure Island (FL): StatPearls Publishing.

Chowdhary, N., Jotheeswaran, A. T., Nadkarni, A., Hollon, S. D., King, M., Jordans, M. J. D., Rahman, A., Verdeli, H., Araya, R., & Patel, V. (2014). The methods and outcomes of cultural adaptations of psychological treatments for depressive disorders: A systematic review. In *Psychological medicine* (Vol 44, pp. 1131–1146). Cambridge University Press. https://doi.org/10.1017/S0033291713001785. Issue 6.

Collins, S., & Arthur, N. (2010). Culture-infused counselling: A model for developing multicultural competence. *Counselling Psychology Quarterly, 23*(2), 217–233. https://doi.org/10.1080/09515071003798212

Devoe, D. (2012). Viktor Frankl's logotherapy: The search for purpose and meaning. *Inquiries Journal/Student Pulse, 4*(7).

Feilzer, M. Y. (2010). Doing mixed methods research pragmatically: Implications for the rediscovery of pragmatism as a research paradigm. *Journal of Mixed Methods Research, 4*(1), 6–16. https://doi.org/10.1177/1558689809349691

Gobo, G. (2023). Mixed Methods and Their Pragmatic Approach: Is There a Risk of Being Entangled in a Positivist Epistemology and Methodology? Limits, Pitfalls and Consequences of a Bricolage Methodology | Mixed Methods und der Pragmatismus: Besteht das Risiko einer Verst. *Forum Qualitative Sozialforschung, 24*(1). https://doi.org/10.17169/fqs-24.1.4005

He, Y. E. (2024). Mixed-methods research. In *Making research relevant applied research designs for the mental health practitioner* (2nd ed.). https://doi.org/10.4324/9781032706139-14

Khazaee-Pool, M., Pashaei, T., Gholami, F., Rafiei, A., Ponnet, K., & Rastegar, H. (2024). Development and psychometric properties of a questionnaire to measure factors affecting the attraction of health tourists. *Journal of Mazandaran University of Medical Sciences, 34*(233), 138–150.

King, A. M., Plateau, C. R., Turner, M. J., Young, P., & Barker, J. B. (2024). A systematic review of the nature and efficacy of rational emotive behaviour therapy interventions. *PLoS One, 19*(7 July). https://doi.org/10.1371/journal.pone.0306835

Längle, A. (2015). From Viktor Frankl's logotherapy to existential analytic psychotherapy. *European Psychotherapy, 12*.

Lee, E., Greenblatt, A., & Hu, R. (2021). A knowledge synthesis of cross-cultural psychotherapy research: A critical review. *Journal of Cross-Cultural Psychology, 52*(6). https://doi.org/10.1177/00220221211028911

Llanas, I. S. (2018). A (very) brief doxographical analysis of constructivism: From pre-Socratics to second-order cybernetics. *Bajo Palabra, 18*, 61–76. https://doi.org/10.15366/bp2018.18.003

Mamud, B. M. (2015). *Cross-cultural issues in comtemporary counselling practice: African experience*. www.britishjr.orgwww.britishjr.org.

McAuliffe, G. J., Grothaus, T., Jensen, M., & Michel, R. (2012). Assessing and promoting cultural relativism in students of counseling. *International Journal for the Advancement of Counselling, 34*(2), 118–135. https://doi.org/10.1007/s10447-011-9142-4

McManus, F. (2022). 3. The theory behind CBT. In *Cognitive behavioural therapy: A very short introduction*. https://doi.org/10.1093/actrade/9780198755272.003.0003

Nagayama Hall, G. C., Kim-Mozeleski, J. E., Zane, N. W., Sato, H., Huang, E. R., Tuan, M., & Ibaraki, A. Y. (2019). Cultural adaptations of psychotherapy: Therapists' applications of conceptual models with Asians and Asian Americans. *Asian American Journal of Psychology, 10*(1). https://doi.org/10.1037/aap0000122

Nelson, J. (2010). *Introducing counselling and therapy approaches*. https://uk.sagepub.com/sites/default/files/upm-binaries/36871_Nelson_Jones_2e_CH_01.pdf?utm_source=chatgpt.com.

Nelson, J. (2014). *Nelson-Jones' theory and practice of counselling and psychotherapy*. https://uk.sagepub.com/sites/default/files/upm-binaries/65524_Nelson_Jones.pdf?utm.

Nelson, J. (2025). *What is counselling and helping? Chapter outcomes*.

O'Callaghan, C., Seah, D., Clayton, J. M., Welz, M., Kissane, D., Georgousopoulou, E. N., & Michael, N. (2020). Palliative caregivers' spirituality, views about spiritual care, and associations with spiritual well-being: A mixed methods study. *American Journal of Hospice and Palliative Medicine, 37*(4). https://doi.org/10.1177/1049909119877351

Opland, C., & Torrico, T. J. (2024). *Psychodynamic therapy*.

Otu, M. S. (2024). Effect of purpose-based career coaching on career decision-making. *Current Psychology, 43*, 25568–25594. https://doi.org/10.1007/s12144-024-06247-3

Otu, M. S., & Eseadi, C. (2024). A psycho-spiritual approach to purpose-based career coaching: A step-by-step guide for practitioners. *Pendekatan Psiko-Spiritual Pada Pelatihan Karir Berbasis Tujuan: Panduan Langkah-Demi-Langkah, 21*(1), 2655–5034. https://doi.org/10.18860/psi.v21i1.26882

Otu, M. S., Otu, F. M., & Ardi, Z. (2023). Purpose-based career coaching as a strategy for increasing employability of graduates: A survey study. *International Journal of Home Economics, Hospitality and Allied Research, 2*(2), 55–80.

Porcino, A. J., & Verhoef, M. J. (2010). The use of mixed methods for therapeutic massage research. *International Journal of Therapeutic Massage and Bodywork Research Education and Practice, 3*(1), 15–25.

Robitschek, C., & Hardin, E. E. (2017). The future of counseling psychology research viewed through the cultural lens approach. *Journal of Counseling Psychology, 64*(4), 359–368. https://doi.org/10.1037/cou0000207

Setia, M. S. (2017). Methodology series module 9: Designing questionnaires and clinical record forms-Part II. *Indian Journal of Dermatology, 62*(3), 258–261. https://doi.org/10.4103/ijd.IJD_200_17

Shaw, J. A., Connelly, D. M., & Zecevic, A. A. (2010). Pragmatism in practice: Mixed methods research for physiotherapy. *Physiotherapy Theory and Practice, 26*(8), 510–518. https://doi.org/10.3109/09593981003660222

Shen, Y.-J., Ting, S.-M., & Shen, H.-J. (2017). Enhancing multicultural counselling competencies and services. *International Journal of Services and Standards, 12*(1), 1–30. https://doi.org/10.1504/IJSS.2017.088167

Skoli, E., Efthymiou, S., Iliopoulou, T., Pilafas, G., & Louka, P. (2025). Trainee integrative therapists' experiences of the role of culture in therapy: An interpretative phenomenological analysis. *International Journal of Research and Review, 12*(9), 443–472. https://doi.org/10.52403/ijrr.20250945

Soto, A., Smith, T. B., Griner, D., Rodríguez, M. D., & Bernal, G. (2019). Cultural adaptations and multicultural competence. In *Psychotherapy relationships that work*. https://doi.org/10.1093/med-psych/9780190843960.003.0004

Spoto, A., Nucci, M., Prunetti, E., & Vicovaro, M. (2023). Improving content validity evaluation of assessment instruments through formal content validity analysis. *Psychological Methods, 30*(2), 203–222. https://doi.org/10.1037/met0000545

Sue, S., Zane, N., Hall, G. C. N., & Berger, L. K. (2009). The case for cultural competency in psychotherapeutic interventions. In *Annual review of psychology* (Vol 60). https://doi.org/10.1146/annurev.psych.60.110707.163651

Welton, D. (2014). The treatment of bipolar disorder in pastoral counseling: Community and silence. In *The treatment of bipolar disorder in pastoral counseling: Community and silence*. https://doi.org/10.4324/9781315808444

Yao, L., & Kabir, R. (2023). *Person-centered therapy (Rogerian therapy)*. StatPearls.

CHAPTER 5

Assessment and diagnosis in multicultural counselling and psychotherapy

Introduction

In today's increasingly diverse and interconnected world, the need for culturally sensitive assessment and diagnostic practices in counselling and psychotherapy has become more critical than ever. As multicultural populations grow, particularly in countries like Nigeria, mental health professionals must adapt their practices to meet the unique needs of individuals from different cultural backgrounds. Nigeria alone is home to over 500 ethnic groups, each with distinct languages, traditions, and beliefs (Nigerian Embassy in Mexico, 2025). A traditional reliance on Western-based psychological models and diagnostic tools, which dominate much of the global mental health field, is problematic when applied to clients from non-Western societies. Such tools often fail to account for cultural, social, and spiritual factors that shape mental health experiences. In fact, research shows that Western diagnostic criteria may not fully capture culturally specific expressions of mental disorders, leading to potential misdiagnosis or underdiagnosis in diverse populations (Fiveable, 2024). This disconnect highlights the importance of integrating cultural perspectives into assessment and diagnosis to provide accurate and effective care.

In many African countries, including Nigeria, mental health conditions are frequently perceived through a cultural or spiritual lens rather than a purely medical one. Emotional struggles are often linked to spiritual, familial, or community-based factors, as opposed to being viewed as isolated psychiatric issues. For example, the etiology of mental illness in some Nigerian communities is commonly attributed to causes like witchcraft, curses, divine punishment, or ancestral spirits (Anjorin & Hassan Wada, 2022). Depression or anxiety might thus be understood as manifestations of spiritual imbalance or as consequences of interpersonal conflicts and moral transgressions, rather than as clinical syndromes. A recent national survey illustrated this perspective: 54% of Nigerians surveyed believed that mental illness is caused by "possession by evil spirits," and about one-third attributed it to hereditary factors ("runs in the family") (Africa Polling Institute & & EpiAfrica, 2020). Such findings highlight how deeply cultural beliefs influence the interpretation of mental health symptoms. In rural areas or among indigenous populations, these interpretations are especially prevalent, meaning that what a Western clinician might

A Pragmatic Approach to Multicultural Counselling and Psychotherapy Skills Acquisition. https://doi.org/10.1016/B978-0-443-33939-4.00008-2

label as depression could be seen by local communities as a spiritual affliction or a family-related issue requiring traditional intervention.

These cultural differences pose a significant challenge for practitioners who rely heavily on standard Western diagnostic tools. Instruments like the DSM-5, MMPI-2, or GAD-7 were largely developed and normed on Western populations and often do not accommodate non-Western idioms of distress or belief systems (Fiveable, 2024). When applied in a multicultural setting without adaptation, such tools may inadvertently lead to misdiagnosis or misunderstanding of clients' symptoms. For instance, a client presenting with somatic complaints (common in some cultures as an expression of emotional distress) might be misdiagnosed if the clinician interprets those symptoms through a strictly Western framework. Studies have noted that overreliance on Western diagnostic criteria can result in clinicians missing the cultural context of symptoms, thereby mistaking culturally normative behaviors or spiritual explanations for psychopathology (Fiveable, 2024). Conversely, genuinely serious conditions might be underdiagnosed because the patient's way of describing distress doesn't fit the expected pattern. In multicultural societies like Nigeria, it is essential that assessment and diagnosis integrate both psychological and cultural perspectives. By doing so, practitioners can more accurately interpret their clients' experiences. The failure to consider culture not only risks clinical inaccuracy but can also alienate clients, who may feel misunderstood or judged if their worldviews are disregarded.

In Nigeria, where traditional healing practices are widely respected and often utilized, many individuals turn to spiritual healers, faith leaders, or community elders for support with mental health issues long before (or in addition to) seeking help from professional psychologists or psychiatrists. In fact, research indicates that more than 70% of people in parts of sub-Saharan Africa (including Nigeria) use traditional or religious healers as their first point of care for mental health concerns (Williams et al., 2025). These healers, ranging from herbalists and spiritualists to religious clergy, are embedded in the community and provide culturally congruent explanations and remedies (prayer, rituals, herbal medicines, etc.) that align with the client's belief system (Anjorin & Hassan Wada, 2022; Nanji & Olivier, 2024). Traditional and faith healers are often more accessible (and affordable) than scarce mental health professionals, and they are trusted figures in many communities. However, their methods and worldview are typically not integrated into Western therapeutic frameworks. Most formal mental health services in Nigeria operate in isolation from traditional practices, leading to a fragmentation of care. Practitioners trained in the Western model may be hesitant to acknowledge or incorporate traditional methods due to lack of training in that area or a perception that such practices are unscientific or incompatible with modern therapy. Likewise, traditional healers may view Western psychology with suspicion. This cultural divide creates a gap in care for clients who navigate both systems. Studies on integration challenges note that attitudinal barriers and mistrust between biomedical practitioners and traditional healers hinder collaboration (Wollie et al., 2025). Many Nigerian mental health professionals have not been formally trained on how to engage with a client's use of traditional healing, and as a result they might dismiss those practices outright. On the other hand, some traditional healers believe their approaches are superior for certain ailments and may discourage clients from seeking psychiatric help. The end result is that clients sometimes feel they must choose one or the other, or they may shuttle between parallel systems of care without any communication between them. This lack of integration can lead to inconsistent or even contradictory treatment plans, and clients can fall through the cracks. Encouragingly, there are calls in the global health community to bridge this gap. Collaborative models have been proposed where, for example, traditional healers are given basic training to identify severe mental illness and refer patients, while clinicians are trained to understand cultural practices. Pilot programmes in some countries have shown improved patient engagement when such collaboration occurs (Anjorin & Hassan Wada, 2022). Integrating traditional and modern approaches—when done with respect and evidence-based guidelines—has the potential to provide more holistic care and reduce the treatment gap for mental illness in places like Nigeria.

The increasing prevalence of immigrant and diaspora populations in Nigeria's urban centers (as well as Nigerians returning from abroad) further complicates the cultural landscape of mental health. These individuals and families bring their own cultural perspectives on mental well-being, which may differ both from the dominant Nigerian culture and from the Western-oriented practices of formally trained clinicians. For instance, immigrants or refugees from parts of Asia or the Middle East settling in Nigeria might interpret mental health symptoms in line with their home culture's beliefs. A client from a Southeast Asian background, for example, might attribute symptoms of anxiety to spiritual causes or ancestral disturbances, diverging from the clinical explanations a Western-trained psychologist would use. Even within Nigeria, internal migrants (people moving from rural to urban areas or from one ethnic region to another) carry distinct cultural frameworks. The ability to assess and diagnose mental health issues in these immigrant or multiethnic populations requires a deep understanding of the various cultural values at play. Cultural factors heavily influence help-seeking behavior. Some groups may prefer family or religious counsel over therapy, and certain symptoms might be expressed differently (such as somatic pain instead of verbalizing "I feel sad"). For example, South Asian immigrant communities worldwide have shown a tendency to prioritize spiritual or religious interventions—like prayer, meditation, or visiting faith healers—over consulting mental health professionals (Vishwani, 2025). Many South Asians view mental illness through a moral or religious lens and may be reluctant to seek Western therapy, considering it a last resort or even feeling that doing so indicates a lack of faith. A therapist in Lagos working with an Indian or Pakistani expatriate family, for instance, might encounter these attitudes. Similarly, immigrants from Middle Eastern backgrounds might talk about jinn or evil eye as causes of psychological distress, which are concepts that standard Western diagnostic interviews do not probe for. If practitioners are not culturally aware, these clients might not receive validation of their experiences, leading to poor rapport or premature dropout from treatment. Therefore, multicultural competence is not only about international differences but also about intra-national diversity and migration. Urban centers like Lagos, Abuja, Uyo, and Port Harcourt are increasingly cosmopolitan, requiring counselors to be adept at navigating a mosaic of cultural narratives about mental health.

Despite these complex challenges, recent studies have shown that culturally adapted assessment tools and multicultural competence training for practitioners can significantly improve the effectiveness of therapy in diverse settings. Training programmes that enhance a therapist's multicultural competence (their awareness, knowledge, and skills for working with diverse clients) correlate with more positive therapeutic alliances and outcomes. In essence, mental health treatments are more effective when they respect and integrate the client's culture, and when therapists are skilled in cultural responsiveness (Soto et al., 2018). Evidence suggests that bridging traditional practices with modern therapy—for example, allowing a client to engage in certain benign cultural rituals as part of their coping strategy while simultaneously receiving counselling—can increase the client's trust and participation in therapy (Wollie et al., 2025). In Nigeria, some forward-thinking practitioners have begun to collaborate with community leaders or incorporate culturally relevant metaphors and stories into therapy sessions, finding that clients respond with greater openness. By acknowledging and valifying clients' cultural experiences, therapists can empower individuals and reduce the sense of alienation that often accompanies conventional therapy in a foreign framework.

However, there remains a significant gap in research specifically addressing how mental health professionals in Nigeria adapt their assessment and diagnostic methods for multicultural populations. Much of the existing literature on multicultural counselling and assessment has centered on challenges and solutions in Western countries (like the United States, Canada, or Western Europe) or in a few well-studied African contexts (such as South Africa or Kenya). Nigeria's unique cultural context with over 250 ethnic groups and myriad indigenous healing traditions coexisting with Western practices is underexplored in scholarly research (Anjorin & Hassan Wada, 2022). While a few studies have highlighted the importance of cultural relevance in psychological testing and diagnosis, they have not fully examined what this looks like in practice within Nigeria's diverse environment. The literature has pointed out that ignoring cultural context can lead to a "category fallacy," where disorders appear homogeneous across cultures when in reality they are expressed differently (Anjorin & Hassan Wada, 2022). Yet, we know little about how Nigerian clinicians are bridging this gap. Do they modify standard questionnaires? Do they use local idioms during clinical interviews? Do they incorporate traditional explanatory models when formulating a case? The scarcity of documented research or case studies on these questions is notable. This gap in the literature is problematic because without context-specific research, policy-makers and educators in Nigeria have limited guidance on training needs or on developing indigenous diagnostic tools. Moreover, Nigerian practitioners themselves have valuable experiential knowledge that has not been formally captured—knowledge about what works and what doesn't when assessing someone from a different tribe, or how to handle a client who simultaneously consults a pastor and a psychiatrist. By not systematically studying these practices, we risk losing insights that could benefit multicultural mental health work globally.

This study seeks to fill the above gap by exploring the use of culturally sensitive assessment and diagnostic practices in multicultural counselling and psychotherapy within Nigeria. It aims to provide in-depth insights into the challenges faced by Nigerian practitioners when working with clients from diverse cultural backgrounds, and to document the strategies these professionals employ to integrate both Western diagnostic tools and traditional cultural practices into their assessment process. Through interviews and surveys with counselors and psychologists across different regions of Nigeria, the study will examine how these practitioners adapt standard diagnostic criteria to be culturally relevant, for example, whether they modify interview questions, use interpreters, consult cultural brokers, or adjust their interpretation of symptoms based on cultural context. By examining the experiences and techniques of Nigerian mental health professionals, this study will offer new perspectives on the effectiveness of culturally adapted tools in real-world practice. It will also shed light on the role of cultural competence in improving client engagement and treatment outcomes in Nigeria's multicultural settings. Ultimately, the findings are expected to contribute to the broader discussion of how mental health professionals worldwide can provide more inclusive, culturally sensitive care. By respecting and integrating the cultural beliefs and practices of clients from diverse backgrounds, therapists can bridge the gap between Western diagnostic frameworks and non-Western worldviews, thereby enhancing the accuracy of diagnoses and the efficacy of subsequent interventions. This research, focusing on Nigeria's rich cultural landscape, will not only benefit local mental health service delivery but also serve as a case study for other multicultural societies striving to reconcile global mental health models with local cultural realities.

Conceptual clarification and framework of assessment and diagnosis in multicultural counselling and psychotherapy

Assessment and Diagnosis in the context of multicultural counselling and psychotherapy refer to the processes of understanding, interpreting, and diagnosing the psychological, emotional, and behavioral concerns of clients from diverse cultural backgrounds. These processes must be adapted to account for the clients' cultural frameworks, including their belief systems, values, worldviews, and social contexts. Without this cultural consideration, standard assessment tools and diagnostic criteria may fail to fully capture or accurately interpret the client's experiences, leading to potential misdiagnosis or misunderstanding.

Conceptual clarification of key terms

Assessment in multicultural counselling

Assessment refers to the process of gathering and evaluating information about a client's psychological functioning, emotional state, life history, and contextual influences. In multicultural counselling, the assessment process goes beyond the application of standardized instruments and includes cultural considerations such as:

- Cultural identity: How the client identifies with various aspects of their background (ethnicity, religion, language, etc.).
- Cultural beliefs: How the client's cultural background influences their understanding of mental health and illness.
- Socio-cultural context: How factors such as family, community, and cultural practices influence the client's mental health.

The process requires that therapists use culturally sensitive tools and approaches, considering that psychological symptoms might be expressed differently across cultures. For example, somatization (the expression of emotional distress through physical symptoms) may be more common in some cultures, and certain behaviors may be misinterpreted when viewed through the lens of a certain diagnostic model (Leong & Lau, 2001).

Diagnosis in multicultural counselling

Diagnosis refers to the identification and classification of mental health disorders based on observed symptoms, client history, and standardized diagnostic criteria (e.g., DSM-5, ICD-10). In multicultural contexts, diagnosis must be:

- Culturally informed: Understanding how cultural context shapes the way individuals express distress, perceive symptoms, and interpret mental health conditions.
- Flexible: Moving beyond the use of rigid diagnostic categories from Western frameworks to include culturally specific symptoms and explanatory models.
- Contextual: Recognizing the role of social, economic, and familial factors in mental health.

A culturally competent diagnostic process helps clinicians make more accurate assessments, as it considers cultural idioms of distress, the culturally specific ways in which individuals articulate their suffering, which may differ from the language of Western psychological tools (Baptiste et al., 1993).

Framework for multicultural assessment and diagnosis

Given the diversity within multicultural counselling settings, a structured framework for integrating cultural factors into assessment and diagnosis is essential. This framework should guide clinicians through culturally competent processes that respect both individual differences and cultural commonalities.

Cultural competence framework

Cultural competence refers to the ability of the therapist to understand and respect the cultural identities of clients while integrating this understanding into assessment and treatment. This framework is often described as having three interrelated components (Sue et al., 2009):

- Cultural Awareness: The therapist's self-awareness regarding their own cultural beliefs, biases, and assumptions.
- Cultural Knowledge: Understanding the client's cultural background, including values, practices, and attitudes toward mental health.
- Cultural Skills: The ability to apply cultural knowledge to therapeutic practice, including modifying diagnostic approaches to accommodate cultural differences.

Incorporating cultural competence into assessment and diagnosis means that therapists should not merely rely on universal diagnostic criteria but should consider the client's cultural worldview, expectations, and experiences.

Cultural formulation interview (CFI)

One of the most prominent tools for integrating cultural competence into the diagnostic process is the Cultural Formulation Interview (CFI), introduced in DSM-5. The CFI is a structured interview guide designed to elicit information about a client's cultural background, including:

- Cultural identity (ethnicity, religion, language).
- Cultural explanations of mental health (e.g., spiritual interpretations, family dynamics).
- Psychosocial stressors (e.g., migration, acculturation, discrimination).
- Help-seeking behaviors (e.g., reliance on traditional healing versus modern mental health services).

The CFI allows clinicians to systematically assess cultural factors that could influence diagnosis and therapeutic engagement. It's especially useful in diverse multicultural settings, such as Nigeria, where cultural identity and beliefs profoundly influence clients' mental health experiences.

Integrative framework for diagnosis

This framework advocates for the integration of culturally specific diagnostic approaches with traditional clinical models (such as the DSM-5 or ICD-10). While DSM-5 and other Western diagnostic systems provide a standardized framework for identifying mental health disorders, they do not always account for cultural variations in symptom expression. This framework involves:

- Flexible adaptation of diagnostic categories to ensure that cultural expressions of distress are understood.
- Combining Western diagnostic criteria with culturally sensitive assessment tools (e.g., CFI) to ensure that the diagnosis is both clinically valid and culturally relevant.
- Consultation with cultural brokers or local healers when needed, particularly in settings where traditional healing plays a key role in the client's worldview.

This approach is vital in a multicultural setting like Nigeria, where mental health issues are sometimes conceptualized as spiritual or familial problems, rather than purely medical or psychological ones. Integrating both traditional and Western perspectives ensures a more holistic approach to diagnosis.

My experience in assessment and diagnosis across cultures in Nigeria

For the past decade, I have worked with clients from diverse cultural backgrounds across Nigeria, offering both counselling services and teaching counselling students. This has provided me with a rich and multifaceted experience in navigating the complexities of assessment and diagnosis in a multicultural context. Working in a country as culturally and ethnically diverse as Nigeria, where over 250 ethnic groups speak hundreds of languages and hold varying belief systems, the nuances of culturally sensitive assessment have become a critical aspect of my practice. In my clinical practice, I have often encountered challenges when using certain standardized assessment tools. Tools like the MMPI-2 or GAD-7, which are commonly used in international clinical settings, sometimes fail to capture the cultural context of mental health in Nigeria. For example, depression and anxiety, as diagnosed in Western settings, might be expressed through physical symptoms (like chronic pain or fatigue) or through somatization, particularly in rural areas or communities with strong spiritual beliefs. In such cases, mental health issues might be viewed as spiritual or familial disturbances, rather than conditions requiring psychiatric intervention.

This has made me realize that diagnostic tools should be adapted to account for cultural beliefs, especially in settings where traditional healing practices hold a prominent place. My experience has taught me to go beyond just ticking off symptom checklists and to incorporate culturally relevant questions during the diagnostic interview. For example, understanding whether a client attributes their distress to spiritual imbalance or family conflict rather than purely psychological factors is essential in making an informed diagnosis. One of the tools I have found particularly helpful in integrating cultural context into the assessment process is the Cultural Formulation Interview (CFI). I've used it in my clinical work to help elicit important cultural details from clients, including their cultural identity, beliefs about the causes of distress, and how they view mental health. This tool has allowed me to ask questions that may not be covered by standard diagnostic instruments but are crucial in understanding a client's lived experience. For instance, Nigerian clients from Indigenous or rural communities often explain their symptoms using metaphysical or spiritual language, which is often overlooked by Western diagnostic criteria.

When I teach my counselling students, I emphasize the importance of cultural competence in diagnosis. I discuss the use of culturally adapted tools like the CFI, but I also encourage them to engage with the community and consider local belief systems when assessing clients. Many of my students initially struggle with the idea of incorporating spiritual or traditional perspectives into therapy, but over time, they come to appreciate how these frameworks shape how clients view and describe their distress.

In the classroom, I focus on the theoretical foundations of multicultural counselling, teaching students about cultural competence and cultural humility in practice. I underscore the importance of being aware of personal biases and stereotypes that may influence diagnostic decisions. I also encourage them to engage in self-reflection on how their own cultural perspectives may shape their understanding of mental health. This self-awareness is critical when they begin to assess clients from diverse backgrounds, especially in Nigeria's multicultural society, where family structures, religious beliefs, and local traditions play a significant role in how clients experience and express psychological distress. I also stress the need for flexibility in diagnostic approaches. Many of my students are initially hesitant to adapt standard diagnostic tools, like the DSM-5 or ICD-10, to account for cultural differences. However, I teach them that it is not about abandoning these tools, but about modifying them to ensure that they are culturally relevant. For example, rather than rigidly applying a diagnosis of Major Depressive Disorder, they can ask clients about how family dynamics, community support, and spiritual beliefs influence their sense of well-being and distress. This approach not only fosters greater client engagement but also leads to more accurate and culturally appropriate diagnoses.

Another key component of my work is integrating spiritual healing practices with modern psychotherapy. In Nigeria, many individuals from rural or indigenous backgrounds often seek out spiritual healers or elders for support with emotional issues. Some clients rely heavily on their pastors or religious leaders for their healing and restoration. I have learned to acknowledge the validity of these faith-based diagnostic practices, particularly when they are deeply intertwined with a client's cultural and spiritual beliefs. In the faith-based context, clients may wish to assess or diagnose their problems through procedures like searching the Scriptures, inquiring from God through prayer, or seeking pastoral counsel. In this process, the will of God concerning the client's distress or concern is sought, and spiritual guidance is provided to help diagnose the underlying cause of the issue troubling them.

While I do not directly engage in spiritual healing, I respect the importance of these practices, especially when clients view their mental health and well-being through a spiritual or communal lens. If a client expresses a desire to incorporate pastoral counselling principles or faith-based diagnostic methods, I am open to integrating these into the therapeutic process, provided it aligns with the client's needs. This could involve supporting the client's spiritual journey by helping them search and learn Scriptures to discover effective spiritual ways of handling their concerns. In such cases, I may also collaborate with community pastors or elders (with the client's consent) to ensure that the healing process is both holistic and culturally responsive. I have found that this integration of spiritual assessment and diagnosis with modern therapeutic techniques fosters a collaborative effort, strengthens the therapeutic relationship, and improves client engagement. When clients feel that both their psychological and spiritual needs are being addressed, they are more likely to remain in therapy and benefit from the intervention. This approach has been particularly effective in my work with clients from Nigeria, where spirituality and faith-based diagnoses are often seen as integral to understanding and resolving mental health concerns.

Despite the successes I've experienced, significant challenges persist in the area of multicultural diagnosis. One of the key obstacles is the lack of standardized, culturally sensitive diagnostic tools tailored for Indigenous Nigerian populations. Many of the tools currently used in therapy are imported from the West, and while they can be effective in certain contexts, they often fall short in fully capturing the cultural nuances and local understandings of mental health in Nigeria. This limitation is especially pronounced in rural areas, where there is also a shortage of trained clinicians who understand the cultural intricacies that shape how mental health issues are expressed and interpreted. Moreover, there remains some resistance among clients who view counselling as a Western practice that is not aligned with their cultural beliefs or spiritual frameworks. Overcoming this resistance requires not only building trust but also a deep understanding of the cultural dynamics that influence how clients perceive mental health and treatment. Addressing these challenges demands a thoughtful, patient approach, rooted in cultural humility and sensitivity.

Research objectives

1. To identify assessment and diagnostic tools in multicultural counselling and psychotherapy.
2. To explore the challenges and strategies for conducting culturally sensitive assessments in multicultural counselling.
3. To provide recommendations for integrating culturally sensitive assessment and diagnostic practices into counselling and psychotherapy.

Research questions

1. What are the commonly used assessment and diagnostic tools in multicultural counselling and psychotherapy?
2. What challenges do practitioners face when conducting assessments and diagnoses in multicultural counselling?
3. What are the key recommendations for integrating culturally sensitive assessment and diagnostic practices into multicultural counselling and psychotherapy?

Research methodology

Approach

A mixed-methods approach was utilized to answer the research questions, integrating both qualitative and quantitative methods to provide a comprehensive and nuanced understanding of the assessment tools, challenges, and strategies for integrating culturally sensitive practices in multicultural counselling and psychotherapy. This approach enabled triangulation, where findings from different data sources could be compared and validated, enhancing the depth and richness of the research.

Research paradigm

This study adopted a pragmatic research paradigm, focusing on practical solutions and outcomes in multicultural counselling and psychotherapy. The pragmatic paradigm is well-suited for addressing complex, real-world issues, such as the challenges of integrating cultural sensitivity into assessment and diagnostic practices, where a combination of both qualitative insights and quantitative data can lead to more actionable results.

Ontology

The ontological stance of this study aligns with constructivism, which posits that reality is socially constructed and context-dependent. The study assumes that multicultural counselors and psychotherapists construct their experiences, assessments, and challenges based on their cultural backgrounds, professional experiences, and the diverse cultural contexts in which they practice. This perspective allows for the exploration of multiple realities and the understanding of cultural diversity in therapeutic settings.

Epistemology

From an interpretivist epistemological perspective, this study recognizes that knowledge is co-constructed through the interactions between researchers and participants. Knowledge about assessment tools, challenges, and recommendations for culturally sensitive practices is seen as subjective and context-specific, requiring understanding through deep engagement with practitioners in multicultural settings. The research process involved interpreting participants' perspectives and lived experiences to generate meaningful insights.

Axiology

The study adopts a value-laden approach, acknowledging that research in multicultural contexts is inherently influenced by the values, beliefs, and cultural perspectives of both the researcher and participants. The research seeks to uphold values of cultural respect, inclusivity, and social justice, ensuring that diverse voices are represented and that the findings promote more culturally sensitive practices in counselling and psychotherapy.

Research design

The research employed a mixed-methods explanatory design, where the quantitative phase (survey) preceded the qualitative phase (interviews, focus groups, and expert panels). This design enabled the researcher to collect broad, generalizable data about the tools and challenges, followed by in-depth qualitative data to explore underlying themes, provide deeper context, and generate actionable recommendations.

Sample and sampling techniques

The study sample initially consisted of 1000 counselors and psychotherapists selected from major cities across Nigeria, including Uyo, Lagos, Abuja, Enugu, Delta, Kano, Sokoto, Benin, Calabar, and Awka. These cities were chosen to represent a broad spectrum of professional practice in multicultural contexts across the country. Stratified random sampling was employed to ensure that each city was proportionally represented in the sample, capturing both urban and semi-urban regions, which contributed to the diversity of the study. To refine the sample, specific inclusion and exclusion criteria were applied. Participants were required to have at least 2 years of professional experience in multicultural counselling settings and be actively engaged in assessment and diagnostic practices. They also needed to be willing to participate in the study, including completing surveys and engaging in qualitative data collection methods. Those with less than 2 years of experience or those not involved in assessment and diagnosis were excluded from the study. Additionally, professionals who did not provide informed consent or were unwilling to participate were also excluded.

From the initial 1000 professionals, 340 met the inclusion criteria and were selected for the quantitative phase of the study. This group was surveyed to gather data regarding their use of assessment tools, diagnostic practices, and challenges faced in multicultural counselling. The selection of these 340 participants was based on purposive sampling to ensure that they were actively engaged in multicultural counselling settings, which was crucial for the study's focus.

For the qualitative phase, a purposive sampling technique was employed to select a sub-sample of 12 professionals from the 340 participants. This group comprised 6 counselors and 6 psychologists, chosen based on their expertise and experience in multicultural counselling. The goal was to ensure a diverse representation of professional perspectives, thereby facilitating in-depth insights through interviews, focus group discussions, and case studies. Additionally, case studies were reported by both the counselors and psychologists, further enriching the qualitative data.

Data collection

In the quantitative phase, data were collected using the Multicultural Counseling and Psychotherapy Assessment and Diagnosis Questionnaire (MCPADQ). This instrument was designed to assess the use of assessment tools and diagnostic practices in multicultural counselling and psychotherapy settings. The MCPADQ consisted of 20 items, which explored various aspects such as the types of tools employed, and the challenges faced by practitioners in ensuring cultural sensitivity in assessments.

The response format for the questionnaire utilized a four-point Likert scale, with response options ranging from "Strongly Agree" to "Strongly Disagree." The scale was assigned numerical values as follows: 1 for "Strongly Disagree," 2 for "Disagree," 3 for "Agree," and 4 for "Strongly Agree." This four-point scale was selected to eliminate the neutral option, compelling participants to express either agreement or disagreement, which can provide clearer insights into their attitudes and practices. This approach ensures that responses are more decisive, capturing the extent to which participants agree or disagree with each statement regarding their multicultural counselling practices. The decision to use this four-point scale was based on the goal of obtaining more specific and actionable data, as the absence of a neutral option encourages stronger responses and avoids ambiguity in the interpretation of the results. Additionally, the four-point scale was designed to keep the questionnaire concise and easy for participants to complete, while still providing enough variation in responses to allow for meaningful analysis.

Each participant's responses were assigned numerical values, and a total score was calculated by summing the scores from all 30 items. The total score provided a composite measure of the participant's use of culturally sensitive assessment and diagnostic practices, with higher scores indicating greater engagement in culturally sensitive practices. For instance, a participant who selected "Strongly Agree" (4) for all items would have the highest possible score, reflecting a strong commitment to cultural sensitivity in their work. Conversely, a participant who consistently selected "Strongly Disagree" (1) would have the lowest possible score, indicating minimal use of culturally sensitive tools.

In the qualitative phase of the study, data were collected through semi-structured interviews and focus group discussions to explore the integration of culturally sensitive assessment and diagnostic practices into multicultural counselling and psychotherapy. The goal was to gather insights from experienced practitioners on the challenges they face and the strategies they employ to ensure cultural sensitivity in their practices. During the interviews, participants were asked open-ended questions, which allowed them to share their experiences and provide detailed responses. Topics explored included the types of assessment and diagnostic tools used, the frequency with which these tools are applied, and the challenges practitioners face when working with clients from diverse cultural backgrounds. Additionally, participants discussed strategies they have found effective for adapting their practices to be culturally sensitive and inclusive.

Data analysis

The data analysis for the quantitative phase of the study was conducted using descriptive statistics, which provided a detailed overview of the responses collected from the Multicultural Counseling and Psychotherapy Assessment and Diagnosis Questionnaire (MCPADQ). The purpose of this analysis was to summarize and interpret the data, offering insights into the use of assessment tools and diagnostic practices in multicultural counselling and psychotherapy settings.

First, the mean score for each item on the questionnaire was calculated. The mean score served as a measure of central tendency, reflecting the average level of agreement or usage of the culturally sensitive practices. A high mean score indicated strong agreement with the use of a particular tool or practice, whereas a lower mean score suggested less frequent engagement with such practices. This helped to identify which assessment tools were most commonly used by the participants. Next, the standard error of the mean (SE) was computed for each item. The standard error provided insight into the precision of the mean estimate. A smaller standard error suggested that the mean was more precise and closer to the true population mean, while a larger standard error indicated more variability in the responses. This measure helped assess the reliability of the mean score and gave context to how confident we could be in the average score for each item.

Additionally, the 95% confidence interval (CI) for the mean was calculated. The confidence interval helped to determine the range within which the true population mean was likely to fall. A narrower confidence interval indicated more precision in the estimate, while a wider interval suggested more uncertainty in the mean score. This interval provided a better understanding of the variability and reliability of the participants' responses, reflecting the extent of agreement or disagreement on each item.

The standard deviation was also calculated to measure the variability or spread of the responses for each item. A higher standard deviation indicated that responses were more spread out, suggesting greater diversity in opinions or experiences among the participants. Conversely, a lower standard deviation indicated more consistency in responses, suggesting that participants had similar views or practices regarding the use of culturally sensitive assessment tools.

In order to assess the normality of the data distribution, the Shapiro–Wilk test was conducted. This test was used to determine whether the data followed a normal distribution, which is crucial for deciding whether parametric tests could be applied. The results of the Shapiro–Wilk test revealed P-values of <0.001, indicating that the data significantly deviated from a normal distribution. This non-normality suggested that further statistical analyses might need to be adjusted, possibly requiring the use of non-parametric methods to analyze the data effectively.

The qualitative data collected from the semi-structured interviews and focus group discussions were analyzed using thematic analysis. Thematic analysis is a method for identifying, analyzing, and reporting patterns or themes within qualitative data. This approach was chosen because it provides a flexible and comprehensive method for interpreting data, allowing the researcher to identify key patterns, insights, and recommendations relevant to the research objectives.

The analysis followed several key steps to ensure a systematic and rigorous process:

1. **Familiarization with the Data**: The first step in the thematic analysis involved familiarizing oneself with the data by reading and re-reading the transcripts from the interviews and focus group discussions. During this stage, the researcher became immersed in the data to gain a broad understanding of the content and to begin identifying initial impressions and potential themes.
2. **Generating Initial Codes**: After familiarization, the next step was to generate initial codes from the data. This involved systematically reviewing the text and marking sections of the data that were relevant to the research objectives. These relevant sections were then given descriptive labels, or "codes." For example, when participants discussed challenges they faced in applying culturally sensitive tools, codes such as "cultural biases," "language barriers," and "lack of training" were applied. The goal was to capture the key features of the data that were of interest.
3. **Searching for Themes**: Once the initial coding was completed, the researcher moved on to the next phase: searching for themes. This step involved grouping related codes into broader themes that captured key aspects of the data. For instance, codes such as "lack of training" and "cultural biases" might have been grouped under a broader theme called "Challenges in Implementing Culturally Sensitive Practices." The researcher looked for patterns and connections in the coded data, organizing them into coherent themes that would help answer the research questions.
4. **Reviewing Themes**: The identified themes were then reviewed to ensure that they accurately represented the data. This involved checking the themes against the original data to confirm that they were grounded in the participants' responses and that they made sense in the context of the study's objectives. In some cases, themes were refined, split into smaller themes, or combined to better reflect the data. This iterative process helped to ensure the validity and relevance of the themes.
5. **Defining and Naming Themes**: After reviewing the themes, the researcher defined each theme and assigned a name that captured its essence. This step was crucial for providing clarity and ensuring that each theme accurately reflected the underlying data. For example, a theme might be defined as "Barriers to Cultural Sensitivity," with subthemes such as "Institutional Barriers" and "Personal Attitudes." Clear definitions helped to ensure that the analysis was consistent and understandable.
6. **Writing the Report**: The final step of thematic analysis involved writing a detailed report that explained the themes and their implications. The report not only described each theme but also illustrated it with direct quotes from the participants. These quotes helped to provide a rich, context-specific understanding of the themes, ensuring that the findings were grounded in the data. The report also included an interpretation of the

themes, linking them back to the study's objectives and providing actionable insights for integrating culturally sensitive assessment and diagnostic practices in multicultural counselling and psychotherapy.

Ethical considerations

In conducting this study, a range of ethical considerations were integral to ensuring the protection of participants' rights, the integrity of the data collected, and the credibility of the findings. Both the quantitative and qualitative phases of the study, including the case studies, involved sensitive data collection from counselors and psychotherapists working in multicultural counselling and psychotherapy settings. Below are the ethical considerations specifically tailored for this study.

Informed Consent: Prior to participating in the study, all participants were fully informed of the purpose, objectives, and procedures involved. In the quantitative phase, participants were made aware of the nature of the questionnaire and the time commitment required. For the qualitative phase, in which in-depth interviews, focus group discussions, and case studies were conducted, participants were informed that their contributions would be audio-recorded, transcribed, and analyzed. They were also assured that participation was voluntary and that they could withdraw from the study at any time without consequence. Written consent was obtained from all participants before data collection began. This ensured that participants understood their rights and provided explicit consent to participate in the study.

Confidentiality and Anonymity: Confidentiality was maintained throughout the study to protect the identities and responses of all participants. In both the quantitative and qualitative phases, all personal identifiers were removed from the data collected. The information provided by the participants, including the case study reports, was anonymized and securely stored to prevent unauthorized access. For the qualitative interviews and focus group discussions, confidentiality was especially important as participants shared personal experiences that could be sensitive. Participants were assured that their names would not be linked to their responses in any published materials or findings, ensuring that they were able to speak openly without fear of their identities being revealed.

Cultural Sensitivity and Respect: Given the multicultural context of the study, particular care was taken to ensure cultural sensitivity throughout the research process. The qualitative phase, which involved interviews and case studies, included culturally adapted methods and tools, such as the Cultural Formulation Interview (CFI) and culturally relevant questionnaires, ensuring that the research methods did not impose cultural biases on the participants. Additionally, researchers and cultural consultants worked collaboratively to ensure that the questions posed were appropriate and respectful of the participants' cultural backgrounds, religious beliefs, and practices. For example, in the case studies, where cultural practices such as traditional healing were involved, the approach was adapted to integrate these practices into the therapeutic process in a manner that was respectful and non-judgmental.

Psychological Safety: Given the potential for participants to discuss sensitive topics related to mental health, such as anxiety, depression, and PTSD, every effort was made to ensure the psychological safety of the participants. In the qualitative phase, the researchers were mindful of the emotional well-being of the participants, particularly during interviews and focus group discussions where sensitive personal experiences were shared. Participants were informed that they could take breaks if needed, and were provided with resources for mental health support should they feel distressed during or after their involvement in the study. Additionally, case study participants were given the opportunity to review the transcripts of their contributions to ensure that their perspectives were accurately represented, and that sensitive information was handled with care.

Right to Withdraw: Participants were informed at the outset of the study that they had the right to withdraw at any time, with no penalty or consequence. This was especially important in the qualitative and case study components, where participants shared personal experiences and narratives about their professional practices and clients. It was made clear that withdrawal would not affect their professional relationships or any future participation in research. This ensured that participants felt no pressure to continue with the study if they felt uncomfortable at any stage.

Data Integrity and Use: The integrity of the data was of paramount importance throughout the study. All data collected from the MCPADQ, interviews, focus group discussions, and case studies were stored securely, and only authorized personnel had access to the data. All findings were reported honestly and transparently, with careful attention to the context of the data, ensuring that no participant's information was misrepresented. The results were analyzed and presented in aggregate form to ensure anonymity and avoid any potential harm to individuals or groups. Furthermore, participants were given the option to review and approve the case study findings that involved their personal experiences, ensuring the accuracy and authenticity of the reported data.

Ethical Approval: Prior to data collection, the study received ethical approval from Department of Counseling and Human Development Studies, University of Nigeria, Nsukka ethics committee. This ensured that the research adhered to the necessary ethical guidelines for studies involving human participants, including the protection of participants' rights, privacy, and well-being.

Cultural and Emotional Impact: Finally, the study was designed to be mindful of the cultural and emotional impact that discussing multicultural counselling practices and mental health issues may have on the participants. Given the diverse range of cultural backgrounds represented in the sample, the research team was trained to approach sensitive topics with care, empathy, and respect. This was particularly important in the qualitative and case study components, where participants shared personal reflections and insights into their professional experiences. To mitigate any potential emotional distress, the counselors and psychologists involved in the study were offered opportunities for debriefing and support throughout the research process.

Results

Table 5.1 presents an analysis of demographic variables and their distributions among 340 participants. The results include counts, proportions, and *P*-values to assess whether the observed proportions deviate significantly from an expected 50% distribution, with the *P*-value tested against a value of 0.5. For professional role, 178 participants (52.4%) identified as psychologists, while 162 participants (47.6%) identified as counselors. The *P*-value of 0.416 indicates that the difference between these two groups is not statistically significant, meaning the distribution of psychologists and counselors in the sample is relatively balanced and does not deviate from the expected 50–50 split.

Regarding years of experience, the participants were distributed across four categories: 81 participants (23.8%) had 2–5 years of experience, 84 participants (24.7%) had 16+ years, 96 participants (28.2%) had 11–15 years, and 79 participants (23.2%) had 6–10 years. The *P*-value for each of these categories is less than 0.001, indicating statistically significant differences from an equal distribution of 50%. This suggests that the distribution of years

Table 5.1: Analysis of demographic variables.

Variable	Level	Counts	Total	Proportion	*P*
Professional role	Psychologist	178	340	0.524	0.416
	Counselor	162	340	0.476	0.416
Years of experience	2–5 years	81	340	0.238	<0.001
	16+ years	84	340	0.247	<0.001
	11–15 years	96	340	0.282	<0.001
	6–10 years	79	340	0.232	<0.001
Region	Both	115	340	0.338	<0.001
	Urban	111	340	0.326	<0.001
	Rural	114	340	0.335	<0.001
Work with diverse clients	Yes	152	340	0.447	0.058
	No	188	340	0.553	0.058

Proportions tested against value: 0.5.

of experience in the sample is not balanced, with a slight overrepresentation of participants with 11–15 years of experience, followed by those with 16+ years.

In terms of region, participants were distributed as follows: 115 participants (33.8%) worked in both urban and rural areas, 111 participants (32.6%) worked in urban areas, and 114 participants (33.5%) worked in rural areas. Again, the *P*-value for each category is less than 0.001, showing that the distribution is significantly different from an equal 50–50 split. However, the distribution across urban, rural, and both settings is relatively even, with no category showing a large imbalance.

For the variable work with diverse clients, 152 participants (44.7%) reported working with diverse clients, while 188 participants (55.3%) did not. The *P*-value of 0.058 indicates that this difference is not statistically significant when compared to a 50% distribution. This suggests that the proportion of participants working with diverse clients is not significantly different from those who do not, and the variation may be due to chance rather than a meaningful difference.

Table 5.2 presents descriptive statistics for the assessment tools used in multicultural counselling and psychotherapy. It includes the mean, standard error of the mean, confidence intervals, standard deviation, and Shapiro–Wilk test results for each assessment tool, which provides insights into the frequency of their use, variability, and the normality of their distributions. For self-report questionnaires, the mean score was 2.532, indicating that, on average, participants "agree" with the use of such tools. These tools typically include instruments like the Beck Depression Inventory and the Generalized Anxiety Disorder Scale. The standard error of the mean was 0.060, suggesting a relatively small variation in the average response across participants. The 95% confidence interval ranged from 2.415 to 2.650, which means that the true mean for the population likely falls within this range. The standard deviation was 1.103, showing moderate spread in responses. The Shapiro–Wilk test yielded a *P*-value of <0.001, indicating that the data were not normally distributed.

Similarly, for structured interviews, the mean score was 2.471, indicating general agreement among participants on the use of interviews in multicultural settings. Structured interviews often involve a set of standardized questions, allowing practitioners to assess clients systematically. An example might include the Structured Clinical Interviews for DSM Disorders (SCID). The standard error of the mean was 0.061, and the 95% confidence interval ranged from 2.351 to 2.590. The standard deviation of 1.117 suggests a moderate level of variability in responses. The Shapiro–Wilk *P*-value of <0.001 again indicates that the data deviate from a normal distribution.

For standardized psychological tools, the mean score was 2.415, slightly lower than that for structured interviews and self-report questionnaires. These tools often include widely-

Table 5.2: Descriptive statistics showing assessment tools used in multicultural counselling and psychotherapy.

	Mean	Std. error of mean	95% confidence interval mean		Std. deviation	Shapiro–Wilk	*P*-value of Shapiro–Wilk
			Upper	Lower			
Self-report questionnaire	2.532	0.060	2.650	2.415	1.103	0.860	<0.001
Structured interviews	2.471	0.061	2.590	2.351	1.117	0.857	<0.001
Standardized psychological tools	2.415	0.063	2.539	2.290	1.168	0.838	<0.001
Standardized assessment tools	2.491	0.061	2.610	2.372	1.117	0.856	<0.001
Cultural formulation method	2.541	0.061	2.661	2.421	1.127	0.853	<0.001
Locally developed instruments	2.432	0.060	2.550	2.315	1.102	0.860	<0.001

used assessments like the Minnesota Multiphasic Personality Inventory (MMPI-2) and the Rorschach inkblot test. The 95% confidence interval ranged from 2.290 to 2.539, and the standard deviation was 1.168, indicating a wider spread in responses. The Shapiro–Wilk P-value showed <0.001, confirming that the data for standardized psychological tools are also not normally distributed.

For standardized assessment tools, the mean score was 2.491, indicating moderate agreement with their use. These tools include well-established assessments like the Wechsler Adult Intelligence Scale (WAIS) and Personality Inventories. The 95% confidence interval ranged from 2.372 to 2.610, with a standard deviation of 1.117. The Shapiro–Wilk P-value of <0.001 suggests that the data deviate from a normal distribution.

For cultural formulation methods, the mean score was 2.541, the highest among the tools, suggesting relatively strong agreement among participants regarding the use of cultural formulation in assessments. This method might include approaches like the Cultural Formulation Interview (CFI), which is used to understand how cultural factors influence mental health. The standard deviation was 1.127, suggesting some variability in responses. The 95% confidence interval ranged from 2.421 to 2.661, with the data once again showing non-normality based on the Shapiro–Wilk P-value of <0.001.

Lastly, for locally developed instruments, the mean score was 2.432, indicating moderate agreement with their use. These tools may include assessments tailored to specific cultural or regional populations, such as locally developed cultural competence scales. The standard deviation of 1.102 reflects a similar spread in responses. The 95% confidence interval ranged from 2.315 to 2.550, and the Shapiro–Wilk P-value of <0.001 again suggests non-normality.

Table 5.3 presents descriptive statistics for cultural sensitivity in assessment practices, based on six statements related to how practitioners adjust, use, and evaluate assessment tools to ensure they are culturally relevant. The data includes mean scores, standard error of the mean, 95% confidence intervals, standard deviation, and Shapiro–Wilk test results.

For "I make adjustments to assessment tools to ensure they are culturally relevant for my clients" (Item 1), the mean score was 2.388, suggesting that participants disagree with the statement. The standard error of the mean was 0.062, indicating a small variation around the average response. The 95% confidence interval ranged from 2.266 to 2.510, suggesting the true population mean is likely within this range. The standard deviation was 1.143, reflecting moderate variation in responses. The Shapiro–Wilk P-value of <0.001 indicates that the data are not normally distributed, suggesting a skewed distribution of responses.

Table 5.3: Descriptive statistics showing cultural sensitivity in assessment practices.

	Mean	Std. error of mean	95% confidence interval mean		Std. deviation	Shapiro–Wilk	*P*-value of Shapiro–Wilk
			Upper	Lower			
Item 7	2.388	0.062	2.510	2.266	1.143	0.845	<0.001
Item 8	2.512	0.062	2.633	2.390	1.141	0.850	<0.001
Item 9	2.482	0.061	2.603	2.362	1.127	0.854	<0.001
Item 10	2.488	0.062	2.610	2.366	1.143	0.848	<0.001
Item 11	2.500	0.061	2.619	2.381	1.117	0.856	<0.001
Item 12	2.353	0.060	2.472	2.234	1.113	0.853	<0.001

For "I have encountered challenges in using assessment tools with clients who speak a different language from the language of the tool" (Item 2), the mean score was 2.512, indicating general agreement with the statement. The standard error of the mean was 0.062, and the 95% confidence interval ranged from 2.390 to 2.633. The standard deviation was 1.141, suggesting variability in responses. The Shapiro–Wilk *P*-value of <0.001 shows that the data are not normally distributed.

For "I receive regular cultural competence training to improve my assessment practices" (Item 3), the mean score was 2.482, indicating agreement. The 95% confidence interval ranged from 2.362 to 2.603, and the standard deviation was 1.127, showing variability in responses. The Shapiro–Wilk *P*-value of <0.001 indicates non-normality.

For "I feel confident that the assessment tools I use are culturally sensitive and appropriate for my clients" (Item 4), the mean score was 2.488, showing agreement. The 95% confidence interval ranged from 2.366 to 2.610, and the standard deviation was 1.143, indicating some spread in the responses. The Shapiro–Wilk *P*-value of <0.001 again shows that the data are not normally distributed.

For "I collaborate with cultural consultants or community leaders to ensure the cultural relevance of the tools I use" (Item 5), the mean score was 2.500, indicating agreement. The 95% confidence interval ranged from 2.381 to 2.619, and the standard deviation was 1.117, showing moderate variation in responses. The Shapiro–Wilk *P*-value of <0.001 confirms non-normality in the data.

For "The cultural background of my clients significantly influences how I interpret their responses during assessments" (Item 6), the mean score was 2.353, suggesting slight disagreement with the statement. The 95% confidence interval ranged from 2.234 to 2.472, with a standard deviation of 1.113, reflecting moderate variability. The Shapiro–Wilk *P*-value of <0.001 shows that the data are not normally distributed.

Table 5.4 provides descriptive statistics for the challenges faced in multicultural assessments, specifically regarding stigmatization, cultural bias, language differences, and the difficulty in adapting traditional assessment tools. The data includes mean scores, standard error of the mean, 95% confidence intervals, standard deviation, and Shapiro–Wilk test results.

For the statement "I face challenges in assessing clients from cultures where mental health issues are stigmatized" (Stigmatization), the mean score was 2.374, indicating that participants slightly disagree with the statement. The standard error of the mean was 0.062, and the 95% confidence interval ranged from 2.252 to 2.495, suggesting that the true population mean likely falls within this range. The standard deviation of 1.136 reflects moderate variability in the responses. The Shapiro–Wilk *P*-value of <0.001 indicates that the data are not normally distributed, suggesting that the responses are skewed and may not follow a standard bell curve.

For "Cultural biases in existing assessment tools make it difficult to assess clients accurately from diverse backgrounds" (Cultural bias), the mean score was 2.491, indicating agreement with the statement. The standard error of the mean was 0.064, and the 95% confidence interval ranged from 2.365 to 2.617. The standard deviation was 1.179, showing moderate variability in responses. The Shapiro–Wilk *P*-value of <0.001 suggests that the data are not normally distributed, indicating significant skewness in responses. For "Language differences significantly affect the reliability of my assessments" (Language differences), the mean score was 2.526, indicating agreement. The 95% confidence interval ranged from 2.404 to 2.649, with the standard deviation being 1.148, reflecting a moderate spread in responses. As with the previous items, the Shapiro–Wilk *P*-value of <0.001 confirms that the data are not normally distributed, meaning the distribution of responses deviates from a standard normal distribution.

For the statement "I struggle with adapting traditional assessment tools to fit the cultural context of my clients" (Difficulty adapting traditional assessment tools), the mean score was 2.521, showing agreement. The standard error of the mean was 0.062, and the 95% confidence interval ranged from 2.399 to 2.642. The standard deviation was 1.138, indicating moderate variability in the responses. The Shapiro–Wilk *P*-value of <0.001 suggests that the data are not normally distributed, indicating a skew in how participants perceive this challenge.

Table 5.5 presents descriptive statistics for the recommendations regarding culturally sensitive assessment practices, based on four statements about the need for ongoing training, new tools, collaboration, and further research. The data includes mean scores,

Table 5.4: Descriptive statistics showing challenges in multicultural assessment.

			95% confidence interval mean				
	Mean	Std. error of mean	Upper	Lower	Std. deviation	Shapiro–Wilk	*P*-value of Shapiro–Wilk
Stigmatization	2.374	0.062	2.495	2.252	1.136	0.847	<0.001
Cultural bias	2.491	0.064	2.617	2.365	1.179	0.836	<0.001
Language differences	2.526	0.062	2.649	2.404	1.148	0.847	<0.001
Difficulty adapting traditional assessment tools	2.521	0.062	2.642	2.399	1.138	0.850	<0.001

Table 5.5: Descriptive statistics showing recommendations for culturally sensitive assessment practices.

	Mean	Std. error of mean	95% confidence interval mean		Std. deviation	Shapiro–Wilk	*P*-value of Shapiro–Wilk
			Upper	Lower			
Ongoing cultural sensitivity training	2.544	0.060	2.662	2.426	1.108	0.858	<0.001
Development of new tools	2.526	0.058	2.641	2.412	1.076	0.865	<0.001
Collaboration with cultural consultants	2.488	0.062	2.610	2.367	1.141	0.849	<0.001
More research into culturally inclusive assessment	2.550	0.059	2.666	2.434	1.086	0.863	<0.001

standard error of the mean, 95% confidence intervals, standard deviation, and Shapiro–Wilk test results.

For the statement "I believe that ongoing cultural sensitivity training should be a standard part of professional development for all counselors and psychotherapists" (Ongoing cultural sensitivity training), the mean score was 2.544, indicating general agreement with the statement. The standard error of the mean was 0.060, and the 95% confidence interval ranged from 2.426 to 2.662, showing that the true population mean is likely within this range. The standard deviation was 1.108, reflecting moderate variability in responses. The Shapiro–Wilk P-value of <0.001 indicates that the data are not normally distributed, suggesting a skew in responses, with practitioners possibly holding differing views on the importance of cultural sensitivity training.

For the statement "I think new, culturally valid assessment tools need to be developed to better meet the needs of clients from diverse backgrounds" (Development of new tools), the mean score was 2.526, indicating agreement. The 95% confidence interval ranged from 2.412 to 2.641, and the standard deviation was 1.076, indicating variability in responses. The Shapiro–Wilk P-value of <0.001 suggests non-normality, indicating diverse opinions among participants regarding the need for new culturally valid tools.

For the statement "I believe that collaboration with cultural consultants and community leaders is essential to improve the relevance of assessments" (Collaboration with cultural consultants), the mean score was 2.488, showing agreement with the statement. The standard error of the mean was 0.062, and the 95% confidence interval ranged from 2.367 to 2.610. The standard deviation of 1.141 reflects moderate variability in responses. The Shapiro–Wilk P-value of <0.001 again indicates that the data are not normally distributed, suggesting that while collaboration is generally agreed upon, the strength of agreement varies across participants.

For the statement "More research into culturally inclusive assessment practices is needed to ensure we are using effective and relevant tools in diverse settings" (More research into culturally inclusive assessment), the mean score was 2.550, indicating strong agreement with the statement. The 95% confidence interval ranged from 2.434 to 2.666, and the standard deviation was 1.086, showing moderate variability in responses. The Shapiro–Wilk P-value of <0.001 suggests that the data are not normally distributed, confirming a skewed distribution where some practitioners feel more strongly about the need for research than others.

Qualitative results

Theme 1: Common assessment tools used in multicultural counselling and psychotherapy

Both counselors and psychologists in the study reported using a variety of assessment tools, although the specific tools they employed varied slightly depending on their professional backgrounds. Despite these differences, there was a shared recognition of the importance of using effective, culturally sensitive tools in multicultural counselling and psychotherapy. Participants highlighted the usefulness of a range of assessment methods but also acknowledged the challenges associated with ensuring these tools accurately reflect the cultural contexts of their clients. Counselors commonly used self-report questionnaires, which are designed to allow clients to report on their own emotional and psychological states. Some of the tools most frequently mentioned included the Beck Depression Inventory and the Generalized Anxiety Disorder Scale.

One counselor explained:

> I primarily use the Beck Depression Inventory because it's straightforward and can be applied to a wide range of clients. However, the language used in these self-report tools doesn't always reflect the nuances of different cultural expressions of distress.

In addition to self-report tools, structured interviews were also commonly used by counselors. These interviews often follow a predefined set of questions and are designed to gather consistent information across clients.

One counselor shared:

> Structured interviews help me maintain consistency across cases. I make sure to adapt some of the phrasing in these interviews to make them more relatable to clients from various backgrounds. It's important not just to stick to the script but also to engage in cultural empathy.

Another method frequently employed by counselors was the cultural formulation method, which involves understanding a client's cultural background and how this influences their mental health. This approach was highlighted by a counselor, who stated:

> Cultural formulation is essential for me. It helps to understand the client not only as an individual but also within their cultural context. This method has been invaluable when working with clients from diverse ethnic backgrounds because it allows me to understand the significance of their symptoms in the light of their cultural beliefs and practices.

On the other hand, psychologists in the study frequently used standardized tests such as personality inventories and projective tests. One

Psychologist mentioned:

> I typically use the MMPI-2, which is a standard tool for assessing personality traits and psychopathology. But I do find that it sometimes fails to account for cultural differences in how individuals express their emotions or stress. So, I make adaptations where necessary to make it more culturally relevant.

Psychologists also commonly used projective tests, such as the Rorschach inkblot test, to assess clients' perceptions and emotional functioning. One psychologist explained:

> I find the Rorschach test useful, especially with clients from different cultural backgrounds. It's flexible and can reveal a lot about a person's worldview. However, interpreting the results can be tricky because cultural influences can shape how people perceive these abstract images. I always make sure to contextualize the responses within the client's cultural framework.

A common thread between both groups of professionals was the acknowledgment of the limitations of these tools when applied in multicultural settings. While these tools were seen as valuable for assessment, both counselors and psychologists highlighted the challenges in ensuring that the tools accurately reflect the experiences and expressions of clients from diverse cultural backgrounds. One psychologist remarked:

> Although the tools we use are validated and reliable, they are not always culturally sensitive. For instance, certain symptoms of depression may manifest differently in different cultures, and the tools might not always capture that difference.

Similarly, a counselor shared:

> The tools themselves are good for measuring general symptoms, but when I work with clients from different cultural backgrounds, I sometimes feel like I'm not getting the full picture. For example, some clients may express distress through somatic complaints rather than verbalizing emotional pain, and these tools don't always account for that.

Despite these challenges, both counselors and psychologists acknowledged the usefulness of the assessment tools they used, but emphasized the need for cultural adaptation and a deeper understanding of the client's cultural context in order to improve the accuracy and relevance of the diagnostic process.

A counselor summed up:

> It's not just about using the tools. It's about using them in a way that respects and acknowledges the cultural background of the client. I find myself constantly adapting these tools to make sure I'm truly capturing the client's experience.

On the whole, while both counselors and psychologists reported using a variety of assessment tools, including self-report questionnaires, structured interviews, personality inventories, and projective tests, they all emphasized the necessity of adapting these tools to the cultural context of the clients they served. These adaptations, as mentioned by many participants, were critical to ensuring that the tools accurately captured the experiences and symptoms of clients from diverse cultural backgrounds.

Theme 2: Challenges in conducting culturally sensitive assessments

The participants in this study identified several significant challenges when conducting culturally sensitive assessments. These challenges highlighted the complexities of providing effective care in multicultural counselling and psychotherapy settings and underscored the need for greater cultural awareness and adaptation in assessment practices. The following key challenges emerged from the interviews and focus group discussions:

One of the most frequently cited challenges by both counselors and psychologists was language barriers. Several participants explained how language differences between the client and the assessment tool posed significant hurdles in accurately assessing clients' emotional and psychological states.

A counselor explained:

> Language can be a real barrier. Many of my clients speak languages that aren't represented in the assessment tools, so I often find myself in a position where the tool just doesn't capture the nuance of what the client is going through. This leads to misunderstandings or misinterpretation of responses.

A psychologist elaborated further:

> When a client doesn't speak the same language as the assessment tool, it's difficult to ensure the tool measures what it's supposed to. Even with translators, some concepts just don't translate well. Clients might not be able to express themselves accurately, and it affects the validity of the assessment.

Another major challenge highlighted by participants was the cultural bias in tools. Many discussed how standardized psychological tests, such as personality inventories and intelligence tests, often fail to account for cultural differences, leading to misdiagnosis or incomplete assessments.

A counselor noted:

> Standardized tools are helpful, but they are built on assumptions that might not apply across cultures. For example, the way depression is measured in Western tools might not reflect how someone from a different cultural background expresses or experiences depression. This could easily lead to misdiagnosis.

A psychologist agreed, stating:

> The issue with using standardized tests like the MMPI-2 is that they were developed in a specific cultural context. When these tools are used with clients from different

> backgrounds, they may not capture cultural nuances, potentially misrepresenting the client's psychological condition.

In addition to cultural bias in tools, participants also expressed concerns about the lack of training in cultural sensitivity. Many counselors and psychologists reported receiving some form of cultural competence training, but they felt it was often insufficient or not ongoing.

One counselor remarked:

> I've had some cultural competence training, but it was just a one-off seminar. It's not enough. We need more ongoing training, more hands-on workshops, and better integration of cultural sensitivity into our professional development. Without that, we're not fully equipped to understand or meet the needs of culturally diverse clients.

A psychologist shared a similar perspective:

> Cultural sensitivity training should be an integral part of our continuing education. It's not enough to have one session and think that's sufficient. Our understanding of cultural issues evolves, and so should our training. If we don't keep up, we risk missing important aspects of our clients' experiences.

Finally, stigma and misunderstanding of mental health in certain cultural groups was another challenge frequently mentioned by participants. In some cultures, mental health issues are still heavily stigmatized, which can make it difficult for clients to openly engage in assessments or even admit to psychological distress.

A counselor explained:

> Some of my clients come from communities where mental health is seen as a taboo subject. They may be reluctant to open up, even in assessments, because admitting to emotional or psychological struggles might be seen as a weakness or something shameful.

Another counselor shared a similar sentiment:

> When clients come from backgrounds where mental health issues are heavily stigmatized, they often won't fully engage in the process. They may hold back during assessments, not wanting to disclose certain symptoms, which makes it difficult to get an accurate diagnosis.

These challenges, which range from language barriers and cultural biases in assessment tools to lack of training and stigma surrounding mental health, highlight the significant obstacles that counselors and psychologists face when working with culturally diverse clients. The participants' insights underscore the need for cultural adaptation of assessment tools, more comprehensive and ongoing cultural competence training, and a greater understanding of the role of cultural stigma in mental health care.

Theme 3: Strategies for ensuring cultural sensitivity

Participants highlighted several strategies they had employed to overcome the challenges of conducting culturally sensitive assessments and ensure their practices were appropriately tailored to the diverse needs of their clients. These strategies were vital in fostering a more inclusive and effective therapeutic environment, where the cultural backgrounds of clients were acknowledged and respected. The strategies discussed included the cultural adaptation of tools, building rapport and trust, using culturally relevant case studies, and collaborating with culturally competent practitioners.

One of the most common strategies mentioned by both counselors and psychologists was the cultural adaptation of tools. Many participants explained how they modified existing assessment tools to better suit the cultural contexts of their clients. This included translating tools into local languages, adjusting the language to reflect local cultural nuances, and revising questions to better align with the cultural values and norms of the client population. A psychologist shared:

> I often work with local translators and cultural consultants when adapting the MMPI-2 for use with diverse populations. It's important to ensure that the language is not just translated but culturally relevant, so the client feels that the tool truly reflects their experiences.

Another psychologist added:

> Some standardized assessments just don't fit well with certain cultural groups. For example, I've had to modify certain questions in psychological inventories to make sure that the way we frame things resonates with how clients from different backgrounds view mental health.

In addition to tool adaptation, both counselors and psychologists emphasized the importance of building rapport and trust with clients from diverse cultural backgrounds. Establishing a strong, trusting relationship was seen as essential in ensuring that clients felt comfortable enough to engage openly during assessments. Many participants noted that this was especially crucial for clients who had been previously distrustful of mental health services. One counselor explained:

> Building trust is key. If the client doesn't trust you, they won't fully open up, and you won't get an accurate picture of their needs. With clients from certain cultural backgrounds, it's particularly important to take time to establish a relationship before diving into any assessments.

A psychologist shared a similar sentiment:

> For many of my clients, mental health care is not something they've had positive experiences with in the past. I focus on building a relationship where they feel safe and

> understood, so they're more likely to engage in the assessment process without fear of judgment.

Another strategy that emerged in the data was the use of culturally relevant case studies and narratives. Some counselors explained how they incorporated local cultural stories or examples into their assessment processes to help clients relate better to the questions or scenarios presented during the assessment.

One counselor noted:

> I use culturally relevant case studies that resonate with the client's own experiences. For example, I might incorporate local folklore or community issues into the conversation, which helps the client see that the tools are not foreign or disconnected from their life.

Another counselor added:

> For clients from rural areas or specific ethnic groups, I sometimes use stories or examples from their culture. This not only makes the assessment feel more relevant but also helps the client understand that I'm genuinely interested in their worldview and experiences.

Finally, several practitioners mentioned the importance of collaborating with culturally competent practitioners to improve their assessment practices. Some reported seeking guidance from colleagues who had specific expertise in cultural competence, while others attended workshops or received additional training on culturally sensitive assessment methods. One psychologist stated:

> I've sought out colleagues who have more experience working with diverse populations. I'm always learning from them. The more you collaborate and discuss your cases with others who are culturally competent, the better equipped you are to handle sensitive situations.

A counselor also emphasized the value of training:

> I've attended workshops on culturally competent assessment methods, which have been really helpful. The more exposure I get to culturally inclusive practices, the better I am at addressing the needs of my clients, especially when working with immigrant populations.

These strategies reflect a strong commitment to ensuring cultural sensitivity in both the assessment and diagnostic processes. The participants agreed that, while these methods required additional effort and resources, they were essential for ensuring that clients from diverse backgrounds received accurate and meaningful assessments. Through the cultural adaptation of tools, relationship-building, the use of relevant narratives, and collaboration with culturally competent peers, these practitioners were able to provide more effective and inclusive care.

Theme 4: Recommendations for integrating culturally sensitive practices

Based on the challenges and strategies shared, participants provided several insightful recommendations for integrating culturally sensitive assessment and diagnostic practices into counselling and psychotherapy. These recommendations were aimed at addressing the gaps and enhancing the effectiveness of current practices, ensuring that both clients and practitioners benefit from a more inclusive, culturally aware approach.

A unanimous recommendation from all participants was the need for ongoing cultural sensitivity training. Participants emphasized that such training should not be a one-time event but rather a continuous process embedded within professional development programmes. Several counselors and psychologists argued that training in cultural competence should be tailored to the specific cultural contexts in which practitioners work.

One counselor said:

> Cultural sensitivity training should be continuous, not just something we do once when we start our careers. It needs to be part of our ongoing professional development to ensure we keep learning and adapting to the changing cultural landscape of our clients.

A psychologist also emphasized:

> We can't just rely on the basic training we received when we first became licensed. Cultural competence is an evolving field, and we need more frequent workshops or courses to stay up to date with the latest research and best practices.

Participants also suggested the development of culturally valid assessment tools. They expressed a clear need for new tools that better reflect the unique experiences and perspectives of clients from diverse cultural backgrounds.

As one counselor noted:

> We need to develop tools that actually reflect the lived experiences of the clients we serve, not just the experiences of a single demographic group. A one-size-fits-all approach doesn't work in multicultural contexts. We need culturally specific tools that are validated for different populations.

A psychologist agreed, stating:

> The tools we currently have are largely based on Western psychological frameworks. If we're serious about multicultural counselling, we need tools that take into account cultural differences in how people express emotions, perceive symptoms, and seek help.

Another critical recommendation was increased collaboration with community leaders. Participants argued that working closely with leaders from the communities they serve could provide valuable insights into cultural values and beliefs that influence clients' responses during assessments.

One participant explained:

> By collaborating with community leaders or cultural consultants, we can gain a deeper understanding of the cultural context in which our clients are living. This helps to make the assessment process more relevant and acceptable to them, which ultimately leads to more accurate diagnoses.

A counselor further emphasized:

> Community leaders play a key role in shaping how people view mental health. If we can collaborate with them, we can ensure that the assessments are culturally grounded and resonate with the values of the community, making it easier for clients to engage in the process.

Finally, many participants highlighted the need for increased research into culturally inclusive practices. They argued that more evidence-based research was necessary to identify best practices and strategies for integrating cultural sensitivity into the diagnostic process. A psychologist explained:

> Research is vital. We need more studies on how to make our assessment practices truly inclusive. This research can help us understand what works in different cultural settings and give us practical solutions to apply in our work.

A counselor shared a similar viewpoint:

> We also need research that explores the outcomes of using culturally adapted tools compared to standard tools. Understanding the effectiveness of these approaches will be crucial for advancing cultural competence in our field.

On the whole, participants in this study provided several important recommendations for integrating culturally sensitive practices into counselling and psychotherapy. These included ongoing cultural sensitivity training, the development of culturally valid assessment tools, collaboration with community leaders, and increased research into inclusive practices. These recommendations reflect a strong desire for more practical, evidence-based approaches that can be implemented to address the unique needs of clients from diverse cultural backgrounds.

Case studies

Case Study 1: In City A, a 38-year-old male client, newly relocated from a rural village to the city, presented with symptoms of sadness, fatigue, and a lack of motivation, but did not directly identify these feelings as depression. The client, having recently moved to Enugu for work, appeared withdrawn and expressed emotional exhaustion, but did not frame his issues in terms of mental illness. Initially, he described feeling "tired" and disconnected from his life in the city but rejected the notion that his struggles could be depression.

Understanding that in many rural Nigerian communities, emotional struggles are often not openly discussed, and mental health issues are frequently stigmatized, the counselor recognized the need to use a more culturally sensitive approach. In rural Nigerian settings, particularly within the Igbo community, emotional vulnerability is often seen as a weakness, especially among men, and any admission of mental health issues is frequently avoided. This cultural context made it difficult for the client to openly express his emotions or see his experiences as indicative of a mental health condition.

To address these barriers, the counselor utilized the Cultural Formulation Interview (CFI), a tool designed to assess a client's cultural identity, their explanatory models of illness, and how these influence their experience of mental health symptoms. The CFI explores cultural factors such as family dynamics, spiritual beliefs, and community expectations, which are essential to understanding how individuals from diverse backgrounds perceive and manage mental health. This approach allowed the counselor to explore not just the client's symptoms, but also his cultural worldview and the specific challenges he faced as a migrant to the city.

However, several challenges arose during the use of the CFI. The first challenge was the client's reluctance to express his emotions. In the client's community, men are often taught to suppress vulnerability, and emotional struggles are seen as something that should be dealt with privately, rather than discussed with others. This cultural norm created a barrier to the client fully articulating his feelings, especially in the context of a mental health assessment. The second challenge was the language and communication style. Although the client was fluent in the dominant language spoken in Enugu, he felt more comfortable speaking in his native dialect when discussing personal matters. The third challenge was the client's reluctance to label his emotional struggles as depression, as mental health issues were often not spoken about in clinical terms in his rural community.

To overcome these challenges, the counselor adapted her approach. First, she took the time to build trust and rapport with the client. Understanding the cultural importance of patience and understanding, she allowed the client to speak about his daily life, work, and the challenges of adapting to the city. This helped him feel more comfortable before delving into deeper emotional topics. The counselor also used culturally relevant metaphors and expressions to help the client feel more at ease. When discussing emotional struggles, she avoided clinical terms like "depression" and instead referred to the client's feelings as "emotional exhaustion" or "disconnection," terms that were more relatable to him.

Another strategy employed was to allow the client to speak in his native dialect when necessary. This provided him with the opportunity to express his feelings more comfortably and accurately, as some cultural nuances and emotions might not have been captured adequately in the city's dominant language. Lastly, the counselor reframed the concept of depression in a way that was culturally sensitive. Instead of directly using the term "depression," which the client was hesitant to embrace, the counselor explained that emotional exhaustion and feelings of isolation are common reactions for individuals who experience significant life transitions, such as migration. By validating the client's struggles and normalizing them within his cultural context, the counselor helped him accept that his emotional experiences were legitimate and worthy of attention.

Through the use of the Cultural Formulation Interview, the counselor was able to identify cultural stressors related to migration, including the loss of social support, the pressure of adapting to an urban environment, and the dislocation from familiar cultural practices. By addressing these factors and providing the client with a safe space to open up, the counselor was able to make a more accurate diagnosis of depression, which took into account both the client's emotional symptoms and the cultural context that shaped his experience. This approach not only led to a more accurate diagnosis but also allowed the client to feel understood, respected, and supported.

Case Study 2: A psychologist in City B worked with a 32-year-old woman who had recently immigrated from Portugal to Nigeria. The client presented with significant symptoms of anxiety, including excessive worrying, restlessness, and sleep disturbances, but struggled to express herself clearly due to language barriers. She was fluent in limited English, which made it difficult for her to articulate her feelings and symptoms in a clinical setting where unfamiliar terminology and expressions were used. This language gap created a challenge for the psychologist in fully understanding the extent of the client's anxiety and providing an accurate diagnosis.

The psychologist recognized that language was a major barrier to communication, and without addressing it, an accurate diagnosis would be challenging. Additionally, the psychologist considered that the client's experience as an immigrant could be contributing to her anxiety. Acculturation stress, which refers to the anxiety related to adapting to a new cultural environment, could be a significant factor in the client's symptoms. The psychologist suspected that concerns like navigating a new country, experiencing social isolation, and adjusting to unfamiliar social norms were affecting the client's mental health.

To overcome these challenges, the psychologist collaborated with a bilingual translator who was fluent in both Portuguese and English. With the translator's assistance, the client was able to express herself more clearly in her native language, making it easier for the psychologist to understand her symptoms and gain deeper insight into her emotional state.

This approach alleviated the pressure of language limitations, enabling the client to articulate her concerns with greater clarity.

Furthermore, the psychologist used a culturally adapted version of the Generalized Anxiety Disorder Scale (GAD-7), a widely used tool to assess anxiety symptoms. The adaptation involved rewording certain questions to better reflect the client's immigrant experience and the specific stressors she faced in adjusting to life in Nigeria. For example, questions about excessive worrying were reframed to include concerns related to the stress of adapting to a new culture and the anxiety of language barriers. This adaptation ensured that the client's unique experiences were captured in the assessment, providing a more accurate measure of her anxiety.

With the help of the translator and the culturally adapted GAD-7, the client was able to respond more clearly to the assessment. The psychologist was able to diagnose Generalized Anxiety Disorder (GAD) while also considering the cultural and linguistic factors that played a role in the client's symptoms. This enabled the psychologist to provide a more holistic understanding of the client's anxiety, taking into account both the traditional symptoms of the disorder and the cultural stressors linked to her experience as an immigrant.

While there were several challenges, including language barriers and the cultural context that shaped the client's experience, these were addressed through the use of a bilingual translator and the culturally adapted assessment tool. By incorporating cultural sensitivity into the diagnostic process, the psychologist was able to arrive at a more accurate diagnosis, which included acculturation stress as a significant factor contributing to the client's anxiety.

The treatment plan that followed included cognitive-behavioral therapy (CBT) to address the client's anxiety and stress management techniques to help her cope with the cultural adjustment process. The psychologist also recommended that the client engage in community support groups to reduce the social isolation often experienced by immigrants, thereby helping her integrate into her new environment more comfortably.

Case Study 3: In City C, a 23-year-old female client from a conservative Muslim family presented with symptoms of post-traumatic stress disorder (PTSD) following a violent robbery she had experienced a few months prior. The client displayed classic signs of trauma, such as hypervigilance, flashbacks, and difficulty sleeping, but she was reluctant to openly discuss her emotional struggles. The client feared that acknowledging her mental health issues would lead to negative judgment from her family and community, as mental health challenges are heavily stigmatized in her cultural and religious context. Within her family and community, emotional struggles, especially those related to mental health, are often viewed as signs of weakness, and she worried that seeking help could bring shame to her and her family.

The counselor recognized the cultural challenge presented by the stigma surrounding mental health within the client's conservative Muslim family. In this cultural context, mental health issues were often either ignored or attributed to moral or spiritual failings rather than understood as legitimate medical concerns. Given this, the counselor had to navigate the cultural complexities surrounding mental health, ensuring the client felt understood and supported while respecting her values and social context.

To address this, the counselor adapted her approach to assessment and diagnosis by using a culturally sensitive questionnaire. Rather than directly addressing mental health terms like "PTSD" or "trauma," which could have triggered shame or fear of being stigmatized, the counselor reframed the questions to focus on the client's emotional and physical symptoms without labeling them. This approach allowed the client to discuss her experiences in a way that felt more culturally acceptable, without feeling like she was admitting to a mental illness.

For example, rather than asking the client whether she experienced symptoms of PTSD, the counselor framed questions around the client's experiences of stress, fear, and the physical effects of trauma, such as sleep disturbances and difficulty concentrating. This indirect approach helped the client to engage in the process without feeling judged. Over several sessions, the counselor helped the client articulate her trauma while respecting her cultural values and social context. The result was a diagnosis of PTSD that took into account the cultural stigma and the client's hesitance to directly label her emotional struggles as mental health issues.

Through this culturally sensitive approach, the counselor was able to provide a diagnosis that not only acknowledged the client's symptoms but also recognized the cultural barriers that influenced her willingness to seek help. The treatment plan included trauma-focused therapy, but with a respect for the client's cultural and familial context, ensuring that the therapeutic process was both effective and culturally appropriate.

Case Study 4: In City D, a psychologist was tasked with diagnosing a 6-year-old child who exhibited delays in speech and language development. The child's parents were concerned about their child's ability to communicate, as the child was not speaking as much as other children their age. However, the symptoms did not align with typical Western diagnostic criteria for developmental delays. The parents were unsure if the delay was a cause for concern, especially since speech development in children varies greatly depending on cultural norms, family expectations, and even regional dialects.

The psychologist quickly recognized that the standard diagnostic tools, often based on Western models, might not be appropriate for assessing a child from a rural Sokoto community. These tools, designed around Western developmental milestones and communication styles, did not fully account for the cultural differences in child-rearing practices or the local language used in this region. In Sokoto, children were often raised in close-knit family settings where communication with extended family and community members also plays a vital role in their early socialization. Children were not necessarily expected to speak early in the same manner as their peers in urban settings. Instead, family and community interaction might be more non-verbal or culturally nuanced, which could affect language development differently from what Western diagnostic criteria would anticipate.

To ensure an accurate and culturally sensitive assessment, the psychologist decided to use a locally developed developmental assessment tool, designed specifically for the cultural practices, languages, and social interactions of Sokoto's rural communities. The tool had been tailored to reflect the family communication styles, local linguistic variations, and child-rearing practices common in the area. It included questions and observations based on how children in Sokoto typically engage with family members, elders, and peers. The tool also allowed the psychologist to assess the child's language development in the context of the community's communicative practices, rather than relying solely on rigid developmental norms.

One of the challenges in using the locally developed tool was ensuring that the assessment questions were culturally relevant and understandable for the parents, as many families in rural Sokoto may have limited literacy or formal education. To address this, the psychologist worked closely with the parents, explaining each question and using examples from everyday life to help them understand the assessment. For instance, instead of asking how many words the child could speak, the tool explored the child's interactions during play, conversations with elders, and their use of local expressions. This approach helped ensure that the parents felt comfortable with the process and that the tool captured a broader, more contextually appropriate view of the child's communication abilities.

The psychologist also faced the challenge of distinguishing between a developmental delay and cultural differences in communication. In Sokoto, children often learn through indirect communication or by listening to elders, rather than engaging in direct verbal exchanges, which might be expected in more urban or Western contexts. By using the culturally sensitive tool, the psychologist was able to see that the child's speech delay was not necessarily indicative of a developmental disorder, but rather a reflection of the different modes of communication valued in the community.

Ultimately, the use of the locally developed developmental assessment tool allowed the psychologist to assess the child's development in a manner that was more aligned with the cultural and social context of the family. After completing the assessment, the psychologist diagnosed the child with a developmental delay but recommended early intervention strategies that aligned with the family's cultural practices. These included introducing more structured language-learning opportunities at home, encouraging interaction with extended family members, and incorporating traditional storytelling practices, which are highly valued in the community, as a way to promote language development.

The recommendations were not only grounded in psychological theory but also reflected the family's cultural understanding and practices, which made the intervention more acceptable and likely to be successful. The family felt empowered by the approach, as it did not dismiss their values or methods of communication but instead integrated them into the developmental plan.

This case demonstrates the importance of using culturally relevant diagnostic tools that consider local communication styles, language variations, and family dynamics. By integrating cultural context into the assessment process, the psychologist was able to provide a more accurate diagnosis and develop an intervention plan that respected the family's practices, while also ensuring that the child received the necessary support for their developmental needs.

Case Study 5: In City E, a psychologist working with a group of Nigerian immigrants from Southeast Asia encountered significant challenges while using the Minnesota Multiphasic Personality Inventory (MMPI-2), a widely used psychological tool for assessing personality traits and psychopathology. While the MMPI-2 is a standard tool in Western psychological practice, the psychologist quickly recognized that it did not fully account for the cultural differences in values, social behavior, and emotional expression present in both the Nigerian and Southeast Asian immigrant populations. The tool's original framework, rooted in Western ideas of individualism and personal achievement, was not applicable to the collectivist cultures of these communities, where family-oriented values and communal success are prioritized over personal accomplishments.

The psychologist was particularly concerned about how this disconnect could affect the accuracy of the assessment. In these immigrant communities, family dynamics and social behavior are deeply intertwined with cultural expectations, and individual traits such as assertiveness or self-promotion may not be viewed in the same way as they are in more individualistic societies. Additionally, emotional expression in these cultures often follows different norms, with emotional restraint and respect for social hierarchy taking precedence over open self-expression, which could lead to misinterpretation of the responses on the MMPI-2 if not adapted accordingly.

To overcome these challenges, the psychologist decided to work with cultural consultants who were familiar with both the Southeast Asian immigrant communities and Nigerian cultural practices. Together, they undertook a process of adapting the MMPI-2 to make it more culturally relevant. The adaptation focused on modifying key sections of the inventory, particularly those related to family dynamics, emotional expression, and social behavior. For example, questions about individualism and personal achievement, which are commonly valued in Western contexts, were reworded to emphasize collectivist values such as family cohesion, interdependence, and respect for elders. Questions that implied assertiveness or self-promotion were reframed to focus on group harmony, family support, and communal success. Similarly, questions about emotional expression were adapted to reflect the more restrained approach often seen in Southeast Asian and Nigerian communities, where individuals may downplay emotional distress in public to maintain social harmony.

In addition to the rewording of specific questions, the adaptation process also involved validating the tool's relevance within the cultural contexts of both the Nigerian immigrants and the Southeast Asian community. This was done by seeking feedback from community leaders and participants, ensuring that the modified MMPI-2 did not conflict with or misunderstand cultural norms. As part of the validation process, the psychologist conducted pilot tests of the adapted tool with a small group of immigrants to ensure that the revisions were effective in capturing the relevant psychological traits without bias or misinterpretation.

Once the culturally adapted version of the MMPI-2 was finalized, the psychologist administered it to the group of Nigerian immigrants. The adaptation allowed for a more accurate assessment of their psychological well-being, as it acknowledged the cultural values and expectations that influenced their emotional and social behaviors. By making the assessment process more relatable and respectful of the participants' cultural backgrounds, the psychologist was able to gather more meaningful data that contributed to a better understanding of the group's mental health needs.

This culturally adapted MMPI-2 was instrumental in diagnosing issues such as anxiety, depression, and adjustment disorders, which were prevalent among the immigrants, especially those struggling with the stresses of acculturation and migration. The adaptation process not only led to more accurate diagnoses but also helped the psychologist develop a treatment plan that was more attuned to the specific cultural and emotional needs of the group. The treatment plan incorporated group therapy, family counselling, and stress management techniques, all of which respected the cultural importance of family and community support systems.

One of the key challenges in adapting the MMPI-2 was ensuring that the modified questions accurately captured the nuances of cultural expressions of mental health without distorting the underlying psychological constructs. For example, in certain Southeast Asian cultures, emotional distress might manifest as physical complaints or behavioral withdrawal rather than verbalizing feelings of sadness or anxiety. The cultural consultants helped the psychologist navigate these subtleties, ensuring that the revised tool could assess psychological distress in a way that was both culturally appropriate and clinically effective.

On the whole, this case study underscores the importance of cultural adaptation in psychological assessments, especially when working with immigrant populations or individuals from non-Western cultures. By modifying the MMPI-2 to reflect the cultural values and practices of both Nigerian immigrants and Southeast Asian clients, the psychologist was able to provide a more accurate and culturally sensitive assessment. This led to better diagnosis, more effective treatment planning, and ultimately improved mental health outcomes for the clients. The case highlights how cultural sensitivity is essential not only for accurate assessments but also for building trust and rapport with clients from diverse backgrounds.

Case Study 6: In City F, a counselor worked with a 30-year-old woman from a local Efik-speaking community who had been experiencing symptoms of depression, including persistent sadness and lack of interest in daily activities. The client had been feeling disconnected from her family and had a diminished capacity to enjoy activities that she once found fulfilling. However, she was also actively seeking treatment from a traditional healer, which created a barrier to her fully engaging with the therapy process. The client expressed hesitation about fully committing to therapy because of her deep belief in the healing power of traditional practices, which were highly respected within her community.

The counselor, recognizing the cultural significance of traditional healing practices, decided to take a culturally sensitive approach. Understanding that traditional healing was an integral part of the client's worldview, the counselor initiated a cultural assessment to understand the client's beliefs surrounding both mental health and healing. The counselor used open-ended questions to explore the client's views on mental health, particularly her perceptions of Western therapy and the role of traditional healing. The aim was to understand how the client viewed these two approaches and whether she felt comfortable combining them.

The counselor also explored the client's relationship with the traditional healer, who had been part of her support system. Through these discussions, the counselor was able to recognize that the client viewed traditional healing and Western therapy not as competing or contradictory, but as potentially complementary. The counselor respected the client's cultural beliefs and incorporated both traditional healing practices and modern psychological therapies into the treatment plan. This approach allowed for a holistic model of care, which integrated talk therapy with support from the traditional healer, fostering a sense of respect and inclusivity for the client's cultural context.

By validating the client's cultural beliefs, the counselor created a therapeutic environment where the client felt understood and respected, which led to greater engagement in therapy. The client was more open to discussing her symptoms and began to participate actively in the therapy sessions. This integrated approach not only helped the client feel more comfortable but also provided a more effective treatment strategy, addressing her emotional well-being through both culturally familiar and psychologically supported methods.

Case Study 7: A psychologist in City G was working with a 40-year-old male client from a Nigerian Indigenous community who reported symptoms of schizophrenia, including hearing voices and experiencing paranoia. These symptoms had been ongoing for some time, and the client's family had been deeply concerned. However, the client did not interpret these symptoms in the same way as the psychologist might. Instead of viewing these experiences as signs of mental illness, the client believed they were spiritual experiences, linked to ancestral communication and messages from the spirit world.

The psychologist, aware of the prevalence of spiritual interpretations of mental health within indigenous communities, approached the assessment process with cultural sensitivity. The psychologist recognized that the client's perception of his symptoms was deeply rooted in his belief system and that disregarding this perspective could hinder the therapeutic process. To ensure an accurate diagnosis while respecting the client's belief system, the psychologist used culturally relevant assessment tools that incorporated the client's worldview. This involved combining interviews with culturally adapted psychological tests designed to assess both mental health symptoms and the client's spiritual beliefs.

The assessment allowed the psychologist to gain deeper insights into the client's experiences, recognizing that the client's understanding of his symptoms was tied to his cultural beliefs. By acknowledging the client's spiritual perspective, the psychologist was able to make an accurate diagnosis of schizophrenia while also respecting the client's spiritual worldview. The treatment plan was developed with input from both psychiatric and cultural counselling, creating a balanced approach that addressed the client's mental health through modern psychiatric methods while integrating the client's spiritual beliefs. The client was referred for medication to help manage the symptoms of schizophrenia, while cultural counselling was also offered to help the client and his family understand and accept both psychological and spiritual perspectives on the condition.

Case Study 8: In City H, a psychotherapist worked with a 16-year-old girl who had been experiencing symptoms of anxiety and depression following her move from a rural area to the city. The transition had been difficult for the client, as she struggled to adjust to the faster-paced, unfamiliar urban environment. She had lost her sense of community and connection to her family traditions, which had previously provided a strong support system. The client's family, who came from a deeply traditional background, believed that emotional distress could be caused by ancestral spirits and spiritual imbalances, which were commonly understood within their community.

Recognizing the importance of cultural context in understanding mental health, the psychotherapist decided to use a collaborative approach that incorporated both psychological therapy and the client's family beliefs. The psychotherapist engaged the family in the treatment process, using culturally sensitive assessment tools that explored family structure, the client's relationship with her community, and how spiritual beliefs influenced the client's emotional well-being. Instead of dismissing the family's beliefs, the psychotherapist integrated these into the therapeutic approach, creating a treatment plan that addressed both psychological and cultural needs.

The psychotherapist focused on helping the client understand her anxiety and depression through psychological frameworks such as cognitive-behavioral therapy (CBT), while also working with the family to explain the role of spiritual beliefs in emotional distress. This approach helped the family understand that while spiritual factors could influence the client's mental health, psychological therapy could also provide essential tools for managing her symptoms. The treatment plan included therapy to address the client's anxiety and depression, stress management techniques, and family counselling to improve the client's relationships and help her better integrate into the urban environment.

The collaborative approach led to a better understanding of the client's struggles by both the family and the therapist. It helped the family feel more comfortable with psychological treatment while still respecting their spiritual beliefs. The client felt supported, both by her family and the therapist, leading to a stronger sense of engagement in therapy and ultimately, better mental health outcomes. This case highlights the value of collaborative counselling in a multicultural context, where respecting cultural and spiritual beliefs can enhance the effectiveness of psychological interventions.

Summary of results

The study examined various assessment tools used in multicultural counselling and psychotherapy, revealing a preference for tools such as self-report questionnaires, structured interviews, and standardized psychological assessments. Participants generally agreed on the usefulness of these tools but acknowledged that they often require cultural adaptations. While tools like the Minnesota Multiphasic Personality Inventory (MMPI-2) and Rorschach inkblot test are widely used, they are primarily designed based on Western psychological frameworks, which may not fully capture cultural nuances. The Cultural Formulation Interview (CFI) was identified as an effective method to incorporate cultural context into the diagnostic process, showing the importance of integrating culturally sensitive approaches.

In terms of cultural sensitivity, participants reported mixed feelings. Some professionals felt that adjusting assessment tools to be more culturally relevant is crucial but challenging, particularly when clients speak different languages or come from backgrounds where emotional expressions differ. For instance, language barriers were a significant challenge, with some clients' distress not being captured accurately due to the mismatch between the language of the tools and the client's native language. Additionally, there was recognition of the cultural biases present in existing tools, making it difficult to assess clients from diverse cultural backgrounds fairly. However, participants emphasized the importance of cultural competence training for professionals to navigate these complexities effectively.

The study also highlighted several challenges in conducting culturally sensitive assessments. For example, many counselors and psychologists reported that clients from cultures with a strong stigma against mental health often struggled to engage fully in the assessment process. This stigma often made it difficult for clients to express their mental health struggles openly, which in turn impacted the accuracy of diagnoses. Moreover, there was a consensus that cultural bias in tools designed for Western populations often led to misdiagnosis, particularly when symptoms of mental health disorders manifest differently across cultures.

Despite these challenges, participants shared effective strategies to ensure that their practices were culturally sensitive. One key strategy was the adaptation of assessment tools, including translating tools into local languages or adjusting the language used to better reflect cultural values and norms. Many participants also emphasized the importance of building strong rapport and trust with clients from diverse backgrounds, recognizing that this relationship was essential for accurate and open communication during assessments. Furthermore, some practitioners used culturally relevant case studies and worked with cultural consultants to ensure that their assessments were more reflective of the client's cultural context.

The recommendations for improving culturally sensitive practices were unanimous: ongoing cultural sensitivity training should be a part of continuous professional development. Participants also suggested that new tools should be developed that are specifically validated for diverse cultural groups. Additionally, there was strong support for collaborating with community leaders and increasing research into culturally inclusive practices, which could help professionals better understand and address the unique needs of clients from various cultural backgrounds. Through case studies, the study illustrated how practitioners navigate cultural differences in real-world settings. For example, a counselor working with a migrant client from a rural community in Nigeria used the

Cultural Formulation Interview (CFI) to understand the client's symptoms in the context of migration stress. Similarly, a psychologist working with an immigrant client from Portugal adapted a widely used anxiety assessment tool to reflect the stress of adjusting to a new culture, ensuring a more accurate diagnosis. In another case, a counselor working with a client from an Efik-speaking community incorporated both traditional healing practices and modern psychotherapy into the treatment plan, respecting the client's cultural beliefs.

Conclusion of the chapter

In conclusion, this chapter has explored the critical importance of cultural sensitivity in assessment and diagnosis within multicultural counselling and psychotherapy. As we have seen, the use of traditional Western assessment tools in diverse cultural contexts often poses significant challenges, from language barriers to cultural biases. While tools like self-report questionnaires, structured interviews, and standardized psychological assessments are commonly employed, their application in multicultural settings requires careful adaptation to reflect the unique cultural values and practices of clients. The findings highlight that cultural competence in assessment goes beyond the mere use of specific tools; it involves understanding the intricate relationship between a client's cultural background, their worldview, and how mental health symptoms are expressed. Practitioners must adapt their approach to ensure that these cultural factors are not only acknowledged but incorporated into the diagnostic process. Tools such as the Cultural Formulation Interview (CFI) and culturally tailored versions of standardized assessments have been highlighted as vital in addressing these concerns.

Moreover, the chapter emphasizes the need for ongoing cultural sensitivity training, the development of culturally valid tools, and collaboration with community leaders and cultural consultants to ensure the relevance and accuracy of assessments. These strategies, alongside continued research into culturally inclusive practices, are essential for enhancing the effectiveness of counselling and psychotherapy practices in multicultural contexts. The case studies presented illustrate the practical application of these strategies, showing how professionals have successfully integrated cultural understanding into their therapeutic work. These real-world examples demonstrate that while challenges persist, culturally sensitive assessment practices can lead to more accurate diagnoses and better mental health outcomes for clients from diverse backgrounds.

In closing, the chapter advocates for a holistic, culturally responsive approach to assessment and diagnosis, one that recognizes the diversity of clients' experiences and respects their cultural identities. Only by embracing this approach can practitioners ensure that their work is both effective and truly inclusive, ultimately fostering a more equitable and supportive therapeutic environment for all clients.

References

Africa Polling Institute, & EpiAfrica. (2020). *Mental health in Nigeria survey.* africapolling.org.

Anjorin, O., & Hassan Wada, Y. (2022). Impact of traditional healers in the provision of mental health services in Nigeria. In *Annals of medicine and surgery* (Vol 82). https://doi.org/10.1016/j.amsu.2022.104755

Baptiste, D. A., Sue, D. W., & Sue, D. (1993). Counselling the culturally different: Theory and practice. *Family Relations, 42*(3). https://doi.org/10.2307/585569

Fiveable. (July 2024). *18.2 cross-cultural assessment and diagnosis—Abnormal psychology.*

Leong, F. T., & Lau, A. S. (2001). Barriers to providing effective mental health services to Asian Americans. *Mental Health Services Research, 3*(4). https://doi.org/10.1023/A:1013177014788

Nanji, N., & Olivier, J. (2024). Providing mental healthcare through faith-based entities in Africa: A systematic review. *Christian Journal for Global Health, 11*(1). https://doi.org/10.15566/cjgh.v11i1.795

Nigerian Embassy in Mexico. (2025). *Facts of Nigeria (multilingual and multicultural makeup of Nigeria).*

Soto, A., Smith, T. B., Griner, D., Domenech Rodríguez, M., & Bernal, G. (2018). Cultural adaptations and therapist multicultural competence: Two meta-analytic reviews. *Journal of Clinical Psychology, 74*(11). https://doi.org/10.1002/jclp.22679

Sue, S., Zane, N., Hall, G. C. N., & Berger, L. K. (2009). The case for cultural competency in psychotherapeutic interventions. In *Annual review of psychology* (Vol 60). https://doi.org/10.1146/annurev.psych.60.110707.163651

Vishwani, S.-S. (March 21, 2025). Spirituality versus psychiatry: Why many South Asians turn to religion before therapy or psychiatric medication. *Behaviour Health News.* https://behavioralhealthnews.org/spirituality-versus-psychiatry-why-many-south-asians-turn-to-religion-before-therapy-or-psychiatric-medication/

Williams, S. A., Baldeh, M., Bah, A. J., Dennis, F., Robinson, D. R., & Adeniyi, Y. C. (2025). Pathways to mental health services across local health systems in Sub-Saharan Africa: Findings from a systematic review. *PLoS One, 20*(6 June). https://doi.org/10.1371/journal.pone.0324064

Wollie, A. M., Usher, K., Rice, K., & Islam, M. S. (2025). Challenges and opportunities for integrating traditional healing approaches with biomedical care for mental illness: A scoping review from healers' perspectives. *PLoS One, 20*(6 June). https://doi.org/10.1371/journal.pone.0325353

CHAPTER 6

Treatment planning and intervention in multicultural counselling and psychotherapy

Introduction

Multicultural counselling and psychotherapy represent an evolving field that recognizes the profound influence of cultural factors on counselling, therapeutic relationships, and treatment outcomes. This approach emphasizes the need for culturally responsive strategies in treatment planning and intervention to address the diverse needs of clients across various cultural backgrounds. Globally, multicultural counselling has gained prominence as societies become increasingly diverse due to migration, globalization, and social change. The American Psychological Association (APA) has long advocated for cultural competence, with guidelines emphasizing the integration of cultural awareness, knowledge, and skills into psychotherapy (Gwyer & Hack, 2014; Sue, 1998, 2017). Recent literature underlines that the quality of the therapeutic alliance—a key predictor of successful outcomes—is significantly enhanced when therapists adapt interventions to clients' cultural contexts (Tao et al., 2015). Thus, culturally adapted treatments tend to be more effective compared to standard interventions, particularly for clients from minority groups (Arundell et al., 2021; Huey et al., 2014). Contemporary research also explores the intersectionality of identities—such as race, ethnicity, gender, and socioeconomic status—in shaping mental health needs (Budge et al., 2016). Hays (2009) proposed a 10-step framework for integrating evidence-based practices, like cognitive-behavioral therapy (CBT), with multicultural therapy, emphasizing the need for flexibility in intervention design. This global perspective is critical as it informs the adaptation of Western therapeutic models to non-Western contexts, ensuring ecological validity.

In Nigeria, a country with over 250 ethnic groups and a complex cultural landscape, multicultural counselling is both a necessity and a challenge. The mental health system in Nigeria has historically relied on large psychiatric hospitals, with limited community-based services and a shortage of trained professionals (Gureje et al., 2015). Cultural beliefs significantly shape attitudes toward mental health, often attributing psychological distress to supernatural causes such as spiritual curses or ancestral influences (Ebigbo et al., 2016). It is important to note also that Nigerians frequently perceive mental disorders as resulting from divine punishment or witchcraft, influencing help-seeking

A Pragmatic Approach to Multicultural Counselling and Psychotherapy Skills Acquisition. https://doi.org/10.1016/B978-0-443-33939-4.00002-1

behaviors and treatment preferences (Ikwuka, 2016). This cultural interpretation, deeply rooted in spiritual and supernatural beliefs, significantly impacts not only mental health treatment but also the broader perception and utilization of counselling services. For many Nigerians, life challenges such as career difficulties, relationship issues, or academic struggles are often viewed through a spiritual lens, attributing such problems to forces like divine retribution, ancestral curses, or witchcraft. As a result, individuals may seek help from spiritual leaders, traditional healers, or religious institutions rather than accessing formal counselling services. This tendency reflects a deep-seated mistrust of psychological interventions and a belief that spiritual solutions are more effective in addressing both personal and social issues. Consequently, professional counselling services may be underutilized or misunderstood, with some individuals perceiving them as less relevant or less capable of resolving problems tied to perceived supernatural causes. This dynamic underline the need for culturally sensitive counselling approaches that acknowledge and address these spiritual perspectives while promoting evidence-based psychological interventions.

Recent literature highlights efforts to bridge Western psychotherapeutic approaches with indigenous practices. Hence, counselling in Nigeria must incorporate multicultural competencies to address the nation's diversity and promote national integration. The counselling system has historically been under-resourced, with cultural beliefs often attributing psychological distress to supernatural causes like spiritual curses or witchcraft (Gureje et al., 2015). Recent studies highlight that Nigerians frequently prefer traditional healing over Western psychotherapy due to its cultural congruence, prompting calls to integrate indigenous practices with modern approaches (Jidong et al., 2021). For instance, harmony restoration therapy, an African-derived method, has been proposed to enhance treatment acceptability (Ebigbo et al., 2016). However, stigma and limited mental health literacy remain barriers, necessitating culturally personalized interventions (Abdulmalik et al., 2016).

Enugu State, located in southeastern Nigeria, exemplifies the local application of multicultural counselling within an Igbo-dominated cultural framework. The state's mental health landscape reflects broader national trends, with a reliance on traditional healers and religious institutions alongside emerging community mental health initiatives. This underscores the need for treatment planning that aligns with local worldviews rather than imposing Eurocentric models. Community-based interventions, such as those supported by the Comprehensive Mental Health Program (CMHP) in Enugu and neighboring states, have begun to address these gaps. A study on mental health awareness campaigns demonstrated that training village health workers to promote culturally sensitive mental health education increased service uptake by 15% in targeted areas. Locally, treatment planning often involves collaboration with families and community leaders, reflecting the collectivist orientation of Igbo culture (Igwe et al., 2020). Thus, culturally responsive strategies will foster counselling treatment and interventions.

Statement of the problem

Treatment planning and intervention in multicultural counselling and psychotherapy face significant challenges due to the complex interplay of cultural diversity and counselling needs across international, national (Nigeria), and local (Enugu State) contexts. Globally, the increasing diversity of populations has highlighted a gap in the application of culturally responsive therapeutic practices. While evidence suggests that culturally adapted interventions improve outcomes, many therapists lack the training or resources to effectively adapt treatments to clients' cultural identities, leading to weaker therapeutic alliances and suboptimal results (Jones-Smith, 2020). This problem is compounded by the dominance of Western therapeutic models, which may not fully resonate with non-Western populations, raising questions about their ecological validity (Bernal & Domenech Rodríguez, 2012).

In Nigeria, the challenge is intensified by a counselling system strained by limited resources and a cultural landscape where psychological distress is frequently interpreted through supernatural or spiritual lenses (Gureje et al., 2015). The preference for traditional healing over Western psychotherapy, coupled with widespread stigma and low counselling literacy, creates barriers to effective treatment planning (Abdulmalik et al., 2016). This disconnect between formal counselling services and cultural beliefs results in underutilization of psychotherapy and a lack of integration between indigenous and modern interventions, leaving many individuals without adequate care.

Locally, in Enugu State, these issues manifest within an Igbo cultural framework where somatic expressions of distress, such as "heat in the head," are prevalent but often misunderstood by practitioners trained in Western models (Ikwuka, 2016). Despite efforts like the Comprehensive Mental Health Program to enhance community-based care, the absence of culturally tailored treatment plans limits service uptake and effectiveness (Eaton et al., 2017). Furthermore, the collectivist nature of Igbo society necessitates family and community involvement in therapy, yet this is rarely incorporated into standard interventions, reducing their relevance and impact. The problem, therefore, lies in the lack of culturally congruent treatment planning and intervention strategies that bridge global best practices with Nigeria's national diversity and Enugu State's local realities. Without addressing these gaps, mental health services risk remaining inaccessible, ineffective, or misaligned with the needs of diverse populations, perpetuating disparities in care and outcomes.

Definition of treatment planning and intervention

Treatment planning in counselling and psychotherapy refers to the collaborative, structured process by which therapist and client map out a path for therapy. After an initial assessment (intake), the therapist and client identify the client's problems or challenges, prioritize them, and agree on both short- and long-term therapeutic goals. A treatment plan outlines how to reach those goals by specifying the methods to be used, the timing or frequency of sessions, and how progress will be reviewed. It becomes a "roadmap" for therapy, dynamic, adapted to the individual, and subject to revision as circumstances or treatment outcomes evolve (Polites et al., 2025).

Typically, treatment plan may include background/contextual information, a clear definition of presenting problems, agreed goals and measurable objectives, proposed therapeutic approaches or interventions, a timeline or schedule, and provisions for monitoring progress. This structure ensures clarity of purpose, shared understanding between therapist and client, and a basis for evaluating therapeutic progress. By contrast, "Intervention", denotes the concrete therapeutic actions, techniques, or methods employed to effect change according to the treatment plan. In psychotherapy, interventions can take varied forms such as talk therapy, cognitive restructuring, behavioral techniques, supportive counselling, or other evidence-based modalities, depending on the therapist's orientation and the client's needs (Farquhar et al., 2018).

Psychotherapy (or counselling) is defined broadly as a range of therapeutic approaches often "talk therapy" through which a trained mental health professional works with a client to address psychological, emotional or behavioral difficulties, aiming to improve well-being, functioning, or adjustment (Caitlin & Tyler, 2025). Thus, the treatment plan lays out the "what," "why," and "how" of therapy; the problems to address, the aims, and the proposed methods while intervention delivers the "doing"; the therapeutic work. Because treatment plans are inherently individualized and dynamic, intervention must be responsive to emerging realities, progress, and revisions in the plan (Perkinson, 2007). In professional practice, this dual structure safeguards ethical and effective care: the plan provides transparency and coherence; interventions provide substance and action. Without a sound plan, intervention risks being unfocused or inconsistent; without appropriate interventions, even the best plan remains theoretical.

My teaching experience

Treatment planning is essentially the map or guide for the therapeutic journey. Without a clear plan, therapy can become aimless, much like driving without a GPS. The purpose of treatment planning is to ensure that both the therapist and the client are aligned on the goals and steps involved in therapy.

Problem identification

The first step in treatment planning is identifying the problems that need to be addressed. These are the issues that brought the client to therapy. To make it more tangible for students, I would use a practical example like this: *"Imagine a client named James who is struggling with social anxiety. His presenting problem is that he feels anxious in social situations, which impacts his personal and professional life. This is what we will focus on first - the problem James is facing."*

In multicultural contexts, it's important to explore not just personal or psychological issues but also how cultural factors might shape the client's experience. For example, a client may face stigma or family pressure regarding seeking help, which can complicate the treatment process.

Goal setting

Once the problem is identified, setting goals is the next step. Goals should be SMART (Specific, Measurable, Achievable, Relevant, and Time-bound).

Practical Example: Let's say James' goal is: "To attend a social gathering without feeling overwhelmed by anxiety." This goal is specific, measurable (can be assessed by whether James attends a social event), and achievable within a certain timeframe.

In the classroom, I might use role-play to show how to set goals with a client. For example, if a client feels depressed, a short-term goal might be: "The client will practice 15 minutes of mindfulness three times a week by the end of the first month."

Cultural Sensitivity: For clients from collectivist cultures, the goals might also involve family or community support, not just individual achievements. For instance, a goal for a client from a collectivist culture might be: "The client will participate in a family event without experiencing overwhelming anxiety."

Treatment plan creation

This step outlines the methodology and interventions the therapist will use to achieve the goals. Think of this as the path or route to the destination.

Example: Continuing with James, his treatment plan may include Cognitive Behavioral Therapy (CBT), focusing on challenging negative beliefs about social situations (e.g., "People will judge me if I speak") and replacing them with more realistic thoughts (e.g., "I may feel nervous, but I can manage it and enjoy myself").

Another example might involve using exposure therapy for James to gradually increase his comfort in social settings, starting with small gatherings and slowly building up to larger ones.

If the client holds spiritual or traditional beliefs, these could also be integrated into the treatment plan, such as incorporating prayer, family discussions, or cultural rituals as part of the healing process.

Multicultural Consideration: If a client practices a particular religion or follows indigenous healing practices, the plan might incorporate these elements, such as involving a spiritual leader in the healing process or recommending culturally relevant coping strategies like communal support or prayer.

Ongoing assessment and flexibility

Treatment planning isn't static. As therapy progresses, regular assessments are needed to track whether the client is progressing toward their goals.

Example: After a few sessions, James might report that he still feels nervous in social settings but has learned ways to cope with his anxiety. At this point, the therapist and James can adjust the treatment plan to make sure it continues to meet his needs, perhaps by increasing the frequency of social exposure or adding additional coping strategies, such as relaxation techniques.

This step involves regular feedback from the client about what is working or not working, ensuring that the treatment remains effective.

Intervention in counselling and psychotherapy

Intervention is where therapy comes alive. It refers to the specific techniques, strategies, and actions the therapist employs to address the client's issues and help them achieve their goals. The intervention phase is driven by the treatment plan but is dynamic and adaptable, as it directly involves implementing and adjusting techniques according to the client's progress.

Therapeutic techniques and methods

Interventions vary depending on the therapeutic approach used by the therapist. Common interventions include CBT, psychodynamic therapy, solution-focused therapy, and mindfulness.

Example of Cognitive Behavioral Therapy (CBT): For a client like James, a typical CBT intervention might involve identifying and challenging negative automatic thoughts like,

"If I speak, people will laugh at me," and replacing them with more balanced thoughts like, "I might feel nervous, but people are generally supportive and accepting."

Example of Behavioral Intervention: For James, the therapist might assign gradual social exposure exercises. At first, this might be attending a small gathering with close friends, then gradually progressing to larger events. This incremental approach helps the client build confidence and reduce anxiety step-by-step.

Mindfulness and Relaxation Techniques: Clients with anxiety or stress can be taught mindfulness techniques, such as deep breathing or meditation, which help them manage their emotional and physiological responses in the moment. e.g., James might practice mindfulness before attending social gatherings to stay calm and centered.

Direct and indirect interventions

Direct interventions are structured actions that directly target the issue at hand (e.g., cognitive restructuring, role-playing, and practicing skills).

Example: In a session, the therapist might guide James through a role-play exercise where he practices introducing himself to a stranger at a party. This is a direct intervention to address his social anxiety.

Indirect interventions are more exploratory or supportive, such as narrative therapy, where the client is encouraged to reframe their life story, or family therapy, where the client's support system is engaged.

Example: If James's anxiety is linked to family dynamics, family therapy could be used to explore the interactions within his family, providing a space for his family to express support and understanding.

Cultural sensitivity in intervention

In multicultural contexts, it's vital that interventions are adapted to respect and integrate the client's cultural beliefs, practices, and values. Some cultures place a strong emphasis on family involvement in therapy, while others may prioritize spiritual practices or communal approaches.

Example: If a client from a collectivist culture experiences social anxiety, their treatment might include engaging in community-based events with family support, as this might feel less intimidating than attending alone.

Example: For a client from a religious background, the therapist might encourage the client to practice prayer or attend religious ceremonies as a way to manage anxiety, thereby integrating the client's spiritual beliefs into the intervention process.

Adjusting interventions based on feedback

Intervention in therapy is an evolving process. If a particular technique doesn't seem to work or if the client experiences discomfort, the therapist should be prepared to adjust the intervention.

Example: If James finds that social exposure is too overwhelming early on, the therapist might slow down the process and focus more on relaxation techniques or cognitive restructuring before gradually increasing exposure to social situations again.

Feedback from the client is essential in this stage. Regularly checking in on how the interventions are making the client feel and whether progress is being made allows the therapist to modify the approach accordingly.

Research objectives and questions

Based on the background and the problem of the study, the following specific objectives and questions are addressed:

Research objectives

1. To explore culturally sensitive treatment planning approaches in multicultural counselling and psychotherapy.
2. To examine the integration of cultural competence into intervention strategies in multicultural therapy.
3. To evaluate the effectiveness of culturally adapted interventions in diverse populations.
4. To identify the challenges faced by counselors in implementing culturally sensitive treatment plans and interventions.
5. To provide recommendations for integrating cultural considerations into treatment planning and intervention in multicultural counselling.

Research questions

1. How do counselors develop culturally sensitive treatment plans that reflect the unique cultural backgrounds, values, and beliefs of clients in multicultural counselling and psychotherapy?
   - What strategies are employed to ensure treatment plans are responsive to diverse cultural identities globally, in Nigeria, and specifically in Enugu State?
2. How is cultural competence integrated into intervention strategies in multicultural therapy, and what is the impact of these culturally informed techniques on treatment outcomes?

- In what ways do counselors adapt interventions to align with cultural understanding, and how does this influence therapeutic success across different populations?

3. To what extent do culturally adapted interventions enhance engagement, treatment adherence, and overall therapeutic success in diverse populations?
   - How effective are tailored interventions in improving client outcomes in international settings, Nigeria, and Enugu State?
4. What challenges do counselors face in implementing culturally sensitive treatment plans and interventions across diverse contexts?
   - What specific barriers—such as resource limitations, training deficits, or cultural misunderstandings—impede the application of culturally competent strategies?
5. What practical recommendations can be proposed to enhance the integration of cultural considerations into treatment planning and intervention in multicultural counselling?
   - How can counselors in global, Nigerian, and Enugu State contexts improve their multicultural competence to design and deliver culturally appropriate and effective treatments?

Methodology

The methodology for this study adopts a qualitative research approach to investigate how counselors develop and implement culturally sensitive treatment plans and interventions, as well as the challenges they face, across international, Nigerian, and Enugu State contexts. Rooted in an interpretivist ontology, the study assumes that reality is subjective and socially constructed, varying by cultural and contextual factors. A constructivist epistemology underpins the research, emphasizing that knowledge is co-created through the interactions between researchers and participants, with a value-laden axiology committed to cultural sensitivity, equity, and social justice.

Research approach

Qualitative Research Approach: The study adopts a qualitative research approach to explore the subjective experiences, perceptions, and practices of counselors and clients in multicultural settings. This approach is appropriate for understanding complex social phenomena, such as cultural competence in counselling, by capturing rich, contextual data through thematic analysis. The focus is on interpreting meanings, values, and challenges rather than quantifying variables, allowing for an in-depth exploration of how cultural factors influence therapeutic practices and outcomes across different contexts (international, Nigeria, and Enugu State).

Ontology

Interpretivist Ontology: The ontological stance is interpretivist, positing that reality is subjective, socially constructed, and context-dependent. In this study, cultural competence, treatment plans, and intervention strategies are not universal truths but are shaped by the cultural backgrounds, values, and beliefs of participants. e.g., what constitutes a culturally sensitive intervention in Enugu State may differ significantly from international or Nigerian contexts due to local norms, histories, and systemic factors. This ontology acknowledges multiple realities, such as those of counselors and clients, and seeks to understand how these realities interact and influence therapeutic processes.

Epistemology

Constructivist Epistemology: The epistemological position is constructivist, emphasizing that knowledge is co-constructed through the interaction between researcher, participants, and context. Knowledge about cultural competence and its challenges emerges from the shared experiences and interpretations of counselors and clients, rather than being objective or externally imposed. For instance, understanding how counselors adapt interventions or face barriers relies on interpreting their narratives and the meanings they attribute to cultural factors, which are shaped by their cultural and professional contexts. This approach values the subjective insights of participants as valid sources of knowledge.

Axiology

Value-Laden and Ethical Stance: The axiological perspective recognizes that the research is value-laden, with a commitment to cultural sensitivity, equity, and social justice. The study values diversity and seeks to highlight the importance of culturally competent practices in improving mental health outcomes, particularly for marginalized or underrepresented groups (e.g., clients in Nigeria and Enugu State). The researcher's values influence the choice of research questions, the interpretation of data, and the emphasis on addressing systemic barriers like stigma and resource limitations. Ethical considerations, such as respecting cultural differences and ensuring participant confidentiality, are central to the research process.

Research design

Case Study and Thematic Analysis Design: The research design combines a multiple case study approach with thematic analysis. Each context (international, Nigeria, Enugu State) is treated as a case, allowing for comparative analysis of how cultural competence is developed, integrated, and challenged across diverse settings. The thematic analysis is inductive, meaning themes emerge from the data rather than being predetermined, focusing on patterns in participants' experiences, strategies, and outcomes. This design is flexible and iterative, enabling the researcher to explore nuances and contextual factors while maintaining a structured framework for comparison. The case study approach is suitable for examining complex, context-specific phenomena like multicultural counselling, while thematic analysis provides a systematic way to identify and interpret key themesf, such as cultural awareness, adaptation strategies, and barriers. This design aligns with the qualitative nature of the research and the interpretivist ontology, ensuring that findings are grounded in participants' lived experiences.

Data collection

- **Semi-Structured Interviews**: Data were collected through semi-structured interviews with the 30 participants, consisting of five counselors and five clients from each of the three contexts (international, Nigeria, and Enugu State). These interviews employed open-ended questions designed to deeply explore participants' experiences, perceptions, and practices related to developing culturally sensitive treatment plans, integrating cultural competence into intervention strategies, and identifying the challenges they encountered. For instance, counselors were asked questions such as, "How did you assess a client's cultural background when designing a treatment plan?" and "What specific barriers did you encounter when implementing culturally sensitive strategies?" Clients, on the other hand, were prompted to share their perspectives, such as, "How did you feel about the cultural sensitivity of the treatment you received?" and "Did you face any difficulties during the therapeutic process?" The interviews, which lasted approximately 45–60 minutes each, were audio-recorded and transcribed verbatim to ensure accuracy and capture nuanced responses.
- **Focus Groups**: Optional focus groups were conducted with counselors from each context to facilitate discussions about common challenges and the sharing of strategies, thereby adding further depth and richness to the data. For example, Nigerian and Enugu State counselors participated in separate focus groups where they discussed issues such as resource limitations, stigma surrounding mental health, and the role of community leaders in therapy. These sessions, lasting about 90 minutes, were moderated by the researcher and allowed for interactive dialog, revealing collective insights and contrasting perspectives that individual interviews might not have captured. The focus groups were also recorded and transcribed for analysis.
- **Document Analysis**: Relevant documents were analyzed to provide additional context and identify systemic factors influencing participants' experiences. These documents included training materials used by counselors, cultural competence guidelines such as those from the American Psychological Association (APA), and local mental health policies specific to Nigeria and Enugu State. This analysis helped to situate the

qualitative data within broader structural and cultural frameworks, offering insights into how policy and training environments either supported or hindered culturally sensitive practices. Documents were sourced from professional organizations, government reports, and academic publications, and were reviewed systematically to extract themes related to resource availability, training standards, and cultural norms.

Data analysis

- **Thematic Analysis Process**: The data were analyzed using Braun and Clarke (2006) six-phase thematic analysis framework to systematically identify and interpret patterns. The process unfolded as follows:
  1. **Familiarization with Data**: The researcher transcribed all interviews and focus group discussions and repeatedly read the transcripts, as well as reviewed the document analysis notes, to become thoroughly immersed in the content. This phase involved noting initial impressions, recurring ideas, and emotional tones expressed by participants.
  2. **Generating Initial Codes**: Initial codes were identified to capture key ideas and concepts within the data. Examples of codes included "lack of resources," "cultural misunderstanding," "training gaps," and "client resistance." These codes were applied systematically across all data sources, ensuring that both counselors' and clients' perspectives were represented.
  3. **Searching for Themes**: Codes were grouped into potential themes and sub-themes, such as "resource limitations" (with sub-themes like "insufficient funding" and "access to cultural resources") and "training deficits" (with sub-themes like "lack of specialized training" and "ongoing learning gaps"). This step involved organizing the data into broader categories that reflected the research questions.
  4. **Reviewing Themes**: Themes were refined by checking their coherence and ensuring they accurately represented the data and addressed the research questions. This involved revisiting the original transcripts and documents to confirm that themes were supported by sufficient evidence and were distinct from one another.
  5. **Defining and Naming Themes**: Each theme and sub-theme was clearly defined and named to reflect its content and relevance. For example, "cultural misunderstandings" was defined as challenges arising from misinterpretations of cultural norms, while "mitigating stigma" was named to capture efforts to address societal barriers. This phase ensured that the themes were meaningful and directly linked to the challenges of implementing culturally sensitive strategies.
  6. **Producing the Report**: The findings were written up in a comprehensive report, incorporating direct quotes from participants and interpretations that linked the themes to the research questions. The report, as demonstrated in previous analyses,

highlighted how challenges like resource limitations and training deficits impacted cultural competence in counselling across the three contexts.

- **Software**: Qualitative data analysis software, specifically NVivo, was utilized to organize the data, code transcripts, and visualize themes. This tool enhanced the rigor and efficiency of the analysis by allowing the researcher to track codes, compare themes across contexts, and ensure consistency in interpretation. The use of software also facilitated the identification of patterns that might have been missed in manual analysis, such as subtle differences in how international, Nigerian, and Enugu State participants described their challenges.

Sampling and recruitment

- **Purposeful Sampling**: Participants were purposively selected based on their experience in multicultural counselling and their representation of the three contexts (international, Nigeria, Enugu State). Counselors were licensed professionals with at least 2 years of experience working with diverse cultural groups, ensuring they could provide informed insights into cultural sensitivity and challenges. Clients were individuals who had received or were currently receiving therapy, selected to represent a range of cultural backgrounds, ages, and genders within each context. This approach ensured a diverse set of perspectives that enriched the study's findings.
- **Sample Size**: The sample consisted of 30 participants, with five counselors and five clients from each context, totaling 10 participants per context. This sample size was deemed sufficient for qualitative depth, as it allowed for thematic saturation within each context—meaning no new themes emerged after interviewing this number—while also enabling meaningful cross-contextual comparisons. The selection process involved contacting professional networks, mental health organizations, and community leaders in Nigeria and Enugu State to recruit participants, ensuring representation from both urban and rural areas.

Ethical considerations

- **Informed Consent**: Prior to data collection, participants were required to provide written informed consent after being fully informed about the study's purpose, procedures, potential risks, and benefits. They were also made aware of their rights, including anonymity, confidentiality, and the ability to withdraw from the study at any time without consequences. Consent forms were translated into local languages (e.g., Igbo for Enugu State participants) where necessary to ensure comprehension.
- **Confidentiality**: To protect participant privacy, all data were anonymized by removing any identifying information, such as names, locations, or specific organizational details, from transcripts and reports. Data were stored securely on encrypted servers, accessible

only to the research team, and were destroyed after the study's completion in accordance with ethical guidelines.

- **Cultural Sensitivity**: The research process was designed to respect cultural norms and values. e.g., in Nigeria and Enugu State, the researcher consulted with community leaders and traditional authorities to gain cultural approval and ensure that interview questions did not inadvertently cause distress or reinforce stigma. Care was taken to avoid topics that might be taboo or sensitive, such as certain mental health issues, unless participants raised them voluntarily.

Validity and reliability

- **Triangulation**: Validity was enhanced by using multiple data sources—interviews, focus groups, and documents—and multiple perspectives, including those of counselors and clients. This triangulation allowed the researcher to cross-check findings and ensure that themes were robust and not reliant on a single data type or viewpoint. For instance, challenges identified in interviews were compared with policy documents and focus group discussions to confirm their prevalence and impact.
- **Member Checking**: Preliminary findings were shared with a subset of participants to verify accuracy and ensure that the interpretations resonated with their experiences. This process involved sending summaries of themes and quotes back to participants via email or in person, allowing them to provide feedback, correct misunderstandings, or add further context. This step strengthened the credibility of the findings by ensuring they reflected participants' intended meanings.
- **Reflexivity**: The researcher reflected on their own cultural biases, assumptions, and positionality throughout the study, acknowledging how these might influence data collection and interpretation. e.g., if the researcher had a Western background, they noted potential biases toward individualistic approaches and actively sought to privilege participants' cultural perspectives. A reflexivity journal was maintained to document these reflections, enhancing transparency and rigor in the analysis.

Results

Research question 1: How do counselors develop culturally sensitive treatment plans that reflect the unique cultural backgrounds, values, and beliefs of clients in multicultural counselling and psychotherapy?

- What strategies are employed to ensure treatment plans are responsive to diverse cultural identities globally, in Nigeria, and specifically in Enugu State?

The following themes and sub-themes were generated from the responses the participants gave to the above question.

Theme 1: cultural awareness and self-reflection

Counselors prioritize understanding their own cultural identity and biases as a foundation for developing culturally sensitive treatment plans.

- **Sub-Theme 1.1: Self-Awareness of Cultural Identity**: Counselors globally, including those in Nigeria and Enugu State, engage in self-reflection to recognize how their own cultural background, values, and privileges (e.g., white privilege, Western training) influence their perceptions of clients. This is critical to avoid imposing dominant cultural norms on clients from diverse backgrounds. e.g., international counselors might reflect on ethnocentrism, while Nigerian counselors might consider regional or ethnic biases (e.g., between Igbo, Hausa, or Yoruba cultures). The following are some quotes from the participants.
    - *International Counselor*: "I realized that my Western training made me assume individual therapy was always best, but I had to check my biases and learn that some cultures prioritize family input over personal goals."
    - *Nigerian Counselor*: "As a Yoruba counselor working with Igbo clients, I had to reflect on how my own cultural assumptions about authority might clash with their values, so I make sure to listen more than I assume."
    - *Enugu State Counselor*: "Growing up in Enugu, I thought I understood our Igbo ways, but working with clients, I saw I needed to unlearn some biases about mental health stigma to really help them."
    - *International Client*: "My counselor asked me about my culture upfront, which made me feel she was trying to understand me, not just fit me into her own box."
    - *Nigerian Client*: "I was worried the counselor wouldn't get me, but she said she's learning too, and that made me trust her more."
    - *Enugu State Client*: "At first, I thought she'd judge me for seeing a native doctor, but she asked about it respectfully, and I felt safe."

Cultural awareness and self-reflection are essential qualities that enable counselors to provide effective and culturally responsive care to clients from diverse backgrounds. When counselors are culturally aware, they are able to recognize and appreciate the unique cultural identities, values, traditions, and belief systems that shape their clients' worldviews and experiences. This awareness goes beyond mere acknowledgment—it requires an active effort to understand how cultural factors influence a client's perceptions, behaviors, communication style, coping mechanisms, and mental health concerns.

Equally important is the process of self-reflection, where counsellors examine their own cultural identities, biases, and assumptions. Through self-reflection, counsellors become more mindful of how their personal values and experiences might impact their therapeutic approach. This introspection helps prevent the imposition of the counsellor's worldview on the client and promotes a more empathetic, respectful, and nonjudgmental therapeutic relationship.

- **Sub-Theme 1.2: Acknowledgment of Cultural Differences:** Counsellors assess the cultural distance between themselves and clients, recognizing differences in race, ethnicity, religion, gender, and socioeconomic status. In Enugu State, where Igbo culture predominates, counselors might need to understand local traditions, family structures, and community expectations, which differ from global or even other Nigerian contexts.
  - *International Counselor*: "With clients from Asia, I had to recognize that their collectivist values were so different from mine, and that changed how I approached their treatment plan."
  - *Nigerian Counselor*: "Working in Lagos, I see clients from all over Nigeria—Hausa, Igbo, Yoruba—and each group has unique ways of viewing family and community that I must respect."
  - *Enugu State Counselor*: "Here in Enugu, the Igbo emphasis on community and elders is huge, so I always ask about their family's role before I suggest any plan."
  - *International Client*: "She noticed I was hesitant to talk about my family's expectations, and she said it's okay if our cultures differ—that helped a lot."
  - *Nigerian Client*: "He didn't act like his way was the only way; he asked about my village's traditions, and that made me open up."
  - *Enugu State Client*: "I told her about our respect for elders, and she said she'd include that in how we work together, which made me feel seen."

Counselors' ability to acknowledge and respect cultural differences plays a vital role in delivering effective and inclusive mental health support. Recognizing that each client comes from a unique cultural background—with distinct values, belief systems, customs, and communication styles—enables counselors to avoid a one-size-fits-all approach to treatment. When counselors make a conscious effort to understand and appreciate these differences, they are better positioned to build trust and rapport with clients, which is a critical foundation for successful therapeutic outcomes.

Developing cultural competence involves not only acknowledging diversity but also actively integrating that understanding into the assessment and treatment planning process. This includes considering how cultural identity influences a client's perception of mental health, help-seeking behavior, family dynamics, coping strategies, and even their willingness to engage in counselling. A culturally sensitive treatment plan reflects these nuances, ensuring that interventions are relevant, respectful, and aligned with the client's worldview.

Moreover, when counselors are aware of their own cultural assumptions and remain open to learning from their clients, they can avoid misunderstandings and potential biases that may compromise the counselling process. Ultimately, this culturally responsive approach promotes empowerment, fosters inclusivity, and enhances the effectiveness of counselling interventions across diverse populations.

Theme 2: client-centered cultural assessment

Effective treatment plans begin with a thorough understanding of the client's cultural context, values, and beliefs.

- **Sub-Theme 2.1: Cultural Identity Exploration**Counsellors use intake interviews and ongoing assessments to explore clients' cultural identities, including race, ethnicity, religion, and intersectional factors (e.g., gender, sexual orientation). For Nigerian and Enugu State clients, this might involve understanding the role of community, family hierarchy, and traditional healing practices alongside Western psychotherapy. Example of the participants' quotes are:
  - *International Counselor*: "I use a cultural genogram to map out a client's background—religion, migration history, language—and it helps me see the full picture."
  - *Nigerian Counselor*: "I always ask about their tribe, religion, and whether they've seen a traditional healer, because that tells me what they value."
  - *Enugu State Counselor*: "For my Igbo clients, I explore their connection to the community and ancestors, because that shapes how they see their problems."
  - *International Client*: "She asked about my heritage and how it affects my stress, which no one else ever did—it made me feel she really cared."
  - *Nigerian Client*: "He wanted to know about my church and family roles, and that showed he wasn't just guessing about me."
  - *Enugu State Client*: "She asked if I talk to my elders about my issues, and when I said yes, she said we'd work with that, not against it."
- **Sub-Theme 2.2: Incorporation of Cultural Strengths:** Counsellors identify and leverage cultural strengths, such as community support networks, cultural coping mechanisms (e.g., storytelling, rituals), and spiritual beliefs. In Nigeria, this could include integrating family or elder involvement, while in Enugu State, counselors might draw on Igbo cultural practices like respect for ancestors or communal decision-making. The participants said the following:
  - *International Counselor*: "I found that this client's community support was a huge strength, so I encouraged them to lean on that during tough times."
  - *Nigerian Counselor*: "Many clients here have strong faith, so I suggest prayers or church groups as part of coping, and it works well."
  - *Enugu State Counselor*: "The client's connection to their umunna (extended family) was a strength, so I helped them use that support in their plan."

- *International Client*: "She told me my cultural traditions could help me heal, and that gave me hope I didn't have before."
- *Nigerian Client*: "He said my faith could be a tool, not a problem, and that made me feel stronger about getting better."
- *Enugu State Client*: "She said our community gatherings could help me feel less alone, and it really did."

Cultural strengths play a significant role in helping counselors design effective and personalized counselling plans for their clients. These strengths—such as strong family ties, community support systems, spiritual or religious beliefs, cultural resilience, and traditional coping mechanisms—serve as valuable assets in the therapeutic process. When counselors are able to identify and integrate these strengths into their treatment approach, they create a supportive and empowering environment that resonates with the client's lived experiences.

Understanding and utilizing cultural strengths allows counselors to build upon what is already working in the client's life, rather than focusing solely on deficits or problems. e. g., a client from a collectivist culture may benefit from interventions that involve family or community support, while a client with strong spiritual beliefs may respond well to counselling approaches that align with their faith. By acknowledging and affirming these cultural assets, counselors not only enhance engagement but also promote a sense of cultural pride and identity in the client. Moreover, incorporating cultural strengths into counselling plans also fosters greater trust and collaboration, as clients are more likely to feel seen, understood, and respected. Ultimately, leveraging cultural strengths helps counselors deliver more effective, relevant, and culturally responsive care that improves client outcomes.

Theme 3: adaptive therapeutic strategies

Counselors employ flexible and culturally adapted strategies to ensure treatment plans are responsive to diverse cultural identities.

- **Sub-Theme 3.1: Culturally Adapted Interventions:** Globally, counselors adapt evidence-based therapies (e.g., CBT) to fit cultural contexts, avoiding Western assumptions. In Nigeria, this might mean incorporating local languages, proverbs, or religious frameworks (e.g., Christianity or traditional beliefs). In Enugu State, counselors might use community-based interventions or address stigma around mental health, which is prevalent in many African cultures.
  - *International Counselor*: "Instead of standard CBT, I used storytelling with this Latin American client because it fit their cultural way of processing emotions."

   - *Nigerian Counselor*: "I adapted the therapy to include family sessions because, for my clients, healing isn't just individual—it's communal."
   - *Enugu State Counselor*: "I used proverbs and stories from Igbo culture to explain coping strategies, and it made the plan more relatable."
   - *International Client*: "He changed his approach to match how my culture sees problems, and it felt like he was speaking my language."
   - *Nigerian Client*: "She brought my family in to talk, which is how we solve things at home, and it made the therapy work better."
   - *Enugu State Client*: "He used a story my grandmother would tell, and suddenly the advice made sense in a way it never did before."
- **Sub-Theme 3.2: Building Trust and Rapport:** Establishing a strong therapeutic alliance is crucial, especially across cultural lines. Strategies include active listening, validating client experiences, and demonstrating cultural humility. For Enugu State clients, trust-building might involve respecting hierarchical family structures or addressing fears of judgment due to cultural taboos around mental illness.
   - *International Counselor*: "I make sure to validate their cultural experiences first, so they know I'm not here to judge but to help."
   - *Nigerian Counselor*: "I tell them I respect their beliefs, even if they're different from mine, and that opens the door to trust."
   - *Enugu State Counselor*: "I show I understand their fear of stigma by being patient and never pushing too hard, and that builds their confidence in me."
   - *International Client*: "She listened without judging my cultural practices, and that made me willing to try her suggestions."
   - *Nigerian Client*: "He said he'd learn more about my culture if needed, and that honesty made me trust him completely."
   - *Enugu State Client*: "She never made me feel ashamed of seeing a diviner first, and that respect kept me coming back."

Theme 4: training and continuous learning

Counselors rely on ongoing education and training to enhance their cultural competence, particularly in specific regional contexts like Nigeria and Enugu State.

- **Sub-Theme 4.1: Formal Multicultural Training:** Counsellors participate in workshops, seminars, and academic programs focused on cultural competence. The search results highlight tools like the Multicultural counselling Inventory and guidelines from the American Psychological Association, which could be adapted for Nigerian and Enugu State contexts to address local cultural nuances.
   - *International Counselor*: "I attended a workshop on multicultural competence last year, and it taught me how to use tools like the Multicultural counselling Inventory to better serve diverse clients."

- *Nigerian Counselor*: "I took a seminar on cultural sensitivity in Lagos, and it helped me understand how to adapt Western models to fit our Nigerian context, like involving families more."
- *Enugu State Counselor*: "We had training on Igbo cultural norms and mental health stigma here in Enugu, and it gave me new ways to connect with clients who fear judgment."
- *International Client*: "My counselor mentioned she's been learning about different cultures through courses, and that made me feel she's serious about understanding me."
- *Nigerian Client*: "She said she's been trained to respect our traditions, and I could tell she knew what she was talking about when she suggested involving my pastor."
- *Enugu State Client*: "He told me he's been to workshops about our Igbo ways, and that made me trust that he wouldn't misunderstand my family's concerns."

- **Sub-Theme 4.2: Supervision and Peer Consultation:** Counsellors seek supervision and collaborate with peers from diverse backgrounds to refine their approach. In Nigeria, this might involve consulting with local elders or traditional healers, while in Enugu State, counselors could benefit from networks of Igbo mental health professionals to better understand regional challenges.
  - *International Counselor*: "I meet with a supervisor monthly to discuss cultural challenges, and last time, she suggested I consult a cultural expert for my Middle Eastern client."
  - *Nigerian Counselor*: "I often talk to colleagues and even local elders to make sure my plans respect the client's community, especially in rural areas."
  - *Enugu State Counselor*: "I work with other Igbo counselors and sometimes ask advice from village heads to ensure my approach fits our cultural expectations."
  - *International Client*: "She said she checks with other experts to make sure she's getting my culture right, and that effort made me feel valued."
  - *Nigerian Client*: "He mentioned he talks to other professionals and even traditional healers, and that showed me he's committed to helping me in a way that makes sense."
  - *Enugu State Client*: "She said she learns from other counselors in Enugu and our community leaders, and I felt relieved knowing she's not just guessing about our ways."

Theme 5: addressing structural and systemic factors

Culturally sensitive treatment plans consider broader systemic issues, such as discrimination, stigma, and access to care, which vary by context.

- **Sub-Theme 5.1: Mitigating Stigma and Discrimination:** Globally and in Nigeria, counselors address cultural stigma around mental health, which can be particularly strong in collectivist societies. In Enugu State, this might involve educating communities about mental health to reduce shame and encourage help-seeking behavior.
  - International Counselor: "I work with immigrant clients to challenge the stigma they face, educating them and their communities about mental health as a universal need, not a weakness."
  - Nigerian Counselor: "Here, stigma is a big barrier, so I educate families and communities about mental health, showing it's not a curse but something we can treat."
  - Enugu State Counselor: "In Enugu, people fear being shamed, so I hold community talks to explain that seeking help is strength, not failure, rooted in our Igbo values."
  - International Client: "She helped me see that the stigma I faced wasn't my fault, and she even spoke to my community to support me, which changed everything."
  - Nigerian Client: "He told my family that mental health is like any other health issue, and slowly they stopped seeing me as cursed."
  - Enugu State Client: "She went to my village and explained that therapy isn't shameful, and now my people are more supportive of me getting help."

  Sub-Theme 5.2: Advocacy and Social Justice: Counsellors advocate for clients by challenging oppressive systems and promoting equity. In Nigeria and Enugu State, this could mean addressing socioeconomic disparities, gender inequality, or the impact of colonial histories on mental health, ensuring treatment plans account for these external pressures.
  - *International Counselor*: "I advocate for policies that address racial discrimination, ensuring my clients aren't just treated in therapy but also supported in their daily lives."
  - *Nigerian Counselor*: "I push for better mental health resources in Nigeria, especially for women and poor communities, because those systemic issues affect treatment success."
  - *Enugu State Counselor*: "I work with local leaders to tackle poverty and gender inequality in Enugu, knowing these pressures make mental health worse for my clients."
  - *International Client*: "He fought for me when I faced discrimination at work, and that, plus therapy, helped me feel empowered to heal."
  - *Nigerian Client*: "She helped me get support for my financial struggles, saying it's part of healing, and that made a huge difference."
  - *Enugu State Client*: "He talked to our community about how poverty affects us all, and it made me feel less alone and more hopeful about getting better."

Research Question 2: How is cultural competence integrated into intervention strategies in multicultural therapy, and what is the impact of these culturally informed techniques on treatment outcomes?

- In what ways do counselors adapt interventions to align with cultural understanding, and how does this influence therapeutic success across different populations?

The following themes and sub-themes answered the above questions.

Theme 1: integration of cultural competence into intervention design

Counselors embed cultural competence into their intervention strategies by adapting approaches to reflect clients' cultural backgrounds, values, and beliefs.

- **Sub-Theme 1.1: Assessment of Cultural Factors**
  - *International Counselor*: "I use a cultural genogram to map out a client's background—religion, migration history, language—and it helps me see the full picture before designing any intervention."
  - *Nigerian Counselor*: "I always ask about their tribe, religion, and whether they've seen a traditional healer, because that tells me what they value and how to start."
  - *Enugu State Counselor*: "For my Igbo clients, I explore their connection to the community and ancestors, because that shapes how they see their problems and what solutions might work."
  - *International Client*: "She asked about my heritage and how it affects my stress, which no one else ever did—it made me feel she really cared and understood my struggles."
  - *Nigerian Client*: "He wanted to know about my church and family roles, and that showed he wasn't just guessing about me but really trying to help."
  - *Enugu State Client*: "She asked if I talk to my elders about my issues, and when I said yes, she said we'd work with that, not against it, which made me trust her more."

These quotes highlight that cultural competence begins with a thorough assessment of clients' cultural identities, which is critical for designing relevant interventions. Internationally, counselors use structured tools like genograms to capture broad cultural influences, while in Nigeria and Enugu State, the focus is on specific local factors such as tribal affiliations, religious practices, and community roles. This alignment with cultural understanding fosters trust and lays the groundwork for effective therapy, as clients feel seen and understood, enhancing engagement.

- **Sub-Theme 1.2: Customization of Therapeutic Techniques**
  - *International Counselor*: "Instead of standard CBT, I used storytelling with this Latin American client because it fit their cultural way of processing emotions and made the therapy more relatable."

- *Nigerian Counselor*: "I adapted the therapy to include family sessions because, for my clients, healing isn't just individual—it's communal, and that's how they expect support."
- *Enugu State Counselor*: "I used proverbs and stories from Igbo culture to explain coping strategies, and it made the plan more relatable and effective for my clients."
- *International Client*: "He changed his approach to match how my culture sees problems, and it felt like he was speaking my language, which made therapy easier to follow."
- *Nigerian Client*: "She brought my family in to talk, which is how we solve things at home, and it made the therapy work better because it felt familiar."
- *Enugu State Client*: "He used a story my grandmother would tell, and suddenly the advice made sense in a way it never did before—it felt like therapy was for me, not just anyone."

Customizing interventions to fit cultural norms and practices demonstrates cultural competence by making therapy more accessible and meaningful. Globally, this might involve narrative techniques, while in Nigeria and Enugu State, it includes leveraging communal and traditional methods. This adaptation not only improves client engagement but also increases the likelihood of therapeutic success by ensuring interventions resonate with clients' cultural frameworks.

Theme 2: strategies for culturally informed interventions

Counselors employ specific strategies to ensure interventions are culturally sensitive and effective across diverse populations.

- **Sub-Theme 2.1: Building Cultural Humility and Rapport**
  - *International Counselor*: "I make sure to validate their cultural experiences first, so they know I'm not here to judge but to help, and that builds a strong connection."
  - *Nigerian Counselor*: "I tell them I respect their beliefs, even if they're different from mine, and that opens the door to trust, which is crucial for progress."
  - *Enugu State Counselor*: "I show I understand their fear of stigma by being patient and never pushing too hard, and that builds their confidence in me and the process."
  - *International Client*: "She listened without judging my cultural practices, and that made me willing to try her suggestions, knowing she wasn't forcing her own views on me."
  - *Nigerian Client*: "He said he'd learn more about my culture if needed, and that honesty made me trust him completely to guide me through this."
  - *Enugu State Client*: "She never made me feel ashamed of seeing a diviner first, and that respect kept me coming back, even when I was skeptical."

- Building cultural humility and rapport is a cornerstone of culturally informed interventions, as it mitigates power imbalances and fosters trust. This strategy is universally important but particularly critical in contexts like Nigeria and Enugu State, where stigma and mistrust of Western methods can be barriers. The quotes suggest that clients are more likely to engage when they feel their cultural identity is respected, which directly enhances therapeutic success.

- **Sub-Theme 2.2: Use of Cultural Mediators and Resources**
  - *International Counselor*: "I sometimes bring in a cultural consultant to ensure I'm not missing something important, especially with clients from cultures I'm less familiar with."
  - *Nigerian Counselor*: "I work with local imams or traditional healers to bridge gaps, because their input can make my interventions more acceptable to the client."
  - *Enugu State Counselor*: "I consult with Igbo community leaders or elders to ensure my plan respects our cultural practices, like involving the family in decision-making."
  - *International Client*: "She brought in someone who understood my background, and that made me feel the therapy wasn't just a generic solution but something tailored for me."
  - *Nigerian Client*: "He talked to our village elder, and when he came back with ideas that fit our ways, I knew he was serious about helping me."
  - *Enugu State Client*: "She said she learned from our local leaders how we handle problems, and that made me believe she could really help me with my issues."

Leveraging cultural mediators and resources enhances the cultural relevance of interventions, making them more acceptable and effective. This strategy is especially vital in Nigeria and Enugu State, where community and traditional authorities play significant roles. The quotes indicate that this approach reduces cultural barriers, increases client buy-in, and improves outcomes by ensuring interventions are rooted in familiar cultural frameworks.

Theme 3: impact of culturally informed techniques on treatment outcomes

Culturally competent interventions significantly influence therapeutic success by improving client engagement, reducing dropout rates, and enhancing mental health outcomes.

- **Sub-Theme 3.1: Enhanced Client Engagement and Trust**
  - *International Counselor*: "When I adapt to their cultural needs, clients are more likely to show up and participate, because they feel the therapy is designed for them, not against their values."

- *Nigerian Counselor*: "Once I started involving their families and respecting their religious beliefs, clients stopped dropping out and started opening up more."
- *Enugu State Counselor*: "In Enugu, when I use our cultural stories and involve the community, clients are less afraid and more willing to stick with the process."
- *International Client*: "Because she understood my culture, I felt safe to share more, and that made the therapy work faster for me."
- *Nigerian Client*: "I used to doubt therapy, but when he respected our ways, I started to trust him and kept coming back until I felt better."
- *Enugu State Client*: "She made it clear she wasn't judging our traditions, and that trust helped me stay in therapy and see real change."

Enhanced engagement and trust are direct outcomes of culturally informed techniques, as they address cultural barriers that might otherwise lead to dropout or resistance. The quotes suggest that when clients feel their cultural identity is honored, they are more invested in the therapeutic process, which improves attendance, participation, and ultimately, success rates.

- **Sub-Theme 3.2: Improved Mental Health Outcomes**
  - *International Counselor*: "Clients report better symptom reduction when we tailor interventions to their cultural coping mechanisms, like using community support or spiritual practices."
  - *Nigerian Counselor*: "When I integrate faith-based coping or family support, my clients show less anxiety and depression, and they feel more empowered."
  - *Enugu State Counselor*: "Here, when we address stigma and use Igbo strengths like community resilience, clients recover faster and report feeling less isolated."
  - *International Client*: "The therapy worked because it built on my cultural strengths, like my community network, and I felt stronger afterward."
  - *Nigerian Client*: "After he helped me use my faith and family, my stress went down, and I felt like I could handle life again."
  - *Enugu State Client*: "She showed me how our traditions could help me heal, and now I'm not as scared or ashamed, and I'm doing much better."

Improved mental health outcomes result from culturally informed techniques that leverage clients' cultural strengths and address systemic barriers. The quotes indicate that tailoring interventions to cultural contexts reduces symptoms and increases well-being, particularly in collectivist settings like Nigeria and Enugu State, where community and tradition play central roles.

Research Question 3: What challenges do counselors face in implementing culturally sensitive treatment plans and interventions across diverse contexts?

- What specific barriers—such as resource limitations, training deficits, or cultural misunderstandings—impede the application of culturally competent strategies?

Theme 1: resource limitations

Counselors face significant challenges due to a lack of resources, which hinders the implementation of culturally sensitive treatment plans and interventions.

- **Sub-Theme 1.1: Insufficient Funding and Infrastructure**
  - *International Counselor*: "In some regions, there's just not enough funding for cultural training or materials, so I have to make do with what I have, which isn't always enough to meet diverse client needs."
  - *Nigerian Counselor*: "Here in Nigeria, we lack the infrastructure for mental health services, especially in rural areas, so it's hard to offer culturally tailored interventions without basic resources like translation services."
  - *Enugu State Counselor*: "In Enugu, we don't have enough clinics or trained staff, and that makes it tough to reach clients who need culturally specific help, like involving their communities."
  - *International Client*: "I could tell my counselor wanted to help, but she said her office didn't have the tools to really understand my background, which made me worry about getting proper support."
  - *Nigerian Client*: "He said he'd love to bring in my family, but there's no space or money for that, so I felt like he couldn't do much for me."
  - *Enugu State Client*: "She tried to include our traditions, but she said the clinic doesn't have the resources, so I didn't get the full help I needed."

Resource limitations, particularly insufficient funding and infrastructure, create significant barriers to implementing culturally sensitive strategies. Internationally, this might involve a lack of specialized training programs, while in Nigeria and Enugu State, the challenge is exacerbated by broader systemic issues like poverty and underfunded healthcare systems. These constraints limit counselors' ability to adapt interventions, leading to frustration for both counselors and clients and potentially reducing treatment effectiveness.

- **Sub-Theme 1.2: Access to Cultural Resources**
  - *International Counselor*: "It's hard to find cultural consultants or materials for every client group, especially for less represented cultures, which slows down my ability to be culturally competent."
  - *Nigerian Counselor*: "We don't have easy access to traditional healers or community leaders who could help us adapt our plans, and that's a big gap in our work."

- *Enugu State Counselor*: "In Enugu, it's difficult to connect with Igbo cultural experts consistently, so sometimes I have to guess what's appropriate, which isn't ideal."
- *International Client*: "He said he couldn't find someone to explain my culture to him, and that made me feel like my needs weren't a priority."
- *Nigerian Client*: "She wanted to learn more about our ways, but she said there's no one around to teach her, so I felt like she was starting from scratch."
- *Enugu State Client*: "He tried to understand our customs, but he said it's hard to find people who can guide him, so I wasn't sure if he really got it."
- The lack of access to cultural resources, such as consultants or community leaders, hinders counselors' ability to tailor interventions effectively. This is a particular challenge in Nigeria and Enugu State, where traditional knowledge holders are crucial but often hard to reach. The quotes suggest that this barrier can lead to misunderstandings, reduced trust, and less effective interventions, as counselors struggle to bridge cultural gaps without adequate support.

Theme 2: training deficits

Counselors encounter challenges due to inadequate or incomplete training in cultural competence, which affects their ability to implement culturally sensitive strategies.

- **Sub-Theme 2.1: Lack of Specialized Cultural Training**
  - *International Counselor*: "My initial training didn't cover many cultures in depth, so I'm learning on the job, but that can lead to mistakes when I'm working with diverse clients."
  - *Nigerian Counselor*: "Most of us were trained in Western models, but there's little focus on Nigerian cultural nuances, so I often feel unprepared for local challenges."
  - *Enugu State Counselor*: "Our training here doesn't always address Igbo-specific issues like stigma or family dynamics, so I have to figure things out as I go, which can be risky."
  - *International Client*: "Sometimes I could tell he didn't fully understand my culture because he admitted his training didn't cover it, and that made me doubt his advice."
  - *Nigerian Client*: "She said she's still learning about our ways because her school didn't teach it, and I wondered if she was the right person to help me."
  - *Enugu State Client*: "He told me his training didn't include much about our traditions, so I wasn't sure if he could really handle my problems."

The lack of specialized cultural training leaves counselors ill-equipped to address diverse cultural needs, leading to potential errors and reduced confidence in their abilities. This is a global issue but is particularly acute in Nigeria and Enugu State, where Western training may not align with local cultural realities. The quotes indicate that clients may lose trust when they perceive counselors as unprepared, which can undermine therapeutic success.

- **Sub-Theme 2.2: Ongoing Learning Gaps**
  - *International Counselor*: "Even with some training, keeping up with new cultural trends and research is tough, and I worry I'm falling behind what my clients need."
  - *Nigerian Counselor*: "There's no regular training here on cultural updates, so I rely on experience, but that's not enough when new issues arise."
  - *Enugu State Counselor*: "We don't have ongoing workshops in Enugu to learn about changing cultural dynamics, like how younger generations view mental health differently."
  - *International Client*: "She said she's trying to learn more, but it felt like she was behind, and I wasn't sure if she could keep up with my needs."
  - *Nigerian Client*: "He admitted he hasn't had recent training on our culture, and that made me worry he might miss something important about my situation."
  - *Enugu State Client*: "She said there's no new training here, so I felt like she might not know the latest about how we deal with mental health in our community."

Ongoing learning gaps exacerbate the challenge of maintaining cultural competence, as counselors struggle to stay current without regular training opportunities. This is a significant issue in resource-limited settings like Nigeria and Enugu State, where access to continuing education is scarce. The quotes suggest that this can lead to outdated or ineffective strategies, eroding client confidence and hindering therapeutic outcomes.

Theme 3: cultural misunderstandings

Misunderstandings arising from cultural differences pose a major challenge to implementing culturally sensitive interventions.

- **Sub-Theme 3.1: Misinterpretation of Cultural Norms**
  - *International Counselor*: "Sometimes I misread a client's cultural cues, like thinking silence means agreement when it might mean discomfort, and that can set us back."
  - *Nigerian Counselor*: "I once assumed a client's reluctance was resistance, but it was respect for elders, and that misunderstanding delayed our progress."
  - *Enugu State Counselor*: "I misjudged a client's family involvement as overbearing, but in Igbo culture, it's normal, and I had to adjust my approach quickly."
  - *International Client*: "He didn't get that my silence wasn't disinterest but respect, and that made me feel he didn't understand me at all."

- *Nigerian Client*: "She thought I was avoiding her, but I was just waiting for my elder's approval, and that mix-up made things tense."
- *Enugu State Client*: "He didn't realize our family's role is central, not intrusive, and I had to explain it, which made me doubt his expertise."

Misinterpreting cultural norms can lead to misunderstandings that damage the therapeutic relationship and hinder intervention effectiveness. This challenge is universal but particularly pronounced in multicultural settings like Nigeria and Enugu State, where local norms (e.g., collectivism, respect for authority) differ significantly from Western models. The quotes indicate that such misunderstandings can erode trust and require additional effort to correct, impacting overall success.

- **Sub-Theme 3.2: Resistance from Clients or Communities**
  - *International Counselor*: "Some clients or their families resist Western methods because they see them as foreign, and that makes it hard to implement my plan."
  - *Nigerian Counselor*: "Families here often prefer traditional healers over us, and convincing them to try therapy can feel like an uphill battle."
  - *Enugu State Counselor*: "In Enugu, some communities still see mental health help as shameful, so clients and their families push back, making it hard to move forward."
  - *International Client*: "I wanted to try his methods, but my family said no because they didn't trust outsiders, and that made therapy harder."
  - *Nigerian Client*: "My village elders said therapy was unnecessary, so I had to hide it from them, which made me less committed."
  - *Enugu State Client*: "Our community thinks seeing a counselor is weak, so I was scared to keep going, even though I knew I needed help."

Resistance from clients or communities, often rooted in cultural beliefs or stigma, creates a significant barrier to implementing culturally sensitive interventions. This is particularly evident in Nigeria and Enugu State, where traditional practices and community norms may conflict with psychological approaches. The quotes suggest that such resistance can lead to dropout, reduced engagement, and frustration for both counselors and clients, underscoring the need for strategies to bridge these gaps.

Discussion of findings

The thematic analyses of data collected offer profound insights into the development, implementation, and challenges of culturally sensitive treatment plans and interventions in multicultural counselling. These findings, derived from three research questions, illuminate the strengths, limitations, and contextual nuances of therapeutic practices, while also highlighting their broader implications for theory, practice, and policy.

Developing culturally sensitive treatment plans

The development of culturally sensitive treatment plans hinges on multiple interrelated factors that influence therapeutic effectiveness across diverse populations. This study identified five recurring elements: cultural self-awareness, client-centered assessment, adaptive strategies, ongoing learning, and structural awareness. Each contributes uniquely to a framework that prioritizes both the client's sociocultural identity and the counselor's reflexive stance.

Cultural self-awareness and humility emerged as foundational. Across all settings, counselors acknowledged that recognizing their own biases, privileges, and cultural assumptions was a prerequisite to engaging effectively with clients from different backgrounds. This aligns with Orlowski et al. (2024), who emphasize that cultural humility—unlike competence, which may imply mastery—is an ongoing, relational process. The Enugu State counselor's emphasis on learning from community elders reflects not only a personal openness but also respect for culturally embedded authority structures. This is especially relevant in Igbo culture, where elders often serve as custodians of moral guidance and conflict resolution (Oppong, 2022).

Client-centered cultural assessments were another core strategy. In practice, this involved exploring the client's beliefs, rituals, family structures, and language preferences as part of intake and ongoing sessions. For example, the inclusion of family role mapping and questions about ancestral beliefs provided a culturally coherent understanding of client needs. In the Nigerian context, where religious and traditional beliefs often coexist (sometimes in tension with Western psychological models), these assessments helped bridge conceptual gaps between client and clinician. Similar strategies were observed internationally, albeit with varying cultural anchors—for instance, narrative inquiry with Latinx clients or symbolic rituals with Indigenous populations (Tao et al., 2015).

Adaptive therapeutic strategies were also critical. Counselors reported modifying standard modalities—such as cognitive-behavioral therapy (CBT) or solution-focused therapy—to reflect cultural scripts and communication styles. In Nigeria and Enugu State, metaphors, proverbs, and storytelling (or "folktale-based reflection") were often used to reframe psychological problems, drawing on oral traditions to enhance resonance. This echoes the findings of (Domenech Rodríguez et al., 2011), who argue that fidelity to cultural values in therapy may require altering not only the content but the delivery of interventions.

Ongoing professional learning featured strongly, particularly among international counselors who expressed the need for continuous exposure to different cultural perspectives. In contrast, Nigerian counselors often resorted to informal learning—consulting with colleagues, community leaders, or religious figures—to compensate for gaps in formal education. While both groups recognized the importance of lifelong learning, their access to structured training varied greatly. Previous research stressed that this disparity reinforces the need for localized, context-driven education programs (Melbourne, 2023).

Lastly, **awareness of structural and systemic influences** shaped how treatment plans were designed and delivered. In Nigeria and Enugu State, poverty, stigma, limited access to clinics, and weak policy support were frequently cited. Counselors in these contexts often engaged in advocacy roles—educating families, working with churches, or liaising with traditional leaders to reduce resistance and promote treatment uptake. This multifaceted role extends beyond clinical work and reflects the broader ecological approach recommended in mental health service design (Saade et al., 2023).

Thus, the development of culturally sensitive treatment plans is not simply a matter of adapting tools but involves a deeper commitment to relational ethics, contextual learning, and cultural attunement. While international best practices provide a foundation, meaningful interventions in local contexts like Enugu State require rooted, flexible, and community-embedded approaches.

Integrating cultural competence into intervention strategies and impact on outcomes

The integration of cultural competence into intervention strategies was found to significantly enhance client engagement, therapeutic alliance, and clinical outcomes across all contexts studied. However, the form and effectiveness of these strategies varied depending on cultural setting, counselor training, and institutional support. Four major dimensions emerged from the data: cultural assessment, tailoring of therapeutic modalities, the use of cultural mediators, and the influence of systemic resources.

Comprehensive cultural assessment was the first step toward culturally informed intervention. In both international and Nigerian contexts, counselors emphasized the need to assess not only individual psychopathology but also cultural identity, spiritual beliefs, acculturation levels, and community dynamics. For instance, in Enugu State, therapists reported routinely exploring the client's family lineage, religious affiliations, and the influence of traditional healers. These assessments were not ancillary but central to case formulation and intervention design. This mirrors Kumpfer et al. (2017), who stress that culturally competent interventions begin with a systemic understanding of the client's lived environment, including familial, communal, and spiritual dimensions.

Tailoring therapeutic modalities involved modifying evidence-based techniques to fit cultural schemas. In international contexts, this included the adaptation of CBT to reflect clients' metaphorical or narrative communication styles—such as integrating storytelling and spiritual reflection with Latinx, Asian, and Indigenous clients (Kumpfer et al., 2017).

Similarly, in Enugu State, CBT was sometimes reframed using parables, proverbs, and indigenous wisdom traditions that emphasized collective responsibility and moral conduct. For example, one counselor used a proverb-based reappraisal method to help clients reframe irrational thoughts—an approach consistent with cognitive interventions (MacGill, 2018).

The use of cultural mediators—including family members, religious leaders, and respected elders—was particularly prominent in Nigerian and Enugu State settings. These individuals often functioned as bridges between the therapeutic process and cultural norms. Their involvement not only increased community buy-in but also served as a buffer against stigma. One Enugu counselor shared that including a family elder in a session helped validate the therapy process for the client, reducing feelings of alienation. This strategy aligns with the argument that culturally endorsed authority figures can legitimize mental health services in communities where psychotherapy may be viewed as foreign or suspicious (Huang & Zane, 2016).

Therapeutic alliance and treatment outcomes were consistently improved when cultural competence was integrated with relational attunement. Clients across contexts described feeling more understood and less judged when counselors respected their cultural norms and refrained from imposing unfamiliar paradigms. In the Nigerian context, clients often reported that validation of traditional coping mechanisms—such as prayer, ancestor consultation, or herbal remedies—fostered trust and sustained participation. These observations are supported by Jones et al. (2017), who highlight cultural responsiveness as a key predictor of treatment retention and symptom reduction. However, the extent of positive outcomes was moderated by resource availability. In Nigeria and particularly in rural Enugu State, systemic constraints—such as limited clinic infrastructure, lack of supervision, and inconsistent access to psychotropic medications—diminished the potential benefits of culturally competent interventions. Many counselors indicated that while they had the knowledge and willingness to provide culturally sensitive care, they lacked the tools, space, or staffing to sustain these efforts. This reflects findings by researchers who caution that the absence of institutional support can undermine even the most well-intentioned culturally adapted interventions in low-resource settings (Semrau et al., 2019).

In contrast, counsellors in international settings had greater access to supervision, cross-cultural training, and multidisciplinary teams, allowing for a more structured application of cultural adaptations. Yet, they often faced challenges related to client mistrust, especially among minority populations who had experienced systemic discrimination. This paradox underscores that while resource-rich settings may offer more institutional support, they are not immune to cultural barriers in practice (Chu et al., 2022; Saade et al., 2023). In summary, culturally competent interventions—when grounded in accurate assessment, relational humility, and context-sensitive adaptation—lead to improved outcomes.

However, their efficacy is not determined by clinical strategies alone but is shaped by broader structural and cultural ecosystems. The Nigerian and Enugu State experiences illustrate both the promise and limitations of culturally integrated counselling in settings where communal life, spirituality, and social hierarchies play pivotal roles in healing.

Challenges in implementing culturally sensitive strategies

While the value of culturally sensitive counselling was evident across contexts, its practical implementation revealed persistent and multifaceted challenges. These challenges were grouped into three primary categories: structural and resource limitations, gaps in culturally relevant training, and the complexities of navigating cultural misunderstandings. Together, these factors illuminate the systemic and interpersonal barriers that constrain the realization of culturally competent practice, especially in under-resourced and culturally diverse settings such as Nigeria and Enugu State.

Structural and resource limitations were a dominant theme, particularly in the Nigerian context. Counselors consistently reported insufficient funding, inadequate physical infrastructure, and a shortage of trained personnel. In Enugu State, for example, therapists operated in facilities lacking privacy, consistent electricity, or access to digital tools for case management and training. These limitations hindered their ability to engage in culturally nuanced practice and often forced them to prioritize immediate crises over long-term therapeutic planning. Previous researcher identify this resource inequity as one of the principal reasons mental health systems in LMICs struggle to scale up culturally competent services (Alloh et al., 2018). The scarcity of interpreters, culturally relevant educational materials, and psychometrically validated tools in local languages further intensified the problem.

In addition to physical constraints, counselors noted the **absence of institutional support** for culturally sensitive models. Many reported that national mental health policies did not prioritize or even reference cultural competence, resulting in an overreliance on imported models of care. This top-down imposition of Western paradigms, without space for local adaptation, risks cultural misalignment and reduces the efficacy of interventions. As researchers argue, culturally competent care must be institutionalized through health policy, not left to the individual discretion of overburdened practitioners (Fadele et al., 2024).

Training deficits also emerged as a critical barrier. Counselors across all regions acknowledged that their formal education lacked depth in cultural issues, especially those specific to their client populations. In Nigeria and Enugu State, many described training programs that emphasized Western diagnostic categories and therapeutic techniques without considering indigenous knowledge systems, traditional beliefs about mental illness, or culturally appropriate engagement strategies. One Enugu-based practitioner shared that she had to "learn on the job" about local stigma and familial hierarchies—an experience not uncommon in contexts where counselling is still a developing profession. These insights are consistent with previous findings that many African training institutions remain under-resourced and theoretically disconnected from their sociocultural environments (Melbourne, 2023).

Internationally, while training tended to be more robust and diverse, practitioners still expressed concern that cultural competence was treated as an "elective" topic rather than a foundational component of clinical education. This superficial integration led to knowledge gaps that undermined practice, particularly when working with minoritized clients or refugee populations. Researchers have long critiqued this trend, arguing that without sustained, experiential learning opportunities, cultural competence remains performative and incomplete (Soto et al., 2019; Tao et al., 2015).

Cultural misunderstandings—stemming from both counselor and client perspectives—formed the third major challenge. These misunderstandings often led to miscommunication, therapeutic rupture, and premature termination. e.g., clients' culturally shaped behaviors such as silence, indirect speech, or deferral to authority were sometimes misinterpreted by counselors as signs of resistance or avoidance. One international client recounted how their cultural expression of respect (e.g., not making direct eye contact) was read as disengagement, which eroded the therapeutic alliance. There is emphasis that such interpretive failures arise when clinicians lack the cultural empathy necessary to decode client behavior within its sociocultural frame (Soto et al., 2018; Varela, 2019). In Enugu State, misunderstandings were further complicated by community-level stigma and suspicion of counselling. Counselors described clients who disengaged after initial sessions due to family pressure, fear of social labeling, or concerns that their problems would be misunderstood through a "Western lens." This aligns with previous findings that traditional beliefs about mental health—particularly spiritual or moral explanations for distress—can lead communities to reject or mistrust formal mental health services (Saade et al., 2023). In these cases, culturally competent engagement required not only individual adaptation but broader community outreach, psychoeducation, and trust-building.

Moreover, role strain among practitioners emerged as a latent challenge. Many Nigerian counselors reported taking on multiple roles—therapist, advocate, educator, cultural translator, and sometimes mediator between traditional and biomedical systems. While this holistic engagement was often necessary, it also led to burnout and ethical dilemmas, especially in the absence of supervision or institutional safeguards. It should be cautioned that the overextension of counselors in resource-poor settings risks compromising the quality and sustainability of care (Mechael & Searle, 2010). In summary, while the ideal of culturally sensitive counselling is widely endorsed, its practical application is constrained by systemic inequities, educational limitations, and interpersonal complexity. Addressing these challenges requires a multi-level response—reform in training curricula, investment in culturally relevant infrastructure, and the co-production of mental health models that integrate local values and knowledge systems. Without such interventions, the potential of culturally responsive care will remain aspirational rather than achievable, particularly in marginalized communities.

Comparative insights across contexts

A comparative analysis of international, Nigerian, and Enugu State counselling contexts revealed both shared values and distinctive challenges in the implementation of culturally sensitive interventions. While all counselors emphasized the centrality of cultural responsiveness, their approaches and constraints varied significantly due to contextual factors such as resource availability, training access, sociopolitical frameworks, and prevailing cultural norms. International settings—especially those in high-income countries—tended to offer more formalized infrastructure and institutional support for multicultural counselling. Counselors in these environments reported access to professional development, supervision, and research-based guidelines tailored to diverse populations. Nevertheless, they grappled with cultural heterogeneity and the risks of ethnocentrism, especially when counselling clients from immigrant, Indigenous, or refugee backgrounds. Even with system-level support, therapists sometimes defaulted to individualistic paradigms ill-suited for collectivist cultures, revealing the limitations of applying Western theoretical models to non-Western clients. Furthermore, international practitioners acknowledged that despite policies promoting diversity, unconscious biases, language barriers, and power imbalances could subtly undermine therapeutic alliances (Ben-Arye et al., 2024).

By contrast, Nigerian counsellors operated in a markedly different environment. Their work was often shaped by systemic underinvestment in mental health, lack of institutionalized training, and limited access to culturally appropriate tools. Yet, they also benefited from a deep contextual understanding of their clients' cultural worlds, allowing for more intuitive integration of indigenous values into counselling. In Nigeria, counselling frequently intersected with religious, spiritual, and traditional systems, requiring therapists to navigate multiple epistemologies simultaneously. This dynamic created both opportunities and tensions: on one hand, it enhanced cultural alignment; on the other, it placed heavy demands on counsellors to reconcile conflicting worldviews within therapeutic frameworks. Within Enugu State, the study found a unique convergence of opportunity and constraint. As a subnational unit with a strong Igbo cultural identity, Enugu offered a more cohesive sociocultural backdrop, allowing for targeted interventions grounded in specific community norms—such as respect for elders, communal decision-making, and deference to ancestral traditions. Counsellors in Enugu often collaborated with community leaders or traditional healers to bridge the gap between psychological and cultural models of healing. However, they also faced acute shortages of trained personnel and health infrastructure, worsened by rural-urban disparities and limited state-level funding. The localized nature of stigma was also more pronounced; community resistance to therapy was shaped not only by religion or tradition but also by fears of social ostracization.

Across all contexts, one consistent finding was that clients highly valued cultural sensitivity in therapy. Whether expressed through language, rituals, metaphors, or the acknowledgement of familial roles, culturally attuned practices fostered trust and therapeutic engagement. However, when counsellors failed to recognize or incorporate cultural cues, clients often disengaged or rejected treatment altogether. This pattern reinforces the idea that cultural congruence is not a peripheral consideration but a core component of effective counselling across sociocultural settings. Therefore, while international contexts may offer better resources and training, they are not immune to cultural blind spots. Similarly, Nigerian and Enugu State practitioners, though constrained by resources, demonstrated innovative and culturally grounded practices that can enrich global understandings of effective counselling. A cross-contextual learning model—where practitioners from different regions exchange culturally specific strategies—could strengthen the field globally by challenging ethnocentric assumptions and valuing local expertise.

Implications

The findings of this study have significant implications for the future of multicultural counselling in both resource-rich and resource-constrained settings. First and foremost, the evidence suggests that cultural competence must be conceptualized as both a personal and systemic endeavor. It requires not only individual counselors to engage in reflective, adaptive, and respectful practice but also demands institutional frameworks that support culturally embedded care.

For counselling practice, this means moving beyond superficial inclusion of cultural references to deeper engagement with clients' worldviews. Practitioners must be trained to elicit cultural narratives, adapt therapeutic models to local logics, and recognize non-Western healing traditions as valid components of the therapeutic process. In regions like Enugu State, this could involve structured partnerships with traditional healers, religious leaders, and community elders to co-create treatment plans that are socially and spiritually coherent.

For training and education, there is a clear need to overhaul existing curricula to ensure that cultural competence is not relegated to elective modules or stand-alone workshops.

Multicultural training must be infused across foundational counselling theories, techniques, and ethics courses. Moreover, experiential learning—such as cultural immersion, case-based simulations, and community-engaged practice—should become standard features of counselor education, particularly in diverse societies.

Policy and systems-level implications are also critical. In Nigeria and similar LMICs, increased investment in mental health infrastructure is essential. This includes funding for training programmes, community-based services, culturally relevant research, and policy frameworks that formalize cultural competence as a standard of care. Ministries of health and education must recognize that sustainable mental health care cannot succeed without grounding interventions in local cultural realities. Internationally, counselling bodies and accreditation agencies should revise competency frameworks to emphasize cultural responsiveness not as a supplementary skill but as a core ethical responsibility.

Limitations

Despite the relevance of these findings, the study is not without limitations. First, the scope of the study was limited to three contexts—international, Nigerian national, and Enugu State subnational. While these provide useful comparative insight, the findings may not fully generalize to other cultural or geopolitical settings, such as Northern Nigeria, West African francophone countries, or diasporic African communities. Broader comparative studies are needed to capture the full diversity of cultural experiences in mental health care.

Second, the study did not measure client outcomes quantitatively, such as symptom reduction, functional improvement, or satisfaction indices. Incorporating mixed-methods or longitudinal designs would provide a more comprehensive understanding of how cultural competence affects measurable outcomes over time.

Nevertheless, this study contributes meaningfully to the growing discourse on culturally responsive counselling, particularly in underrepresented regions. It underlines the need to honor both the cultural depth of clients and the professional responsibility of counselors to engage with difference ethically, intelligently, and relationally.

References

Abdulmalik, J., Kola, L., & Gureje, O. (2016). Mental health system governance in Nigeria: Challenges, opportunities and strategies for improvement. *Global Mental Health, 3*. https://doi.org/10.1017/gmh.2016.2

Alloh, F. T., Regmi, P., Onche, I., Teijlingen, E. Van, & Trenoweth, S. (2018). Mental health in low-and middle income countries (LMICs): Going beyond the need for funding. *Health Prospect, 17*(1). https://doi.org/10.3126/hprospect.v17i1.20351

Arundell, L. L., Barnett, P., Buckman, J. E. J., Saunders, R., & Pilling, S. (2021). The effectiveness of adapted psychological interventions for people from ethnic minority groups: A systematic review and conceptual typology. *Clinical Psychology Review, 88*. https://doi.org/10.1016/j.cpr.2021.102063

Ben-Arye, E., Lopez, G., Rassouli, M., Ortiz, M., Cramer, H., & Samuels, N. (2024). Cross-cultural patient counseling and communication in the integrative medicine setting: Respecting the patient's health belief model of care. *Current Psychiatry Reports, 26*(8), 422–434. https://doi.org/10.1007/s11920-024-01515-2

Bernal, G., & Domenech Rodríguez. (2012). Cultural adaptations: Tools for evidence-based practice with diverse populations. In *Cultural adaptations: Tools for evidence-based practice with diverse populations*. https://doi.org/10.1037/13752-000

Braun, V., & Clarke, V. (2006). Using thematic analysis in psychology. *Qualitative Research in Psychology, 3* (2), 77–101. https://doi.org/10.1191/1478088706qp063oa

Budge, S. L., Thai, J. L., Tebbe, E. A., & Howard, K. A. S. (2016). The intersection of race, sexual orientation, socioeconomic status, trans identity, and mental health outcomes. *The Counseling Psychologist, 44*(7). https://doi.org/10.1177/0011000015609046

Caitlin, O., & Tyler, J. T. (2025). *Psychotherapy and therapeutic relationship*. StatPearls Publishing.

Chu, W., Wippold, G., & Becker, K. D. (2022). A systematic review of cultural competence trainings for mental health providers. *Professional Psychology: Research and Practice, 53*(4). https://doi.org/10.1037/pro0000469

Domenech Rodríguez, M. M., Baumann, A. A., & Schwartz, A. L. (2011). Cultural adaptation of an evidence based intervention: From theory to practice in a Latino/a community context. *American Journal of Community Psychology, 47*(1), 170–186. https://doi.org/10.1007/s10464-010-9371-4

Eaton, J., Nwefoh, E., Okafor, G., Onyeonoro, U., Nwaubani, K., & Henderson, C. (2017). Interventions to increase use of services; mental health awareness in Nigeria. *International Journal of Mental Health Systems, 11*(1). https://doi.org/10.1186/s13033-017-0173-z

Ebigbo, P. O., Oluka, J., Ezenwa, M., & Obidigbo, G. (2016). Harmony restoration therapy. In *An African contribution to psychotherapy*.

Fadele, K. P., Igwe, S. C., Toluwalogo, N.-O., Udokang, E. I., Ogaya, J. B., & Lucero-Prisno, D. E. (2024). *Mental health challenges in Nigeria: Bridging the gap between demand and resources, 11*. Cambridge Prisms: Global Mental Health. https://doi.org/10.1017/gmh.2024.19

Farquhar, J. M., Stonerock, G. L., & Blumenthal, J. A. (2018). Treatment of anxiety in patients with coronary heart disease: A systematic review. *Psychosomatics, 59*(4). https://doi.org/10.1016/j.psym.2018.03.008

Gureje, O., Abdulmalik, J., Kola, L., Musa, E., Yasamy, M. T., & Adebayo, K. (2015). Integrating mental health into primary care in Nigeria: Report of a demonstration project using the mental health gap action programme intervention guide. *BMC Health Services Research, 15*(1). https://doi.org/10.1186/s12913-015-0911-3

Gwyer, J., & Hack, L. (2014). In search of cultural competence. *Journal, Physical Therapy Education, 28*(1). https://doi.org/10.1097/00001416-201410000-00001

Hays, P. A. (2009). Integrating evidence-based practice, cognitive-behavior therapy, and multicultural therapy: Ten steps for culturally competent practice. *Professional Psychology: Research and Practice, 40*(4). https://doi.org/10.1037/a0016250

Huang, C. Y., & Zane, N. (2016). Cultural influences in mental health treatment. *Current Opinion in Psychology, 8*. https://doi.org/10.1016/j.copsyc.2015.10.009

Huey, S. J., Tilley, J. L., Jones, E. O., & Smith, C. A. (2014). The contribution of cultural competence to evidence-based care for ethnically diverse populations. *Annual Review of Clinical Psychology, 10*. https://doi.org/10.1146/annurev-clinpsy-032813-153729

Igwe, P. A., Newbery, R., Amoncar, N., White, G. R. T., & Madichie, N. O. (2020). Keeping it in the family: Exploring Igbo ethnic entrepreneurial behaviour in Nigeria. *International Journal of Entrepreneurial Behaviour & Research, 26*(1), 34–53. https://doi.org/10.1108/IJEBR-12-2017-0492

Ikwuka, U. (2016). Perceptions of mental illness in South-Eastern Nigeria: Causal beliefs, attitudes, help-seeking pathways and perceived barriers to help-seeking. *Journal of Mental Health, 13*(1).

Jidong, D. E., Bailey, D., Sodi, T., Gibson, L., Sawadogo, N., Ikhile, D., Musoke, D., Madhombiro, M., & Mbah, M. (2021). Nigerian cultural beliefs about mental health conditions and traditional healing: A qualitative study. *The Journal of Mental Health Training, Education and Practice, 16*(4). https://doi.org/10.1108/JMHTEP-08-2020-0057

Jones, J., Lee, L., Zigarelli, J., & Nakagawa, Y. (2017). Culturally responsive adaptations in evidence-based treatment: The impact on client satisfaction. *Contemporary School Psychology, 21*(3). https://doi.org/10.1007/s40688-016-0118-6

Jones-Smith, E. (2020). Culturally diverse counseling: Theory and practice. In *Culturally diverse counseling: Theory and practice*. https://doi.org/10.4135/9781071800744

Kumpfer, K., Magalhães, C., & Xie, J. (2017). Cultural adaptation and implementation of family evidence-based interventions with diverse populations. *Prevention Science, 18*(6), 649–659. https://doi.org/10.1007/s11121-016-0719-3

MacGill, V. (2018). Reframing cognitive behaviour theory from a systems perspective. *Systemic Practice and Action Research, 31*(5). https://doi.org/10.1007/s11213-017-9440-9

Mechael, P., & Searle, S. (2010). Barriers and gaps affecting mHealth in low and middle income countries: Policy white paper. *Health San Francisco, 54*. https://doi.org/10.4103/0019-557X.73274

Melbourne, E. (2023). Challenges and opportunities in counsellor education in Nigeria: A comprehensive analysis. *International Journal of Innovative Education Research, 11*(2), 218–224. www.seahipaj.org.

Oppong, S. (2022). Indigenous psychology in Africa: Centrality of culture, misunderstandings, and global positioning. *Theory & Psychology, 32*(6), 953–973. https://doi.org/10.1177/09593543221097334

Orlowski, E. W., Moeyaert, M., Monley, C., & Redden, C. (2024). The effects of cultural humility on therapeutic alliance and psychotherapy outcomes: A systematic review and meta-analysis. *Counselling and Psychotherapy Research, 25*(2), Article e12835.

Perkinson. (2007). In *The treatment plan*.

Polites, A., Sewick, B., Florin, J., & Trytek, J. (2025). In *Addictions counseling essentials*. https://LibreTexts.org.

Saade, S., Lamarche, A. P., Khalaf, T., Makke, S., & Legg, A. (2023). What barriers could impede access to mental health services for children and adolescents in Africa? A scoping review. *BMC Health Services Research, 23*(1). https://doi.org/10.1186/s12913-023-09294-x

Semrau, M., Alem, A., Ayuso-Mateos, J. L., Chisholm, D., Gureje, O., Hanlon, C., Jordans, M., Kigozi, F., Lund, C., Petersen, I., Shidhaye, R., & Thornicroft, G. (2019). Strengthening mental health systems in low- and middle-income countries: Recommendations from the Emerald programme. *BJPsych Open, 5*(5). https://doi.org/10.1192/bjo.2018.90

Soto, A., Smith, T. B., Griner, D., Domenech Rodríguez, M., & Bernal, G. (2018). Cultural adaptations and therapist multicultural competence: Two meta-analytic reviews. *Journal of Clinical Psychology, 74*(11). https://doi.org/10.1002/jclp.22679

Soto, A., Smith, T. B., Griner, D., Rodríguez, M. D., & Bernal, G. (2019). Cultural adaptations and multicultural competence. In *Psychotherapy relationships that work*. https://doi.org/10.1093/med-psych/9780190843960.003.0004

Sue, S. (1998). In search of cultural competence in psychotherapy and counseling. *American Psychologist, 53*(4). https://doi.org/10.1037/0003-066X.53.4.440

Sue, S. (2017). In search of cultural competence in psychotherapy and counseling. In *Counseling psychology*. https://doi.org/10.4324/9781315259178-36

Tao, K. W., Owen, J., Pace, B. T., & Imel, Z. E. (2015). A meta-analysis of multicultural competencies and psychotherapy process and outcome. *Journal of Counseling Psychology, 62*(3), 337–350. https://doi.org/10.1037/cou0000086

Varela, O. E. (2019). Multicultural competence: An empirical comparison of intercultural sensitivity and cultural intelligence. *European Journal of International Management, 13*(2). https://doi.org/10.1504/EJIM.2019.098146

CHAPTER 7

Multicultural counselling for youth and families

Introduction

Multicultural counselling for youth and families recognizes that helping young people and their relatives thrive requires more than generic therapeutic techniques. It demands deliberate attention to cultural identities, power dynamics, and contextual realities that shape experience and behavior. Contemporary frameworks in multicultural and social-justice counselling underline the need for counselors' self-awareness, understanding of clients' worldviews, culturally grounded relationships, and advocacy-oriented interventions. At multiple levels, individual, institutional, community, and policy, competent counselors engage in ongoing development of attitudes, knowledge, skills, and concrete action to address privilege, marginalization, and systemic barriers (Manivong et al., 2016). In practice, youth and family counselling in multicultural settings must be sensitive to how ethnicity, language, religion, socioeconomic status, migration history, and community norms influence development, communication, decision-making, and wellbeing. Youth often value counselor qualities that foster a sense of safety, choice, and autonomy; these relational conditions are necessary for forming and maintaining therapeutic alliances that support transformation (Dimic et al., 2023). When families bring differing cultural expectations, intergenerational tensions, or varied worldviews into counselling, the therapist's cultural responsiveness becomes central to both engagement and outcomes.

Against this backdrop, the present chapter centers youth and family counselling within multicultural contexts, drawing on theoretical foundations, empirical insights, and practical experience. It aims to clarify guiding principles and common practices that support culturally responsive work; examine barriers and challenges that therapists face when serving diverse youths and families; and offer concrete recommendations to strengthen cultural competence and effectiveness.

Research objectives guiding the chapter are:

1. to explore the principles and practices of family and youth counselling in multicultural contexts;

A Pragmatic Approach to Multicultural Counselling and Psychotherapy Skills Acquisition. https://doi.org/10.1016/B978-0-443-33939-4.00004-5

2. to identify challenges faced by therapists in providing effective multicultural counselling for youth and families;
3. to provide recommendations for improving the cultural competence of therapists working with youth and families.

Together, these objectives frame an inquiry that is both scholarly and practice-oriented. The chapter seeks to advance counselling that is ethically grounded, culturally attuned, and practically effective for diverse youth and family systems, recognizing that meaningful change occurs not only within individuals but through relationships, communities, and broader social structures.

What is youth counselling?

Youth counselling is a professional, developmentally attuned form of therapeutic support aimed at adolescents and young people as they face emotional, social, academic, and identity-related challenges. It involves a trained practitioner helping a young person explore experiences, strengthen coping skills, and make adaptive decisions within the context of their life circumstances. Crucially, it relies on a strong, collaborative therapeutic relationship, with respect to the youth's perspective, autonomy, and cultural background, to improve engagement, reduce dropout, and support positive outcomes. Empirical work highlight this relational emphasized that young people prioritize clinicians who connect well, protect their space, treat them as equals, and work in ways that feel right to them, and such qualities are linked to sustained engagement in mental health care (Stubbing & Gibson, 2022). In multicultural or migration-affected settings, youth counselling also attends to unique post-migration stressors, developmental shifts, and intersecting cultural identities that influence a young person's well-being and integration. Scholars note that as newcomer youth populations grow, service providers must be knowledgeable about these cultural and developmental challenges and employ culturally responsive competencies to meet their needs effectively. Thus, youth counselling is not merely problem-solving; it is a culturally sensitive, relationship-based process that supports young people's psychological and social development during a pivotal life stage.

Youth counselling in Nigeria is a specialized form of guidance and psychological support designed to help adolescents navigate the developmental, educational, social, and emotional challenges that arise within the country's unique cultural and socioeconomic environment. Nigerian youths grow up within diverse ethnic traditions, communal value systems, religious expectations, extended-family structures, and sometimes conflicting influences of modernization and globalization. Counselling therefore functions as a safe, structured space where young people can explore identity questions, manage peer pressure, understand emotional difficulties, and make informed decisions about education, career, relationships, and personal behavior. Furthermore, in the Nigerian context, youth counselling also plays a preventive role. Many young people face pressures such as academic competition, unemployment anxieties, family expectations, exposure to social media, substance use, and in some regions, insecurity or community violence. Counselling helps them develop resilience, problem-solving skills, and healthy coping strategies. Schools, faith-based organisations, and community centers often serve as the primary settings for youth counselling, underscoring the country's collective approach to child development.

Culturally, Nigerian youth counselling recognizes that adolescents rarely make decisions independently of family and community norms. Counselors must therefore understand cultural hierarchies, respect for elders, extended family involvement, and religious influences when working with young people. For example, discussions about career choices, relationships, or personal values must be handled with sensitivity, acknowledging that many Nigerian youths balance personal aspirations with expectations from parents, kinship groups, or religious communities. Additionally, because mental health stigma remains significant in many Nigerian communities, counselors often adopt a strengths-based, culturally responsive, and educational approach, focusing on guidance, empowerment, and mentorship rather than labels. Effective youth counselling in Nigeria, therefore, is not only therapeutic but developmental, culturally grounded, and oriented toward helping young people become well-adjusted, responsible, and socially engaged adults.

What is family counselling?

Family counselling, often used interchangeably with family therapy, is a psychotherapeutic approach that views relational patterns within a family or close interpersonal system as central to understanding and alleviating problems. A widely cited definition describes it as an approach focused on changing interactions among family members or between a family and other interpersonal systems, with the goal of easing problems initially presented by one or more individuals, subsystems, or the family as a whole (Yoshikawa et al., 2012). From a global practice standpoint, family-based interventions are among the most commonly used modalities in mental health care. Systematic reviews note that reasons for seeking therapy frequently involve family conflicts, and that family systems approaches rank highly alongside other prominent models such as cognitive behavioral therapy in international practice (Todd et al., 2025).

The core logic is systemic distress or dysfunction experienced by one member is understood in relation to patterns of communication, roles, boundaries, and interactional sequences within the family system rather than solely within the individual. Interventions therefore aim to shift these patterns, improving communication, reducing conflict, strengthening cooperation, or mobilizing family strengths, so that changes ripple through the system, benefiting multiple members. Studies further emphasize relational ingredients of helpful family counselling globally, including therapist warmth, respectful collaboration, and techniques that enhance reflection, emotional expression, and perspective-taking (Todd et al., 2025). This emphasize that, worldwide, effective family counselling is not merely about problem-solving for one person, but about fostering healthier relationships and systemic change through a culturally attuned, participatory therapeutic process.

Family counselling in Africa and in Nigeria remains a relational, systemic form of professional support aimed at improving the wellbeing of family units by addressing interaction patterns, communication, roles, and broader social forces that shape family life. From an African perspective, contemporary scholarship stresses that systemic family work cannot be divorced from sociocultural, historical, and political realities colonial legacies, social justice issues, economic disparities, and community structures all influence how families experience distress and healing. Recent work argues for Afrocentric or socially-just paradigms that foreground local worldviews, communal resilience, and indigenous values, rather than importing models that may overlook African contexts (Asiimwe et al., 2026). Similarly, research on the development of systemic family therapy across Africa notes a growing recognition that family health is deeply embedded in relational and contextual structures. While family therapy is expanding on the continent, there remain barriers related to training, implementation, and adapting Western-derived models to local realities. Scholars describe a shift toward systemic perspectives that better fit African social and cultural contexts, acknowledging both the promise and the challenges of building locally relevant family therapy capacity (Asiimwe et al., 2023).

In Nigeria, family counselling is understood within a partly developing professional landscape where counselling and psychotherapy specialties including marriage and family counselling are still being strengthened through education, research, and practice. Nigerian scholarship calls for more practice-oriented training, stronger research base, and integration of indigenous approaches, so that counselling becomes more relevant and accessible to the population. This includes expanding training beyond theory to community practice, developing local counselling specialties, and promoting indigenous therapeutic models alongside global ones (Kate & Ekwe, 2021). Empirical studies within Nigeria also illustrate the positive role of counselling for families facing specific challenges. For instance, research on families of children with intellectual disability in Cross River State found that counselling had significant positive impacts on parents' emotional stability and on stabilizing families, highlighting how family-focused therapeutic support can strengthen family functioning in Nigerian settings (Akinwumi et al., 2024). Taken together, family counselling in Africa and Nigeria is framed not merely as an import of Western therapy techniques but as a culturally grounded, systemic practice. It aims to strengthen dialog, shared understanding, and adaptive family functioning while attending to local cultural values, communal ties, and the socio-political forces that shape family life.

Theoretical perspectives

A robust framework for youth and family counselling draws on several complementary theories. Below are four widely cited perspectives that together help explain how problems arise, how change occurs, and what counselors should attend to, especially in culturally diverse settings.

Multicultural counselling competencies and responsiveness

A foundational perspective emphasizes the counselor's awareness, knowledge, and skills to work effectively across cultural differences. Sue and colleagues' model, long referenced in multicultural counselling literature, specifies three core components:

- cultural awareness of one's own biases and values,
- cultural knowledge of the client's worldview, and
- culturally appropriate intervention skills (Sue et al., 2009).

Subsequent discussions highlight that cultural competence is not merely a personal trait but a process involving adaptive strategies and responsive relationships. Research reviewing definitions stresses that competent care incorporates culture into assessment, remains vigilant to cultural dynamics, and adapts interventions to clients' cultural needs. More recent empirical work with newcomer youth explicitly links counselor awareness, knowledge, and skills with multicultural counselling relationships, underscoring their practical relevance in diverse contexts (Zak et al., 2025). Why this theoretical perspective matters for youth and families is that cultural responsiveness shapes trust, engagement, and perceived relevance of therapy. A systematic synthesis of youth perspectives on the therapeutic alliance also found that adolescents value safety, choice, autonomy, and relational quality elements that overlap strongly with culturally responsive practice (Dimic et al., 2023). This implies that counselors should guide assessment of family or youth needs with attention to cultural meanings; individualized communication and interventions to reflect clients' cultural values; prioritize ongoing self-reflection and learning.

Family systems theory

Family systems perspectives conceptualize individual symptoms or struggles as embedded in patterns of relationships, roles, and emotional processes within the family. Bowen-inspired formulations remain central, particularly the construct of differentiation of self the ability to balance emotional connection and independent thinking in relationships. A recent scoping review of Bowen's core construct reports substantial evidence linking higher differentiation to better psychological health, marital quality, and intergenerational relationships, signifying its continuing relevance for practice (Calatrava et al., 2022). A contemporary overview of Bowen family systems theory reiterates its role in guiding family therapy, showing how theory informs therapist stance and interventions with parents and adolescents (Brown & Errington, 2024).

This theory matters for youth and families because:

- Many youth problems manifest within ongoing family cycles conflict, enmeshment, or disengagement so systems perspectives prompt counselors to work with interactions, not only individual symptoms.
- The theory supports exploring intergenerational patterns, emotional reactivity, and boundaries, all critical in culturally layered families where roles and authority may be strongly influenced by tradition or community norms.

To apply the theory in counselling, counselors should map family interaction patterns, coach family members to maintain clarity under stress, and help parents and youth reduce reactive patterns that escalate conflict or hinder autonomy.

Ecological or socio-ecological systems theory

Ecological perspectives stress that youth development and family functioning occur within multiple, interacting environments school, community, institutions, and broader cultural and social structures. While Bronfenbrenner's classic bio-ecological ideas underlie this viewpoint, contemporary applications emphasize practical partnerships among families, schools, communities, and other stakeholders. For instance, recent work using Bronfenbrenner's framework advocates expanding collaboration beyond just families and schools to include community and higher-education partners, illustrating the practical relevance of ecological thinking for real-world youth support (Stanley & Kuo, 2022).

This perspective is relevant for youth and families counselling because:

- It broadens the lens from individual or family issues to contextual factors such as community resources, social norms, economic pressures, or policy environments that influence youth outcomes.
- Helps counselors identify leverage points beyond the immediate family, e.g., school relationships or community programs, that can reinforce therapeutic gains.

To apply the theory in counselling, counselor should assess influences at multiple levels, coordinate with schools or community services, and design interventions that consider not just the family but also their broader social ecology.

Relationship-centered perspectives emphasizing autonomy and collaboration

While not a single formal school like the others, a growing body of youth-focused research emphasized how the quality of the therapeutic relationship, marked by safety, autonomy, and meaningful collaboration, drives engagement and change. The systematic review of young people's experiences cited above highlights that youth value therapist qualities and conditions fostering autonomy and choice, and perceive the relationship as central to the therapy process (Dimic et al., 2023). Coupling this relational emphasis with multicultural competencies creates a framework where counselors attend closely to both culture and the youth's sense of ownership over therapy. For families, it also signals the importance of respectful collaboration, joint decision-making, and listening to multiple voices parents, children, extended family in shaping goals and methods. To apply this perspective, counselors need to:

- Establish shared goals, invite youth and family members to contribute preferences, and adapt session flow based on clients' responses.
- Monitor alliance and autonomy regularly; adjust strategies if youth or family members feel pressured, misunderstood, or sidelined.

Integrating the perspectives

These theoretical lenses are complementary rather than mutually exclusive. Multicultural competence provides the ethical and practical foundation for culturally attuned care; family systems guide attention to interaction patterns; ecological theory expands the focus to wider contexts; and relationship-centered approaches keep the alliance and client autonomy at the heart of practice. Together they offer a coherent framework for work with diverse youth and families, whether in global, African, or Nigerian settings.

My experience as a relationship and marriage counselor

My work as a relationship and marriage counselor has exposed me to the depth and complexity of couple and family dynamics within culturally diverse settings. Over the years, I have encountered couples whose challenges were not merely interpersonal but deeply rooted in cultural expectations, family traditions, gender roles, and community pressures. These experiences have strengthened my appreciation for the fact that no two relationships exist in isolation; every marital or relational issue is embedded within a broader cultural narrative. This understanding has shaped my counselling approach, prompting me to treat culture not as an external variable but as a central lens through which couples interpret love, commitment, conflict, and healing.

In practice, many couples come into therapy carrying unspoken assumptions formed by their upbringing, religious values, and extended family systems. For example, some partners operate with strong communal or collectivist orientations where family elders influence marital decisions, while others adopt more individualistic interpretations of marriage driven by personal autonomy and modern aspirations. Navigating these differences requires sensitivity, patience, and the ability to hold space for multiple cultural truths. My sessions often involve helping partners articulate the cultural stories that shape their expectations of marriage stories about respect, authority, finances, emotional expression, or parenting and guiding them toward shared meanings that honor both backgrounds.

Furthermore, my experiences have taught me that conflict in relationships often arises from cultural misalignment rather than a lack of love or commitment. In many cases, partners struggle not because they are incompatible, but because they speak "different cultural languages" about responsibility, affection, or communication. By gently helping couples uncover these hidden cultural scripts, therapy becomes a journey of understanding rather than blame. This culturally reflective process has consistently led to breakthroughs, allowing couples to appreciate one another's perspectives and negotiate healthier relational patterns. Additionally, working with married couples from different ethnic, linguistic, or religious backgrounds has enhanced my competence in multicultural counselling. It has challenged me to remain aware of my own biases, to avoid imposing external standards on clients, and to practice deep listening, especially when clients express culturally sensitive issues such as gender roles, fertility expectations, or extended-family involvement. Over time, I have integrated approaches that blend systemic thinking, empathy, narrative exploration, and cultural humility. These experiences continue to shape my identity not only as a counselor but also as an educator who trains future practitioners to approach family and marital counselling with cultural intelligence and reflexivity.

Ultimately, my work has reinforced a key insight that effective relationship and marriage counselling requires more than therapeutic techniques; it demands an authentic understanding of how culture shapes emotional life and interpersonal behavior. This awareness has enriched my practice and strengthened my conviction that culturally responsive counselling is essential for supporting healthy relationships in our increasingly diverse society.

My experience as a career coach

My experience as a career coach has been deeply shaped by years of dedicated work with young people across different cultural, socioeconomic, and educational backgrounds. Motivated by the desire to empower youths and strengthen families, I have consistently pursued innovative and culturally sensitive approaches to career development, employability enhancement, and purpose discovery. Over the years, I have done extensive work in career coaching and youth employability, recognizing that career uncertainty often creates tension in families and affects young people's self-esteem, decision-making ability, and future stability. This realisation drove my commitment to designing interventions that support both youths and their parents, ultimately promoting peace, understanding, and harmony in homes. As part of this commitment, I have organized numerous career seminars, workshops, and coaching sessions for students from secondary through tertiary institutions, often inviting parents to participate so that both sides gain clarity, communicate effectively, and work toward shared career goals. These family-inclusive programmes have contributed significantly to reducing conflict, improving parental support, and fostering more holistic career development outcomes.

In my professional journey, I developed two major frameworks that have shaped my coaching practice. The first is the Rational Emotive Career Coaching (RECC) model, which integrates Rational Emotive Behavior Therapy principles into career guidance (Otu, 2025; Otu & Omeje, 2021; Otu & Sefotho, 2024). This model emerged from my observation that many youths' career struggles stem from irrational beliefs fear of disappointing parents, pressure to conform, anxiety about failure, or internalised negative comparisons. Through RECC, I help young people identify, challenge, and refocus these unhelpful thoughts, building healthier belief systems that lead to more confident and objective career decisions. Building on my experience, I later developed the Purpose-Based Career Coaching Framework (PBCCF), a more holistic model that guides individuals to align their unique purpose, identity, and values with their career choices. I also tested the effect of this framework on career decision-making, demonstrating its positive influence on clarity, motivation, and long-term planning (Otu et al., 2023, Otu, 2024; Otu & Eseadi, 2024; Victor-Aigbodion & Eseadi, 2025). This purpose-oriented approach has proven particularly effective for youths navigating complex cultural expectations, economic realities, and shifting labor market demands.

My contribution to the field extends to scholarship as well. I have co-edited a book on career coaching and employability, reflecting my commitment to expanding the body of knowledge available to practitioners, educators, policymakers, and families. This publication, along with my practical work, reinforces my focus on empowering young people with the skills, mindsets, and opportunities needed to become employable, productive, and fulfilled adults. My career coaching practice is also deeply informed by my background in multicultural counselling. Working with youths and families in Nigeria's richly diverse environment has strengthened my sensitivity to cultural norms, family dynamics, belief systems, economic disparities, and regional variations that influence career choices. I approach every coaching relationship with respect for cultural identity, understanding that career decisions do not occur in a vacuum they are shaped by family expectations, community values, religious beliefs, and social realities. This multicultural lens enables me to tailor interventions that are culturally appropriate, inclusive, and sustainable. General, my journey as a career coach has been characterized by innovation, cultural responsiveness, and a strong commitment to youth empowerment and family harmony. Through research, teaching, coaching, and community engagement, I continue to contribute to a future where young people confidently pursue their purpose, families support their growth, and communities benefit from their potential.

The role of educators in promoting youth and family counselling in a multicultural context

Educators play a central role in supporting the psychological, social, and emotional wellbeing of young people, particularly within multicultural societies where learners navigate diverse cultural expectations, intersecting identities, and varying family dynamics. In such contexts, educators contribute significantly to youth and family counselling by fostering culturally responsive learning environments, identifying emerging psychosocial concerns, and linking students and parents to appropriate counselling services. First, educators serve as early identifiers of behavioral, emotional, and academic challenges among youths. Due to their daily interaction with students, they are often the first professionals to observe patterns such as withdrawal, aggression, sudden academic decline, or distress associated with family or cultural conflict. Research highlights that teachers and school counselors in multicultural settings are essential in providing preliminary support and referrals, ensuring that students are connected to counselling services before challenges escalate. This early detection is particularly critical in contexts like Nigeria, where stigma surrounding mental health often delays help-seeking.

Second, educators play a vital role in promoting cultural competence and sensitivity within the school environment. In multicultural settings, such as Nigeria, where ethnicity, language, religion, and family norms vary widely, culturally competent educators help students feel understood and valued. By acknowledging cultural differences in communication, parenting styles, emotional expression, and conflict resolution, educators contribute to a school climate that supports both youth development and positive family relationships. This culturally responsive approach aligns with global calls for educational systems to integrate multicultural principles into teaching and counselling practices. Furthermore, educators facilitate family–school partnerships, which are essential for effective youth and family counselling. Through parent conferences, workshops, open-day dialogs, and community outreach, educators help parents understand their children's developmental needs, academic challenges, and psychosocial concerns. These interactions not only support counselling efforts but also reduce misunderstandings between parents and their children, especially in homes where generational or cultural value clashes exist. In multicultural societies, such partnerships promote communication and trust, thereby strengthening the family unit and enhancing youth resilience.

Educators also contribute through advocacy and curriculum integration. By incorporating topics such as emotional intelligence, conflict management, mental health literacy, and career awareness into classroom instruction, educators prepare young people to navigate personal and interpersonal challenges. Globally, scholars emphasize that embedding psychosocial skills within the curriculum enhances youths' ability to cope with stress, communicate effectively, and make informed decisions. In Nigeria, where formal counselling services are still developing in many schools, educators' involvement in psychosocial education is particularly vital. Finally, educators serve as collaborators with counselors and mental health professionals. Working alongside school counselors, psychologists, and social workers, they share insights into student behavior, cultural contexts, and family backgrounds information essential to effective counselling. Collaborative practices ensure that interventions are holistic, culturally grounded, and responsive to the lived realities of the youth.

Characteristics of youth and family counselors in a multicultural context

Working with youths and families in multicultural settings requires specialized competencies that go beyond conventional counselling skills. Youth and family counselors must understand how culture shapes identity development, communication patterns, parenting practices, emotional expression, conflict management, and expectations within the family system. The following characteristics are essential for counselors working effectively with young people and their families in culturally diverse contexts.

Competence in multicultural family dynamics

Effective counselors must possess deep knowledge of how different cultures define family roles, hierarchy, parenting styles, gender expectations, and intergenerational communication.

This competence enables them to interpret youth behavior within a cultural lens rather than through bias. For example, a behavior viewed as "rebellion" in one culture may be normal assertion of independence in another. Understanding these nuances helps counselors avoid misinterpretation and strengthen family functioning.

Sensitivity to youth development across cultures

Youth counselors require strong grounding in adolescent development cognitive, emotional, social, and moral but must also recognize how culture shapes these developmental tasks.

In multicultural contexts, counselors must understand:

- How cultural norms shape identity formation
- The impact of collectivist versus individualistic values on youth choices
- Cultural expectations for obedience, independence, or career pathways

This sensitivity helps counselors support youths in navigating tensions between cultural expectations and personal goals.

Advanced communication skills for intergenerational dialog

Youth and family counselling often involves bridging communication gaps between adolescents and parents.

Counselors must be skilled in:

- Mediating intergenerational conflict
- Facilitating respectful dialog
- Translating emotional experiences across cultural and age differences

These communication skills are critical in multicultural families where value clashes or acculturation gaps commonly arise.

Cultural humility and non-judgmental attitude

Youth and family counselors must approach clients with humility, recognizing that:

- Every family's cultural interpretation of problems is valid
- The counselor is a collaborator, not an authority figure
- Families often have indigenous wisdom and practices

Cultural humility allows the counselor to co-create solutions with the family rather than impose Western or personal values.

Flexibility in integrating culturally relevant interventions

Youth and family counselling in multicultural settings demands flexibility.

Counselors must adapt evidence-based practices to respect:

- Cultural rites
- Religious beliefs
- Parenting philosophies
- Extended family involvement

A flexible counselor recognizes when to integrate storytelling, communal decision-making, elders' involvement, or culturally familiar metaphors into the counselling process.

Advocacy skills for youth and family wellbeing

Many youths from multicultural backgrounds experience academic, economic, or social barriers.

Effective counselors advocate by:

- Linking youths to school supports
- Engaging parents in educational and developmental processes
- Navigating social service systems
- Addressing discrimination or exclusion where needed

Advocacy is crucial in contexts like Nigeria, where counselling services are still emerging and families often require guidance in accessing support.

Emotional stability and empathy for complex family issues

Youth and family counselors often encounter:

- Intergenerational conflicts
- Cultural identity struggles
- Mental health stigma in families
- Parenting stress
- Career decision conflicts

Empathy, patience, and emotional stability help the counselor remain calm, supportive, and effective, especially when navigating sensitive family issues influenced by culture.

Collaboration with schools, communities, and religious institutions

Youth and family counselors in multicultural societies work best when they collaborate with:

- Teachers
- School counselors
- Community leaders
- Religious leaders
- Parents' associations

Such collaboration ensures a holistic support system for youths and strengthens family cohesion across cultural groups.

Confidentiality and ethical adaptability

Ethical issues are more delicate in multicultural family counselling.

Counselors must navigate:

- Collective family decision-making
- Parental expectations for information access
- Youth confidentiality rights
- Cultural norms around disclosure

Being ethically grounded and culturally sensitive ensures trust and effectiveness.

Counselling LGBTQ+ youths and families

The acronym LGBTQ+ is an inclusive term used to describe diverse sexual orientations and gender identities. L refers to lesbian (women who experience emotional or romantic attraction to women), G to gay (commonly used for men attracted to men, though sometimes used more broadly), B to bisexual (individuals attracted to more than one gender), T to transgender (individuals whose gender identity differs from the sex assigned at birth), and Q to queer or questioning (those who either identify outside traditional categories or are exploring their identity). The "+" symbol recognizes additional identities and experiences that do not fit neatly within these categories, such as intersex, asexual, or other emerging identity labels. The term is primarily descriptive and is used in counselling and research to acknowledge human diversity in sexual orientation and gender identity, without implying uniform experiences or beliefs among individuals so identified.

Counselling LGBTQ+ youths and their families requires a developmentally sensitive, ethically grounded, and culturally responsive approach. Young people navigating questions of sexual orientation and gender identity often face complex psychological, social, and familial challenges, including stigma, identity confusion, value conflicts, and fear of rejection. These challenges may be intensified in sociocultural contexts where marriage, family continuity, and religious beliefs are strongly emphasized. Within professional counselling practice, the counselor's role is not to direct clients toward a particular sexual orientation, but to facilitate informed, reflective, and autonomous decision-making. This includes helping clients understand the social realities, potential challenges, and lived experiences associated with different sexual orientations, such as societal acceptance, family expectations, legal recognition, and personal wellbeing. Exploring both perceived benefits and limitations of various identity pathways allows clients and families to engage in realistic appraisal rather than idealized or fear-based assumptions.

Counselors may also support clients in examining their personal, cultural, religious, and relational values, including beliefs about marriage and family life. This process involves explaining the historical, cultural, and social purposes of marriage, such as companionship, mutual support, social stability, procreation, and intergenerational continuity, while acknowledging that definitions and expectations of marriage vary across cultures, faith traditions, and legal systems. Rather than imposing a singular or "true" definition, counselors encourage clients to critically reflect on how their identity, aspirations, and values align with their understanding of marriage and long-term relational goals.

Family counselling further focuses on dialog, psychoeducation, and emotional processing, helping families articulate fears, expectations, and hopes without resorting to rejection or coercion. The counselor maintains a neutral, non-judgmental stance, supporting respect for human dignity while recognizing the tensions that may arise between individual identity, cultural norms, and familial expectations. In multicultural and Global South contexts, ethical practice requires heightened sensitivity to legal constraints, religious convictions, and communal values. Counselors must balance cultural respect with professional responsibility, prioritizing psychological wellbeing, informed consent, and the client's right to self-determination. Ultimately, effective counselling in this area seeks not to prescribe identity choices, but to empower youths and families to make thoughtful, values-congruent decisions that promote mental health, relational stability, and personal integrity.

Nonetheless, a critical responsibility of the counselor in working with LGBTQ+ youths and families is to provide accurate, balanced, and developmentally appropriate enlightenment, ensuring that clients' decisions are not shaped primarily by ignorance, misinformation, fear, or external pressure. In many contexts, individuals may arrive at particular identity positions amid confusion, emotional vulnerability, social coercion, peer influence, traumatic experiences, or limited exposure to alternative perspectives. Counselling therefore serves an important educative function which is to help clients clearly understand concepts related to sexual orientation, identity development, relational commitments, and long-term psychosocial implications. Through structured psychoeducation and reflective dialog, counselors assist clients in disentangling personal convictions from imposed expectations, emotional distress, or situational pressures. This process does not involve directing clients toward predetermined outcomes, but rather equips them with knowledge, self-awareness, and critical reflection, enabling choices that are genuinely informed and freely made. By addressing gaps in understanding and creating space for thoughtful exploration, counselors help prevent decisions driven by fear, secrecy, or social conformity, thereby promoting autonomy, psychological wellbeing, and responsible life planning.

A faith-based counselling framework for working with LGBTQ+ youths and families

Within a faith-based counselling framework, enlightenment and guidance are grounded in religious teachings, moral traditions, and spiritual anthropology, while still upholding core counselling principles such as dignity, compassion, and informed choice. Faith-based counselling does not deny the psychological and emotional realities faced by LGBTQ+ youths; rather, it situates identity exploration within a broader understanding of purpose, meaning, and moral order as defined by a particular faith tradition. A central responsibility of the faith-based counselor is to clearly explain the faith's understanding of human identity, sexuality, relationships, and marriage, tracing these concepts to their theological and historical foundations. Marriage is presented not merely as a social institution, but as a purposeful covenant originally intended to foster companionship, moral responsibility, family stability, and, in many traditions, procreation and intergenerational continuity. Counselors help clients understand how these purposes inform the faith's definition of marriage and relational life, while acknowledging that contemporary societies hold multiple, often competing interpretations.

In this context, the counselor provides structured moral and spiritual enlightenment, explaining how different sexual orientations and relational pathways may align or conflict with the faith's teachings. This includes open discussion of perceived merits, challenges, and moral implications as understood within the faith tradition, as well as the psychological, familial, and communal consequences of various life choices. Importantly, this process is framed as guidance rather than coercion. Clients are encouraged to reflect prayerfully and thoughtfully, examining how their identity experiences, personal convictions, and long-term aspirations relate to the faith's vision of marriage, family, and purposeful living. Faith-based counselling also pays careful attention to conscience and free will. While the counselor may clearly articulate doctrinal positions, clients are not forced into predetermined outcomes. Instead, the counselor supports clients in making decisions that are informed, internally coherent, and consistent with their faith commitments, should they choose to uphold them. Where tension arises between personal experience and religious belief, counselling focuses on meaning-making, self-discipline, spiritual support, and coping strategies rather than rejection or condemnation.

Family engagement is a vital component of this framework. Counselors work with families to promote understanding, patience, and compassion, discouraging responses rooted in fear, shame, or hostility. Families are guided to uphold their faith values while maintaining relational bonds, emotional safety, and pastoral care for their children. The emphasis is on truth communicated with love, recognizing that harsh or punitive reactions often exacerbate psychological distress. In pluralistic and multicultural settings, faith-based counselors must clearly state the scope and limits of their approach, ensuring informed consent and respecting clients who may not fully share the same beliefs. Ethical practice requires transparency, referral when appropriate, and a commitment to non-violence, non-coercion, and psychological wellbeing. When practised responsibly, faith-based counselling offers clients a structured moral framework, spiritual resources, and supportive relationships that assist them in navigating complex identity questions with clarity, integrity, and hope.

Empirical research perspective

Approach

The approach to this study is qualitative in nature. Qualitative research is appropriate for this type of study because it allows for an in-depth exploration of the experiences, practices, challenges, and perceptions of therapists and youth in the context of multicultural family counselling. This approach prioritizes rich, descriptive data and aims to understand the subjective experiences of participants, rather than seeking to quantify data or establish causal relationships.

Research paradigm

The research paradigm guiding this study is interpretivism. Interpretivism is rooted in the belief that reality is socially constructed and that knowledge is subjective, shaped by cultural, social, and personal contexts. In this study, the focus is on understanding how therapists and youth from diverse backgrounds perceive and navigate therapeutic interventions in multicultural settings. Interpretivism aligns well with this research because it emphasizes understanding people's lived experiences and the meanings they attach to their cultural identities and therapeutic processes.

The interpretivist paradigm emphasizes the importance of understanding the subjective and contextual nature of participants' experiences. The researcher does not seek to predict or generalize findings but rather to understand how cultural backgrounds shape counselling practices and youth experiences.

Ontology

Ontology is concerned with the nature of reality and what we can know about it. In this study, the ontological assumption is that reality is socially constructed. The researcher assumes that the experiences of the therapists and youth in multicultural settings are subjective and influenced by their unique cultural backgrounds, values, and worldviews. Each participant's reality is seen as valid and meaningful within the context of their lived experiences.

This ontological stance aligns with the interpretivist paradigm, as it acknowledges that individuals' experiences of therapy and multicultural interactions cannot be understood outside the cultural, social, and familial contexts in which they occur. Reality is viewed as dynamic, influenced by cultural and societal factors that shape how individuals understand their roles, challenges, and interactions within therapy.

Epistemology

Epistemology concerns the theory of knowledge and how we come to know what we know. The epistemological stance in this study is constructivism. According to constructivism, knowledge is co-constructed between the researcher and participants. It emphasizes the idea that understanding is not objectively "discovered" but is actively constructed through social interaction, experiences, and dialog. The researcher's role is not to discover an objective truth, but to interpret and understand the meanings that participants attach to their experiences.

In line with the interpretivist paradigm and constructivism, this study emphasizes participant perspectives as central to understanding multicultural counselling. The researcher seeks to understand how therapists and youth make sense of their experiences, acknowledging that knowledge is subjective and context-specific. The researcher's interpretation is shaped by interactions with the participants, and reflexivity (awareness of the researcher's influence on the research process) is an important component of the epistemological approach.

Axiology

Axiology is the study of values and ethics in research. This study recognizes the inherent subjectivity and values that both the researcher and participants bring to the research process. The researcher is guided by a commitment to cultural respect, empathy, and ethical integrity in all stages of the research process. This includes acknowledging the cultural values and beliefs of participants, ensuring that their voices are heard and respected, and promoting a non-judgmental approach to understanding their experiences.

Ethically, the researcher maintains a strong focus on informed consent, confidentiality, and participant welfare, as outlined in the ethical considerations. Additionally, the researcher remains sensitive to the cultural norms of participants, ensuring that their values and practices are respected throughout the research process. The researcher's goal is to create a space where participants feel safe to share their perspectives, without feeling pressured to conform to dominant cultural norms or practices.

Research design

The research design for this study is qualitative, specifically utilizing a case study and phenomenological approach. The case study design allows for an in-depth exploration of individual and family experiences in multicultural counselling settings, focusing on a small, targeted group of participants. This design is ideal for examining the complexities of real-life cases and understanding the contextual factors that influence therapeutic outcomes.

In addition to case studies, the researcher uses phenomenological methods to explore the lived experiences of youth and therapists. Phenomenology focuses on understanding how individuals experience the world and make meaning of their experiences. The aim is to capture the essence of how participants experience multicultural family and youth counselling, considering the cultural contexts that shape these experiences.

Sample and sampling techniques

The study was conducted in Nigeria, with participants selected to provide a diverse representation of multicultural counselling practices. A total of eight counselors were chosen from major cities across Nigeria, including Abuja, Lagos, Enugu, Kano, Benin, Calabar, Sokoto, and Delta. These cities were selected to ensure a broad range of cultural, regional, and socioeconomic diversity, allowing for a comprehensive understanding of the challenges and practices involved in multicultural family and youth counselling in different contexts.

Purposive sampling was employed to select therapists with a minimum of 3 years of experience in providing multicultural counselling, particularly with youth and families from diverse cultural backgrounds. This method ensured the inclusion of professionals who had relevant expertise in addressing the unique cultural dynamics encountered in family and youth therapy. The selected therapists participated in in-depth interviews or focus groups, sharing insights into their therapeutic practices, challenges, and recommendations for improving cultural competence.

In addition to the therapists, youth participants were also included in the study. These participants were selected through a combination of purposive and snowball sampling techniques. The youth had received multicultural counselling and were aged 18 and above. To ensure that they had sufficient experience with the therapeutic process, participants were required to have engaged in therapy for at least 6 months. This criterion allowed for an in-depth exploration of their experiences, perspectives on cultural considerations in therapy, and the challenges they faced.

The inclusion of both therapists and youth participants provided a holistic view of multicultural family and youth counselling, capturing the perspectives of those directly involved in the therapeutic process. This approach ensured that the study reflected the diverse cultural contexts in Nigeria and addressed both the practices of therapists and the experiences of the youth they counsel.

Method of data collection

The data collection for this study primarily relied on qualitative methods to explore the principles and practices of family and youth counselling in multicultural contexts, identify challenges faced by therapists, and provide recommendations for improving the cultural competence of therapists. In-depth interviews were conducted with experienced multicultural family and youth therapists, as well as supervisors or trainers in the field. These semi-structured interviews allowed participants to share their experiences and expertise in a flexible manner, providing rich insights into the principles and practices of multicultural counselling. The interviews also addressed the challenges therapists encountered and gathered recommendations for enhancing cultural competence.

Additionally, focus groups were held with a diverse group of therapists or counselors who worked in multicultural settings. These focus groups fostered interactive discussions, allowing participants to elaborate on each other's experiences and collaborate on identifying common challenges and effective strategies for multicultural counselling. By facilitating group dialog, this method offered a more holistic view of the issues therapists faced and allowed for a range of perspectives on how to improve practice.

Furthermore, case studies were conducted with youth and family clients who had received counselling in multicultural settings. These case studies provided an in-depth understanding of how cultural competence in therapy influenced outcomes for youth and families. Detailed examinations of individual or family therapy sessions revealed the strategies employed by therapists to address cultural differences, as well as the challenges encountered and how these challenges were navigated. This qualitative approach offered valuable insights into the application of multicultural principles in real-world therapeutic contexts.

Method of data analysis

The analysis of the qualitative data collected through in-depth interviews, focus groups, and case studies followed a thematic approach to provide a rich understanding of the experiences of both therapists and youth clients in multicultural family and youth counselling.

The process began with familiarization with the data, where the researcher carefully reviewed the transcribed interviews and focus group discussions to immerse themselves in the data and gain a comprehensive understanding of the content. This step ensured that no important details were overlooked.

Next, initial coding was done, where the researcher systematically tagged significant sections of the data that were relevant to the study's objectives. These included aspects such as the principles and practices of multicultural counselling, the specific challenges faced by therapists, and the recommendations for improving cultural competence.

After the initial coding, the data underwent a process of theme generation. The researcher examined the codes and organized them into broader themes that best represented the recurring ideas and patterns across the data. This stage allowed for the identification of key issues and practices within multicultural counselling, as expressed by both therapists and youth clients.

Once the themes were established, a review of the themes was conducted to ensure they accurately reflected the data and the research questions. During this phase, the researcher checked the coherence and consistency of the themes, revising them as necessary to ensure they aligned with the study's objectives.

The final refinement of the themes involved naming and defining each theme to ensure clarity and focus. These themes were then used to interpret the findings and draw conclusions about the key factors influencing multicultural family and youth counselling in Nigeria.

Finally, the findings from the thematic analysis were written up in a narrative format, using direct quotes from participants to illustrate each theme. This approach helped maintain the authenticity of the data, ensuring that the voices of both therapists and youth clients were captured and reflected in the study.

This qualitative analysis provided a detailed understanding of the principles, challenges, and practices in multicultural family and youth counselling, contributing valuable insights into how cultural competence can be improved in therapeutic settings (Fig. 7.1).

Ethical considerations in the study

In conducting this study on multicultural family and youth counselling, several key ethical considerations were taken into account to ensure the protection of participants, maintain the integrity of the research, and respect the cultural values and beliefs of those involved.

1. Informed Consent: Informed consent was obtained from all participants involved in the study. Prior to participation, the researcher provided clear, accessible information about the purpose of the study, the nature of participation, the potential risks, and the expected benefits. Participants were informed that they had the right to withdraw from the study at any time without any consequences. For youth participants, parental consent was also sought, alongside the youth's assent, ensuring that both the family and the youth understood the study's aims and were willing to participate voluntarily.
   The informed consent process included detailed explanations about the confidentiality of responses, the use of data, and the potential for publication. The researcher emphasized that participation was voluntary and that refusal to participate would not affect any services the participants might be receiving.
2. Confidentiality and Privacy: The confidentiality of participants' personal and sensitive information was strictly maintained throughout the study. All data, including interviews and focus group discussions, were anonymized to protect the identities of participants.

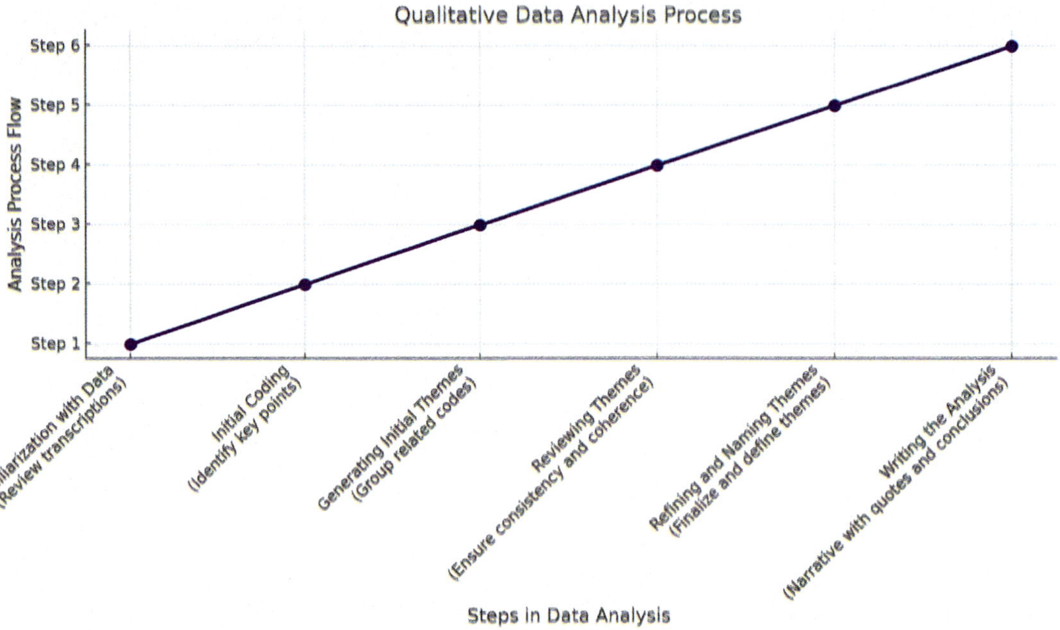

Figure 7.1
Qualitative data analysis process.

Identifying information was removed or coded to prevent traceability, and all recordings and transcripts were stored securely.

Participants were assured that their identities would remain confidential, and the results of the study would be presented in aggregate form. Any information that could potentially identify an individual or family was excluded from the analysis and final reporting.

The researcher also considered the cultural expectations regarding privacy, especially in multicultural contexts where some communities may have different views on confidentiality. The researcher ensured that these views were respected while still upholding the ethical requirement of confidentiality in the research process.

3. Cultural Sensitivity and Respect for Diversity: Given the diverse cultural backgrounds of the participants, the researcher ensured that the study was conducted with cultural sensitivity. This involved understanding the cultural norms and values of the participants, particularly in relation to mental health, therapy, and family dynamics. The researcher took care to avoid any biases or assumptions that could influence the interpretation of data. The researcher actively sought to recognize and respect the values and beliefs of each participant, especially when cultural differences were present in the therapeutic approaches discussed. For example, in discussing the role of traditional healers

or spiritual practices in therapy, the researcher ensured that these cultural aspects were approached with respect and without judgment.

The researcher also acknowledged their own cultural biases and worked to remain neutral and objective throughout the study. Cultural humility was an essential part of the researcher's approach, ensuring that the voices and experiences of participants from all cultural backgrounds were valued equally.

4. Protection from Harm: Participants were protected from harm throughout the research process. The researcher ensured that no participant was exposed to any risks or discomforts beyond what would be considered part of normal therapy discussions. Given the sensitive nature of the topics (mental health, family dynamics, and cultural practices), the researcher made it clear that participants could choose not to answer any questions they found uncomfortable or intrusive.

   In cases where the research process triggered emotional distress or discomfort, the researcher ensured that appropriate referrals for support or additional therapeutic services were provided. This included referrals to local mental health professionals or community support services. The researcher also provided a list of mental health resources for participants to access should they need further assistance.
5. Voluntary Participation and Right to Withdraw: All participants were informed that their participation was voluntary, and they had the right to withdraw from the study at any time without any negative consequences. The researcher emphasized that withdrawal from the study would not affect any ongoing therapy or support the participants were receiving, ensuring that no participant felt coerced into participating. The right to withdraw was also explained to the youth participants, with their autonomy being respected. The researcher maintained an open line of communication, ensuring that participants felt comfortable voicing any concerns about their involvement in the study.
6. Ethical Use of Data: The data collected during the study were used strictly for the purposes of the research. The researcher adhered to ethical guidelines regarding the analysis, interpretation, and presentation of data. All findings were presented in an anonymized and aggregated form, ensuring that no individual participant or family could be identified in the final report. The researcher ensured that any sensitive information shared by participants was treated with the utmost care and respect, and no personal data was published without prior consent. The researcher also acknowledged the limitations of the study, such as the potential for cultural misunderstandings in interpreting responses, and was transparent about these limitations in the reporting of findings.
7. Integrity and Transparency in Reporting: The researcher maintained integrity and transparency in reporting the findings of the study. The findings were presented in a way that accurately reflected the data, without exaggeration or misrepresentation. The researcher made every effort to present the perspectives of participants authentically, without letting personal biases influence the interpretation of the data.

Results

Principles and practices of family and youth counselling in multicultural contexts

In exploring effective counselling practices within multicultural environments, three major themes emerged from both therapist and youth perspectives. These themes reflect the complexities and opportunities inherent in delivering culturally responsive care in diverse societies.

Theme 1: cultural sensitivity and awareness (youth and therapist perspective)

Therapists' perspective

Cultural sensitivity emerged as a central principle among therapists working with diverse youth and families. Many therapists described cultural awareness as the starting point for building rapport and ensuring that interventions are not only effective but also respectful and contextually appropriate. They recognized that cultural norms deeply influence how clients interpret emotional distress, cope with conflict, and seek help.

> *Understanding a client's cultural background isn't optional—it's essential. If I don't grasp how their culture influences family roles or emotional expression, I risk misinterpreting their experience.*
>
> – ***Therapist participant.***

Therapists emphasized that failing to consider cultural dynamics can lead to mismatched interventions and a breakdown in trust.

> *In one session, I suggested open confrontation to resolve a family issue, not realizing that in their culture, direct confrontation with elders is considered deeply disrespectful. That was a turning point for me, I had to slow down and listen better.*
>
> – **Therapist participant.**

Several therapists shared that they invested time in learning about the cultures represented in their client populations, often beyond formal training.

> *I make it a point to read up on my clients' cultural practices, but more importantly, I ask them to teach me what I don't know. It's a partnership.*
>
> – **Therapist participant.**

Therapists also stressed the importance of avoiding stereotypes or assumptions.

> *Cultural awareness isn't just about knowing facts. Two families from the same ethnic group can have completely different worldviews. I try to stay curious rather than assume I already understand.*
>
> – **Therapist participant.**

Youth perspective

Youth participants frequently echoed the importance of cultural sensitivity but noted that it was often lacking in their therapeutic experiences. Some youth reported that therapists appeared unaware of the cultural pressures they faced, especially regarding family expectations, gender roles, and religious practices.

> *I had to explain why I couldn't talk about certain things at home. My therapist didn't get why it wasn't just about me—it was about my whole family and how we are supposed to act.*
>
> – **Youth participant.**

Others described feeling invalidated or dismissed when cultural factors were ignored or misunderstood.

> *My therapist once told me to just 'stand up for myself' at home. But in my family, speaking back to your parents is not okay. I felt like she didn't respect my way of life.*
>
> – ***Youth participant.***

In contrast, when therapists actively engaged with the youths' cultural identities, it created a safer and more affirming therapeutic environment.

> *One of the first things my counsellor asked was, 'What should I know about your background that will help me support you better?' That question made all the difference.*
>
> – **Youth participant.**

Youth expressed appreciation for therapists who learned about their languages, attended cultural events, or simply took the time to ask respectful questions about their traditions.

> *When my therapist greeted me in my language one day, it made me smile. It showed she cared about me beyond the sessions.*
>
> – **Youth participant.**

Importantly, youth also valued therapists who were open about what they didn't know and who approached cultural discussions with humility rather than expertise.

> *It's okay if they don't know everything. But I want them to care enough to ask and not make me feel weird for being different.*
>
> – **Youth participant.**

Theme 2: holistic and family-centered approaches (youth and therapist perspective)

Therapists' perspective

Therapists working with youth in multicultural settings commonly emphasized the importance of **holistic and family-centered approaches**, recognizing that in many cultures, the individual is embedded within a larger family and community system. Rather than focusing solely on the presenting problem or the individual client, these practitioners adopted an integrative view that considered relational dynamics, intergenerational patterns, and systemic influences.

> *In many of families I work with, decisions aren't made by individuals. They are made collectively. So if I only focus on the young person, I'm missing half the story.*
>
> – **Therapist participant.**

Several therapists shared that involving the family in counselling sessions, particularly parents or caregivers, allowed them to understand the root causes of conflicts, address communication breakdowns, and clarify misunderstandings shaped by cultural expectations.

> *A lot of issues stem from unspoken expectations between parents and youth. Involving both parties gives us a chance to unpack what's really going on beneath the surface.*
>
> – **Therapist participant.**

Holistic approaches also meant addressing emotional, social, academic, and spiritual needs in tandem, especially in communities where mental health is understood through a broader lens.

> *In some cultures, distress is not described in psychological terms. People will say things like 'my heart is heavy' or 'I'm cursed.' We have to listen to those metaphors and work with them, not against them.*
>
> – **Therapist participant.**

Some therapists noted that working with the entire family system allowed for culturally grounded healing, especially when traditional values were acknowledged and respected within the therapeutic process.

> *Sometimes, the most progress comes when we bring elders into the room; those with authority in the family. They help bridge the gap between tradition and the youth's emerging identity.*
>
> – **Therapist participant.**

Youth perspective

Youth participants expressed mixed but generally positive views about family involvement in therapy. Many acknowledged the value of including their parents or guardians in sessions, especially when it led to improved communication, understanding, and emotional support.

> *My mom never really listened to me before, but in therapy, she actually heard what I was saying. It was like a breakthrough for both of us.*
>
> – **Youth participant.**

Others felt that involving their families helped reduce the stigma they faced within the household and allowed for shared growth.

> *I used to feel like I was the problem. But when my parents joined a few sessions, they started to see that we all needed to change, not just me.*
>
> – **Youth participant.**

However, not all youth found family involvement beneficial. Some were concerned about privacy, judgment, or cultural taboos around sharing personal feelings in front of parents or relatives.

> *I didn't feel safe talking about everything when my dad was in the room. In my culture, we're taught to keep things private, especially from elders.*
>
> – **Youth participant.**

Several youth participants preferred a hybrid approach—starting with individual sessions and gradually involving family members once a foundation of trust and clarity had been established.

> *I needed time to figure out what I was feeling before bringing my parents in. Once I understood myself better, it was easier to let them be part of the process.*
>
> – **Youth participant.**

Some youth also expressed that therapists needed to be careful not to side with parents or reinforce family hierarchies during sessions.

> *Sometimes I felt like the therapist was trying to please my parents more than helping me. It's important they stay neutral, or it doesn't feel fair.*
>
> – **Youth participant.**

Theme 3: integration of traditional and modern therapeutic techniques (youth and therapist perspective)

Therapists' perspective

In multicultural counselling contexts, therapists often find themselves navigating between traditional belief systems and contemporary psychological frameworks. Many therapists acknowledged the necessity of integrating both approaches to meet the cultural and emotional needs of youth and families in a respectful and effective manner.

> *In my practice, I've learned not to dismiss traditional beliefs, even when they don't align with Western psychological models. They carry meaning, and we have to honour that.*
>
> – **Therapist participant.**

Some therapists reported that their clients came from backgrounds where mental health issues were interpreted through spiritual, religious, or communal lenses, rather than clinical or individualistic terms. In such contexts, ignoring these perspectives would risk alienating the client and undermining the therapeutic relationship.

> *For some families, emotional distress is seen as spiritual imbalance, or the result of ancestral issues. I've found ways to respectfully engage with these beliefs while introducing modern strategies like cognitive reframing or emotion regulation.*
>
> – **Therapist participant.**

A few therapists described using storytelling, metaphor, or proverbs from the client's cultural background to explain therapeutic concepts. Others spoke about working in collaboration with traditional healers, faith leaders, or community elders, especially in rural or conservative communities where these figures still hold strong influence.

> *There were cases where therapy only became acceptable to the family once a religious leader gave their blessing. We had to build a bridge, not a wall, between belief and psychology.*
>
> – **Therapist participant.**

This kind of integration was not always straightforward. Therapists emphasized the importance of ethical sensitivity, collaborative dialog, and client autonomy when negotiating traditional practices, especially when such practices were in tension with human rights or clinical safety.

> *I always ask: Is this belief harming or helping the client? If it's helping, I honour it. If it's harmful—like in the case of stigma around mental illness—I address it gently, without dismissing their culture.*
>
> – **Therapist participant.**

Youth perspective

Youth participants offered complex insights into their experiences with traditional and modern approaches to mental health. Many described feeling torn between loyalty to cultural traditions and curiosity or appreciation for modern psychological methods.

> *At home, we talk to elders or pray when someone is stressed. But in school or online, I learned about therapy and wanted to try it. I didn't want to choose—I wanted both to be okay.*
>
> – **Youth participant.**

Some youth valued the emotional language and coping tools provided by modern therapy, which helped them make sense of internal experiences in ways that traditional methods did not always provide.

> *In therapy, I learned how to name my feelings—anxiety, shame, pressure. That was new to me. Before, I just thought I was weak.*
>
> – **Youth participant.**

At the same time, traditional healing practices remained significant for many. Youth spoke of the comfort, familiarity, and communal aspect of rituals, spiritual guidance, and ancestral beliefs.

> *When my grandmother did a prayer for me, I felt something shift. I don't know how to explain it. It's not the same as therapy, but it helped in its own way.*
>
> – **Youth participant.**

However, some participants noted challenges when therapists were dismissive or unaware of their cultural frameworks.

> *I once told a therapist about a dream my aunt said had spiritual meaning, and they laughed it off. That was the last time I brought it up.*
>
> – **Youth participant.**

Conversely, when therapists expressed interest in learning about these practices—or even asked how they could be incorporated—youth felt more understood and empowered.

> *My counsellor didn't know much about my tradition, but she asked me to explain it. That respect made me want to keep coming back.*
>
> – **Youth participant.**

A few youth described themselves as "cultural navigators," seeking to blend both worlds—drawing strength from their traditions while also benefiting from the insights of modern therapy.

> *I go to therapy, but I also light a candle and say my prayers the way my mom taught me. I've made peace with both.*
>
> – **Youth participant.**

Challenges faced by therapists and youth in multicultural counselling

Theme 1: communication barriers and language limitations

Description

Communication emerged as a significant challenge in multicultural counselling, particularly where there were differences in language fluency, cultural expressions, and nonverbal cues. Both therapists and youth participants reported that language barriers—whether overt or subtle—often hindered the effectiveness of therapy. These challenges extended beyond just vocabulary, encompassing emotional expression, cultural idioms, tone, silence, and body language.

Therapists' perspective

Therapists described struggling to fully understand the emotional depth or contextual meaning of what youth were trying to convey, particularly when English was not their first language. They noted that nuances often got lost in translation, and that standard therapeutic language sometimes felt foreign or clinical to the clients.

There are times when a youth is clearly upset but says very little, and I know it's not because they're unwilling to share—but because they don't have the words in English to describe what they're feeling.

– Therapist participant.

Therapy is built around verbal expression. But when the client comes from a culture where feelings are expressed differently—or not at all in words—I have to find other ways to connect.

– Therapist participant.

Some therapists also expressed concern about using Western psychological terms (e.g., "depression," "trauma," or "self-actualization") that may not exist or carry the same meaning in the client's native language or cultural framework.

I've had clients look confused when I used words like 'boundaries' or 'assertiveness.' In their world, these are not just unfamiliar—they're sometimes unacceptable or meaningless.

– Therapist participant.

Additionally, therapists noted that nonverbal cues, such as eye contact, silence, or body posture, carried different meanings across cultures, which sometimes led to misinterpretation.

In one case, a youth rarely made eye contact. Initially, I thought it was social anxiety, but later I learned that in their culture, looking an adult in the eyes is seen as rude.

– Therapist participant.

Youth perspective

Youth participants, especially those from immigrant or non-dominant language backgrounds, spoke of feeling restricted or misunderstood during therapy sessions conducted in English or another second language. They expressed that while they might be conversationally fluent, they often lacked the vocabulary to convey emotions, family dynamics, or cultural values in a way that felt authentic.

I can speak English fine at school, but when I talk about deep stuff—like how I feel inside—it doesn't come out right. I wish I could speak in my own language.

– Youth participant.

Sometimes I wanted to explain things about my family or culture, but there just aren't words for it in English. It's like something important gets lost.

– Youth participant.

Others expressed that therapy felt like a foreign space because the way emotions were talked about didn't match their cultural upbringing.

> *My therapist asked me to describe my emotions, but in my home, we don't really talk like that. I felt weird and didn't know what to say.*
>
> **– Youth participant.**

In addition to verbal challenges, youth highlighted that their nonverbal expressions were sometimes misread.

> *I was quiet in sessions, and my therapist thought I was hiding something. But in my culture, we're taught to listen first and only speak when needed. I wasn't trying to avoid her—I was just being respectful.*
>
> **– Youth participant.**

Some youth wished for therapy to include language flexibility, such as allowing bilingual expression or having the option of code-switching when needed.

> *I feel safest when I can mix languages. Some words just feel more powerful in my mother tongue, especially when I'm upset.*
>
> **– Youth participant.**

Theme 2: cultural misunderstandings and stereotyping

Description

Cultural misunderstandings and stereotyping emerged as a significant barrier to effective counselling in multicultural settings. Youth participants shared that they often felt misrepresented, judged, or forced into cultural categories by therapists who lacked a nuanced understanding of their lived experiences. On the other hand, therapists admitted that, despite their best intentions, they sometimes struggled to separate clinical impressions from cultural norms—particularly when behaviors were unfamiliar or clashed with Western counselling models.

Youth perspective

Many youth described feeling *invisible* or *misunderstood* when therapists made generalizations about their culture or failed to explore their individual experiences within a broader cultural context.

> *Just because I wear a hijab doesn't mean I'm oppressed. My therapist kept tiptoeing around topics, assuming I had no freedom. But that's not my story.*
>
> ***– Youth participant.***

Some youth reported that their cultural practices or family values were pathologized or seen as "problems" rather than culturally grounded differences.

My therapist said I was 'too dependent' on my family. But in my culture, we stick together. It's not a weakness—it's how we survive.

– Youth participant.

There were also instances where youth felt that therapists oversimplified their identity by focusing only on race or religion without acknowledging the complexity of intersecting factors such as gender, class, immigration status, and generational dynamics.

It felt like once she knew I was Nigerian, she thought she knew everything about me. But my experience is not the same as someone who just moved here or lives in a big city.

– Youth participant.

In some cases, youth withdrew from the therapeutic process due to feeling misrepresented or unheard.

I stopped talking in sessions because she didn't get me. Everything I said was seen through this 'cultural lens' that wasn't mine.

– Youth participant.

Therapists' perspective

Therapists acknowledged the **tension between avoiding stereotypes** and needing to consider cultural context in assessment and intervention. Some shared that they were afraid of offending clients or making incorrect assumptions, which sometimes led to hesitation or avoidance of culturally relevant conversations.

I want to be culturally sensitive, but I also need to ask difficult questions. Sometimes I worry—am I being respectful or am I being overly cautious and missing something important?

– Therapist participant.

Therapists also recognized that certain cultural values and behaviors—such as emotional restraint, reverence for elders, or family hierarchy—could easily be misinterpreted through a Western therapeutic lens.

When a youth is quiet and deferential, it's easy to label it as avoidance or anxiety. But often, it's just how they've been raised—to listen more than speak, especially to adults.

– Therapist participant.

Several therapists admitted that they had unintentionally applied clinical frameworks that clashed with the client's worldview, especially in the early stages of their multicultural practice.

I once encouraged a young girl to assert herself more with her father, thinking I was empowering her. Later, I realized I was asking her to break a cultural code of respect, which only increased her anxiety.

– Therapist participant.

Others highlighted that cultural generalizations—such as assuming collectivist families are always supportive or that certain groups always stigmatize mental health—can be harmful if not critically examined.

> *Culture is not a script. Two clients from the same background may have completely different values. I try to ask, not assume.*
>
> – **Therapist participant.**

Theme 3: conflicting values between clients and therapists

Description

One of the most pervasive challenges in multicultural counselling was the tension between therapeutic values—often grounded in Western individualism—and the cultural values held by youth and their families. Youth participants shared that standard counselling approaches sometimes clashed with their upbringing, especially when the advice encouraged behaviors seen as inappropriate or even disrespectful in their cultural contexts. Therapists, on the other hand, described the difficulty of facilitating change without invalidating cultural norms or imposing their own value systems.

Youth perspective

Youth often described feeling conflicted when they were encouraged to prioritize personal independence, express emotions openly, or challenge family expectations—actions that were not culturally acceptable in their households.

> *My therapist told me to 'speak my truth' to my parents. But in my family, children don't confront elders. If I said half of what she suggested, I'd be seen as rude and ungrateful.*
>
> – **Youth participant.**

Several youth participants mentioned that they understood the intent behind the therapist's advice but felt that it was out of sync with their cultural realities.

> *I get that she wanted me to make my own decisions. But where I'm from, you don't just do what you want. You think of your parents, your siblings—it's a collective thing.*
>
> – **Youth participant.**

Others shared that being encouraged to express vulnerable emotions like sadness, frustration, or anger in therapy conflicted with cultural norms of emotional control or silence.

> *In my culture, you don't cry in front of people or talk about your feelings like that. Even saying 'I'm depressed' feels wrong. I was taught to be strong, to keep it inside.*
>
> – **Youth participant.**

Youth also felt frustrated when they sensed therapists did not fully understand the weight of cultural and family obligations.

> *My therapist kept asking why I don't just move out and focus on myself. But in my community, we take care of our parents. That's not something I can walk away from.*
>
> **– Youth participant.**

Therapists' perspective

Therapists acknowledged that value conflicts frequently arose, especially when their counselling goals—such as promoting self-expression, autonomy, or boundary-setting—clashed with collectivist values like obedience, harmony, and family loyalty.

> *I often find myself caught between helping the youth find their voice and respecting a culture that prioritizes silence, obedience, or sacrifice. It's a tightrope.*
>
> **– Therapist participant.**

Several therapists expressed concern about unintentionally offending families or undermining cultural authority structures, especially when working with clients from hierarchical or patriarchal communities.

> *Once, I encouraged a young girl to make decisions independently. Her parents saw it as rebellion. It caused more harm than good. I had to rethink my entire approach.*
>
> **– Therapist participant.**

Others shared that they had to unlearn assumptions about what "progress" looked like, especially when their professional values were shaped by Western therapeutic ideals.

> *For a long time, I thought empowerment meant asserting yourself and setting boundaries. But I've learned that for some clients, strength means endurance, patience, or finding peace within a system—not necessarily changing it.*
>
> **– Therapist participant.**

A few therapists also noted the internal struggle of trying to avoid imposing their values, while still addressing issues like emotional suppression, parental overcontrol, or gender-based restrictions.

> *There's a fine line between respecting culture and allowing harm. If a client feels silenced or controlled, I need to address it—but with great care, and in ways that honour their worldview.*
>
> **– Therapist participant.**

Theme 4: lack of cultural competency training for therapists

Description

This theme highlights a critical systemic gap in multicultural counselling: the insufficient training and support therapists receive in developing cultural competence. Many therapists acknowledged that their formal education did not adequately prepare them to engage meaningfully with clients from diverse cultural, religious, or linguistic backgrounds. Youth participants often perceived this lack of cultural awareness, which contributed to feelings of disconnection, invalidation, and mistrust during therapy. The absence of culturally responsive models, ongoing supervision, and institutional investment further exacerbated the challenge.

Therapists' perspective

Numerous therapists expressed frustration with the limited cultural content in their professional training, noting that most models emphasized Western, individualistic frameworks that did not account for cultural variations in family structures, emotional expression, or concepts of well-being.

> *Most of what we were taught in graduate school was based on Western norms. We barely touched on how culture affects therapy—except for maybe one elective.*
>
> **– Therapist participant.**

> *There's this assumption that one model fits all. But that's not true. Without proper training, we risk doing more harm than good.*
>
> **– Therapist participant.**

Some therapists revealed that they often had to "learn on the job", turning to self-study, trial-and-error, or informal peer discussions when working with culturally diverse youth.

> *I've had to do a lot of my own reading and research outside work hours. There's no structured guidance from my agency on how to support clients from different cultural backgrounds.*
>
> **– Therapist participant.**

Others noted the lack of culturally relevant supervision or case consultation, which left them feeling isolated or uncertain when navigating complex cultural dynamics in therapy.

> *I've wanted to bring up cultural issues in supervision, but my supervisor also doesn't know what to say. It's like we're all learning as we go, which doesn't feel right.*
>
> **– Therapist participant.**

Youth perspective

Youth participants were highly perceptive of therapists' cultural blind spots. Many reported that they could tell when a therapist lacked understanding of their background, leading to awkwardness, miscommunication, or a loss of confidence in the therapeutic process.

> *I didn't expect my therapist to know everything about my culture, but I wanted her to at least try. Instead, it felt like she avoided the topic or ignored it.*
>
> – **Youth participant.**

Some youth felt frustrated by the burden of having to explain basic cultural concepts or correct stereotypes during therapy sessions.

> *I had to teach my therapist what it meant to be a second-generation immigrant. That's not why I came to therapy. I needed help, not a classroom.*
>
> – **Youth participant.**

Others described experiences where their therapist's lack of cultural awareness led to harmful assumptions or inappropriate advice.

> *He told me to 'just say no' to my parents, like it was that simple. He didn't get how disrespectful that would be in my family. It's not that easy.*
>
> – **Youth participant.**

There was also a sense that some youth withdrew or disengaged from therapy when they sensed that the therapist lacked cultural sensitivity.

> *After a few sessions, I stopped opening up. She kept bringing everything back to individual freedom, but I don't live like that. She didn't get me.*
>
> – **Youth participant.**

Theme 5: stigma and family resistance to counselling

Description

In many multicultural contexts, stigma surrounding mental health remains a pervasive barrier to accessing and engaging in counselling. Youth participants often reported hesitation or fear in seeking support due to anticipated judgment from their families, religious communities, or cultural networks. Therapy was sometimes perceived as a sign of weakness, madness, or family failure. Therapists, in turn, described encountering parental resistance or outright rejection of therapeutic interventions—especially when counselling was viewed as conflicting with spiritual beliefs, traditional healing practices, or familial pride. This resistance not only limited youth engagement but also hindered collaborative, family-centered approaches.

Youth perspective

Youth participants consistently described an internal conflict between their desire to seek help and their fear of being stigmatized or shamed by family members.

> *I didn't tell my parents I was in therapy. They think it's only for 'crazy people.' I just said I had extra classes after school.*
>
> – **Youth participant.**

For many, the stigma extended beyond the household and into the broader community, where seeking mental health support was often seen as airing private matters or exposing family weaknesses.

> *In my culture, we don't talk about our problems outside the home. If you do, it means you're disrespecting your parents or bringing shame to the family.*
>
> – **Youth participant.**

Several youth shared that the fear of judgment or rejection kept them from being open during therapy sessions, especially if there was a risk their parents might find out.

> *I couldn't really open up because I knew my parents didn't support therapy. I kept holding back because I was scared it would get back to them.*
>
> – **Youth participant.**

In some cases, youth reported that their families preferred spiritual or traditional solutions, such as prayer, fasting, or visiting a religious leader, instead of professional counselling.

> *My mom said I should just pray more. She thought going to therapy meant I didn't have enough faith.*
>
> – **Youth participant.**

Therapists' perspective

Therapists echoed these concerns, describing parental and family resistance as a major obstacle in delivering effective multicultural counselling. Many families, especially from collectivist, religious, or conservative backgrounds, viewed therapy with suspicion or even hostility.

> *Some parents think therapy will turn their children against them. They worry that we'll encourage rebellion or question their authority.*
>
> – **Therapist participant.**

Therapists also noted that mental health stigma was often tied to cultural notions of shame, secrecy, and family honor.

> *I've had families refuse to let their child continue therapy because they didn't want the neighbours or church members to know. Mental health is still seen as a disgrace in some circles.*
>
> – **Therapist participant.**

Resistance was particularly strong when therapy was perceived as contradicting spiritual or religious teachings.

> *In some communities, emotional suffering is viewed as a spiritual test or demonic attack. Therapy is dismissed in favour of fasting, deliverance, or faith healing.*
>
> **– Therapist participant.**

This created a challenge for therapists attempting to involve families in treatment plans, as many parents resisted even the basic language of mental health or psychological intervention.

> *It's hard to talk about anxiety or depression when the family doesn't believe those are real things. They see it as laziness, weakness, or lack of discipline.*
>
> **– Therapist participant.**

Some therapists reported progress when they approached families respectfully and collaboratively, framing therapy in ways that aligned with their values—for example, as a tool to strengthen family relationships or enhance resilience.

> *I've learned to start with language that resonates—like talking about family harmony or supporting the child's academic success. Once there's trust, then we can introduce more psychological terms.*
>
> **– Therapist participant.**

Theme 6: power dynamics and generational tensions

Description

In multicultural counselling contexts—particularly within collectivist or traditional cultures—intergenerational power dynamics often create significant challenges. Youth participants expressed difficulty voicing concerns, asserting boundaries, or sharing personal struggles in the presence of elders or parents, due to deeply rooted norms around hierarchy, obedience, and respect. Therapists, while aiming to empower young clients, found themselves needing to navigate these cultural hierarchies delicately, balancing the youth's voice with family authority. This often led to tension in therapy sessions involving multiple generations, where cultural expectations clashed with therapeutic goals.

Youth perspective

Many youth shared that therapy became uncomfortable or ineffective when their parents or elders were present, as they felt unable to speak freely due to cultural norms that discourage questioning or contradicting adults.

> *In my family, you're not supposed to talk back. So even in therapy, I just sat there while my mom talked. I couldn't say what I really felt.*
>
> **– Youth participant.**

Others expressed that they feared being punished or misunderstood if they disclosed family issues or negative emotions in a family-based session.

> *If I told the therapist that my dad yells at me, he would get angry later. So I just kept quiet to avoid trouble.*
>
> – **Youth participant.**

Some youth felt that their emotional needs and personal identities were overlooked when the therapy sessions centered on adult narratives or decisions.

> *It felt like the session was all about making my parents happy—not helping me. The therapist kept trying to 'mediate' instead of listening to me.*
>
> – **Youth participant.**

Still, youth valued when therapists advocated for their voice in culturally sensitive ways, helping to open dialog without causing disrespect or family conflict.

> *One therapist helped me talk to my mom without sounding disrespectful. She showed me how to express myself and still honour my parents.*
>
> – **Youth participant.**

Therapists' perspective

Therapists acknowledged that traditional family structures and authority dynamics posed challenges, particularly when working with families where elders held unquestioned power and expected deference from youth.

> *In some sessions, the parents dominated the conversation. The youth barely spoke. If I tried to redirect, I risked appearing disrespectful to the adults.*
>
> – **Therapist participant.**

Several therapists described ethical dilemmas around whose voice to prioritize—the youth client's or the parental authority figure—especially when the goals of therapy differed between the two.

> *The youth wanted space and independence. The parents wanted obedience and discipline. I had to tread carefully so neither side felt attacked.*
>
> – **Therapist participant.**

Therapists also noted that generational worldviews often clashed. While younger clients leaned toward autonomy, mental health awareness, and emotional openness, older family members prioritized tradition, control, and silence around emotional issues.

> *There's often a huge gap in worldview between the youth and their parents. Bridging that gap without offending anyone requires a lot of cultural sensitivity and flexibility.*
>
> – **Therapist participant.**

Some therapists adopted indirect approaches, such as storytelling, metaphors, or culturally relevant communication styles, to help elders consider the youth's perspective without feeling challenged.

> *Instead of saying, 'your child needs more freedom,' I might say, 'many young people today benefit from guided independence.' That small shift helps parents feel respected while still hearing the message.*
>
> – **Therapist participant.**

Theme 7: emotional suppression and cultural norms of expression

Description

In many cultural traditions, emotional restraint is a sign of strength, dignity, or self-control, while open displays of vulnerability may be seen as weakness, shameful, or inappropriate—especially in public or therapeutic settings. This cultural norm of emotional suppression poses significant challenges in multicultural counselling, where emotional expression is often central to therapeutic progress. Therapists reported difficulty in helping youth clients articulate or even acknowledge emotions due to internalized norms of emotional silence. At the same time, youth expressed a desire to be heard and understood but struggled with the fear of cultural backlash or emotional exposure.

Youth perspective

Many youth shared that they had been raised to suppress emotions—particularly sadness, fear, or anger—as a way to protect family honor or avoid being perceived as weak.

> *In my culture, we don't talk about our feelings. We're told to be strong, especially in front of others. So opening up in therapy was really hard.*
>
> – **Youth participant.**

Several youth explained that even when they wanted to express emotions, they didn't know how, having never been taught a language of emotional literacy.

> *I was never asked how I felt growing up. I didn't have the words. So in therapy, when I was asked to talk about emotions, I just froze.*
>
> – **Youth participant.**

Some youth also feared that expressing strong emotions would disappoint or embarrass their families, or be interpreted as rebellion or disrespect.

> *I didn't want to cry or complain too much in case my therapist thought my parents were problem. I still want to protect them.*
>
> – **Youth participant.**

Despite these struggles, many youth valued therapists who approached emotional expression gently and respectfully, without pressuring them to "perform" emotions.

> *My therapist didn't force me to talk. She gave me space. Over time, I started to open up when I felt safe.*
>
> – **Youth participant.**

Therapists' perspective

Therapists reported that emotional suppression among youth clients was one of the most difficult barriers to address, especially when it was culturally reinforced by family, community, or religion.

> *Some youth were very guarded. I sensed deep emotional pain, but they'd smile or say 'I'm fine' because that's what they were taught to do.*
>
> – **Therapist participant.**

Therapists explained that Western counselling models, which emphasize catharsis, emotional vulnerability, and self-disclosure, often clashed with cultural expectations of emotional control or stoicism.

> *In some families, emotional control is a virtue. So when I encouraged the youth to cry or talk about fear, they felt ashamed—or even guilty—for breaking that norm.*
>
> – **Therapist participant.**

They also observed that emotional suppression sometimes masked underlying mental health conditions, such as depression or anxiety, which went unnoticed by both the family and the youth themselves.

> *A youth came in with physical complaints—headaches, fatigue—but wouldn't talk about stress or sadness. Eventually, we realized it was unspoken depression, shaped by a cultural belief that emotions shouldn't be voiced.*
>
> – **Therapist participant.**

To overcome this barrier, therapists described using creative and culturally sensitive techniques—such as art, metaphors, storytelling, or nonverbal tools—to help youth explore emotions in less direct but effective ways.

> *I used drawing and music therapy with one client. It allowed her to express what she couldn't say out loud. That was a turning point.*
>
> – **Therapist participant.**

Recommendations for enhancing cultural competence in therapists working with youth and families

The recommendations provided by therapist participants in this study reflect a deep commitment to improving the cultural responsiveness and effectiveness of counselling services, especially in multicultural contexts. The therapists' suggestions emphasize the need for systemic changes, personal development, and structural adjustments to make counselling more inclusive, accessible, and effective for culturally diverse populations. These recommendations are intended to help therapists better engage with youth and families from various cultural backgrounds and enhance the therapeutic outcomes in multicultural settings.

Theme 1: culturally responsive training and education

Therapist participants in this study consistently emphasized the importance of culturally responsive training as a critical factor in improving the effectiveness of counselling services for youth and families from diverse cultural backgrounds. Many therapists expressed that while they were well-trained in general therapeutic approaches, they often lacked the specific cultural knowledge necessary to address the unique needs of their clients in multicultural settings. The therapists noted that incorporating cultural competence into both their formal education and ongoing professional development could greatly enhance their ability to serve culturally diverse populations.

One therapist highlighted this need by stating:

> *In my early years as a therapist, cultural competence wasn't a major focus in my training. I learned a lot from experience, but formal education in how to navigate cultural differences would have been invaluable. We need training that prepares us for the nuances of working with clients from different backgrounds, especially in the context of youth and families.*

Another therapist echoed similar sentiments, pointing out that multicultural training should be a foundational element of therapist education:

> *Cultural awareness should be part of our core training, not something we pick up later. It's crucial to understand not just the diversity in client backgrounds but how those backgrounds influence family dynamics, youth development, and coping strategies. Without this knowledge, we risk missing important cultural factors in therapy.*

Therapists expressed the need for training programs that would provide practical tools to engage with diverse communities. One participant suggested:

> *We need more than just theoretical knowledge about different cultures. There should be more practical training on how to conduct therapy in ways that are respectful and*

> *effective in multicultural settings. Things like how to ask culturally relevant questions or how to recognize cultural stressors that affect the family unit.*

The importance of continuous professional development was another key point raised by therapists. Several participants stressed that cultural competence is an ongoing process, and therapists must remain open to learning throughout their careers. One therapist explained:

> *Cultural competence isn't something you just learn once. It's something that requires continuous learning and self-reflection. I participate in workshops and attend conferences, but it's also about being open to feedback and making sure I'm constantly adapting my approach to the unique needs of each family.*

Therapists also suggested that training should be dynamic and evolving, reflecting the changing nature of multicultural dynamics in society. As one participant noted:

> *The world is constantly changing, and so are the cultures we interact with. As therapists, we need training that evolves to address new challenges. What worked five years ago might not be effective today, and we need to be prepared for that.*

Overall, the therapists agreed that a strong foundation in culturally responsive training would enable them to work more effectively with youth and families from diverse backgrounds, enhancing the therapeutic experience for both clients and practitioners. By incorporating cultural competence into education and ongoing professional development, therapists would be better equipped to address the complex cultural issues that arise in therapy and build stronger therapeutic relationships with their clients.

Theme 2: cultural sensitivity in therapeutic practices

Therapists highlighted the critical importance of cultural sensitivity in their therapeutic practices, emphasizing that understanding and respecting the cultural backgrounds of their clients is essential for building trust, fostering open communication, and providing effective therapy. Therapists recognized that each cultural group has unique values, beliefs, and expectations that influence how individuals perceive and engage with therapy. They acknowledged that a lack of cultural awareness could create barriers to effective therapeutic work, particularly when it comes to working with youth and families from multicultural backgrounds.

One therapist shared their approach to ensuring cultural sensitivity in therapy:

> *I always start by getting to know the cultural background of the family. It's not just about asking questions about their culture—it's about learning how their culture influences their perspective on therapy and family dynamics. It helps me tailor my approach so that I don't impose a framework that feels foreign to them.*

Many therapists expressed that cultural assessments at the beginning of therapy were a key part of their practice. They found that this helped both the therapist and client better understand the client's cultural values and expectations, and allowed the therapist to adjust their therapeutic strategies accordingly. One therapist explained:

> *Before we begin any work, I ask questions to understand their cultural identity, family roles, and how they view mental health. This isn't just about ticking boxes—it's about creating a safe space where the family feels understood and respected. I also acknowledge that their culture plays a big part in how they view therapy and the outcomes they expect.*

Therapists also emphasized the need to be flexible in their approach. They pointed out that not every client fits into a standardized model of therapy, and a flexible, culturally sensitive approach was necessary to meet the specific needs of each family or youth client. One therapist shared:

> *Sometimes, you have to adapt your techniques to match the client's cultural needs. For example, in some cultures, discussing personal issues with a stranger isn't acceptable, so I might involve the family in the process more or use less direct approaches, like storytelling or role-playing, that align with their cultural practices.*

Some therapists recognized that clients, especially from non-Western cultural backgrounds, may prefer traditional or spiritual healing practices in conjunction with formal therapy. These therapists highlighted the importance of incorporating these practices into their therapeutic methods to build rapport and increase client engagement. One therapist reflected:

> *For clients from more traditional backgrounds, there might be an expectation that therapy should include spiritual or community-based support. In some cases, I've worked alongside local healers or elders, especially in rural communities. It's important that I honor their traditions while providing the psychological support they need.*

Therapists also discussed the challenge of balancing cultural respect with evidence-based therapeutic practices. While they were committed to using methods that aligned with the clients' cultural values, they also recognized that they must not compromise on therapeutic effectiveness. One participant shared:

> *There's always a fine balance between being culturally sensitive and adhering to evidence-based practices. Sometimes, clients will want to follow traditional healing practices exclusively, but I need to explain the benefits of combining those with psychological methods to ensure they receive comprehensive support. It's about finding common ground.*

Youth participants, when asked about their experiences with cultural sensitivity in therapy, also expressed appreciation for therapists who took the time to understand and integrate their cultural context into the therapeutic process. One youth participant noted:

> *I had a therapist who took the time to ask me about my family traditions and beliefs. At first, I didn't think it mattered, but it made me feel like she understood where I was coming from. She even suggested some cultural resources that could help me in therapy, and that felt really supportive.*

However, youth also mentioned that when cultural sensitivity was lacking, it made it difficult to engage in therapy. One youth participant said:

> *I had another therapist who didn't understand my background. She kept pushing for me to talk about things in a way that didn't make sense to me. It felt like she was trying to force me into her way of thinking, which didn't work for me. I stopped going to therapy after a few sessions because I didn't feel heard.*

The insights from both therapists and youth participants highlight that cultural sensitivity goes beyond just knowing about a client's background—it involves a continual process of adapting one's therapeutic approach to ensure that it is respectful, relevant, and effective. Therapists who were successful in building strong relationships with their culturally diverse clients were those who took the time to understand the role that culture plays in the client's worldview, family structure, and approach to mental health.

Theme 3: building trust and rapport with culturally diverse clients

Building trust and rapport was consistently highlighted by therapists as a foundational element in multicultural counselling, particularly when working with youth and families from diverse cultural backgrounds. Therapists emphasized that for effective therapy to occur, especially in culturally diverse contexts, clients need to feel understood, respected, and safe. Trust is a crucial element in establishing a productive therapeutic relationship, and without it, clients—particularly youth—are less likely to engage fully in the process.

Therapists shared various strategies for building trust and rapport with their culturally diverse clients. One therapist described how they approach initial sessions with an open and non-judgmental attitude:

> *I always approach the first session with humility, knowing that I don't have all the answers. I let the client share their culture, their values, and what is important to them. It's all about listening first. I ask open-ended questions that allow them to lead the conversation and build a space where they feel heard and respected. Without that initial trust, the work is much harder.*

Several therapists emphasized the importance of active listening as a tool for building rapport. Active listening goes beyond simply hearing what a client is saying—it involves paying close attention to non-verbal cues, understanding the emotional context of the client's words, and responding in ways that validate the client's experience. One therapist shared:

> *I've learned that the key to building rapport is not just talking but really listening. When you listen to what's unsaid, when you read between the lines, you can begin to understand the deeper layers of their experience. It's not just about what they say, but how they feel, how their culture shapes what they think, and how they react.*

Another therapist discussed how cultural humility is essential for trust-building, especially when working with clients from cultures that may be skeptical of formal mental health practices:

> *Cultural humility is something I take to heart in every session. I don't assume I know the right way to help someone just because I have a degree. I recognize that clients are the experts on their own lives. It's important to constantly check my own biases and assumptions, and approach the work with curiosity and respect.*

Therapists also mentioned that engaging with families and respecting the family unit is particularly important when working with youth. In many cultures, family plays a central role in decision-making, and it's essential for therapists to acknowledge and integrate this dynamic into the therapy process. One therapist explained:

> *When working with youth, especially from cultures where family is the cornerstone, I often invite the family into the conversation. It helps the youth feel supported and less isolated in their struggles. But it's also important to be sensitive to the family dynamics—some families are very involved, while others may have more complex or strained relationships. You need to adjust how you work with the family based on their unique needs.*

In addition to family involvement, therapists noted that language barriers and the use of interpreters could be significant barriers to building trust. They emphasized that it's important to use trained, culturally aware interpreters who are sensitive to the emotional context of the conversation. One therapist shared their experience:

> *Language is a huge barrier in multicultural therapy. I've had sessions where a family speaks a language I don't understand, and we rely on an interpreter. It's crucial that the interpreter is not just a translator of words, but also understands the emotional nuances of the conversation. That way, trust is maintained not just between me and the client, but also between the family and the interpreter.*

Despite these challenges, many therapists agreed that consistency in their approach was key to maintaining trust. Regular follow-ups and open communication about the therapy process can help clients feel that they are supported over time. As one therapist shared:

> *Trust doesn't develop overnight, especially when you're working with families from a background where mental health is stigmatized or misunderstood. It takes time, patience, and consistency. Every session is a step toward building that rapport. I've found that letting the client and family know that I'm here for the long haul helps them feel less alone in the process.*

From the youth perspective, many participants noted that therapists who were culturally sensitive and showed genuine interest in their backgrounds were more likely to earn their trust. One youth participant said:

> *The best therapist I've had was the one who didn't make me feel like I had to change who I was. She was interested in my family and how we do things back home. She took the time to understand my culture, and that made me feel like I could open up more. I didn't feel judged or like I was 'wrong' for thinking differently.*

However, some youth participants mentioned that trust was harder to build with therapists who did not show cultural awareness. One youth participant expressed:

> *It was hard to trust a therapist who didn't understand where I came from. I had one who kept pushing me to talk about things I wasn't comfortable with. I felt like she didn't respect my boundaries, and that made it hard to trust her.*

On the whole, the therapists' reflections underscore that building trust and rapport in multicultural therapy involves more than simply establishing a connection—it requires ongoing sensitivity, openness, and flexibility in response to the cultural dynamics at play. Youth participants emphasized that their engagement in therapy was closely linked to whether they felt their culture was respected and understood. Both therapists and youth agreed that trust was foundational to the success of therapy, and it required consistent effort, humility, and cultural awareness on the part of the therapist.

Theme 4: collaboration with community leaders and traditional healers

The integration of community leaders and traditional healers into the therapeutic process emerged as a significant recommendation among therapists working with culturally diverse clients. Many therapists acknowledged that cultural factors play a pivotal role in the mental health of youth and families, and they recognized the need for a collaborative approach that includes not only formal therapy but also the support of trusted community figures and traditional healers. This collaboration was particularly emphasized in communities where traditional healing practices are deeply rooted and may conflict with or complement modern therapeutic approaches.

Therapists noted that by working alongside community leaders or traditional healers, they could build trust with clients and help bridge the gap between cultural expectations and contemporary therapy. One therapist explained:

> *In some communities, traditional healers and spiritual leaders hold a great deal of influence. For clients from these communities, therapy can be more effective if we recognize and respect those figures. In some cases, I've had the opportunity to collaborate with a local healer to provide more holistic care for the family. It shows the clients that we are*

not dismissing their cultural beliefs but integrating them with modern psychological practices.

Another therapist shared their experience of collaborating with community leaders:

I've found that involving a community elder in the therapeutic process can make a huge difference, particularly when working with families who are new to therapy. The elders often serve as intermediaries, helping to explain the therapeutic process in a way that resonates with the family's cultural values. It's not about taking over the therapy process, but about creating a collaborative environment where the client feels supported in every way.

Therapists emphasized that collaboration with traditional healers can also be beneficial when dealing with sensitive or stigmatized issues, such as mental health concerns. For example, some cultural groups may have reservations about engaging with mental health professionals, viewing mental health issues through a spiritual or community lens rather than a psychological one. One therapist shared:

In some communities, mental health issues are seen as spiritual problems or as a family curse. Rather than pushing back against these beliefs, I try to work with the traditional healer to understand how we can address both the cultural and psychological aspects of the client's experience. It's about finding a middle ground where both healing traditions are respected.

The benefits of collaboration with traditional healers were not only evident in the rapport-building process but also in addressing holistic aspects of mental health. Many therapists reported that traditional healing practices, which often involve a strong sense of community and spirituality, could complement modern therapeutic techniques. One therapist shared:

I've seen clients open up more when they know we're acknowledging the spiritual and community support they rely on. For example, when a client attends a community healing ceremony and then comes to therapy to process their emotions afterward, it allows for a more integrated approach to their care. It's about providing options, not telling them they must choose one path over the other.

However, while many therapists supported the idea of collaboration, they also acknowledged that boundaries and clear roles need to be established in these partnerships. Therapists stressed the importance of maintaining professional ethics and ensuring that the integration of traditional practices does not undermine or conflict with the goals of therapy. One participant explained:

I always make it clear that while I respect traditional healers, my role as a therapist is to offer evidence-based psychological interventions. I ensure that when I collaborate with a healer or community leader, it's clear that we are working together to support the client, not to confuse or overwhelm them with conflicting advice.

From the youth participants' perspective, many expressed a sense of comfort and reassurance when traditional healing practices were respected or integrated into their therapy. One youth participant shared:

> *I felt more comfortable when my therapist didn't just tell me to forget about my culture. She asked about the things I believe in and suggested ways that we could work together with my community. It felt like she understood me, and that made therapy easier.*

Some youth also noted that the involvement of community leaders helped them feel less isolated in the therapeutic process, especially when there were language barriers or cultural misunderstandings. One youth participant remarked:

> *Sometimes, it's hard to talk to someone who doesn't understand where you come from. But when my therapist talked to someone from my community who understood our way of life, it made me feel like therapy was more for me and not just something that was forced on me.*

While there was a consensus among therapists and youth that collaboration with community figures and traditional healers can enhance cultural relevance in therapy, it was also acknowledged that such collaborations must be approached ethically and carefully. Therapists were advised to ensure that any collaboration or involvement of community leaders did not undermine the therapeutic process or perpetuate practices that could potentially harm the client.

Theme 5: development of culturally personalized resources

The development of culturally personalized resources was identified as a crucial recommendation for improving the effectiveness of therapy in multicultural contexts. Therapists highlighted the importance of creating resources that reflect the cultural values, traditions, and needs of the diverse populations they serve. Such resources would not only enhance the therapeutic experience but also improve client engagement by making therapy feel more relevant and accessible. These culturally appropriate materials could range from educational handouts to multimedia tools, which would provide practical support for both therapists and clients.

Therapists emphasized that resources should be linguistically appropriate and reflect the cultural context of the client, ensuring that the materials resonate with the values, beliefs, and practices of different cultural groups. One therapist shared their experience:

> *When I work with families from different cultural backgrounds, I make sure to incorporate resources that reflect their cultural values. For example, I've worked with families from a community where spirituality plays a significant role. I've created pamphlets and exercises that combine spiritual practices with therapeutic activities, making it easier for families to connect with the content.*

Another therapist pointed out the importance of bilingual materials, especially when working with clients who do not speak the same language as the therapist. This was particularly important for communities where the primary language was different from the official language used in therapy. One therapist explained:

> *When I work with clients who speak another language, I try to use bilingual resources, or at least provide translated materials, so they don't feel disconnected from the process. It's not just about translation; it's about making sure the resources reflect the cultural nuances and values that are important to the client.*

Therapists also recommended that therapeutic resources be designed to help clients understand the therapy process within the framework of their own cultural beliefs. Many therapists suggested that by adapting common therapeutic models to reflect cultural perspectives, they could make therapy more relatable. For example, therapists working with clients from collectivist cultures could create materials that focus on family dynamics, community involvement, and collective healing. One participant shared:

> *For some families, therapy might feel too individualistic, especially in cultures that prioritize the collective. I've developed resources that focus on family-based healing, so the whole family can be part of the therapeutic process. This shift makes clients feel like they're participating in something that aligns with their cultural understanding of support.*

Youth participants also spoke about the importance of having culturally relevant resources that reflect their personal experiences and backgrounds. One youth participant noted:

> *It was helpful when my therapist gave me materials that talked about things I could relate to, like the way my family deals with problems or the values we hold. It made me feel like the therapy wasn't just about 'fixing me' but also about understanding where I came from.*

Some youth highlighted the need for resources that were easy to understand and accessible, especially for those from low-income communities or educational backgrounds. One participant shared:

> *I've had therapists give me worksheets that were difficult to follow, especially because of the way they were written. But when they gave me simple handouts that used examples from my culture or community, it felt easier to relate to what they were saying. It was like they were speaking my language, and that helped me understand what I needed to do.*

Therapists also recognized the potential of multimedia resources, such as videos, audio recordings, and interactive apps, which could be more engaging and effective in certain contexts. For example, therapists working with youth mentioned that videos or storytelling techniques based on cultural narratives could be powerful tools to explain therapeutic concepts. One therapist remarked:

> *In some cultures, storytelling is a key way of imparting wisdom. I've used culturally relevant stories or folk tales in therapy, explaining psychological concepts through stories that youth can relate to. It brings therapeutic principles to life in a way that feels meaningful and respectful of their culture.*

Moreover, therapists emphasized that resources should be adaptable to the specific needs of individual clients and families, ensuring that they are not overly rigid or prescriptive. As one therapist pointed out:

> *The resources I use are just tools. I always ensure they are flexible enough that we can adapt them to the unique needs of each client. What works for one family may not work for another, so the key is personalization and relevance to their specific cultural context.*

Another point raised by therapists was the importance of collaborative resource development, where both the therapist and the client contribute to the creation and customization of the materials. One therapist suggested:

> *Sometimes, I invite families to co-create certain parts of the therapy process. For example, if we are developing coping strategies, I'll ask the family what methods or practices from their culture they've used successfully. Then, we combine these with evidence-based practices, creating a resource that is both culturally respectful and clinically effective.*

In summary, therapists and youth participants alike emphasized that culturally tailored resources could significantly enhance the therapeutic process by making therapy feel more accessible, relevant, and respectful of clients' backgrounds. By integrating cultural values, language, and community practices into therapeutic resources, therapists can improve engagement, foster trust, and ensure that therapy resonates with culturally diverse youth and families. Culturally sensitive materials help bridge the gap between Western therapeutic models and clients' lived experiences, creating a more inclusive and supportive environment for all.

Theme 6: overcoming stigma and resistance to therapy

Stigma surrounding mental health and therapy was frequently discussed by therapists as a significant challenge in multicultural settings, particularly when working with youth and families from cultures where mental health issues are often misunderstood or taboo. Therapists recognized that in many cultural contexts, mental health issues are stigmatized, and seeking therapy may be seen as a sign of weakness or a last resort. This stigma can create significant barriers to effective therapeutic engagement, especially in communities where mental health is viewed through a cultural or spiritual lens rather than a psychological one.

Therapists' experiences with stigma

Therapists emphasized that educating clients and their families about the benefits of therapy was vital in overcoming the stigma. They acknowledged that the perception of therapy as a foreign or unnecessary practice in some communities required a thoughtful, culturally sensitive approach to introduce and normalize the idea of seeking help. One therapist explained:

> *In many cultures, therapy is seen as something to be avoided, or even something that reflects badly on family. I've found that educating families about how therapy can help improve their relationships or help their child with challenges like school or behavior goes a long way. It's about reframing therapy as something that is part of the solution, not the problem.*

Another therapist shared how important it is to address the cultural views on mental health early in therapy:

> *One of the first things I do is have a conversation with the family about mental health from their perspective. I ask about their beliefs and perceptions, which opens up a dialogue and helps me understand where they are coming from. From there, I can gently correct any misconceptions about therapy and mental health, which often helps to reduce the stigma.*

Youth experiences with stigma

Youth participants also reflected on how cultural stigma around mental health impacted their willingness to seek therapy. Many mentioned that family expectations and community judgment made it difficult to openly engage in therapy. One youth participant described:

> *My family never really talked about mental health. When I first told them I wanted to go to therapy, they didn't understand why. They thought it meant I was weak or that I had something seriously wrong with me. It wasn't until I explained that therapy wasn't about being 'crazy' that they started to be more supportive.*

Some youth also shared their experiences of feeling ashamed or embarrassed to seek therapy due to societal perceptions. One participant noted:

> *In my community, mental health is really stigmatized. I felt embarrassed at first to go to therapy because I didn't want people to think something was wrong with me. It wasn't until my therapist made it clear that asking for help is a sign of strength that I felt okay with the process.*

Overcoming resistance through culturally relevant interventions

Therapists shared strategies for overcoming resistance to therapy, often by incorporating culturally relevant interventions that respected the family's values while addressing their mental health concerns. One therapist explained:

> *I find that resistance often comes from the perception that therapy is not part of their cultural traditions. By blending culturally relevant practices, such as spiritual or community support, with modern therapy, I've been able to ease the family's concerns. This approach shows them that therapy can align with their values while still addressing the issues they face.*

Another approach discussed by therapists was the use of storytelling and other culturally familiar methods as tools to introduce therapy. A therapist shared:

> *Storytelling is big in many cultures, and I use that to my advantage. I might share stories or parables that highlight the value of seeking help or overcoming challenges, which is something people can relate to in their own lives. It helps clients see therapy as just another step in overcoming obstacles, not as something foreign or shameful.*

Youth support in navigating stigma

Youth participants also expressed that peer support was a powerful tool in overcoming stigma. They shared that when peers openly discussed their experiences with therapy, it made seeking help feel more normalized. One youth said:

> *When I found out that some of my friends had gone to therapy and it helped them, it made me feel more comfortable. If they can do it, then it's okay for me to do it too. I think having peers who talk openly about it would really help break the stigma.*

Therapists noted that creating a supportive environment within the therapy process, where clients and their families could express their fears or concerns about therapy without judgment, was also key to overcoming resistance. One therapist described their approach:

> *I often invite families to ask any questions they might have about therapy at the beginning. They need to feel like they can be open with me about their doubts. It's a slow process, but as we continue to work together and see positive changes, the resistance begins to fade.*

Recommendations for reducing stigma

Based on their experiences, therapists recommended several strategies to reduce stigma and resistance to therapy:

- **Community Education:** Therapists suggested that mental health education campaigns within communities could help change perceptions of therapy. One therapist shared:

  > *I think community-wide workshops or talks that include not just clients, but their families, could help educate people about the importance of mental health and therapy. If we normalize these discussions, people might be more likely to seek help before things escalate.*

- **Family Involvement:** Incorporating family members into the therapy process was another recommendation. Therapists believed that family acceptance and understanding were critical to overcoming stigma. One therapist mentioned:

  > *When families see the positive impact therapy has on their loved one, they're more likely to embrace it and view it as a helpful tool rather than something shameful. It's key to involve them early and throughout the therapy process.*

Theme 7: socioeconomic barriers and access to therapy

In many multicultural contexts, socioeconomic factors can significantly affect access to therapy, particularly for youth and families from low-income or marginalized communities. Therapists and youth participants both emphasized that financial constraints, lack of insurance, and limited access to affordable mental health services were major challenges in providing or seeking therapeutic care. This theme highlights how socioeconomic status can directly impact the availability and effectiveness of mental health support.

Therapists' perspectives on socioeconomic barriers

Therapists acknowledged that financial limitations often hindered families' ability to access necessary therapy services. One therapist described:

> *I see many families who are struggling financially, and therapy is often something they can't afford. Even when therapy could benefit the whole family, cost becomes a barrier. I've had to refer clients to community programs or try to adjust my fees, but the lack of financial resources is a major issue.*

Another therapist shared their concern about the lack of affordable, community-based services:

> *In some areas, especially rural or low-income neighborhoods, therapy is seen as a luxury. There aren't enough low-cost or sliding-scale services available, and the families who need therapy the most often don't know where to turn. We need more outreach programs that specifically target these communities and provide affordable, culturally competent care.*

Youth participants' experiences with socioeconomic barriers

Youth participants also shared their struggles with affordability and access to therapy. Many mentioned that their families couldn't afford private therapy, and public health services were often overburdened or inaccessible. One youth participant explained:

> *I wanted to go to therapy because I was dealing with a lot, but my mom couldn't afford it. We don't have insurance that covers mental health, and the waitlist for the public*

services is really long. So, I had to wait and deal with things on my own. It was frustrating because I knew I needed help.

Some youth also noted that the lack of mental health awareness in their communities contributed to the issue of access. One participant said:

Mental health is not something people talk about where I come from, so when I needed help, I didn't know where to go. I had to rely on my school counselor, but they don't always have the resources or time to give me the support I need.

Strategies to overcome socioeconomic barriers

Therapists discussed various strategies they had implemented to help clients navigate these challenges, such as referrals to community organizations, pro bono services, or working on a sliding scale to make therapy more affordable. One therapist shared:

I try to connect clients with local organizations that offer free or low-cost therapy services. There are also a lot of grant programs and scholarships for therapy that families might not be aware of. It's important for us, as therapists, to help them navigate these resources and make therapy as accessible as possible.

Additionally, some therapists mentioned the possibility of group therapy as a more affordable option for families who could not afford individual sessions. One therapist explained:

I've started offering group therapy sessions for families or youth who can't afford individual therapy. It's more cost-effective for them, and it also helps create a sense of community and shared understanding. It's a way to reduce isolation and provide support without the cost of individual therapy.

Youth suggestions for improving access

Youth participants recommended that schools and community organizations play a larger role in facilitating access to therapy. They suggested that mental health services should be available on-site at schools or through youth centers, which would reduce the logistical and financial barriers to accessing care. One youth participant shared: "I think schools should offer therapy as part of the curriculum. If we had mental health services in schools, it would be easier for us to get help without having to worry about cost or making an appointment somewhere else." Some youth also proposed that mental health awareness campaigns be integrated into community programs to increase knowledge about available resources. One participant suggested: "There should be more community programs where people talk about mental health and let you know where to find help. If people knew what was available, they might be more likely to seek out therapy."

Case studies

The Johnson family, of Nigerian descent, resides in Lagos. The family consists of Mr. and Mrs. Johnson, their two teenage children, Ade and Amina, and the elderly maternal grandmother, who plays a significant role in the family's dynamics. The family is deeply rooted in traditional Nigerian cultural values, with strong emphasis on respect for elders and maintaining family honor. The family practices Christianity, but the maternal grandmother is a devout believer in indigenous African spiritual practices.

Ade, a 16-year-old male, has been exhibiting signs of depression, including withdrawal from social activities, a drop in academic performance, and increased irritability. His parents are concerned, but they have difficulty understanding his behavior. Mrs. Johnson, in particular, insists that Ade's issues are a "spiritual matter" and often consults with traditional healers for remedies. The family has been reluctant to seek professional psychological help due to the stigma surrounding mental health in their community. The grandmother, while supportive, believes that Ade's behavior is a result of spiritual disharmony, which complicates the family's willingness to engage in therapy. The therapist, recognizing the family's cultural background, begins by acknowledging the family's traditional beliefs and practices. In the initial session, the therapist asks open-ended questions to understand the family's perspective on mental health and spirituality. The therapist reassures the family that therapy does not negate their cultural practices but rather complements them by helping Ade navigate his challenges in a holistic way.

The therapist incorporates family-centered therapy, inviting the entire family to the sessions. This allows Ade to express his feelings in a supportive environment where his family can participate in his healing process. The therapist also integrates spiritual elements into the therapeutic process by allowing space for the grandmother's beliefs, while gently explaining the psychological aspects of Ade's depression. This combined approach helps bridge the gap between traditional healing practices and modern therapeutic techniques. Through the course of therapy, Ade begins to open up about the pressure he feels to meet his family's high expectations, as well as the conflict between adhering to traditional values and his own evolving identity. The family becomes more supportive, especially after the therapist educates them about mental health issues and how they are not linked to spiritual failure but can coexist with their beliefs. Ade's academic performance improves as he begins to manage his stress better, and the family becomes more accepting of therapy, which they now see as an extension of their care for him.

Hassan, a 17-year-old youth, is from a conservative Muslim family in Sokoto, northern Nigeria. His family practices a strict interpretation of Islam, and mental health issues are often viewed with suspicion. Hassan's family holds the belief that therapy is unnecessary and may even be seen as shameful, particularly for males, as it may reflect poorly on the family. Hassan has struggled with social anxiety and has had trouble making friends at school, which has led to a sense of isolation.

Hassan has been referred to therapy after his school counselor noticed his reluctance to participate in class activities and his withdrawal from group interactions. Hassan's social anxiety is manifesting in physical symptoms, including sweating, heart palpitations, and frequent stomach aches when he anticipates social situations. He feels increasingly isolated, as his anxiety prevents him from engaging with his peers. Hassan's parents, particularly his father, are resistant to therapy, seeing it as a weakness and an issue that should be dealt with within the family. The therapist begins the sessions with individual youth-focused therapy, creating a safe, confidential space where Hassan can discuss his fears without the judgment or scrutiny of his family. Recognizing the cultural stigma surrounding therapy, the therapist first works on building trust with Hassan, emphasizing that seeking help is a strength, not a weakness. The therapist uses cognitive-behavioral therapy (CBT) to address Hassan's anxiety, helping him to recognize and challenge negative thought patterns and develop healthier coping strategies.

The therapist also introduces the concept of mental health literacy to Hassan, educating him about the psychological nature of anxiety and normalizing his experiences. Hassan is encouraged to open up gradually about his struggles, with the therapist offering positive reinforcement for every small step he takes toward socializing. Through the course of therapy, Hassan begins to engage more in class and seeks out social opportunities, though at a slow and manageable pace. His anxiety symptoms decrease as he learns to challenge irrational thoughts and gain confidence in social situations. The therapist also educates Hassan's family about mental health, helping them understand that therapy is a constructive step toward personal growth. Although initially hesitant, Hassan's parents become more supportive as they witness his gradual improvement. Hassan feels more empowered, and his social interactions begin to improve.

The Okafor family lives in a rural part of Enugu State. The family, originally from the Igbo ethnic group, practices a mixture of Christianity and traditional Igbo spiritual beliefs. Mr. and Mrs. Okafor have three children, and their youngest son, Chijioke, aged 14, has been struggling with behavioral issues and academic difficulties. The family has consulted traditional healers in their village to address what they perceive as Chijioke's "spiritual problems," believing that his behavioral issues are linked to ancestral spirits and family curses. Chijioke's disruptive behavior at school and at home has caused significant stress in the family. He refuses to comply with authority figures and often becomes aggressive when confronted about his academic underperformance. The family is torn between seeking psychological help and relying on traditional healing practices. Chijioke's father, in particular, insists that the boy's problems are linked to ancestral spirits and has been resistant to professional therapy, viewing it as incompatible with their spiritual beliefs.

The therapist recognizes the cultural importance of traditional healing practices in the Okafor family's life. Rather than dismissing their beliefs, the therapist works collaboratively with the family and introduces the idea of integrating traditional healing practices with modern therapeutic methods. The therapist invites a community elder and a local healer in the initial therapy sessions to discuss how therapy can be used alongside traditional practices to address Chijioke's behavior. In the first session, the therapist listens to the community leader and healer's perspective, acknowledging the family's cultural context. The therapist then educates the healer about the benefits of family therapy, explaining that it can be a complementary practice to traditional healing. The therapist introduces family therapy sessions, focusing on improving communication within the family and addressing the underlying stressors that may be contributing to Chijioke's behavior.

Over time, Chijioke's behavior improves as the family learns healthier ways to communicate and set boundaries. The family begins to view therapy as a holistic process that respects both their traditional values and the benefits of modern psychological support. The involvement of the community elder and healer helps the family feel more comfortable with the therapy process, and Chijioke becomes more open to discussing his issues in therapy. The integration of traditional healing practices with therapy creates a sense of cultural relevance, and the family is more engaged in the therapeutic process.

Conclusion

Youth and family counselling in multicultural contexts requires a delicate balance of cultural awareness, systemic understanding, and relational sensitivity. This chapter has shown that young people and their families do not experience emotional or developmental challenges in isolation; rather, their experiences are deeply shaped by cultural identities, intergenerational expectations, historical influences, and the broader social ecology in which they live. Effective counselling therefore demands a holistic, culturally grounded approach that honors these complexities. The theoretical perspectives reviewed multicultural competence, family systems theory, ecological frameworks, and relationship-centered approaches together provide a comprehensive foundation for practice. They emphasize that counselors must not only understand cultural norms and family dynamics but also engage in ongoing self-reflection, collaborative meaning-making, and flexible intervention strategies. The lived experiences shared by both youth and therapists further highlight the importance of humility, empathy, and active partnership in addressing cultural misunderstandings, communication barriers, emotional suppression, and conflicting values.

The empirical findings reinforce that culturally responsive counselling is both necessary and challenging. Therapists must navigate linguistic differences, stigma, generational tensions, and the integration of traditional and modern healing practices. Youth, on their part, desire safety, validation, and counselors who genuinely seek to understand their cultural worlds without judgment or stereotyping. The recommendations offered emphasize the need for stronger cultural competence training, institutional support, collaborative community partnerships, and counselling models that reflect local realities and indigenous wisdom. Ultimately, multicultural youth and family counselling is a relational, contextual, and evolving practice. It requires counselors to meet clients where they are, honor their cultural narratives, and co-create pathways toward healing, resilience, and harmonious family functioning. As societies continue to diversify, counselors, educators, institutions, and communities must work together to ensure that all young people and families receive support that is respectful, responsive, and firmly rooted in cultural dignity and human understanding.

References

Akinwumi, A. S., Philip, A. O., Ayorinde, A. O., Obioma, A. M., Emmanuel, A., Etukudo, O. B., Sade, O. J., Osa, I. P., Ayibeya, A. M., Eunice, A. N., Bullem, A. G., Etta, B. A., Omowumi, A. F. O., Odey, O. J., Okorn, O. O., Ademola, S. F., & Emmanuel, E. (2024). Impact assessment of counselling on family of children with intellectual disability in Cross River State, Nigeria. *Journal of Intellectual Disability - Diagnosis and Treatment, 12*(3). https://doi.org/10.6000/2292-2598.2024.12.03.3

Asiimwe, R., Karume, M., & Kasujja, R. (2023). Systemic family therapy in Africa. In *The Routledge international handbook of couple and family therapy*. https://doi.org/10.4324/9781003297871-14

Asiimwe, R., McIntosh, D. L., Nyambura, R. G., & Kasujja, R. (2026). Cultural threads: An Afrocentric paradigm for integrating social justice principles in the practice of family therapy in Africa. *Journal of Marital and Family Therapy, 52*(1). https://doi.org/10.1111/jmft.70091

Brown, J., & Errington, L. (2024). Bowen family systems theory and practice: Illustration and critique revisited. *Australian and New Zealand Journal of Family Therapy, 45*(2). https://doi.org/10.1002/anzf.1589

Calatrava, M., Martins, M. V., Schweer-Collins, M., Duch-Ceballos, C., & Rodríguez-González, M. (2022). Differentiation of self: A scoping review of Bowen family systems theory's core construct. *Clinical Psychology Review, 91*. https://doi.org/10.1016/j.cpr.2021.102101

Dimic, T., Farrell, A., Ahern, E., & Houghton, S. (2023). Young people's experience of the therapeutic alliance: A systematic review. *Clinical Psychology & Psychotherapy, 30*(6). https://doi.org/10.1002/cpp.2885

Kate, C., & Ekwe, N. (2021). Counselling and psychotherapy encounter with the Nigerian cultural context. *International Journal for Psychotherapy in Africa, 6*.

Manivong, J. R., Singh, A. A., Kent Butler, S., Nassar-McMillan, S., & Rafferty McCullough, J. (2016). *Multicultural and social justice counseling competencies: Practical applications in counselings.* American Counselling Association. https://www.counseling.org/publications/counseling-today-magazine/article-archive/article/legacy/multicultural-and-social-justice-counseling-competencies-practical-applications-in-counseling#:~:text=Competencies%3A%20Counselors%20who%20are%20multicultural,the%20cultural%20worldview%20of%20clients.

Otu, M. S., Otu, F. M., & Ardi, Z. (2023). Purpose-based career coaching as a strategy for increasing employability of graduates: A survey study. *International Journal of Home Economics, Hospitality and Allied Research, 2*(2), 55–80.

Otu, M. S. (2024). Effect of purpose-based career coaching on career decision-making. *Current Psychology, 43*, 25568–25594. https://doi.org/10.1007/s12144-024-06247-3

Otu, M. S. (2025). The effectiveness of rational emotive career coaching in enhancing recent first-degree graduates' entrepreneurial intentions. *The International Journal of Interdisciplinary Educational Studies, 20*(1), 77–94. https://doi.org/10.18848/2327-011X/CGP/v20i01/77-94

Otu, M. S., & Eseadi, C. (2024). A psycho-spiritual approach to purpose-based career coaching: A step-by-step guide for practitioners. *Pendekatan Psiko-Spiritual Pada Pelatihan Karir Berbasis Tujuan: Panduan Langkah-Demi-Langkah, 21*(1), 2655–5034. https://doi.org/10.18860/psi.v21i1.26882

Otu, M. S., & Omeje, J. C. (2021). The effect of rational emotive career coaching on dysfunctional career beliefs in recent university graduates. *Journal of Rational-Emotive and Cognitive-Behavior Therapy, 39*(4). https://doi.org/10.1007/s10942-020-00383-y

Otu, M. S., & Sefotho, M. M. (2024). Increasing graduates' employability skills through rational emotive career coaching. *African Journal of Career Development, 6*(1). https://doi.org/10.4102/ajcd.v6i1.106

Stanley, K., & Kuo, N.-C. (2022). "It takes a village": Approaching the development of school-family-community partnerships through bronfenbrenner's socio-ecological perspectives. *Journal of Human Sciences and Extension, 10*. https://doi.org/10.54718/cqbw6379

Stubbing, J., & Gibson, K. (2022). What young people want from clinicians: Youth-informed clinical practice in mental health care. *All About You, 2*(4). https://doi.org/10.3390/youth2040039

Sue, S., Zane, N., Hall, G. C. N., & Berger, L. K. (2009). The case for cultural competency in psychotherapeutic interventions. *Annual Review of Psychology, 60*. https://doi.org/10.1146/annurev.psych.60.110707.163651

Todd, E., Pond, R., & Coomber, K. (2025). Client perspectives of family therapy: A qualitative systematic review. *Journal of Marital and Family Therapy, 51*(3). https://doi.org/10.1111/jmft.70024

Victor-Aigbodion, V., & Eseadi, C. (2025). Effect of purpose-based career coaching on career transition self-efficacy among college students with autism spectrum disorder. In *EDULEARN25 proceedings: 17th international conference on education and new learning technologies* (pp. 8088–8101).

Yoshikawa, H., Aber, J. L., & Beardslee, W. R. (2012). The effects of poverty on the mental, emotional, and behavioral health of children and youth. *American Psychologist, 67*(4). https://doi.org/10.1037/a0028015

Zak, M., Kalchos, L. F., & Kassan, A. (2025). Multicultural responsiveness with newcomer youth: A counsellors' perspective. *All About You, 5*(4). https://doi.org/10.3390/youth5040102

CHAPTER 8

Supervision and consultation in multicultural counselling and psychotherapy

Introduction

Supervision and consultation represent the principal vehicle through which counselling and psychotherapy practitioners develop professional competence, ethical clarity, and quality of care. In increasingly multicultural settings, these processes must extend beyond technical oversight to deliberate engagement with culture, power, and social context. Multicultural counselling therefore requires that supervisors and consultants guide practitioners not only in clinical skills but also in critically examining assumptions, navigating cultural difference, and managing ethical complexities that arise when clients' identities or worldviews differ from those of practitioners. Contemporary scholarship emphasizes that culturally responsive supervision is both theoretically imperative and empirically consequential.

Foundational texts on clinical supervision have evolved to give added emphasis to multicultural supervision and competence, alongside ethics, client outcomes, and broader professional responsibilities. For example, the sixth edition of Bernard and Goodyear's widely cited resource notes expanded coverage of multicultural supervision and competence, signaling the centrality of these matters to current supervisory discourse (Bernard & Goodyear, 2014). Empirical studies further bolster the case for culturally attuned supervision. Research on cultural humility reports that higher client perceptions of a therapist's cultural humility are associated with stronger working alliances and improved therapy outcomes (Hook et al., 2013). Similarly, investigations of supervisors' multicultural competence document positive associations with supervisory processes and satisfaction, illustrating how supervisor orientation to culture can shape the quality of supervision itself (Inman, 2006). These theoretical and empirical developments highlight supervision as a critical site for integrating multicultural principles into everyday practice. Yet, meaningful translation from theory to practice is uneven, especially in contexts that differ from those in which many models were developed. In African countries such as Nigeria, supervision and consultation occur within culturally complex environments marked by ethnic plurality, linguistic diversity, religious variation, and diverse communal norms concerning mental health and help-seeking. Moreover, professional systems may

A Pragmatic Approach to Multicultural Counselling and Psychotherapy Skills Acquisition. https://doi.org/10.1016/B978-0-443-33939-4.00007-0

rely on imported frameworks that do not fully mirror local realities, generating a tension between global models and contextual needs. This situation raises pressing questions about how principles of multicultural supervision are actually interpreted, operationalized, and sustained by supervisors and consultants working in such settings.

Conceptual clarification

Supervision and consultation, at their core, are purposeful professional relationships in which more experienced practitioners guide, support, and oversee the work of less experienced colleagues. Supervision is a structured professional relationship in which a more experienced practitioner guides, supports, and oversees the work of another practitioner. It is typically formal, ongoing, and aimed at helping the supervisee grow in knowledge, skill, and professionalism while ensuring the quality and safety of services. In many fields, supervision includes regular discussion of casework, feedback, and sometimes evaluation, distinguishing it from purely informal help or mentoring. Descriptions of clinical supervision emphasize its structured nature, its role in developing expertise, and its function in maintaining service quality; one widely referenced summary notes that supervision involves regular meetings to discuss professional work and progress in expertise, and it differs from mentoring or coaching by including evaluative elements (Bernard & Goodyear, 2014; Haggerty & Hilsenroth, 2011; Kagee, 2007). On the other hand, consultation is typically advisory interaction between professionals, often focused on a particular issue or set of concerns. It may be short-term or occasional, formal or informal, and usually centers on exchanging experience, advice, or perspectives to address a specific challenge or improve practice in a focused way. Unlike supervision, consultation does not inherently carry an ongoing evaluative or hierarchical relationship; instead, it is collaborative and sought as needed. Professional guidance for counselors describes consultation as a voluntary practice where practitioners share experiences, advice, questions, or concerns potentially in one-on-one or group settings, primarily to support professional growth or tackle a particular difficulty.

In counselling and psychotherapy these processes help ensure ethical care, ongoing learning, and the translation of theory into effective practice. When viewed through a multicultural lens, the meaning of supervision and consultation expands. They become not only forums for technical skill development, but also intentional spaces for recognizing, exploring, and navigating cultural difference, power, and context. Thus, in multicultural settings, supervision and consultation signal a commitment to understanding how clients' cultural identities shape their experiences, presenting issues, and help-seeking behaviors. They also require supervisors and consultants to attend to how their own backgrounds, assumptions, and positions of privilege or marginality may influence interpretation, decision-making, and the supervisory relationship itself. Practices that emphasize openness, respect, and mutual learning toward cultural difference are thus integral to the very meaning of supervision. Empirical work on cultural humility emphasizes that such interpersonal orientations are linked to stronger working alliances and better therapeutic outcomes (Hook et al., 2013). Extending these insights to supervision means that the process is not merely an administrative or evaluative function, but a relational practice that models and cultivates cultural awareness, humility, and reflective dialog. Furthermore, contemporary scholarship on supervision has increasingly framed multicultural competence as a central, not peripheral, element of professional guidance. Authoritative texts note expanded coverage of multicultural supervision and competence alongside ethics and client outcomes, reflecting the view that culture is essential to how supervision is understood and enacted in current practice (Bernard & Goodyear, 2014). In other words, in a multicultural context, the meaning of supervision and consultation includes the deliberate integration of culture into ethical deliberations, case discussions, and overall professional growth. They become sites where culturally informed values, knowledge, and attitudes are actively cultivated rather than assumed to ensure that the care practitioners offer is both technically sound and genuinely responsive to the varied cultural realities of the people they serve.

Key characteristics of an effective multicultural supervisor

1. **Cultural humility and openness to learning:** The supervisor actively models a stance of respectful curiosity about cultural difference, rather than claiming expertise or certainty. This means recognizing that one's own cultural knowledge is limited, inviting correction, and being willing to learn from supervisees and clients about their cultural worlds. Empirical and conceptual work on cultural humility in supervision emphasizes modeling and teaching this stance through interpersonal interactions, suggesting it is central to nurturing culturally responsive practice (Zhang et al., 2022).
2. **Awareness of cultural complexity and intersectionality:** An effective supervisor understands that culture is not a single, uniform trait but involves intersecting identities, norms, and experiences. They guide supervisees to see how clients' cultural backgrounds, and even the diversity within cultural groups, shape presenting issues, therapeutic relationships, and ethical considerations. Professional commentary stresses that awareness of cultural complexity and the need to avoid stereotyping or monolithic views of cultural groups is critical to preventing bias and strengthening alliance (Holly, 2023).
3. **Reflective self-awareness about bias and positionality:** The supervisor routinely examines their own assumptions, potential biases, and power or privilege in relation to supervisees and clients. They encourage supervisees to do the same, using reflection as a routine part of case discussion and professional growth. Guidance from experienced supervisors underlines the importance of identifying and checking one's own biases,

and helping supervisees acknowledge theirs, as a foundation for culturally inclusive supervision (Holly, 2023).

4. **Knowledge of multicultural principles and contextual resources:** Beyond attitude, the supervisor has a working understanding of multicultural counselling principles and relevant cultural or contextual materials. This includes familiarity with culturally grounded models, local practices, and resources that can inform case conceptualization and interventions. Effective supervisors not only use, but also help supervisees to find, culturally based curricula, texts, or locally appropriate frameworks when needed.
5. **Ability to translate principles into concrete practice:** The supervisor helps supervisees move from abstract ideals to tangible actions; framing ethical dilemmas through cultural lenses, discussing specific cultural dynamics in cases, or adapting strategies to fit clients' cultural realities. Professional discussions observe that embedding multiculturalism in supervision provides supervisees with tools that might otherwise be overlooked, fostering deeper sensitivity and authenticity in clinical work (Holly, 2023).
6. **Capacity to address difficult or sensitive cultural issues:** The supervisor creates a safe, respectful space for addressing microaggressions, cultural misunderstandings, or power dynamics that surface in practice. When such issues arise, they guide supervisees in naming them, understanding their impact, and exploring corrective or preventative steps. Commentary emphasizes the supervisor's duty to proactively address attitudes or biases related to cultural variables, indicating that avoiding cultural conversations can itself be harmful (Holly, 2023).
7. **Collaborative, supportive communication style:** Communication is both clear and compassionate. The supervisor encourages dialog rather than top-down instruction, invites supervisees' perspectives, and balances feedback with encouragement, especially when cultural topics may feel unfamiliar or challenging. A collaborative style helps reduce defensive reactions, promote trust, and invite supervisees to share cultural insights or concerns without fear of judgment, aligning with the ethos of cultural humility.
8. **Commitment to ongoing professional development:** The supervisor remains committed to learning through training, lived experience, or community engagement about cultural issues, systemic inequities, and effective multicultural practices. They model lifelong learning and encourage supervisees to pursue similar growth. Evidence from professional experience suggests that supervisors' own exposure to diverse contexts and reflective learning shapes their competence in multicultural practice over time.
9. **Sensitivity to institutional and contextual factors:** The supervisor understands how organizational norms, policies, or resource constraints can affect multicultural supervision and client care. They strive to navigate or advocate within these systems to ensure cultural issues are not sidelined. Literature reviews of multicultural supervision note

the importance of supervisor and supervisee competencies among broader themes and emphasize the role of context and institutional support in effective practice (Kemer et al., 2022).

10. **Ethical integrity and responsibility toward client welfare:** The supervisor holds firmly to ethical standards that include cultural considerations to ensure supervisees attend to clients' cultural realities, respect their rights, and avoid harm arising from cultural ignorance or insensitivity. This characteristic integrates the supervisor's role in maintaining professional quality with the moral imperative to treat clients' cultural identities with care, fairness, and respect.

Key characteristics of an effective multicultural counselling consultant

1. **Collaborative, advisory stance:** A multicultural consultant operates from a partnership mindset, offering guidance, perspective, or problem-solving help on specific clinical or cultural issues, rather than directing or formally evaluating the other professional's work. This collaborative orientation aligns with how consultation is typically defined. Such a stance supports open dialog about cultural concerns, because clients or peers do not feel coerced or judged; instead, they can weigh cultural suggestions alongside their own judgment.
2. **Cultural humility and respect for diverse perspectives:** An effective consultant demonstrates genuine openness to learning from the client's and the consultees' cultural worlds. They recognize that cultural knowledge is never complete and that each situation may offer new insights. This humility encourages consultees to share their own cultural understandings, questions, or uncertainties without fear of being corrected or shamed. A humble, respectful consultant can thus facilitate deeper exploration of cultural meaning in a case, helping the practitioner better understand how cultural beliefs or values shape clients' experiences and responses to treatment.
3. **Sensitivity to power, context, and positionality:** Though consultation is less hierarchical than formal supervision, a multicultural consultant still pays attention to how differences in authority, training, or social background can influence the exchange. They remain mindful of how institutional, societal, or relational power dynamics may affect the practitioner's ability to implement culturally sensitive recommendations. By acknowledging these dynamics, the consultant avoids assuming that their advice will automatically fit every context and instead invites discussion about feasible, culturally congruent strategies within the practitioner's environment.
4. **Practical knowledge of cultural factors and local resources:** Beyond general awareness, an effective multicultural consultant possesses usable, context-relevant knowledge about cultural norms, linguistic nuances, local community practices, or available services that can directly inform case work. They can quickly suggest culturally appropriate assessment questions, intervention ideas, or referral options. When they lack

specific information, they transparently identify gaps and help the consultee find trustworthy local sources or culturally grounded materials. This practical orientation prevents consultation from remaining abstract and makes cultural adaptation more achievable in real cases.

5. **Skill in translating cultural insights into concrete actions:** A consultant's value is not only in interpreting culture but in showing how that understanding can shape real-world clinical steps. Effective multicultural consultants help practitioners move from recognizing cultural differences to deciding what to say, how to engage, or which techniques to adjust. They might propose culturally relevant examples, phrasing, or engagement strategies that practitioners can test immediately, making the consultation directly useful for client care.
6. **Clear, respectful communication:** Because consultation often occurs on an as-needed basis, sometimes briefly or remotely, the consultant must communicate clearly and respectfully. They present ideas in straightforward language, check the practitioner's understanding, and invite questions or alternative viewpoints. This communication style is especially important when discussing sensitive cultural issues, where misunderstandings or defensive reactions could otherwise hinder progress.
7. **Ability to navigate ethical and cultural dilemmas without imposing one-size-fits-all solutions:** A multicultural consultant recognizes that ethical choices and cultural norms vary across settings. Instead of insisting on a single correct approach, they offer options that consider cultural values, client autonomy, community expectations, and professional ethics. They help practitioners weigh possible actions in light of the client's cultural context, the practitioner's responsibilities, and any relevant standards or norms, thus supporting ethically sound decision-making that respects cultural variation.
8. **Commitment to ongoing learning and community engagement:** Effective multicultural consultants stay current with cultural developments, community changes, and emerging issues that may affect practice. They seek learning opportunities, engage with diverse communities, or consult other experts when needed. This ongoing growth enables them to bring updated, relevant insights to each consultation, strengthening the practitioner's confidence that the advice is grounded in both cultural reality and professional competence.
9. **Sensitivity to practical constraints and feasibility:** A consultant understands that practitioners may have limited time, resources, or institutional support. They offer culturally responsive suggestions that are realistic within those constraints, such as brief interventions, low-cost resources, or simple language adaptations. By focusing recommendations on what is feasible, they increase the likelihood that cultural considerations will actually be used, not dismissed as too difficult or time-consuming.

10. **Ethical integrity and responsibility toward client welfare:** Although consultation is voluntary and non-evaluative, a multicultural consultant remains ethically responsible for providing well-considered guidance that supports client welfare. They avoid offering advice based on stereotypes or insufficient understanding and clarify when issues exceed their expertise. They also encourage practitioners to seek additional support or supervision when cultural or clinical complexity demands more thorough attention.

My experiences as a multicultural counselling supervisor and consultant

My experiences as a multicultural counselling supervisor and consultant have been shaped by sustained engagement with culturally diverse practitioners, clients, and institutional contexts. Working within multicultural settings has required continuous negotiation between professional standards of counselling and supervision and the cultural realities that influence how distress, healing, authority, and ethics are understood and enacted. These experiences have reinforced the view that supervision and consultation are not culturally neutral processes but are deeply embedded within social, cultural, and relational contexts.

In my role as a supervisor, I have observed that supervisees often bring culturally shaped assumptions about hierarchy, communication, and learning into the supervisory relationship. In some cases, supervisees expect directive guidance and clear authority, reflecting cultural norms that emphasize respect for seniority and expertise. In others, supervisees may hesitate to openly discuss uncertainty, ethical dilemmas, or cultural tensions due to fear of appearing incompetent or disrespectful. Navigating these dynamics has required cultural sensitivity, patience, and the intentional creation of a supervisory climate that values openness, mutual respect, and reflective dialog. Supervising in multicultural contexts has also highlighted the centrality of culture in case conceptualization and ethical decision-making. I have encountered situations where Western counselling models did not fully capture clients' lived realities, particularly when communal values, spiritual beliefs, or traditional healing practices played a central role in clients' experiences. These encounters have reinforced the importance of encouraging supervisees to critically examine dominant theoretical frameworks and to integrate culturally relevant perspectives into their clinical work. Supervision thus becomes a space for expanding professional understanding rather than merely reinforcing standardized approaches.

My experiences as a consultant in multicultural counselling contexts have further emphasized the advisory and collaborative nature of consultation. Unlike supervision, consultation has often involved working with practitioners who seek support voluntarily, usually in response to specific cultural, ethical, or practice-based challenges. In these settings, I have found that effective consultation depends heavily on cultural humility, active listening, and respect for the consultee's professional autonomy. Consultants are frequently required to navigate sensitive cultural issues without imposing solutions, instead facilitating reflection and culturally informed problem-solving.

Across my roles as a multicultural counselling supervisor and consultant, I have encountered persistent and often complex challenges that reflect the realities of working within culturally diverse academic and professional environments. The university context in which I currently serve is characterized by significant cultural diversity, encompassing differences in ethnicity, language, religion, educational background, and worldview. These internal dynamics are further complicated by my international professional engagements, which have exposed me to additional layers of multicultural difference shaped by global counselling traditions, professional norms, and sociocultural expectations. Together, these contexts have made multicultural supervision and consultation both deeply enriching and consistently demanding.

Among the most recurring challenges are language differences, culturally shaped communication styles, and divergent understandings of professional roles and boundaries. In supervision, for example, variations in indirect versus direct communication, attitudes toward authority, and culturally informed expectations of guidance or evaluation often shape supervisees' engagement. Similarly, in consultation contexts, cultural norms regarding autonomy, feedback, and problem ownership influence how advice is sought, interpreted, and applied. These challenges are not merely technical but relational and ethical, requiring sustained attentiveness to power, respect, and mutual understanding. International engagements have further revealed how counselling and supervision practices are embedded in broader cultural and institutional traditions. Approaches that are taken for granted in one context may be perceived as inappropriate, insufficient, or even unethical in another. Navigating these differences has required deliberate effort, humility, and a willingness to question dominant assumptions about best practice. Rather than diminishing the supervisory or consultative process, these tensions have underscored the necessity of ongoing self-reflection, particularly regarding one's own cultural assumptions, biases, and positionality.

Despite the reality of these challenges, I have worked intentionally to confront and overcome them.

This effort has involved continuous learning, reflective practice, dialog with colleagues across cultures, and a commitment to culturally responsive ethical practice. Importantly, it has also involved recognizing the limitations of existing supervision and consultation models, many of which are grounded in Western epistemologies and do not always adequately address the lived realities of culturally diverse or non-Western contexts. Part of this sustained effort is the conviction that scholarship must respond to practice realities. The development of a book such as this is therefore not incidental, but a deliberate attempt to contribute to the growth of culturally grounded knowledge that speaks directly to these challenges.

These experiences point to the urgent need for empirical inquiry into how multicultural supervision and consultation are enacted in real-world settings, particularly within culturally diverse institutions and international professional spaces. There remains a critical gap in understanding how supervisors and consultants negotiate cultural complexity, what obstacles hinder culturally responsive practice, and which strategies practitioners themselves identify as most viable for improvement. Addressing these questions is essential for advancing supervision and consultation models that are not only theoretically sound but also practically relevant within local and global contexts. Against this background, the present chapter is guided by three interrelated research objectives. First, it seeks to investigate the principles and practices of supervision and consultation in multicultural counselling and psychotherapy, with particular attention to how cultural considerations are integrated into ethical discussions, supervisory relationships, and everyday professional activities. Second, it aims to identify the challenges faced by supervisors and consultants in multicultural supervision and consultation, including structural, institutional, interpersonal, and cultural barriers that shape how cultural issues are recognized, discussed, and addressed in practice. Third, the chapter seeks to determine strategies for improving multicultural supervision and consultation practices, focusing on research, policy, training, and reflective approaches that professionals consider necessary, feasible, and contextually appropriate. By addressing these objectives, this chapter contributes to the growing scholarship on multicultural supervision and consultation while foregrounding perspectives that remain underrepresented, particularly those emerging from culturally diverse and non-Western contexts. The chapter offers insights relevant to supervisors, consultants, educators, and policymakers who are committed to strengthening the cultural integrity, ethical quality, and practical effectiveness of supervision and consultation in multicultural counselling and psychotherapy.

Methodology

Study area

This study was conducted across six states in Nigeria, carefully selected to represent each of the country's six geopolitical zones: North Central, North East, North West, South East, South South, and South West. This deliberate design choice was guided by the multicultural nature of Nigeria itself, a nation characterized by significant cultural, ethnic, linguistic, and religious diversity. By including one state from each zone, the study sought to ensure that the voices and experiences captured would not reflect the reality of a single region alone but rather illustrate a broader national perspective on supervision and consultation practices in multicultural counselling and psychotherapy. The selection of states across these zones also served to explore potential regional variations in professional practices, challenges, and strategies related to multicultural supervision and consultation. For example, cultural beliefs, educational structures, and institutional support systems may differ between northern and southern zones, between predominantly Muslim and predominantly Christian states, or between urbanized and rural contexts. Including participants from these diverse areas helped the study to identify both shared principles and region-specific nuances in multicultural counselling practice.

Research approach

This study adopted a quantitative research approach complemented by qualitative case studies, forming a mixed-methods framework designed to provide a richer, more comprehensive understanding of supervision and consultation practices in multicultural counselling and psychotherapy across Nigeria. The quantitative component enabled the collection of structured data from a large sample of counselors, psychologists, supervisors, and consultants, allowing for statistical analysis of patterns, differences, and relationships among variables related to multicultural supervision and consultation. The qualitative component, through carefully designed case study templates, offered an opportunity to explore in depth the lived experiences, practical challenges, and strategies employed by professionals in real multicultural practice settings. Together, this combined approach ensured the research questions were examined both broadly and deeply, producing findings that are statistically grounded and contextually meaningful to inform policy, training, and professional development in multicultural counselling and psychotherapy.

Design of the study

The study employed a descriptive survey design integrated with qualitative case studies to systematically investigate supervision and consultation practices within multicultural counselling and psychotherapy across Nigeria. The descriptive survey design was appropriate because it allowed for the collection of data from a large, geographically diverse participant group, providing an overview of professionals' perceptions, practices, and challenges related to multicultural supervision. To deepen this understanding, a case study component was included, inviting selected participants to provide narrative accounts of specific challenges they had encountered and strategies they had implemented in real-world multicultural contexts. This design not only captured general trends and statistical patterns but also illuminated the nuanced, practice-based realities behind the numbers. By bringing together these complementary strands of evidence, the study's design increased the relevance, credibility, and practical value of its findings and recommendations for the field of multicultural counselling and psychotherapy.

Research paradigm

This study was guided by a pragmatic research paradigm, which recognizes that both objective measurement and subjective interpretation are valuable for understanding complex social phenomena. Pragmatism supports methodological pluralism, making it well suited for a study that combined quantitative survey data with qualitative case studies. Through this paradigm, the study sought to answer practical research questions about supervision and consultation practices in multicultural counselling and psychotherapy by drawing on the strengths of numerical data and narrative insights. This approach enabled the integration of broad statistical patterns with rich, context-specific accounts, ensuring the findings were both generalizable and grounded in professional realities.

Ontology

The study's ontological stance reflects a pluralistic view of reality, acknowledging that multiple realities coexist: some that can be measured objectively and others that are shaped by individuals' professional experiences and cultural contexts. In the quantitative part of the study, reality was viewed as relatively stable and measurable—captured through structured survey responses reflecting shared practices and perceptions. In the qualitative case studies, reality was seen as constructed through participants' lived experiences, shaped by their interactions with clients, institutions, and multicultural contexts. Together, this ontological approach accepted that reality is both objectively describable and subjectively interpreted.

Epistemology

Epistemologically, the study combined positivist and constructivist perspectives, consistent with a mixed-methods approach. The quantitative component was grounded in a positivist orientation, seeking objective knowledge through statistical analysis of survey responses from 400 professionals. It aimed to identify general patterns and relationships that could be generalized across settings. In contrast, the qualitative case study component aligned with a constructivist epistemology, valuing participants' subjective accounts and contextual insights into challenges and strategies. This dual epistemological stance allowed the study to produce knowledge that is both broadly applicable and deeply contextual.

Axiology

The study's axiological position recognized that research, especially in multicultural contexts, is inherently value-laden. Ethical sensitivity, cultural respect, and inclusivity were prioritized at every stage—from instrument design to data collection and interpretation. By including both quantitative and qualitative data, the study intentionally honored diverse voices and professional perspectives, acknowledging the importance of cultural competence and humility. The researcher's values also shaped choices such as seeking participant consent, ensuring confidentiality, and interpreting findings with awareness of cultural dynamics and ethical responsibilities.

Sampling technique

The sample for this study comprised 400 counselors, supervisors, and psychologists actively practising in multicultural counselling and psychotherapy across Nigeria. A purposive sampling technique was initially applied to identify qualified professionals directly engaged in supervision and consultation roles, ensuring participants had relevant practical experience aligned with the study's objectives.

Within each of the six selected states, representing the six geopolitical zones, stratified sampling was then used to achieve proportional representation across key categories: professional role (supervisors, consultants, and practising therapists), level of professional qualification (bachelor's, master's, and doctorate degrees), and primary work settings (educational institutions, hospitals, and private practice). This layered approach strengthened the study's capacity to capture diverse professional viewpoints.

In addition to collecting quantitative data through the structured questionnaire, the sampling design also supported the integration of a case study component. From within the same stratified groups, participants with notably rich or illustrative supervision experiences were purposively identified and invited to share anonymized examples of challenges faced and strategies applied in multicultural supervision and consultation. These case narratives were used to complement the quantitative findings, providing context-specific insights and enhancing the depth of the analysis.

Instrument for data collection

In this study, data were collected using a self-developed instrument titled the Questionnaire for Supervision and Consultation in Multicultural Counselling and Psychotherapy (QSCMCP). The development of the QSCMCP was informed by a careful review of relevant literature and existing models of supervision and consultation within multicultural contexts. Its design aimed to capture a comprehensive understanding of professional practices, perceived challenges, and potential strategies for improvement as they relate to multicultural counselling and psychotherapy. The questionnaire is organized into four sections to ensure clarity and focus. The first section gathers demographic information such as gender, age, highest qualification, professional role, years of experience in counselling or psychotherapy, and whether respondents have received formal training in multicultural supervision and consultation. This background information helps situate the responses within participants' professional contexts.

The second section explores the principles and practices underlying multicultural supervision and consultation. It consists of 10 statements addressing areas such as cultural competence, cultural humility, the integration of clients' cultural backgrounds into supervision discussions, and the encouragement of supervisees to reflect on their cultural assumptions and biases. These items aim to assess the extent to which supervisors and consultants actively incorporate multicultural considerations into their professional practice. The third section focuses on challenges encountered in multicultural supervision and consultation. This section also comprises 10 items, which identify potential barriers including limited institutional support, language differences, time constraints, power dynamics, stereotypes, and insufficient research evidence guiding practice. These items were designed to reveal practical and structural issues that professionals may face when engaging in multicultural supervision and consultation. The fourth section presents 10 items related to strategies for improvement. These items cover suggestions such as organizing training workshops specifically on multicultural supervision, developing institutional policies that promote culturally responsive practices, encouraging ongoing self-reflection among supervisors and supervisees, and providing access to multicultural resources and peer supervision opportunities.

All items in Sections B, C, and D are rated on a five-point Likert scale ranging from 1 (Strongly disagree) to 5 (Strongly agree). Higher scores indicate greater endorsement of the described practice, recognition of challenges, or agreement with suggested strategies for enhancing multicultural supervision and consultation. To ensure the clarity and relevance of the questionnaire items, the instrument was reviewed by experts in counselling psychology and multicultural education, which contributed to its content validity. The QSCMCP was intentionally structured to be concise and accessible, allowing supervisors, consultants, and therapists to reflect meaningfully on their practices within multicultural counselling and psychotherapy settings. To enrich the quantitative data and illustrate real-world professional experiences, a separate instrument, the Case Study Template for Supervision and Consultation in Multicultural Counselling and Psychotherapy (CST–SCMCP), was also used. This template invited selected participants to share detailed, anonymized narratives describing specific challenges faced and strategies adopted in multicultural supervision and consultation. The case study template consisted of two main parts: one focusing on challenges, where participants described the cultural factors involved and their professional impact; and another focusing on strategies, detailing how specific initiatives were implemented and what outcomes they produced.

Validation of the instrument

To establish the validity and reliability of the Questionnaire for Supervision and Consultation in Multicultural Counselling and Psychotherapy (QSCMCP), a systematic process of instrument validation was undertaken. This process included content validation, face validation, construct validation through pilot testing, and reliability analysis. The first step involved content validation, aimed at ensuring that the items adequately covered the domains reflected in the research objectives: principles and practices, challenges, and strategies for improving multicultural supervision and consultation. To achieve this, the initial draft of the questionnaire was reviewed by a panel of five experts comprising senior academics and practitioners in counselling psychology, multicultural education, and psychotherapy. The experts were asked to assess each item in terms of relevance, clarity, and representativeness of the construct it was intended to measure. Based on their feedback, some items were reworded for clarity, and redundant items were removed to enhance the focus of the instrument.

Following content validation, face validation was conducted to ascertain the comprehensibility and appropriateness of the questionnaire from the perspective of potential respondents. The revised instrument was shared with a small group of practising supervisors, consultants, and therapists ($n = 10$) who provided comments on the clarity of language, the suitability of the Likert scale, and the overall organization of the questionnaire. Minor adjustments were made, including refining some statements to use more accessible language and ensuring consistent formatting across all sections. For construct validation, the instrument underwent a pilot study involving 30 professionals engaged in multicultural supervision and consultation across various practice settings. Data from this pilot study were subjected to exploratory factor analysis (EFA) to assess whether items clustered into the expected dimensions reflecting the three main constructs of the study: principles and practices, challenges, and strategies for improvement. The factor loadings generally supported the proposed structure, indicating that the instrument effectively captured distinct yet related aspects of multicultural supervision and consultation.

To evaluate reliability, the internal consistency of the instrument was assessed using Cronbach's alpha. The overall instrument achieved a Cronbach's alpha coefficient of 0.88, indicating a high level of reliability. The subscales also showed satisfactory internal consistency: the principles and practices subscale ($\alpha = 0.75$), the challenges subscale ($\alpha = 0.67$), and the strategies for improvement subscale ($\alpha = 0.58$). These coefficients suggest that the items within each subscale are measuring coherent constructs and that the questionnaire is suitable for use in empirical research.

Procedure for data collection

The data collection process was structured to ensure broad representation and methodological rigor. The study focused on counselors and psychologists practising in multicultural counselling and psychotherapy across Nigeria, drawing participants from one state in each of the country's six geopolitical zones: North Central, North East, North West, South East, South South, and South West. This approach ensured geographical diversity and helped capture variations in supervision and consultation practices influenced by cultural and regional contexts.

Before initiating data collection, ethical approval was secured from the relevant institutional review board. Letters of permission and introduction were sent to heads of counselling units, state ministries of education, hospitals, universities, and professional associations within the selected states to formally request their collaboration in facilitating access to qualified participants. A total sample of 400 counselors and psychologists was determined for the study. Using purposive and stratified sampling techniques, participants were selected to include supervisors, consultants, and practising therapists actively engaged in multicultural counselling and psychotherapy. This sampling strategy ensured that the perspectives gathered were relevant to the study objectives and reflected a balance of professional roles, years of experience, and educational backgrounds.

The Questionnaire for Supervision and Consultation in Multicultural Counselling and Psychotherapy (QSCMCP), which included an informed consent section and clear instructions, served as the primary instrument for data collection. Data were gathered through both digital and printed formats to accommodate participants' preferences and ensure broader participation. For digital administration, the questionnaire was distributed via email and secure online survey platforms, with support from professional networks and counselling associations. For printed administration, the researcher and five trained research assistants visited selected counselling centers, hospitals, schools, universities, and professional meetings within the chosen states to distribute and collect completed questionnaires. Participants were encouraged to complete the questionnaire individually at a convenient time, and were assured of confidentiality and anonymity. Completed questionnaires were reviewed for completeness and consistency before being included in the final dataset. This wide-ranging procedure ensured that data collection was ethical, inclusive, and reflective of multicultural supervision and consultation practices across Nigeria's diverse geopolitical landscape.

Method of data analysis

The study adopted a mixed-methods data analysis approach to capture both the breadth and depth of supervision and consultation practices within multicultural counselling and psychotherapy. The analysis integrated quantitative statistical procedures and qualitative thematic interpretation, thereby aligning with the study's design to explore professional principles, challenges, and strategies across diverse practitioner contexts in Nigeria.

For the quantitative data, responses from the Questionnaire for Supervision and Consultation in Multicultural Counselling and Psychotherapy (QSCMCP), completed by 400 counselors, supervisors, and consultants, were entered into SPSS (version 26) for analysis. Descriptive statistics, including means, standard deviations, and standard errors, were computed to summarize participants' views on the principles and practices of multicultural supervision and consultation. To assess the precision of these estimates, 95% confidence intervals were calculated for mean scores and proportions.

The demographic characteristics of participants were further examined using tests of proportions against a hypothesized value of 0.5, allowing the study to determine whether the sample distribution was balanced or skewed in categories such as gender, age group, professional role, qualification, and years of experience. For each proportion test, *P*-values were reported to indicate statistical significance, while the Vovk-Sellke Maximum p-Ratio (VS-MPR) was calculated to provide a measure of the maximum possible odds in favor of the alternative hypothesis over the null hypothesis, especially useful where *P*-values alone might be insufficient to express evidence strength. Confidence intervals were reported alongside these statistics to show the likely range of the true population proportions. To evaluate the distributional properties of the data, the Shapiro–Wilk test for normality was conducted for each continuous variable derived from Likert scale items. This step ensured that subsequent analyses and interpretations accounted for whether data distributions deviated significantly from normality.

For the qualitative component, narrative data were collected through the Case Study Template for Supervision and Consultation in Multicultural Counselling and Psychotherapy (CST–SCMCP). Participants provided detailed, anonymized descriptions of real challenges encountered and strategies adopted in multicultural supervision and consultation contexts. These narratives were transcribed and subjected to thematic analysis, following an inductive process. The researcher coded recurring concepts, organized them into broader categories, and refined them into central themes that reflected shared professional experiences. Finally, a triangulation process was employed to integrate findings from both data sources. Quantitative patterns (e.g., high mean scores on cultural competence and cultural humility) were compared with the themes emerging from case narratives. This step helped illustrate how practitioners' lived experiences confirmed, deepened, or nuanced the statistical trends observed in the survey data. By combining numeric evidence with contextual stories, the analysis produced a balanced interpretation that is both statistically robust and practically grounded in real-world multicultural supervision practice.

Ethical considerations

Ethical principles were carefully observed throughout the planning and execution of this study to protect the rights, dignity, and welfare of all participants. Before data collection commenced, the research proposal and instruments were reviewed and approved by ethics committee of Department of Counselling and Human Development Studies, University of Nigeria, Nsukka to ensure compliance with established ethical standards in social science research. Participation in the study was entirely voluntary, and all potential respondents were provided with a detailed informed consent statement attached to the questionnaire. The consent statement explained the purpose of the research, the expected duration of participation, and the nature of the questions to be asked. It also clarified that participants could decline to answer any question or withdraw from the study at any point without facing any penalty or negative consequences.

To safeguard participants' privacy and confidentiality, no personal identifiers such as names, contact details, or institutional affiliations were collected alongside their responses. All completed questionnaires were securely stored—both physically and digitally—and access was limited to the researcher and designated members of the research team. Data were reported only in aggregate form, ensuring that individual responses could not be traced back to any participant. Furthermore, the study paid careful attention to cultural sensitivity, given the diverse cultural contexts represented by counselors and psychologists from different geopolitical zones of Nigeria. Questions were framed to avoid language that might be perceived as biased or insensitive, and the research process was designed to respect cultural values and professional norms of participants.

Finally, participants were provided with contact information should they wish to ask questions or seek clarification about the study. By adhering to these ethical principles, the study aimed to maintain the highest standards of respect, transparency, and responsibility throughout the research process.

Results

Table 8.1 presents the demographic breakdown of the 400 participants in the study, covering gender, age, highest qualification, professional role, and years of experience. The analysis included the proportions of each category, P-values comparing these proportions against an expected value of 0.5, confidence intervals, and the Vovk-Sellke Maximum p-Ratio (VS-MPR) which quantifies evidence strength against the null hypothesis. Gender distribution was nearly balanced, with 199 males (49.7%) and 200 females (50.0%). The P-values (0.960 for males and 1.000 for females) are well above 0.05, indicating no significant difference from the expected proportion of 0.5. The narrow 95% confidence

Table 8.1: Analysis of demographic characteristics.

Variable	Level	Counts	Total	Proportion	P	VS-MPR[a]	95% CI for proportion	
							Lower	Upper
Gender	Male	199	400	0.497	0.960	1.000	0.447	0.548
	Female	200	400	0.500	1.000	1.000	0.450	0.550
Age	20–30	69	400	0.172	<.001	$9.870 \times 10^{+38}$	0.137	0.213
	31–40	99	400	0.247	<.001	$7.759 \times 10^{+21}$	0.206	0.293
	41–50	78	400	0.195	<.001	$1.704 \times 10^{+33}$	0.157	0.237
	51–70	69	400	0.172	<.001	$9.870 \times 10^{+38}$	0.137	0.213
	5	84	400	0.210	<.001	$5.052 \times 10^{+29}$	0.171	0.253
Qualification	Bachelors	103	400	0.258	<.001	$1.082 \times 10^{+20}$	0.215	0.303
	Masters	124	400	0.310	<.001	$5.505 \times 10^{+11}$	0.265	0.358
	Ph.D	172	400	0.430	0.006	12.163	0.381	0.480
	Highest qualification	1	400	0.003	<.001	$4.378 \times 10^{+114}$	6.329×10^{-5}	0.014
Role	Consultant	196	400	0.490	0.726	1.000	0.440	0.540
	Supervisor	203	400	0.507	0.803	1.000	0.457	0.558
Experience	5–10 years	97	400	0.242	<.001	$7.122 \times 10^{+22}$	0.201	0.288
	11–20 years	154	400	0.385	<.001	6140.951	0.337	0.435
	21–30 years	106	400	0.265	<.001	$5.037 \times 10^{+18}$	0.222	0.311
	31 years and above	42	400	0.105	<.001	$1.960 \times 10^{+60}$	0.077	0.139

Proportions tested against value: 0.5.

[a]Vovk-Sellke Maximum P -Ratio: Based on the P -value, the maximum possible odds in favor of H_1 over H_0 equals $1/(-e\, P \log(P))$ for $P \leq .37$ (Sellke et al., 2001).

intervals (e.g., male: 44.7%–54.8%) also reflect this balance, suggesting the sample is representative in terms of gender.

For age groups, the distribution was more uneven and significantly different from equal proportions (all $P < 0.001$). The largest age group was 31–40 years (24.7%), followed by those coded as "5" (likely representing 51–60 years, 21.0%), 41–50 years (19.5%), and 20–30 and 51–70 years (each 17.2%). The small *P*-values and large VS-MPR values (e.g., 9.870×10^{38} for 20–30 years) indicate very strong evidence that the age distribution is not evenly spread, with a concentration in mid-career age brackets. In terms of highest qualification, 43.0% of respondents held a Ph.D., followed by 31.0% with a Master's degree and 25.8% with a Bachelor's degree. The *P*-value for Ph.D. holders (0.006) is below 0.05, suggesting this proportion significantly differs from the hypothesized proportion of 0.5, though the VS-MPR (12.163) shows moderate evidence strength compared to the very large values in other categories. These results highlight that the sample is academically diverse but slightly skewed toward higher academic qualifications.

Regarding professional roles, the sample was split between supervisors (50.7%) and consultants (49.0%). Both *P*-values (0.803 and 0.726) are well above 0.05, indicating no significant difference from equal distribution. The confidence intervals for these roles are also closely aligned, suggesting a balanced professional composition within the sample. For years of experience, the largest group had 11–20 years of practice (38.5%), followed by 21–30 years (26.5%), 5–10 years (24.2%), and those with over 31 years of experience (10.5%). The *P*-values (all $< .001$) and very large VS-MPR values (e.g., 1.960×10^{60} for 31+ years) provide strong evidence that these proportions differ significantly from 0.5, indicating the sample is weighted toward mid-career professionals rather than novices or those with very long tenure.

The Vovk-Sellke Maximum p-Ratio values add further depth by quantifying how strongly the data support the alternative hypothesis over the null hypothesis, especially in age and experience groups where the evidence of uneven distribution is most pronounced.

Results for research question one: what are the principles and practices of supervision and consultation in multicultural counselling and psychotherapy?

Table 8.2 presents descriptive statistics on key principles and practices reported by professionals in supervision and consultation within multicultural counselling and psychotherapy. The analysis includes mean scores, standard deviations, confidence intervals, and normality tests. Overall, the mean ratings for the listed practices range from approximately 2.85–3.13 on the scale used, suggesting a moderate level of agreement among respondents regarding the importance or frequency of these multicultural supervision practices. The relatively consistent means across items point to a shared

Table 8.2: Descriptive statistics showing principles and practices of supervision and consultation in multicultural counselling and psychotherapy.

Principles and practices	Mean	Std. error of mean	95% Confidence interval mean		Std. deviation	Shapiro–Wilk	*P*-value of Shapiro–Wilk
			Upper	Lower			
Incorporation of cultural background in supervision/ consultation	2.852	0.071	2.992	2.712	1.423	0.883	<.001
Cultural competence in supervision/consultation	2.880	0.070	3.017	2.743	1.393	0.890	<.001
Encouraging supervisees to explore cultural factors affecting clients	3.063	0.071	3.202	2.923	1.417	0.887	<.001
Culturally discussing cultural identities and their influence on practice	2.972	0.075	3.119	2.826	1.489	0.870	<.001
Supervisors/consultants should model cultural humility	3.020	0.073	3.164	2.877	1.458	0.878	<.001
Adapting supervision methods to reflect cultural differences among supervisees.	2.982	0.070	3.119	2.845	1.392	0.892	<.001
Including multicultural topics are part of supervision session plans.	2.997	0.070	3.136	2.859	1.403	0.889	<.001
Helping supervisees recognize their cultural biases and assumptions.	2.925	0.071	3.064	2.785	1.416	0.887	<.001
Culturally relevant ethical considerations should be discussed in supervision.	3.125	0.073	3.269	2.981	1.463	0.874	<.001
The use of multicultural resources (e.g., case studies, literature) during supervision	3.028	0.070	3.165	2.890	1.395	0.891	<.001

understanding of the role of cultural awareness in supervision and consultation. Among the practices, "Culturally relevant ethical considerations should be discussed in supervision" recorded the highest mean score ($M = 3.125$, SD = 1.463), indicating that respondents place slightly greater emphasis on integrating ethical discussions framed by cultural contexts. Similarly, "Encouraging supervisees to explore cultural factors affecting clients" ($M = 3.063$) and "The use of multicultural resources such as case studies and literature" ($M = 3.028$) also had higher mean values, suggesting these practices are more widely endorsed or observed.

Practices such as "Incorporation of cultural background in supervision/consultation" ($M = 2.852$) and "Cultural competence in supervision/consultation" ($M = 2.880$) had slightly lower mean scores compared to the other items. Nevertheless, these means still reflect moderate support, indicating that although respondents recognize the importance of these principles, they may be applied less consistently in practice. The standard deviations, which range roughly from 1.39 to 1.49, show some variability in responses, suggesting differences in how these principles are practised across settings or among individual professionals. Tests of normality, assessed by the Shapiro–Wilk statistic (all values below 0.890) and significant P-values ($< .001$), suggest that the distribution of responses deviates from normality. This is common in applied social science research and indicates that while central tendencies are meaningful, some respondents report markedly higher or lower levels of engagement with these multicultural supervision practices.

Results for research question two: what are the challenges faced by supervisors and consultants in multicultural supervision and consultation?

The results presented in Table 8.3 offer a descriptive overview of the challenges faced by supervisors and consultants in multicultural supervision and consultation. The data reveal that, overall, respondents moderately agree that a range of issues hinder effective multicultural supervision, as reflected in the mean scores, which cluster around the midpoint of the 5-point Likert scale. Among the most prominent challenges identified were the lack of sufficient research to guide multicultural supervision (mean = 3.113), differences in cultural values (mean = 3.088), and language barriers (mean = 3.085). These relatively higher mean scores suggest that these issues are particularly salient in the practice of multicultural supervision and consultation. Other challenges such as the avoidance of cultural discussions due to discomfort or fear of conflict (mean = 3.045), the influence of stereotypes and biases (mean = 3.020), and perceived low prioritization of multicultural supervision compared to clinical topics (mean = 3.003) were also acknowledged by respondents, indicating that these are relevant and ongoing concerns. Challenges such as limited institutional support (mean = 3.000), time constraints (mean = 2.917), power dynamics (mean = 2.947), and lack of formal training in

Table 8.3: Descriptive statistics showing the challenges faced by supervisors and consultants in multicultural supervision and consultation.

Challenges	Mean	Std. error of mean	95% Confidence interval mean		Std. deviation	Shapiro–Wilk	*P*-value of Shapiro–Wilk
			Upper	Lower			
Lack of training in multicultural supervision	2.960	0.073	3.103	2.817	1.454	0.878	<.001
Differences in cultural values sometimes	3.088	0.072	3.229	2.946	1.435	0.883	<.001
Limited institutional support	3.000	0.074	3.145	2.855	1.468	0.876	<.001
Time constraints	2.917	0.071	3.058	2.777	1.427	0.884	<.001
Language barriers complicate.	3.085	0.071	3.224	2.946	1.410	0.887	<.001
Insufficient research to guide.	3.113	0.067	3.245	2.981	1.341	0.895	<.001
Supervisors and supervisees may avoid cultural discussions.	3.045	0.069	3.180	2.910	1.368	0.897	<.001
Power dynamics make.	2.947	0.069	3.083	2.812	1.376	0.894	<.001
Stereotypes and biases.	3.020	0.070	3.158	2.882	1.398	0.891	<.001
Multicultural supervision is sometimes seen as less important than clinical topics.	3.003	0.072	3.145	2.860	1.445	0.881	<.001

multicultural supervision (mean = 2.960) received slightly lower mean scores, though still indicating moderate agreement. These results reflect a consistent perception that systemic, organizational, and interpersonal factors can hinder the effectiveness of multicultural supervision.

Importantly, the standard errors of the mean were relatively low (ranging from 0.067 to 0.074), and the confidence intervals were narrow, suggesting that the responses were relatively stable and reliable across the sample. Standard deviations ranged from approximately 1.34–1.47, indicating moderate variability in how strongly participants perceived each challenge. Furthermore, the Shapiro–Wilk test results revealed statistically significant deviations from normality for all items ($P < 0.001$), indicating that the distribution of responses was not normal. This implies that any subsequent inferential statistical analyses should consider using non-parametric methods.

Results for research question three: what are the strategies for improving multicultural supervision and consultation practices?

The findings presented in Table 8.4 show that participants moderately agreed on a range of strategies for improving multicultural supervision and consultation, with mean scores ranging from 2.950 to 3.148. The highest-rated strategy was "Promoting research on multicultural supervision and consultation practices," which had a mean score of 3.148, a standard error of 0.072, and a 95% confidence interval ranging from 3.006 to 3.290. This item also had a standard deviation of 1.439, indicating some variability in responses, though the mean suggests general agreement among respondents.

Following closely was the strategy "Developing formal policies that promote multicultural supervision," which recorded a mean of 3.075, a standard error of 0.070, and a confidence interval of 2.938–3.213, with a standard deviation of 1.398. Similarly, "Including cultural competence in supervision performance evaluations" was moderately endorsed, with a mean of 3.025, standard error of 0.071, and confidence interval of 2.885–3.165. Other strategies with comparable levels of agreement included "Providing access to multicultural supervision resources" (mean = 3.023), "Creating peer supervision groups to share multicultural experiences" (mean = 3.018), and "Organizing specialized multicultural supervision training workshops" (mean = 3.005). These strategies were all within the same moderate range of endorsement. Additional strategies such as "Allocating dedicated time for cultural discussions in supervision" (mean = 3.000) and "Encouraging self-reflection on cultural identity and biases" (mean = 2.960) also received moderate support, though slightly lower in comparison. The least endorsed strategies, though still approaching agreement, were "Using multicultural case studies in training" (mean = 2.952) and "Adapting supervision models to address cultural diversity explicitly" (mean = 2.950). Despite having the lowest means in the table, both items remained close to the midpoint of

Table 8.4: Descriptive statistics showing the strategies for improving multicultural supervision and consultation.

Strategies	Mean	Std. error of mean	95% Confidence interval mean		Std. deviation	Shapiro–Wilk	*P*-value of Shapiro–Wilk
			Upper	Lower			
Organizing specialized multicultural supervision training workshops.	3.005	0.072	3.147	2.863	1.446	0.881	<.001
Developing formal policies that promote multicultural supervision.	3.075	0.070	3.213	2.938	1.398	0.890	<.001
Including cultural competence in supervision performance evaluations.	3.025	0.071	3.165	2.885	1.419	0.887	<.001
Encouraging self-reflection on cultural identity and biases.	2.960	0.072	3.101	2.818	1.438	0.880	<.001
Using multicultural case studies in training.	2.952	0.071	3.091	2.814	1.411	0.888	<.001
Creating peer supervision groups to share multicultural experiences.	3.018	0.069	3.154	2.881	1.384	0.893	<.001
Adapting supervision models to address cultural diversity explicitly.	2.950	0.072	3.092	2.808	1.445	0.880	<.001
Allocating dedicated time for cultural discussions in supervision.	3.000	0.069	3.136	2.864	1.382	0.894	<.001
Providing access to multicultural supervision resources (books, guidelines).	3.023	0.072	3.164	2.882	1.433	0.882	<.001
Promoting research on multicultural supervision and consultation practices.	3.148	0.072	3.290	3.006	1.439	0.878	<.001

the scale. Across all strategies, the Shapiro–Wilk test indicated significant deviation from normality, with test statistics ranging from 0.878 to 0.894 and P-values less than 0.001. This suggests that the distribution of responses for each item was not normally distributed.

Case studies on principles and practices of supervision and consultation

To enrich the quantitative findings and illustrate how multicultural supervision and consultation principles appear in real practice, the study includes five detailed case studies. These cases, drawn from diverse regions of Nigeria, provide practical context to the statistical patterns identified earlier.

Case study 1: incorporation of cultural background

A supervisor in Abuja routinely asks supervisees to complete cultural genograms. This exercise revealed, for instance, how a supervisee's ethnic background shaped perceptions of client behavior. Reflecting on this helped the team understand culturally influenced biases and adapt interventions accordingly.

Case studies on challenges in multicultural supervision and consultation

Case study 1: limited time for cultural exploration

In Lagos, a supervisor working at a busy community mental health center described how the sheer number of supervisees and administrative demands often constrained the time available to explore cultural issues in depth. Although supervisees occasionally raised cultural questions, supervision sessions were usually dominated by urgent clinical or procedural matters. The supervisor recognized that cultural exploration was appreciated but admitted that systemic pressures and limited supervision slots meant it was frequently postponed or compressed into brief discussions.

Case study 2: lack of formal training in multicultural supervision

A consultant in Kano State noted that although both supervisors and supervisees expressed willingness to address cultural dimensions of counselling, they lacked structured training or frameworks to guide these conversations. During a reflective meeting, supervisees voiced uncertainty about how to balance cultural respect with ethical boundaries when client values conflicted with professional codes. The consultant acknowledged relying on personal experience rather than formal models, highlighting a gap in systematic multicultural supervision training.

Case study 3: language and communication barriers

In Enugu State, a supervisor shared how supervisees sometimes worked with clients who spoke dialects unfamiliar even to them as Nigerians. These language gaps complicated case discussions during supervision, as supervisees struggled to fully convey client narratives or nuances. The supervisor recounted a specific instance where the subtle meaning of a proverb central to a client's disclosure was lost, limiting the group's ability to explore cultural significance. This barrier reduced the depth and accuracy of cultural understanding in supervision.

Case studies on strategies for improving multicultural supervision and consultation

Case study 1: organizing multicultural competence workshops

At a counselling center in Abuja, supervisors initiated monthly workshops dedicated to multicultural topics. Each session centered on a real or hypothetical case illustrating cultural complexity, followed by group discussion and invited commentary from culturally diverse staff. One session focused on reconciling religious beliefs with therapeutic goals, which helped supervisees develop practical strategies for similar real-life cases. The supervisor reported increased supervisee confidence and openness in later supervision meetings.

Case study 2: establishing peer consultation groups

In Port Harcourt, a group of experienced consultants formed an informal peer consultation circle to share and discuss multicultural challenges they encountered in practice. Meeting once every 2 months, members presented cases, reflected on cultural biases, and brainstormed culturally respectful interventions. One consultant shared that the group helped her recognize a blind spot in her assumptions about rural clients, leading to more culturally responsive supervision.

Case study 3: developing locally adapted case resources

A supervisor in Benin City observed that supervisees engaged more deeply when presented with localized case examples reflecting familiar cultural scenarios. To address this, she compiled a casebook based on anonymized supervision experiences and local cultural dilemmas. During sessions, supervisees analyzed these vignettes, discussed ethical implications, and proposed culturally grounded interventions. Feedback suggested that the resource made multicultural discussions more concrete and relatable.

Case study 2: cultural competence in supervision

In Port Harcourt, a consultant used local case studies to explore how cultural beliefs influence mental health stigma. Supervisees discussed how clients sometimes seek traditional healing before therapy and how to respond respectfully yet professionally.

Case study 3: modeling cultural humility

In Lagos, a senior supervisor acknowledged gaps in knowledge about minority cultural groups and invited supervisees to teach him. This created a collaborative learning atmosphere and modeled humility as an ongoing professional stance.

Case study 4: discussing culturally relevant ethics

An Enugu-based supervisor included discussions of culturally shaped ethical dilemmas in every supervision meeting. For example, when cultural norms pressured a supervisee to share confidential information, the group debated how to uphold ethical codes while respecting cultural values.

Case study 5: use of multicultural resources

In Kano, a consultant introduced local-language materials and culturally adapted vignettes into supervision. This helped supervisees develop strategies for working with clients across language and cultural barriers.

Triangulation of quantitative findings and case studies

The triangulation of quantitative results and qualitative case studies shows clear convergence around the importance of culturally relevant ethics, cultural humility, and the use of multicultural resources.

- Quantitatively, discussing culturally relevant ethics received the highest mean score ($M = 3.125$). Case Study 4 directly illustrates this, showing how supervisors guide ethical decisions in cultural contexts.
- The use of multicultural resources ($M = 3.028$) is echoed in Case Study 5, highlighting practical strategies to enrich supervision.
- Modeling cultural humility ($M = 3.020$) is vividly captured in Case Study 3, showing supervisors' openness to learning from supervisees.

General, the qualitative cases deepen understanding of the statistical findings by showing what these practices look like in everyday professional life. Together, these two strands of evidence reinforce the conclusion that multicultural supervision and consultation are recognized and practized, although with varying emphasis.

Discussion of findings

Principles and practices of multicultural counselling and psychotherapy

The findings reveal that among Nigerian supervisors and consultants, there is a shared but moderately expressed commitment to integrating multicultural principles into supervision and consultation. The strongest endorsement was for the principle of discussing culturally relevant ethical considerations, which indicates that practitioners perceive ethics as inseparable from cultural context. This supports previous work (Bernard & Goodyear, 2014; Sue et al., 2019) arguing that effective multicultural supervision must move beyond generic ethical codes to embrace culturally situated ethical reflection. This suggests a growing recognition that what is considered ethical in practice often depends on cultural values, communal norms, and local expectations.

The moderately high endorsement of practices such as encouraging supervisees to explore cultural influences on clients, and the use of multicultural resources (e.g., culturally adapted case studies), suggests that Nigerian supervision is beginning to take practical steps toward cultural responsiveness. This aligns an argument that supervision becomes more impactful when cultural competence is translated from abstract ideals into concrete actions (Benuto et al., 2019). By emphasizing real-life resources and reflective discussions, supervisors appear to acknowledge that cultural learning must be dynamic and grounded in actual practice contexts rather than limited to theoretical knowledge. Interestingly, the practice of modeling cultural humility by supervisors also received notable, though not the highest, emphasis. This reflects a shift from viewing supervisors as cultural "experts" toward recognizing them as co-learners, which echoes global discussions on cultural humility (Hook et al., 2013). This finding suggests that Nigerian supervisors recognize the importance of openly acknowledging their cultural blind spots and encouraging supervisees to do the same. Yet, the relatively lower mean scores for broader concepts like "incorporation of cultural background" and "cultural competence" suggest that while these principles are valued in theory, they may be perceived as harder to operationalize in daily supervision practice. This resonates with critiques in the literature (Hook et al., 2013) that cultural competence frameworks, when left abstract, often fail to guide day-to-day supervisory dialog and decision-making.

Challenges in multicultural supervision and consultation

The findings indicate that supervisors and consultants in Nigeria perceive a range of systemic, institutional, and interpersonal challenges that complicate the practice of multicultural supervision and consultation. Notably, the most consistently identified challenges include insufficient research to guide multicultural supervision, differences in cultural values, and language barriers. These highlight how the multicultural context is deeply shaped by structural gaps in local evidence, cultural complexity, and communication constraints. The concern over the lack of research resonates with the observation Johnston (2019) that multicultural supervision in African contexts often relies on imported frameworks that may not fully reflect local realities. Without locally grounded models and empirical studies, supervisors face uncertainty in applying multicultural principles in ways that are culturally meaningful and ethically sensitive. This gap reinforces what (Bernard & Goodyear, 2014) argue globally. Hence, the effectiveness of supervision depends heavily on context-specific evidence and guidance. The identified challenge of differing cultural values aligns with previous scholarship (Chung & Bemak, 2012) which notes that cultural clashes can lead to tension in supervision, especially when supervisors and supervisees come from different backgrounds. In Nigeria's highly diverse setting, where ethnic, linguistic, and religious identities intersect, these differences can complicate shared understanding of client issues and professional ethics.

Language barriers were also perceived as significant, echoing studies that highlight how language differences undermine depth of case discussions and reduce supervisees' ability to articulate cultural nuances (Hook et al., 2013; Mosher et al., 2017). In multilingual countries like Nigeria, where even shared national languages may not fully capture local cultural meanings, these barriers can affect the richness of supervision dialog and ultimately client care. Other challenges, such as the avoidance of cultural discussions, stereotypes, and power dynamics, show that beyond structural gaps, relational and attitudinal factors remain significant. This may prevent the critical self-reflection that multicultural supervision ideally promotes. Lower but still relevant challenges like time constraints and limited institutional support highlight organizational barriers. These findings are consistent with previous research showing that even where supervisors are committed to multicultural practice, institutional pressures and competing clinical demands can reduce the time and resources available for culturally focused supervision (Bernard & Goodyear, 2014). Importantly, the collective pattern across these findings suggests that Nigerian supervisors and consultants do not view multicultural supervision challenges as isolated issues but rather as systemic shaped by gaps in training, research infrastructure, institutional priorities, and broader sociocultural complexities. This mirrors global observations (Chung & Bemak, 2012) that multicultural supervision must be understood within broader organizational and societal contexts, not just individual attitudes or skills.

Strategies for improving multicultural supervision and consultation

The findings reveal that professionals see multiple, complementary strategies as important for improving multicultural supervision and consultation in Nigeria, with strongest support for structural and research-focused initiatives. The most endorsed strategy is promoting research on multicultural supervision, highlighting practitioners' recognition that local, contextually grounded evidence is urgently needed to shape effective supervision practices. A stronger research base would help supervisors respond to cultural complexities specific to Nigerian society, such as navigating ethnicity, language diversity, and traditional beliefs.

Developing formal policies that promote multicultural supervision was also highly supported. This reflects an awareness that beyond individual motivation, institutional commitment is essential to normalize multicultural supervision practices (Bernard & Goodyear, 2014). Policies can set expectations for supervisors and protect time and resources needed for culturally focused supervision, which is often sidelined in favor of clinical or administrative tasks. Similarly, including cultural competence in supervision performance evaluations points to a desire to embed multicultural values into accountability structures. Prior studies (Chung & Bemak, 2012) have noted that supervisors may neglect multicultural issues if these are not explicitly included in evaluation systems. Formal assessments can encourage supervisors to engage actively with cultural issues rather than treating them as optional.

Moderate endorsement was also given to practical strategies, such as creating peer supervision groups and providing access to multicultural resources. These strategies align with findings from Hook et al. (2013), who argue that ongoing, shared reflection and access to culturally relevant materials help supervisors stay updated and self-aware. Peer groups, in particular, create safe spaces to discuss cultural challenges and reduce feelings of isolation among supervisors facing complex cultural dynamics. In addition, encouraging self-reflection on cultural identity and biases, while slightly lower in mean rating, remains critical. This finding reflects ongoing awareness that supervisors must address their own cultural positioning, consistent with other findings (Sue et al., 2019), who stress that supervision quality is linked to supervisors' willingness to examine their biases and privilege. The relatively lower endorsement of strategies like using multicultural case studies and adapting supervision models does not suggest these are unimportant, but may reflect practical barriers. For instance, case studies and culturally adapted models often depend on having access to local examples and frameworks which are limited in the Nigerian context. This gap reinforces why respondents rated promoting research so highly, without local case materials and validated supervision models, practical strategies become harder to implement.

Conclusion

This chapter has examined supervision and consultation in multicultural counselling and psychotherapy, highlighting their ethical, relational, and contextual foundations. The findings show that supervisors and consultants value multicultural principles, particularly culturally informed ethical reflection and practical supervisory strategies, yet face significant challenges in translating broader concepts of cultural competence into daily practice. These challenges, including language barriers, differing cultural values, power dynamics, limited institutional support, and insufficient locally grounded research, are not isolated but systemic, shaped by organizational and sociocultural contexts. The chapter also identifies key strategies for strengthening multicultural supervision and consultation, such as promoting context-specific research, developing supportive policies, enhancing training opportunities, embedding cultural competence in evaluation processes, and fostering reflective and peer-based learning spaces.

Recommendations

Based on the study's findings regarding principles, challenges, and strategies in multicultural supervision and consultation in counselling and psychotherapy, the following recommendations are proposed for practitioners, training institutions, professional associations, and policymakers:

1. Strengthen multicultural supervision training: Training institutions and professional development providers should design and implement dedicated workshops and modules that focus on multicultural supervision. These should cover practical skills, cultural humility, self-reflection, and the use of multicultural resources such as culturally relevant case studies and literature.
2. Develop and enforce formal institutional policies: Professional associations and mental health organizations should establish formal policies that explicitly require multicultural considerations in supervision and consultation processes. Policies should set expectations for discussing cultural identities, biases, and ethical considerations as integral components of supervision.
3. Integrate cultural competence into supervision evaluations: Supervision performance evaluations should include criteria that assess how well supervisors and supervisees engage with cultural issues. This would help ensure accountability and encourage supervisors to adopt and model culturally responsive practices.
4. Encourage reflective practice and peer learning: Supervisors and institutions should promote regular reflective exercises, such as cultural genograms or journaling, to help supervisees recognize their cultural assumptions and biases. Establishing peer supervision groups can further provide spaces for sharing experiences and challenges related to multicultural work.
5. Prioritize research and context-specific resources: Academic researchers and professional bodies should invest in contextually grounded research to develop and validate supervision models tailored to Nigeria's diverse cultural settings. Additionally, efforts should be made to produce and disseminate locally relevant multicultural supervision resources, including guidelines, toolkits, and case compilations.

6. Address systemic and organizational barriers: Organizations should work to reduce barriers such as limited institutional support and time constraints by allocating dedicated time within supervision sessions to discuss multicultural issues. Furthermore, strategies like adapting supervision models to local cultural contexts should be formally supported.
7. Raise awareness of the value of multicultural supervision: It is recommended that supervisors, educators, and professional bodies advocate for multicultural supervision to be recognized as equally important as clinical topics. This could be achieved through seminars, conferences, and publications that highlight the positive impact of culturally competent supervision on client outcomes.

References

Benuto, L. T., Singer, J., Newlands, R. T., & Casas, J. B. (2019). Training culturally competent psychologists: Where are we and where do we need to go? *Training and Education in Professional Psychology, 13*(1). https://doi.org/10.1037/tep0000214

Bernard, J. M., & Goodyear, R. K. (2014). Fundamentals of clinical supervision. *Journal of Counseling and Development, 92*(1).

Chung, R., & Bemak, F. (2012). Social justice counseling: The next steps beyond multiculturalism. In *Social justice counseling: The next steps beyond multiculturalism.* https://doi.org/10.4135/9781452240503

Haggerty, G., & Hilsenroth, M. J. (2011). The use of video in psychotherapy supervision. *British Journal of Psychotherapy, 27*(2). https://doi.org/10.1111/j.1752-0118.2011.01232.x

Holly, S. (2023). *Incorporating multiculturalism in clinical supervision.* NBCC.

Hook, J. N., Davis, D. E., Owen, J., Worthington, E. L., & Utsey, S. O. (2013). Cultural humility: Measuring openness to culturally diverse clients. *Journal of Counseling Psychology, 60*(3). https://doi.org/10.1037/a0032595

Inman, A. G. (2006). Supervisor multicultural competence and its relation to supervisory process and outcome. *Journal of Marital and Family Therapy, 32*(1). https://doi.org/10.1111/j.1752-0606.2006.tb01589.x

Johnston, E. R. (2019). South African clinical psychologists' multicultural clinical and supervisory experience. *South African Journal of Psychology, 49*(2). https://doi.org/10.1177/0081246318801122

Kagee, A. (2007). Multicultural aspects of supervision: Considerations for South African supervisors in the helping professions. *Social Work, 43*(4). https://doi.org/10.15270/43-4-263

Kemer, G., Li, C., Attia, M., Chan, C. D., Chung, M., Li, D., Neuer Colburn, A., Peters, H. C., Ramaswamy, A., & Sunal, Z. (2022). Multicultural supervision in counseling: A content analysis of peer-reviewed literature. *Counselor Education and Supervision, 61*(1). https://doi.org/10.1002/ceas.12220

Mosher, D. K., Hook, J. N., Captari, L. E., Davis, D. E., DeBlaere, C., & Owen, J. (2017). Cultural humility: A therapeutic framework for engaging diverse clients. *Practice Innovations, 2*(4). https://doi.org/10.1037/pri0000055

Sellke, T., Bayarri, M. J., & Berger, J. O. (2001). Calibration of p values for testing precise null hypotheses. *The American Statistician, 55*(1), 62–71. https://doi.org/10.1198/000313001300339950

Sue, D. W., Sue, D., Neville, H. A., & Smith, L. (2019). *Counseling the culturally diverse: Theory and practice, 8th edition.* NJ: Wiley.

Zhang, H., Watkins, C. E., Hook, J. N., Hodge, A. S., Davis, C. W., Norton, J., Wilcox, M. M., Davis, D. E., DeBlaere, C., & Owen, J. (2022). Cultural humility in psychotherapy and clinical supervision: A research review. *Counselling and Psychotherapy Research, 22*(3). https://doi.org/10.1002/capr.12481

CHAPTER 9

Research in multicultural counselling and psychotherapy

Introduction

Research in multicultural counselling and psychotherapy has become increasingly vital in response to the growing cultural, ethnic, linguistic, and religious diversity of contemporary societies. Counselors and psychotherapists are now more likely than ever to work with clients whose cultural backgrounds, value systems, and lived experiences differ significantly from their own. In this context, research serves as the foundation for developing counselling theories, assessment tools, and intervention strategies that are culturally responsive, ethically sound, and empirically supported. Without systematic and culturally informed research, counselling practice risks reinforcing cultural bias, misdiagnosis, and ineffective or even harmful interventions.

Multicultural counselling research seeks to examine how culture influences psychological development, help-seeking behaviors, therapeutic relationships, and treatment outcomes. Culture shapes individuals' understanding of distress, coping strategies, family roles, spirituality, communication styles, and expectations of therapy. Consequently, research that ignores cultural context often fails to capture the complexity of clients' experiences, particularly among marginalized, minority, and indigenous populations. This limitation has led to increasing calls for research approaches that move beyond universalist assumptions and instead recognize the contextual and relational nature of mental health and healing.

Historically, much of the empirical foundation of counselling and psychotherapy has been derived from Western, individualistic, and Eurocentric frameworks (Draguns, 2013; Martin, 2025; Moodley & Kinha, 2015). Research samples have frequently been homogeneous, instruments culturally narrow, and interpretations grounded in dominant cultural norms. As a result, the applicability of many established counselling models to culturally diverse populations has been questioned. Multicultural research challenges these limitations by interrogating whose knowledge is represented, whose voices are excluded, and how power dynamics influence both research processes and therapeutic practice. In recent decades, multicultural counselling research has expanded to include qualitative,

A Pragmatic Approach to Multicultural Counselling and Psychotherapy Skills Acquisition. https://doi.org/10.1016/B978-0-443-33939-4.00003-3

mixed-methods, and participatory approaches that prioritize clients' narratives and cultural meanings (Kuo et al., 2023). Indigenous and community-based research methodologies have also gained prominence, particularly in non-Western contexts, as scholars seek to generate knowledge that is locally relevant and culturally grounded. These approaches emphasize collaboration, reflexivity, and respect for cultural traditions, thereby aligning research practices with the ethical principles of multicultural counselling.

Ethical considerations are central to research in multicultural counselling and psychotherapy. Issues such as informed consent, cultural sensitivity, language use, researcher positionality, and the potential for exploitation require careful attention. Researchers must critically reflect on their own cultural assumptions and biases, ensuring that research designs and interpretations do not perpetuate stereotypes or systemic inequities. In this regard, multicultural research is closely linked to social justice, advocacy, and the promotion of equitable mental health services.

The field of multicultural counselling and psychotherapy has matured considerably over recent decades, yet its research foundations continue to face distinctive conceptual and methodological challenges. As culturally diverse populations grow and intercultural encounters become routine in therapeutic contexts, scholars and practitioners are pressed to examine not only what works in counselling, but how research can validly capture the complex dynamics of culture, power, and healing relationships. Seminal discussions in the literature have long highlighted issues such as cultural hegemony, marginalization of minority perspectives, and the need to integrate local healing practices into mainstream counselling discourse (Moodley, 1999). These debates indicate that research in this domain must move beyond conventional paradigms to embrace approaches that are both culturally responsive and methodologically rigorous.

Against this backdrop, the present chapter sets out three interlinked objectives. First, it explores the methodologies employed in multicultural counselling and psychotherapy research. Second, it identifies persistent challenges that hinder the production of credible and useful knowledge. Empirical work on cross-racial therapy, for example, illustrates how client experiences and therapeutic alliance processes demand careful, culturally attuned inquiry (Chang & Berk, 2009). Third, the chapter offers recommendations aimed at strengthening research practices, encouraging innovations that enhance validity, inclusivity, and practical relevance for diverse client populations. Together, these aims seek to chart a more reflective and effective research agenda for multicultural counselling and psychotherapy.

Conceptual foundations of research in multicultural counselling and psychotherapy

The conceptual foundations of research in multicultural counselling and psychotherapy are grounded in the recognition that human behavior, psychological distress, and healing processes are deeply embedded within cultural, social, and historical contexts. Multicultural research is therefore informed by theoretical perspectives that challenge monocultural assumptions and emphasize cultural diversity, contextual meaning, and relational understanding. These foundations provide the philosophical and theoretical lens through which research questions are framed, methodologies selected, and findings interpreted. At the core of multicultural counselling research is the concept of culture as a dynamic and multifaceted construct. Culture encompasses shared values, beliefs, traditions, language, worldviews, and social norms that influence how individuals perceive themselves and the world around them (Stephen, 2017). In research, culture is not viewed as a static variable but as an evolving process shaped by intersecting factors such as ethnicity, gender, religion, socioeconomic status, age, and migration experiences. This perspective underscores the need for research designs that capture cultural complexity rather than relying on simplistic categorizations.

Another key foundation is the principle of cultural relativism, which asserts that behaviors and experiences must be understood within their cultural context rather than judged against dominant or universal standards. In multicultural counselling research, this principle challenges deficit-based models that pathologize cultural differences. Instead, it encourages researchers to examine how culturally specific coping strategies, family structures, and healing practices contribute to psychological well-being. Cultural relativism thus promotes respectful inquiry and guards against ethnocentric interpretations of research findings (Maratsos, 2012). Social constructionism also plays a significant role in shaping multicultural research. From this perspective, psychological realities such as mental health, illness, and normality are constructed through social and cultural interactions. Research informed by social constructionism emphasizes language, narratives, and meaning-making processes, making qualitative methods particularly valuable (Demiray, 2020). This foundation highlights the importance of clients' voices and lived experiences, especially those from historically marginalized groups whose perspectives have often been excluded from mainstream research.

The concept of intersectionality further strengthens the theoretical base of multicultural counselling research. Intersectionality recognizes that individuals simultaneously occupy multiple social identities, which interact to shape experiences of privilege, oppression, and access to mental health services. Research grounded in this framework avoids isolating culture from other identity dimensions and instead examines how overlapping identities influence counselling processes and outcomes. This approach enhances the relevance and accuracy of research findings in diverse populations. Ethical and social justice principles are integral to the conceptual foundations of multicultural research. Multicultural counselling research is not value-neutral; it is inherently linked to issues of power, equity, and representation. Researchers are expected to adopt reflexive practices, critically examining their positionality and the power dynamics between researchers and participants. This ethical stance aligns research with the broader goals of multicultural counselling, which include advocacy, empowerment, and the reduction of systemic barriers to mental health care. Finally, multicultural counselling research is informed by contextual and indigenous frameworks, particularly in local settings. These frameworks emphasize communal values, spirituality, oral traditions, and culturally embedded healing practices. By valuing indigenous knowledge systems, researchers contribute to the development of culturally congruent theories and interventions. This foundation challenges the dominance of foreign paradigms and supports the creation of research that is both culturally meaningful and practically applicable.

Characteristics of a multicultural counselling researcher

A multicultural counselling researcher possesses specific personal, ethical, and professional qualities that enable culturally responsive and socially just inquiry. Given the complex role of culture in shaping human behavior and mental health, researchers in this field must move beyond technical competence to embody values and practices that respect diversity, equity, and contextual understanding. First, cultural self-awareness is a fundamental characteristic. Multicultural counselling researchers must critically examine their own cultural identities, values, assumptions, and biases, and understand how these influence the research process. This reflexive awareness helps researchers avoid imposing their worldview on participants and supports more accurate interpretation of culturally situated experiences.

Second, cultural sensitivity and humility are essential. Rather than assuming expertise over participants' cultural realities, multicultural researchers adopt a stance of openness, respect, and lifelong learning. Cultural humility acknowledges that understanding culture is an ongoing process and that participants are the experts of their own lived experiences. This attitude fosters trust and ethical engagement, particularly with marginalized or historically oppressed groups.

Third, a multicultural counselling researcher demonstrates a strong commitment to ethical practice and social justice. Such researchers recognize that research is not value-neutral and that it often reflects power dynamics between researchers and participants. They are attentive to issues of informed consent, confidentiality, language use, representation, and potential harm, and they actively work to ensure that research outcomes benefit the communities involved rather than exploiting them.

Another key characteristic is competence in culturally appropriate research methodologies. Multicultural researchers are skilled in selecting and adapting research designs, instruments, and data collection methods that are culturally congruent. This may include the use of qualitative, mixed-methods, participatory, or indigenous approaches that prioritize context, narrative, and community collaboration over rigid standardized measures.

Additionally, openness to multiple ways of knowing distinguishes multicultural counselling researchers. They value indigenous knowledge systems, spiritual perspectives, communal values, and non-Western healing practices as legitimate sources of psychological understanding. This epistemological flexibility challenges the dominance of Western paradigms and broadens the scope of counselling research.

Effective multicultural researchers also possess strong interpersonal and communication skills. These skills are critical for building rapport, negotiating cultural meanings, working with interpreters when necessary, and engaging respectfully with individuals and communities from diverse backgrounds. Clear and culturally appropriate communication enhances data quality and ethical engagement.

Finally, a multicultural counselling researcher demonstrates ongoing professional development and advocacy orientation. They remain informed about emerging multicultural theories, ethical guidelines, and cultural issues affecting mental health. Beyond knowledge generation, they view research as a tool for advocacy, policy development, and the promotion of equitable counselling and psychotherapy services.

My experiences as a multicultural counselling researcher

My work as a multicultural counselling researcher has involved conducting studies within Nigeria and other African contexts, as well as collaborating with researchers based outside Africa. These experiences have provided sustained engagement with diverse cultural, institutional, and academic environments, allowing for a deeper understanding of how counselling and psychotherapy research is shaped by context. Working across local and international settings has revealed important contrasts in how mental health is conceptualized, how research is designed, and how knowledge is evaluated and disseminated.

Research conducted in Nigeria and across Africa has consistently highlighted the influence of culture, community structures, spirituality, and socio-economic realities on counselling and psychotherapy processes. In many African settings, psychological distress is not understood solely as an individual or clinical issue but is often linked to family relationships, communal responsibilities, spiritual beliefs, and broader social conditions. These realities present challenges when applying conventional research instruments and frameworks that were developed in Western, individualistic contexts. As a result, research in these settings often requires methodological flexibility and cultural adaptation to ensure that participants' experiences are accurately represented. My experience has shown that qualitative and mixed-methods approaches are particularly valuable in African and multicultural contexts. Such approaches allow participants to express their experiences in culturally meaningful ways and provide space for narrative, context, and interpretation. However, employing these methodologies is not without difficulty. Researchers must navigate language diversity, translation concerns, varying literacy levels, and differences in how psychological concepts are understood. These factors complicate data collection and analysis, requiring careful planning and culturally informed decision-making throughout the research process. Collaboration with researchers outside Africa has been intellectually enriching, offering opportunities for interdisciplinary dialog, shared expertise, and access to wider academic networks. At the same time, these collaborations have revealed tensions related to research priorities, methodological preferences, and publication expectations. In some cases, dominant research standards privilege foreign epistemologies, which can limit the recognition of indigenous knowledge systems and culturally grounded methodologies. Negotiating these differences has required ongoing dialog and a deliberate effort to ensure that African perspectives are meaningfully integrated rather than treated as supplementary.

Several recurring challenges have shaped my experience as a multicultural counselling researcher. These include limited funding for mental health research, inadequate research infrastructure, delays in ethical approval processes, and difficulties in participant recruitment due to stigma surrounding counselling and psychotherapy. In cross-national collaborations, additional challenges arise in relation to authorship expectations, data ownership, and ethical standards, which may vary across institutions and regions. These challenges affect not only the conduct of research but also the interpretation and application of findings. Engaging in research across multiple cultural contexts has also reinforced the importance of reflexivity. My position as a researcher situated within African cultural realities while interacting with global academic communities has influenced how research questions are framed and how findings are interpreted. This positioning requires continuous self-reflection, particularly in relation to power, representation, and voice in the research process. Recognizing one's positionality is essential for maintaining ethical integrity and cultural responsiveness in multicultural counselling research. These experiences form the basis for the focus of this chapter. The need to adapt research methodologies to diverse cultural contexts, the practical and ethical challenges encountered in multicultural and cross-continental research, and the ongoing negotiation between local relevance and global academic standards all point to the importance of critically examining research practices in multicultural counselling and psychotherapy. In response to these realities, this chapter is guided by the following research objectives and questions.

Research objectives

1. To explore the methodologies used in research within multicultural counselling and psychotherapy.

2. To identify the challenges in conducting research in multicultural counselling and psychotherapy contexts.
3. To provide recommendations for improving research practices in multicultural counselling and psychotherapy.

Research questions

1. What methodologies are commonly used in research within multicultural counselling and psychotherapy?
2. What are the key challenges faced in conducting research in multicultural counselling and psychotherapy contexts?
3. What recommendations can be made to improve research practices in multicultural counselling and psychotherapy?

Research methodology

This study adopted a mixed-methods research design, integrating both quantitative and qualitative approaches to gain a holistic understanding of research practices within multicultural counselling and psychotherapy. This methodological choice was informed by the complexity of multicultural contexts, where combining numerical trends with rich, contextually grounded narratives enhances the depth and validity of findings (Creswell & Plano Clark, 2018).

Research design

The study utilized an exploratory sequential mixed-methods design. Initially, qualitative data were collected to explore prevailing methodologies and contextual challenges in multicultural research. The insights from this phase informed the development of a quantitative survey instrument used to validate and generalize the qualitative findings across a broader sample.

Population and sample

The study targeted researchers, counselors, psychotherapists, and postgraduate students engaged in multicultural counselling and psychotherapy research. Purposive sampling was used in the qualitative phase to select 15 participants with substantial experience in multicultural research from universities, research institutes, and professional associations across Nigeria and other multicultural contexts. For the quantitative phase, a stratified random sampling technique was used to distribute the survey to 250 respondents, ensuring representation across gender, region, and years of professional experience.

Data collection methods

Qualitative phase: In-depth semi-structured interviews were conducted, exploring participants' experiences with research methodologies, challenges faced in multicultural contexts, and suggestions for improving research practices. Interviews were audio-recorded and transcribed verbatim with participants' consent.

Qualitative interview protocol

The qualitative interview protocol consisted of semi-structured, open-ended questions designed to explore methodologies, challenges, and recommendations in multicultural counselling research. Questions were developed to elicit detailed narratives from 15 participants (researchers, counselors, psychotherapists, and postgraduate students) about their experiences, focusing on cultural distinctions in Nigeria and with African American and South Asian populations. The protocol included prompts such as, "What methodologies do you use to study multicultural counselling, and why?" and "What cultural factors influence your research challenges?" to ensure depth and flexibility in responses.

Validation process

Content Validity: To ensure content validity, the interview questions were developed based on a comprehensive literature review of multicultural counselling research. A panel of five experts three multicultural counselling researchers and two Nigerian community-based practitioners with expertise in Yoruba and Hausa cultural contexts reviewed the protocol to confirm that questions adequately covered the research questions and were relevant to Nigeria's ethnic diversity. Feedback led to revisions, such as adding prompts to explore intra-cultural variability (e.g., differences within Igbo communities) and diaspora-specific experiences (e.g., African American historical trauma).

Construct Validity: Construct validity was established by aligning questions with theoretical frameworks, such as cultural competence and community-based participatory research (Benz et al., 2024). For example, questions about participatory methods were grounded in empowerment theories to ensure they captured the intended constructs. Pilot testing with three Nigerian researchers (one each from Yoruba, Igbo, and Hausa backgrounds) confirmed that questions elicited responses aligned with these constructs, with minor adjustments to clarify terminology (e.g., replacing "cultural sensitivity" with "cultural responsiveness" to avoid ambiguity).

Reliability: To enhance reliability, the protocol was standardized with a guide for interviewers, including probes and follow-up questions to ensure consistency across interviews. Two trained interviewers conducted mock interviews during pilot testing, and inter-rater agreement was assessed by comparing coded responses from pilot transcripts, achieving a Cohen's kappa of 0.82, indicating strong reliability (Landis & Koch, 1977). Training ensured interviewers used culturally sensitive language, such as avoiding Western-centric terms when discussing Hausa mental health beliefs.

Cultural Sensitivity: To ensure cultural appropriateness, the protocol was reviewed by community consultants from Yoruba, Igbo, and Hausa backgrounds, as well as an African American counselor familiar with diaspora issues. They suggested incorporating culturally relevant examples, such as references to Yoruba family dynamics or South Asian stigma, to make questions resonate with participants. The protocol was translated into Hausa for Northern Nigerian participants, with back-translation to ensure accuracy, following guidelines for cross-cultural research (Brislin, 1970). Pilot testing confirmed that questions were culturally acceptable and elicited meaningful responses across diverse groups.

Quantitative phase: A structured questionnaire titled "Questionnaire for Research in Multicultural Counselling and Psychotherapy" was developed based on themes emerging from the qualitative phase. The questionnaire included Likert-scale items and demographic questions, and it was administered both online and in-person to maximize participation. The questionnaire used a 5-point scale (e.g., 1 = Never to 5 = Very frequently for methodologies; 1 = Strongly disagree to 5 = Strongly agree for challenges; 1 = Not important to 5 = Very important for recommendations).

Validation process

Content Validity: The survey items were developed based on a literature review of multicultural counselling methodologies, challenges, and recommendations (Hair et al., 2010). A panel of six experts four academic researchers (two from Nigeria, one specializing in African American populations, one in South Asian contexts) and two community practitioners reviewed the items to ensure comprehensive coverage of the constructs. Feedback led to the inclusion of items specific to Nigeria's context, such as challenges related to Hausa language barriers and recommendations for Yoruba-specific scales. The panel confirmed that items were clear, relevant, and culturally appropriate.

Construct Validity: Construct validity was established by mapping items to theoretical constructs, such as cultural competence for methodologies (Sodowsky et al., 1994), trust barriers for challenges, and capacity building for recommendations (Ratts et al., 2016). Exploratory factor analysis (EFA) during pilot testing with 30 Nigerian researchers and practitioners confirmed that items loaded onto expected constructs (e.g., qualitative methods, trust challenges, funding recommendations), with factor loadings above 0.6, indicating strong construct alignment (Hair et al., 2010). Items with low loadings (e.g., a vague question about "general barriers") were revised for clarity.

Reliability: Internal consistency was assessed using Cronbach's alpha during pilot testing, yielding values of 0.87 for methodologies, 0.85 for challenges, and 0.89 for recommendations, indicating high reliability. Test-retest reliability was evaluated by administering the survey to 20 pilot participants 2 weeks apart, achieving a correlation coefficient of 0.81, suggesting stable responses over time. Items were standardized to ensure consistency across Nigeria's regions, with translations into Hausa and Yoruba for accessibility, verified through back-translation (Brislin, 1970).

Cultural Sensitivity: To ensure cultural appropriateness, the survey was reviewed by community consultants from Yoruba, Igbo, and Hausa backgrounds, as well as an African American practitioner. They suggested rephrasing items to reflect local terminology (e.g., "community trust" instead of "participant trust" for Hausa respondents) and adding context-specific examples (e.g., Igbo collectivism, South Asian stigma). Pilot testing with 30 participants across Nigeria's regions confirmed that items were culturally relevant and comprehensible, with no reported discomfort or misunderstanding.

Data analysis

Qualitative data were analyzed thematically, following (Braun & Clarke, 2006) six-step framework. Themes were identified to address each research objective, providing nuanced insights into methodologies, challenges, and recommended practices. The quantitative data were analyzed using descriptive and inferential statistical methods. Prior to the analysis, all responses were carefully reviewed for completeness and accuracy. Incomplete questionnaires were excluded to ensure the integrity of the results, and the remaining data were entered and processed using IBM SPSS Statistics (Version 26). Descriptive statistics were used to summarize the demographic characteristics of the respondents, including gender, age, professional role, years of experience, region, and population experience. Frequencies and proportions were calculated for each demographic variable to provide a clear overview of the sample distribution. Additionally, mean scores, standard deviations, and 95% confidence intervals were computed for responses related to the frequency of research methodologies used, the challenges encountered, and strategies for improving research practices in multicultural counselling and psychotherapy.

To determine the normality of the data, the Shapiro–Wilk test was applied to the Likert-scale responses. The results showed that all variables significantly deviated from a normal distribution ($P < 0.001$). However, given the sufficiently large sample size and the ordinal nature of the Likert data, the use of means and standard deviations was maintained for interpretive purposes.

Inferential statistical tests were also employed to compare the observed proportions of demographic variables to a hypothesized value, typically 0.50. These tests helped to assess whether certain groups were overrepresented or underrepresented in the sample.

Trustworthiness and rigor

For the qualitative phase, credibility was ensured through member checking, where participants reviewed and confirmed the accuracy of transcriptions and interpretations. Triangulation of data sources and peer debriefing further enhanced trustworthiness. In the quantitative phase, the survey instrument underwent pilot testing to refine clarity and reliability, and Cronbach's alpha coefficients were calculated to assess internal consistency.

Ethical considerations

Ethical approval was obtained from the Institutional Review Board of the Department of Counselling and Human Development Studies, University of Nigeria, Nsukka. Informed consent was secured from all participants, who were assured of confidentiality and their right to withdraw at any stage without consequence. Data were anonymized and securely stored to protect participants' identities.

Qualitative results

Research question 1: what methodologies are commonly used in research within multicultural counselling and psychotherapy?

Analysis of the interview transcripts revealed that researchers in multicultural counselling and psychotherapy employ a diverse range of methodologies, including qualitative, quantitative, mixed-methods, participatory, and context-rich approaches. These methods are deliberately chosen to address the complex, culturally situated nature of the field, ensuring that research captures the nuances of cultural identities, systemic influences, and client-therapist dynamics. Participants emphasized that methodological choices are guided by the research objectives, the cultural context of the study population, and the need to balance depth, rigor, and ethical responsibility. The following themes emerged from the analysis, each reflecting a distinct approach to studying multicultural counselling.

Theme 1: qualitative exploration of lived experiences

Qualitative methodologies were the most frequently cited approaches, with 12 out of 15 participants highlighting their use of phenomenology, grounded theory, and narrative inquiry. These methods were valued for their ability to delve into the subjective experiences, cultural meanings, and lived realities of clients and therapists, particularly in culturally diverse contexts.

- Phenomenology focuses on understanding the essence of participants' lived experiences, making it ideal for exploring how cultural factors shape perceptions of therapy. For example, a researcher might use phenomenology to study how Southeast Nigerian clients experience trust in therapeutic relationships.
- Grounded theory enables researchers to develop culturally informed theories by systematically analyzing data, especially when existing frameworks lack cultural specificity. This approach is often used to create models for culturally responsive interventions, such as integrating African spiritual practices into therapy.
- Narrative inquiry centers on clients' stories, allowing researchers to explore how cultural narratives influence mental health. This method is particularly effective for amplifying the voices of marginalized groups, such as Indigenous or queer communities of color.

One participant, a researcher studying Caribbean diaspora communities in his postdoctoral research, shared:

> *Qualitative methods let us uncover the layers of meaning behind a client's experience. For instance, when a Jamaican client talks about 'strength' in therapy, it's not just resilience—it's tied to cultural expectations of family and community. Numbers can't capture that.*

Another participant, working with Middle Eastern refugee populations in a postgraduate study, noted:

> *Narrative inquiry gives us access to stories that are often silenced. When a client shares their journey of displacement, we learn how cultural trauma shapes their mental health in ways no survey could reveal.*

Applications: Qualitative methods are widely used in exploratory studies, such as understanding barriers to mental health access or exploring cultural stigma. They are also employed in training programs to provide rich, narrative-based case examples for therapists.

Challenges: Participants acknowledged that qualitative research is time-intensive and requires significant researcher reflexivity to mitigate bias. One researcher emphasized:

> *We have to constantly check our own cultural lenses to avoid misinterpreting participants' experiences. Cultural humility is non-negotiable in this work.*

Theme 2: mixed-methods for inclusive insights

Eight out of 15 participants advocated for mixed-methods designs, which combine qualitative and quantitative approaches to balance depth with generalizability. These designs were valued for their ability to explore culturally specific issues qualitatively and then test or scale findings quantitatively across diverse populations.

- **Sequential designs** typically begin with qualitative methods, such as interviews or focus groups, to identify cultural themes, followed by quantitative surveys to test their prevalence. For example, a study on Latinx youth might use interviews to explore cultural identity conflicts and then survey a larger sample to quantify their impact on mental health.
- **Concurrent designs** collect qualitative and quantitative data simultaneously to triangulate findings. A study on therapist cultural competence might pair interviews with therapists about their practices with client satisfaction surveys using validated scales.

One researcher working with Nigerian communities explained:

> *We start with interviews to understand how cultural values like collectivism influence therapy, then we design surveys to see if those patterns hold across a broader population. It's about building a bridge between stories and statistics.*

Another participant, studying multicultural training programs, added:

> *Mixed-methods let us show both the 'why' and the 'how much.' For example, we can explore therapists' challenges in cultural adaptation qualitatively and then measure improvements in their skills quantitatively after training.*

Applications: Mixed-methods approaches are often used to evaluate culturally adapted interventions, assess training programs, or influence policy by combining rich qualitative insights with measurable outcomes.

Challenges: Participants noted that mixed-methods research requires expertise in both qualitative and quantitative methodologies, which can strain resources. One researcher cautioned:

> *Integrating qualitative and quantitative findings is tricky—you have to ensure the cultural nuances from interviews aren't lost when you move to numbers.*

Theme 3: quantitative measurement of constructs

While less dominant than qualitative or mixed-methods approaches, quantitative methodologies were recognized for their role in measuring specific constructs, such as multicultural competencies, client outcomes, intervention effectiveness or attitudes toward therapy. Participants used these methods to provide measurable evidence for stakeholders like funders or policymakers.

- Validated scales, such as the Multicultural Counselling Inventory (MCI) or the Cross-Cultural Counselling Inventory-Revised (CCCI-R), were commonly used to assess therapists' cultural competence or clients' perceptions of culturally responsive care.
- Outcome measurement involved tracking changes in mental health outcomes, such as reductions in anxiety or depression, using culturally validated scales. Statistical

techniques like regression analysis or structural equation modeling were employed to explore relationships between cultural variables and therapeutic outcomes.

One participant, a policy researcher, stated:

> *Quantitative data are crucial when you're trying to convince funders or institutions to invest in multicultural training. Showing a correlation between therapist cultural competence and client retention speaks their language.*

Another researcher, studying African American clients in a postdoctoral research, added:

> *We use scales like the MCI to measure how well therapists adapt to cultural needs. It's not perfect, but it gives us a starting point to quantify something as complex as cultural responsiveness.*

Applications: Quantitative methods are often used in program evaluation, policy advocacy, or research requiring generalizable findings, such as studies on the effectiveness of culturally tailored interventions.

Challenges: Participants highlighted the need for culturally validated measures, as many standardized tools were developed with Western populations. One researcher noted:

> *We can't just apply a scale designed for White clients to a multicultural population—it risks missing the mark. We need more work on culturally specific instruments.*

Theme 4: participatory and community-based approaches

Four out of 15 participants emphasized participatory action research (PAR) and community-based approaches, which prioritize collaboration with the communities being studied. These methods were seen as ethically and culturally essential for empowering underrepresented groups and ensuring research relevance.

- Participatory Action Research (PAR) involves community members in designing, conducting, and interpreting research, ensuring that findings address community needs. For example, a PAR study with Indigenous communities might involve elders in developing research questions about integrating traditional healing into therapy.
- Community-based approaches focus on conducting research within the cultural and social contexts of the target population, often in partnership with community organizations. These methods build trust and ensure actionable outcomes.

One therapist-researcher working with Somali immigrant communities shared:

> *PAR isn't just research—it's a partnership. When we involve community leaders in studying mental health stigma, the solutions we develop are grounded in their reality, not our assumptions.*

Another participant, researching rural Latinx populations, noted:

> *Community-based research means meeting people where they are—literally and figuratively. We work with local organizations to ensure our research respects cultural values and leads to real community benefit.*

Applications: These approaches are common in research with marginalized groups, such as refugees, Indigenous populations, or low-income communities, and are used to develop culturally tailored interventions or advocate for systemic change.

Challenges: Building community trust requires significant time and resources, and researchers must navigate power dynamics carefully. One participant reflected:

> *You can't just parachute into a community and expect trust. It takes years of relationship-building to do this work ethically.*

Theme 5: context-rich case studies and ethnography

Participants also highlighted case studies and ethnographic methods for capturing detailed cultural contexts, particularly in settings where formal data collection is challenging or culturally inappropriate. These methods bridge theory and practice, providing vivid, real-world insights.

- Case studies explore individual or small-group experiences in depth, often highlighting unique cultural dynamics. For example, a case study might examine how a therapist navigates cultural differences with a client from a collectivist culture in an individualistic society.
- Ethnographic methods involve immersive observation to understand cultural practices and social dynamics. A researcher might spend time in a Nigerian community to study how family dynamics influence therapy engagement.

One researcher working with Northen Nigerian clients explained:

> *Case studies let us show how theory meets practice in real-world multicultural counselling scenarios. A single case can reveal how cultural values shape a client's journey in ways a survey might miss.*

Another participant, studying South-east communities in Nigeria, added:

> *Ethnography is about immersion. By spending time in the community, we see how cultural practices—like church-based support systems—shape mental health in ways no questionnaire could capture.*

Applications: These methods are used in exploratory research, clinical training, or studies with underrepresented populations where standardized methods may be impractical.

Challenges: Generalizability is a limitation, and ethical considerations, such as protecting anonymity, are critical. One researcher noted:

> *Ethnography requires us to be deeply respectful of cultural boundaries. We have to ensure our presence doesn't disrupt the community we're trying to understand."*

Future Directions: Participants called for more culturally validated quantitative measures, the integration of digital tools like online ethnography to reach diverse populations, and expanded participatory approaches to include more marginalized voices. One researcher summarized:

> *The future of this field lies in blending rigor with cultural authenticity. We need methods that honor both the science and the humanity of our work.*

Research question 2: what are the challenges in conducting research in multicultural counselling and psychotherapy contexts?

Analysis of the interview data revealed a range of interconnected challenges that researchers encounter when conducting studies in multicultural counselling and psychotherapy. These challenges, which impact the design, implementation, and dissemination of research, clustered into four major themes: cultural complexity and sensitivity, methodological limitations, access and trust, and institutional and systemic constraints. Participants emphasized that these challenges require careful navigation to ensure that research is culturally responsive, ethically sound, and practically impactful. Each theme is explored below, with expanded details and additional quotations to provide a deeper understanding of the issues and their implications.

Theme 1: cultural complexity and sensitivity

Nearly all participants (13 out of 15) highlighted the difficulty of accounting for the intricate and dynamic nature of cultural identities, traditions, and beliefs, which vary not only between cultural groups but also within them. This complexity poses significant challenges in designing culturally valid research instruments, interpreting findings responsibly, and avoiding overgeneralization.

- Inter- and Intra-Cultural Variability: Participants noted that cultural groups are not monolithic, and factors such as intersectionality (e.g., race, gender, socioeconomic status, and migration status) add layers of complexity. For example, studying mental health stigma among Latinx communities requires recognizing differences between Mexican, Puerto Rican, or Salvadoran subgroups, as well as individual variations influenced by acculturation or generational status.
- Risk of Researcher Bias: A key concern was the potential for researchers to impose their own cultural lenses on study design, data collection, or analysis, which could lead to misinterpretations or culturally insensitive conclusions. This risk is particularly

pronounced when researchers lack deep familiarity with the cultural context of their participants.

One participant, a researcher studying Western Nigerian communities, reflected:

> *Culture isn't static even within the same community, people can see things differently. Capturing this diversity without overgeneralising is always difficult. For instance, mental health beliefs among Indian immigrants vary widely depending on whether they're first- or second-generation.*

Another participant, working with Indigenous populations, added:

> *If we don't approach cultural complexity with humility, we risk misrepresenting communities. I've seen studies where researchers assumed all Indigenous clients share the same spiritual beliefs, and that's just not true, it erases the diversity within tribes.*

Applications and Implications: Cultural complexity affects all stages of research, from formulating research questions to interpreting data. For example, a study on therapy engagement among African clients must consider cultural factors like distrust in mental health systems due to historical abuses, as well as variations in how urban versus rural clients perceive therapy.

Strategies to Address: Participants suggested strategies such as involving cultural consultants or community advisors in study design, conducting pilot studies to refine instruments, and employing reflexive practices to monitor and mitigate researcher bias. One researcher emphasized: "Working with community elders as co-researchers has been a game-changer. They help us see nuances we'd otherwise miss, like how cultural shame influences therapy-seeking in certain groups."

Challenges: Navigating cultural complexity requires time, resources, and cultural expertise, which may not always be available. Additionally, balancing specificity with generalizability remains a persistent challenge, as overly narrow findings may limit the broader applicability of research.

Theme 2: methodological limitations

Ten out of 15 participants identified methodological limitations as a significant barrier, particularly the scarcity of culturally validated tools and measures. This shortage often forces researchers to adapt or translate existing instruments, which may have uncertain reliability or validity in diverse cultural contexts. Additionally, balancing the depth of qualitative approaches with the breadth of quantitative methods poses challenges, especially when resources are limited.

- **Lack of Culturally Validated Tools**: Many standardized scales, such as those measuring depression or cultural competence, were developed with Western populations

and may not capture culturally specific expressions of mental health or therapeutic dynamics. For example, a scale measuring anxiety might miss culturally unique manifestations, such as somatic complaints common in some populations.
- **Balancing Depth and Breadth**: Participants noted that qualitative methods, while ideal for capturing cultural nuances, are often resource-intensive and limited in generalizability. Mixed-methods designs, which could address this by combining qualitative depth with quantitative breadth, are challenging to implement due to time, funding, or expertise constraints.

One researcher studying multicultural training programs shared:

> *Most standardised scales weren't developed for our contexts, so we constantly question if they truly reflect the realities of the populations we study. Adapting a scale for a South-south population, for instance, often means rethinking entire constructs like 'well-being.'*

Another participant, working on cross-cultural therapy outcomes, noted:

> *We'd love to use mixed-methods more, but it's tough when you're a small team with limited funding. You end up choosing between deep qualitative insights or broader quantitative data, and both are critical.*

Applications and Implications: Methodological limitations impact the validity and reliability of research findings, potentially undermining their applicability in multicultural counselling practice. For example, using a non-validated scale to measure cultural competence in therapists working with Native Yoruba clients could produce misleading results, affecting training program development.

Strategies to Address: Participants recommended developing and validating culturally specific instruments, collaborating with interdisciplinary teams to enhance methodological rigor, and leveraging open-source or community-driven data to create new tools. One researcher suggested:

> *We need to invest in creating measures that reflect cultural realities like how collectivism shapes mental health in Latinx communities. It's slow work, but it's essential.*

Challenges: Developing culturally validated tools is resource-intensive and requires extensive testing across diverse populations. Additionally, the pressure to publish quickly can discourage researchers from investing in time-consuming methodological development.

Theme 3: access and trust

Building trust and gaining access to culturally diverse communities was a significant challenge, cited by seven participants. Historical marginalization, negative experiences with research, and cultural differences in perceptions of research often lead to skepticism or reluctance among potential participants, complicating recruitment and data collection.

- **Community Skepticism**: Communities with histories of exploitation in research may view research as intrusive or irrelevant. Participants noted that potential participants often question the tangible benefits of research for their communities.
- **Language and Privacy Barriers**: Language differences and cultural norms around privacy can hinder informed consent and data collection. For example, in some cultures, discussing mental health openly may be stigmatized, making participants hesitant to share personal experiences.

One counselor-researcher working with refugee communities explained:

> *Community members often ask, 'How will this help us?'—and if we can't answer clearly, recruitment becomes very hard. For refugees who've faced systemic betrayal, trust is a huge hurdle.*

Another participant, researching rural Black communities, added:

> *Language barriers are just the start. In some communities, even the concept of 'informed consent' feels foreign or suspicious, it's seen as a bureaucratic hurdle rather than a protection.*

Applications and Implications: Trust and access issues directly affect participant recruitment and data quality. For instance, a study on therapy access among Southeast Nigeria may struggle if participants fear stigma or mistrust researchers' intentions, leading to low response rates or incomplete data.

Strategies to Address: Participants emphasized the importance of community engagement, such as partnering with local organizations, hiring community members as research assistants, and clearly communicating the benefits of research. One researcher shared:

> *We've had success by holding community forums before starting research. It's a chance to listen, build trust, and show that we're not just here to take data were here to give back.*

Challenges: Building trust is time-intensive and may require long-term relationship-building, which can conflict with tight research timelines. Additionally, navigating cultural norms around privacy requires sensitivity to avoid alienating participants.

Theme 4: institutional and systemic constraints

Nine out of 15 participants highlighted structural barriers within academic and funding systems that complicate multicultural counselling research. These include limited funding, institutional pressure for generalizable findings, and ethical review processes that may not account for cultural nuances.

- **Limited Funding**: Research on multicultural counselling often receives less funding than mainstream psychological research, as it may be perceived as niche or less generalizable. This limits the scope and scale of studies, particularly those requiring resource-intensive methods like participatory action research.
- **Pressure for Generalizability**: Academic institutions and journals often prioritize findings that apply broadly, which can discourage context-specific research critical to multicultural counselling. Participants noted that culturally specific studies are sometimes undervalued or harder to publish.
- **Ethical Review Challenges**: Institutional review boards (IRBs) may apply standardized ethical guidelines that do not fully account for cultural considerations, such as community-based consent processes or culturally appropriate recruitment strategies.

One participant, a researcher studying Indigenous mental health, commented:

> *Ethics committees often apply a one-size-fits-all model, which doesn't always fit cultural realities on the ground. For example, requiring individual consent in a collectivist community can feel disrespectful to their values.*

Another participant, working on a grant-funded project, noted:

> *Funders want big, generalizable results, but multicultural research often needs to be hyper-local to be meaningful. That tension makes it hard to secure grants for the kind of work we want to do.*

Applications and Implications: Systemic constraints limit the scope and impact of multicultural counselling research, potentially perpetuating gaps in knowledge about underrepresented populations. e.g., underfunded studies may rely on small sample sizes, reducing their influence on policy or practice.

Strategies to Address: Participants suggested advocating for funding dedicated to multicultural research, educating IRBs about cultural considerations, and building coalitions with community organizations to strengthen grant applications. One researcher proposed:

> *We need to push for funding streams specifically for culturally responsive research. It's about showing funders that this work isn't niche it's essential for equitable mental health care.*

Challenges: Overcoming systemic barriers requires long-term advocacy and institutional change, which can be slow and resource-intensive. Researchers may also face career pressures to prioritize mainstream topics over culturally specific ones.

Future Directions: Participants called for increased investment in culturally validated measures, training for researchers in cultural competence, and reforms to funding and ethical review processes to better support multicultural research. One researcher summarized:

> *We're at a turning point where multicultural research can reshape mental health care, but only if we address these barriers head-on. It starts with listening to communities, to each other, and to the gaps in our own systems.*

Research question 3: what are the recommendations for improving research practices in multicultural counselling and psychotherapy?

Thematic analysis of the interview data revealed an inclusive set of recommendations aimed at enhancing the quality, cultural relevance, and impact of research in multicultural counselling and psychotherapy. These recommendations, grounded in participants' experiences, clustered into four key themes: capacity building through training and mentorship, methodological innovation and localisation, strengthening community engagement and trust, and advocacy for institutional and policy support. Participants emphasized that implementing these recommendations requires collaboration across researchers, communities, and institutions to address the unique challenges of multicultural research and produce findings that are ethically sound, culturally responsive, and practically impactful. Each theme is explored below:

Theme 1: capacity building through training and mentorship

Eleven out of 15 participants highlighted the critical need to equip researchers with specialized skills in multicultural research methods, cultural competence, ethics, and reflexivity. They argued that ongoing training and mentorship are essential to prepare researchers, particularly early-career scholars, for the complexities of studying diverse populations, ensuring that research practices are both rigorous and culturally sensitive.

- **Specialized Training Programmes**: Participants recommended developing workshops and courses focused on culturally responsive research methods, such as qualitative approaches (e.g., phenomenology, narrative inquiry) and participatory designs. These programs should also cover ethical considerations, such as navigating cultural norms around consent or addressing power imbalances in research.
- **Mentorship and Cross-Cultural Collaboration**: Mentorship programmes pairing early-career researchers with experienced scholars in multicultural counselling were seen as vital for building practical skills. Participants also advocated for cross-cultural research collaborations, such as international partnerships or interdisciplinary teams, to broaden perspectives and share best practices.

- **Interdisciplinary Learning**: Drawing insights from fields like anthropology, sociology, and education was recommended to enrich research approaches. For example, anthropological methods like ethnography can enhance understanding of cultural contexts, while sociological frameworks can inform analyses of systemic inequities in mental health care.

One participant, a senior researcher mentoring graduate students, explained:

> *We need ongoing training to understand our own biases and learn culturally responsive methods, it shouldn't stop after postgraduate studies. A workshop on reflexive interviewing completely changed how I approach data collection with diverse populations.*

Another participant, working with Igbo communities, added:

> *Mentorship is key. My advisor helped me navigate cultural distinctions in my research with Hausa clients, it's not something you learn from a textbook. We need more programmes to pass that knowledge on.*

Applications and Implications: Capacity building ensures that researchers are equipped to design studies that respect cultural diversity and produce valid, meaningful findings. For instance, training in reflexive practices can help researchers studying African clients recognize how their own cultural assumptions might influence interpretations of data on therapy engagement.

Strategies for Implementation: Participants suggested integrating multicultural research training into graduate curricula, offering professional development workshops through academic associations, and fostering interdisciplinary research networks. One researcher proposed:

> *Universities should partner with community organizations to offer hands-on training in cultural competence. It's not just theory—it's about learning from the communities we serve.*

Impact: Enhanced training and mentorship can lead to more culturally valid research, reduce biases, and increase the pipeline of skilled researchers in multicultural counselling, ultimately improving the quality and impact of studies.

Theme 2: methodological innovation and localisation

Ten out of 15 participants emphasized the need for methodological innovation, particularly the development and validation of research instruments tailored to local cultural contexts. They also advocated for greater use of mixed-methods and participatory approaches to capture both individual experiences and broader trends, ensuring that research is culturally relevant and scientifically robust.

- **Culturally Validated Instruments**: Participants highlighted the importance of co-creating or adapting research tools, such as surveys or scales, with input from community members to ensure cultural fit. For example, a scale measuring mental health stigma might be redesigned with input from Nigerian communities to reflect culturally specific attitudes toward therapy.
- **Mixed-Methods Designs**: Combining qualitative and quantitative methods was recommended to balance depth and generalizability. For instance, qualitative interviews could identify cultural barriers to therapy, while quantitative surveys could test their prevalence across a larger population.
- **Participatory Approaches**: Involving communities in designing research tools and interpreting findings was seen as a way to enhance cultural relevance and ethical responsibility. Participatory methods, such as community-based participatory research (CBPR), ensure that research aligns with community priorities.

One researcher studying Indigenous mental health shared:

> *Instead of borrowing instruments wholesale, we should work with communities to design measures that speak their language and reality. For example, we co-created a wellness scale with tribal elders that incorporates traditional healing concepts.*

Another participant, researching therapy outcomes in Nigerian populations, noted:

> *Mixed-methods give us the best of both worlds. We used focus groups to understand cultural attitudes toward therapy, then tested those themes with a survey across multiple African communities, it's powerful when you combine stories with data.*

Applications and Implications: Methodological innovation enables researchers to produce findings that accurately reflect the cultural realities of diverse populations. e.g., a culturally validated scale for measuring cultural competence in therapists working with Middle Eastern clients could improve training programmes by providing precise, context-specific metrics.

Strategies for Implementation: Participants suggested forming research consortia to develop and validate culturally specific tools, leveraging technology (e.g., online surveys in multiple languages) to reach diverse populations, and publishing open-access toolkits to share validated instruments. One researcher emphasized:

> *We need to make culturally validated tools freely available. Sharing our work with other researchers can accelerate progress in this field.*

Impact: Localized and innovative methods enhance the validity and applicability of research findings, ensuring that interventions and policies are grounded in the lived experiences of diverse communities.

Theme 3: strengthening community engagement and trust

Eight participants stressed the importance of building trust and involving communities in the research process to improve recruitment, ensure cultural relevance, and maximize the impact of findings. They recommended proactive engagement strategies to foster collaboration and demonstrate the value of research to participants.

- **Community Involvement in Research Design**: Engaging community leaders, clients, or cultural mediators early in the research process was seen as critical for aligning studies with community needs. This could involve forming advisory boards or holding community forums to co-develop research questions and methods.
- **Transparent Communication**: Participants emphasized clearly communicating the purpose and benefits of research to communities, addressing concerns about exploitation or irrelevance. Sharing findings back with communities through accessible formats, such as workshops, translated reports, or community presentations, was also recommended.
- **Cultural Mediators**: Employing cultural mediators or community liaisons who share the cultural background of participants was suggested to bridge trust gaps and facilitate recruitment and data collection.

One participant, working with refugee communities, noted:

> *When communities see themselves in the process and the outcomes, they're more willing to participate and benefit. We held a community dialogue session before starting our study, and it made all the difference in recruitment.*

Another researcher, studying rural Nigerian populations, added:

> *We hired community members as research assistants—they knew the cultural distinctions and helped us explain the study in a way that resonated. It's about showing communities you're not just here to take data.*

Applications and Implications: Strong community engagement ensures that research is relevant, ethical, and trusted by participants. For example, a study on therapy access among Nigerian communities could benefit from involving tribal leaders to ensure that findings respect cultural values and address community priorities.

Strategies for Implementation: Participants suggested establishing long-term partnerships with community organizations, offering training for community members to participate in research, and using culturally appropriate dissemination methods, such as storytelling or visual media. One researcher proposed:

> *We should create community advisory boards for every study. They keep us accountable and ensure our work actually matters to the people we're studying.*

Impact: Enhanced community engagement builds trust, increases participation rates, and ensures that research findings are actionable, leading to interventions and policies that directly benefit diverse populations.

Theme 4: advocacy for institutional and policy support

Nine out of 15 participants called for systemic changes within academic institutions, funding bodies, and ethical review processes to better support multicultural counselling research. They emphasized that institutional barriers, such as limited funding and rigid evaluation criteria, must be addressed to legitimize and resource this work.

- **Dedicated Funding Streams**: Participants advocated for grants specifically earmarked for multicultural research, recognizing its importance in addressing mental health disparities. Such funding would support resource-intensive methods like participatory action research or longitudinal studies.
- **Flexible Ethical Review Processes**: Simplifying and adapting ethical review processes to accommodate cultural considerations, such as community-based consent or non-traditional recruitment methods, was seen as essential for facilitating context-sensitive research.
- **Valuing Diverse Research Outputs**: Participants urged institutions and journals to recognize the value of qualitative, participatory, and context-specific research outputs, rather than prioritizing only generalizable or quantitative studies. This shift would encourage researchers to pursue culturally responsive methodologies without career penalties.

One counselor-researcher working with Southeast Nigerian communities highlighted:

> *We need policies that see cultural research as essential, not optional—this shift could unlock resources and legitimise the work. Right now, we're fighting for scraps while mainstream research gets the big grants.*

Another participant, a junior faculty member, added:

> *Ethics boards need to understand that a one-size-fits-all approach doesn't work for multi-cultural research. Requiring individual consent in a collectivist community can alienate participants—we need flexibility.*

Applications and Implications: Institutional support is critical for scaling up multicultural research and ensuring its sustainability. For example, dedicated funding could enable a longitudinal study on the effectiveness of culturally adapted therapy for Nigerian clients, producing robust evidence to inform policy.

Strategies for Implementation: Participants suggested forming advocacy coalitions to lobby for funding, educating ethical review boards about cultural considerations, and creating journal policies that prioritize diverse research outputs. One researcher proposed:

We should push for a multicultural research task force within academic associations to advocate for policy changes—it's time to make this work a priority.

Impact: Stronger institutional support would increase the resources, legitimacy, and visibility of multicultural counselling research, enabling researchers to address systemic mental health inequities more effectively.

Future Directions: Participants called for sustained efforts to implement these recommendations, including cross-disciplinary collaborations, global research networks, and policy reforms to prioritize multicultural research. One researcher summarized:

This work isn't just about better research—it's about justice. By centering culture and community, we can build a counselling system that serves everyone, not just a select few.

Quantitative results

A total of 250 participants were involved in the study. An analysis of their demographic characteristics is presented in Table 9.1 shows that out of the 250 respondents, 136 (54.4%) identified as male while 114 (45.6%) identified as female. The difference in gender proportions was not statistically significant ($P = .184$), indicating a relatively balanced gender representation. Participants were drawn from a diverse age range. Those aged 50–59 years accounted for the highest proportion at 22.0% ($n = 55$), followed by respondents aged 30–39 years at 20.4% ($n = 51$), 60 years and above at 20.0% ($n = 50$), and those under 30 years at 19.6% ($n = 49$). The smallest age group was 40–49 years, representing 18.0% ($n = 45$). All age group proportions significantly differed from the 0.5 test value ($P < 0.001$), indicating a wide age spread among participants.

The sample included a diverse range of professional backgrounds. Counselors and psychotherapists each constituted 22.8% of the sample ($n = 57$), while postgraduate students accounted for 17.6% ($n = 44$). Researchers made up 17.2% ($n = 43$), and those identifying with multiple roles (e.g., researcher–counselor or psychotherapist–student) represented 19.6% ($n = 49$). The distribution across professional roles was statistically significant ($P < 0.001$), suggesting meaningful variability in the professional identity of respondents. In terms of experience, the largest group had 3–5 years of practice, making up 26.8% ($n = 67$), closely followed by those with less than 3 years' experience at 25.6% ($n = 64$), and those with 6–10 years at 24.8% ($n = 62$). Participants with over 10 years of experience accounted for 22.8% ($n = 57$). The distribution of experience levels was statistically significant ($P < 0.001$), indicating that early and mid-career professionals were well represented.

The respondents were fairly distributed across Nigerian regions. The West had the highest representation at 22.0% ($n = 55$), followed by the South (21.6%, $n = 54$), the North (20.8%,

Table 9.1: Analysis of demographic variables.

Variable	Level	Counts	Total	Proportion	*P*
Gender	Male	136	250	0.544	0.184
	Female	114	250	0.456	0.184
Age	30–39	51	250	0.204	<.001
	40–49	45	250	0.180	<.001
	50–59	55	250	0.220	<.001
	60 and above	50	250	0.200	<.001
	Under 30	49	250	0.196	<.001
Professional role	Counselor	57	250	0.228	<.001
	Researcher	43	250	0.172	<.001
	Psychotherapist	57	250	0.228	<.001
	Multiple roles	49	250	0.196	<.001
	Postgraduate student	44	250	0.176	<.001
Years of experience	6–10 years	62	250	0.248	<.001
	3–5 years	67	250	0.268	<.001
	Less than 3 years	64	250	0.256	<.001
	More than 10 years	57	250	0.228	<.001
Region	North-Central	45	250	0.180	<.001
	South	54	250	0.216	<.001
	West	55	250	0.220	<.001
	North	52	250	0.208	<.001
	East	44	250	0.176	<.001
Population experience	Nigerian populations	48	250	0.192	<.001
	Mixed/Other	53	250	0.212	<.001
	African American	42	250	0.168	<.001
	South Asian	46	250	0.184	<.001
	Global populations	61	250	0.244	<.001

Proportions tested against value: 0.5.

$n = 52$), the North–Central region (18.0%, $n = 45$), and the East (17.6%, $n = 44$). All regional proportions were statistically significant ($P < 0.001$), reflecting a broad geographical diversity among participants. In terms of population groups with which respondents had professional experience, 24.4% ($n = 61$) reported working with global populations, followed by 21.2% ($n = 53$) with mixed or other populations, 19.2% ($n = 48$) with Nigerian populations, 18.4% ($n = 46$) with South Asian populations, and 16.8% ($n = 42$) with African American populations. All proportions were significantly different from 0.5 ($P < 0.001$), suggesting a high level of international and cross-cultural engagement.

The findings presented in Table 9.2 provide insights into the frequency with which different research methodologies are employed in multicultural counselling and psychotherapy research, based on a 5-point Likert scale ranging from 1 (Never) to 5 (Very frequently). The analysis captures both the central tendency and the variability of use among respondents, as well as the distribution characteristics of each method. Among the six methodologies

Table 9.2: Descriptive statistics for the research methodologies in multicultural counselling and psychotherapy.

	Mean	Std. error of mean	95% Confidence interval mean		Std. deviation	Shapiro–Wilk	*P*-value of Shapiro–Wilk
			Upper	Lower			
Qualitative methods	2.948	0.090	3.126	2.770	1.429	0.883	<.001
Quantitative methods	2.908	0.089	3.084	2.732	1.413	0.887	<.001
Mixed methods	3.076	0.092	3.257	2.895	1.453	0.878	<.001
Participatory action research	2.948	0.093	3.131	2.765	1.473	0.874	<.001
Case studies	3.040	0.090	3.217	2.863	1.419	0.887	<.001
Ethnographic approaches	3.000	0.090	3.178	2.822	1.426	0.886	<.001

examined, mixed methods emerged as the most frequently used approach, with a mean score of 3.08. This suggests that many researchers value the integration of both qualitative and quantitative strategies to explore complex multicultural issues. The use of case studies and ethnographic approaches followed closely, with mean scores of 3.04 and 3.00 respectively. These findings reflect the importance of context-specific, in-depth exploration in understanding multicultural dynamics in counselling and psychotherapy. Qualitative methods and participatory action research (PAR) both recorded mean frequencies of 2.95, indicating moderate usage. These methods are especially suitable for exploring subjective experiences and empowering marginalized voices, which are central to multicultural practice. Quantitative methods, while slightly lower in mean frequency at 2.91, were still used regularly, indicating that statistical and empirical approaches also play a significant role in the field. The Shapiro–Wilk test results revealed significant deviations from normality for all six methods ($P < 0.001$), suggesting the data distributions were not perfectly normal, likely due to varying usage patterns among participants. However, the standard deviations—ranging from 1.413 to 1.473—indicate a moderate spread of responses, further underscoring the diverse methodological preferences across the research community.

Section C: Challenges in conducting multicultural counselling and psychotherapy research

This section examines the challenges you face in your research. Please respond based on your experiences, including work with Nigerian, African American, or South Asian populations.

Table 9.3: Descriptive statistics for challenges in conducting multicultural counselling and psychotherapy.

	Mean	Std. error of mean	95% Confidence interval mean Upper	Lower	Std. deviation	Shapiro–Wilk	*P*-value of Shapiro–Wilk
Culturally validated instruments	2.928	0.088	3.101	2.755	1.389	0.892	<.001
Gaining community trust	3.144	0.091	3.324	2.964	1.446	0.877	<.001
Institutional pressures	3.068	0.093	3.251	2.885	1.467	0.875	<.001
Ethical review processes	3.032	0.089	3.208	2.856	1.414	0.885	<.001
Resource constraints	3.080	0.091	3.259	2.901	1.440	0.881	<.001
Language barriers	2.980	0.088	3.152	2.808	1.384	0.891	<.001
Intra-cultural diversity	2.868	0.085	3.036	2.700	1.351	0.898	<.001

Level of Agreement: On a scale of 1 (Strongly disagree) to 5 (Strongly agree), indicate your agreement with the following statements about challenges in multicultural counselling research:

The findings presented in Table 9.3 offer a distinct understanding of the challenges faced by researchers engaged in multicultural counselling and psychotherapy, particularly when working with populations such as Nigerian, African American, and South Asian communities. Using a 5-point Likert scale (1 = Strongly disagree, 5 = Strongly agree), the data reflect varying degrees of agreement with specific research challenges. Among the seven challenges assessed, gaining community trust emerged as the most strongly agreed-upon barrier, with a mean score of 3.14. This suggests that establishing rapport and legitimacy within culturally diverse communities remains a significant obstacle, likely due to historical marginalization, power dynamics, or cultural unfamiliarity. Other high-ranking challenges included resource constraints (mean = 3.08) and institutional pressures (mean = 3.07), indicating that both funding limitations and systemic expectations (such as academic or administrative requirements) can hinder culturally responsive research. These findings point to a need for more flexible institutional policies and increased resource allocation to support multicultural inquiry.

The issue of ethical review processes also received considerable agreement (mean = 3.03), suggesting that researchers may encounter difficulties in aligning ethical guidelines with culturally sensitive practices. Standard review frameworks may not always accommodate the complexities of conducting research across diverse cultural contexts. Language barriers (mean = 2.98) and the lack of culturally validated instruments (mean = 2.93) were also identified as moderate challenges. These results underscore the limitations in available tools and the need for better linguistic and cultural adaptation of research instruments to ensure accurate and respectful representation of participants. Interestingly, intra-cultural diversity had the lowest mean score of 2.87, though still relatively high on the scale. This finding reflects the complexity of conducting research within a single cultural group that contains multiple subgroups, traditions, and perspectives, which may challenge overly simplistic or homogenized approaches to multiculturalism. All variables showed statistically significant non-normal distributions according to the Shapiro–Wilk test ($P < 0.001$), indicating variability in how these challenges are experienced across respondents. Standard deviations ranged from 1.351 to 1.467, showing a moderate spread in levels of agreement.

The data presented in Table 9.4 offer insights into the perceived importance of strategies aimed at improving multicultural counselling and psychotherapy research. Participants were asked to rate various strategies on a scale of 1 (Not important) to 5 (Very important), based on their experiences working in culturally diverse settings. Overall, the strategy rated as most important was dedicated funding, with a mean score of 3.12. This suggests a widespread acknowledgment among researchers that financial resources are fundamental to

Table 9.4: Descriptive statistics recommendations for improving research practices.

	Mean	Std. error of mean	95% Confidence interval mean		Std. deviation	Shapiro–Wilk	*P*-value of Shapiro–Wilk
			Upper	Lower			
Training on culturally responsive methods	3.008	0.093	3.190	2.826	1.464	0.875	<.001
Developing culturally specific instruments	3.056	0.088	3.230	2.882	1.393	0.891	<.001
Community involvement	2.968	0.092	3.150	2.786	1.461	0.875	<.001
Dedicated funding	3.120	0.090	3.297	2.943	1.418	0.885	<.001
Ethical review revisions	2.812	0.087	2.984	2.640	1.383	0.889	<.001
Interdisciplinary collaboration	2.932	0.092	3.113	2.751	1.453	0.879	<.001
Community dissemination	3.056	0.086	3.226	2.886	1.367	0.896	<.001

conducting effective, culturally grounded research. Without adequate funding, activities such as community engagement, instrument development, and ethical accommodations become significantly constrained.

Closely following were developing culturally specific instruments and community dissemination, both with mean scores of 3.06. These results highlight a growing emphasis on ensuring that research tools are not only valid across different populations but also that findings are meaningfully shared with the communities involved. The high score for dissemination may reflect a desire to bridge the gap between academic knowledge and real-world application, ensuring research contributes to both scholarship and social change.

Training on culturally responsive methods also scored relatively high (mean = 3.01), indicating the need for ongoing capacity building in culturally competent research practices. This reflects a recognition that many researchers still require support in designing and implementing methods that are ethically and culturally aligned. Interdisciplinary collaboration (mean = 2.93) and community involvement (mean = 2.97) were also seen as moderately important. While still valued, these strategies may be viewed as more logistically challenging or less directly impactful compared to funding or tools development, especially in resource-limited contexts. Interestingly, revising ethical review processes received the lowest mean rating of 2.81, though still above the midpoint of the scale. This may suggest that while current ethical frameworks are sometimes seen as limiting, researchers may not view them as the most immediate priority for reform compared to more tangible supports like funding or training. All responses were significantly non-normally distributed, as indicated by Shapiro–Wilk p-values below 0.001, suggesting diverse perspectives among respondents. The standard deviations, ranging from 1.367 to 1.464, indicate a moderate spread in the importance ratings across different strategies.

Summary of findings

This chapter examined the methodologies used, the challenges encountered, and possible ways forward in research on multicultural counselling and psychotherapy. The findings are presented as follows:

Methodologies used in multicultural counselling research

Qualitative approaches

Qualitative methods were found to be central to research in multicultural counselling and psychotherapy. Approaches such as phenomenology, grounded theory, and narrative inquiry were commonly used to explore lived experiences of clients and practitioners. In the Nigerian context, these methods were especially useful for examining culturally embedded experiences, including family expectations, religious beliefs, and communal understandings of mental health. Participants' narratives reflected how cultural norms shape help-seeking behavior, trust in counselling relationships, and interpretations of psychological distress.

Narrative inquiry allowed participants from marginalized groups to describe their experiences in their own terms. Phenomenological approaches supported detailed exploration of counselling relationships and client engagement, particularly where cultural norms influence openness and disclosure. While these methods provided rich data, they required significant time and researcher reflexivity, which posed challenges in settings with limited resources.

Mixed-methods approaches

Mixed-methods designs were frequently used to combine in-depth qualitative data with broader quantitative findings. These approaches enabled researchers to explore cultural meanings while also producing data that could inform policy and institutional decision-making. In Nigeria, mixed-methods studies were particularly useful in urban areas where diverse populations interact within shared service systems. However, the findings also showed that mixed-methods research placed heavy demands on researchers. Limited funding, inadequate training, and insufficient institutional support restricted the extent to which these designs could be fully implemented. Despite these constraints, mixed-methods approaches were viewed as valuable for capturing both cultural depth and broader patterns across populations.

Quantitative methods

Quantitative methods were used primarily to measure constructs such as counselor cultural competence, attitudes toward counselling, and perceived outcomes. Standardized instruments were often adapted from Western contexts. The findings indicated that many of these tools did not adequately reflect culturally specific expressions of distress or help-seeking, particularly among Nigerian ethnic groups and some diasporic populations. Participants noted that somatic expressions of distress, stigma, and culturally grounded coping strategies were not always captured by existing scales. This limitation affected the validity of findings and reduced their usefulness for local practice. The findings pointed to the need for developing and validating culturally appropriate measurement tools.

Participatory and community-based approaches

Participatory and community-based approaches were identified as effective strategies for conducting research in collectivist settings. In Nigeria, collaboration with community leaders, traditional authorities, and faith-based figures improved access to participants and increased trust. These approaches supported shared decision-making and ensured that research topics reflected community concerns. At the same time, participatory research required sustained engagement, time, and funding. These demands limited the scalability of such approaches, particularly in rural and under-resourced areas. Despite these challenges, participatory methods were viewed as ethically appropriate and culturally respectful.

Case studies and ethnographic methods

Case studies and ethnographic approaches were used to document culturally specific counselling practices and belief systems. These methods were effective in contexts where standardized data collection was impractical. They allowed researchers to examine local meanings of mental health, healing practices, and counselling relationships in detail.

Challenges associated with these methods included limited generalizability and ethical concerns related to confidentiality in close-knit communities. Careful attention to anonymity and informed consent was required.

Challenges in conducting multicultural counselling research

Cultural complexity

One major challenge identified was the complexity of cultural identities. Within Nigerian ethnic groups, significant variations exist in language, belief systems, gender roles, and religious practices. These variations complicated research design, data interpretation, and generalization. Similar challenges were noted when working with diasporic populations whose experiences were shaped by migration, discrimination, and historical trauma. Researchers reported difficulties in fully understanding local meanings without prolonged cultural immersion. The risk of misinterpretation increased when researchers lacked familiarity with the communities involved.

Methodological constraints

The absence of culturally validated research instruments was a persistent challenge. Many standardized tools failed to reflect local expressions of distress or culturally specific counselling outcomes. While mixed-methods designs could address some of these limitations, resource constraints often prevented their effective implementation. Training gaps also affected methodological quality, particularly in advanced qualitative and integrative research designs.

Trust and access

Gaining access to participants and building trust was identified as a significant barrier. Mental health stigma, cultural norms around privacy, and historical mistrust of research limited participation in some communities. Language differences further complicated data collection, particularly in multilingual regions. Engagement with community leaders was essential but required time and negotiation.

Institutional and systemic barriers

Limited funding, publication pressures, and rigid ethical review processes constrained research practice. Ethical guidelines were sometimes misaligned with collectivist consent practices, creating tension between institutional requirements and community norms. These systemic factors reduced the scope and sustainability of multicultural counselling research.

Recommendations for improving research practices

Capacity development

The findings highlight the need for sustained training in culturally responsive research methods. Researchers require skills in qualitative inquiry, reflexivity, participatory methods, and ethical engagement. Mentorship and interdisciplinary collaboration were identified as effective strategies for skill development.

Methodological localisation

Developing culturally appropriate research instruments was identified as a priority. Collaborative tool development involving local communities would improve validity and relevance. Greater use of flexible research designs was also recommended.

Community engagement

Ongoing community involvement was viewed as essential. Advisory boards, cultural mediators, and feedback mechanisms improved trust and relevance. Sharing findings in accessible formats strengthened the connection between research and practice.

Institutional support

Improved funding, flexible ethical guidelines, and recognition of diverse research outputs were identified as necessary for advancing multicultural counselling research. Partnerships with national and international organizations could support these efforts.

Conclusion

This chapter has examined research in multicultural counselling and psychotherapy through conceptual, methodological, and contextual lenses, with particular attention to experiences from Nigeria and collaborative work beyond Africa. It has shown that research in this field must move beyond monocultural assumptions and adopt approaches that are sensitive to cultural diversity, social context, and historical realities. Multicultural counselling research is shaped not only by theory and method but also by the researcher's positionality, ethical responsibility, and engagement with the communities involved.

The findings highlight that qualitative, mixed-methods, and community-based approaches are especially suited to multicultural contexts, as they allow for deeper understanding of lived experiences and culturally grounded meanings of mental health and healing. At the same time, the chapter has identified persistent challenges, including cultural complexity, limited culturally validated research tools, issues of trust and access, and institutional constraints that affect research design and implementation. These challenges are particularly evident in resource-limited and highly diverse settings.

In response, the chapter has emphasized the need for improved training, methodological localisation, sustained community engagement, and stronger institutional support for researchers. By addressing these areas, research in multicultural counselling and psychotherapy can become more culturally responsive, ethically grounded, and practically relevant. Therefore, the chapter affirms that strengthening research practices in this field is essential for developing counselling and psychotherapy interventions that are equitable, effective, and responsive to the needs of diverse populations.

References

Benz, C., Scott-Jeffs, W., McKercher, K. A., Welsh, M., Norman, R., Hendrie, D., Locantro, M., & Robinson, S. (2024). Community-based participatory-research through co-design: Supporting collaboration from all sides of disability. *Research Involvement and Engagement, 10*(1). https://doi.org/10.1186/s40900-024-00573-3

Braun, V., & Clarke, V. (2006). Using thematic analysis in psychology. *Qualitative Research in Psychology, 3* (2). https://doi.org/10.1191/1478088706qp063oa

Brislin, R. W. (1970). Back-translation for cross-cultural research. *Journal of Cross-Cultural Psychology, 1*(3). https://doi.org/10.1177/135910457000100301

Chang, D. F., & Berk, A. (2009). Making cross-racial therapy work: A phenomenological study of clients' experiences of cross-racial therapy. *Journal of Counseling Psychology, 56*(4). https://doi.org/10.1037/a0016905

Creswell, J. W., & Plano Clark, V. L. (2018). Designing and conducting mixed methods research. *Organizational Research Methods, 12*(4).

Demiray, M. R. (2020). Acknowledging and limiting the moral significance of cultural praxis: Reflections on Cassirer's critical philosophy of culture. In *Identities in transition*. https://doi.org/10.1163/9781848880825_003

Draguns, J. G. (2013). Counseling and psychotherapy around the world: Current state and future prospects. In *Handbook of counseling and psychotherapy in an international context*. https://doi.org/10.4324/9780203864906-50

Hair, J. F., Black, W. C., Babin, B. J., & Anderson, R. E. (2010). Multivariate data analysis. *Vector*. https://doi.org/10.1016/j.ijpharm.2011.02.019

Kuo, B. C. H., Hussein, N., Makhzoum, N., Sabhnani, P., & Zvric, M. (2023). Evaluating the effects of cultural immersion on counselor trainees' multicultural development and intercultural competence: A metasynthesis of qualitative evidence. *International Journal of Intercultural Relations, 94*. https://doi.org/10.1016/j.ijintrel.2023.101798

Landis, J. R., & Koch, G. G. (1977). The measurement of observer agreement for categorical data. *Biometrics, 33*(1). https://doi.org/10.2307/2529310

Maratsos, M. (2012). Two senses of cultural relativity. In *Minnesota symposia on child psychology series, 38* (pp. 299–341). John Wiley and Sons Ltd. https://doi.org/10.1002/9781119301981.ch8

Martin, K. (2025). The individual and society in psychotherapy: Reflections from anthropology. *European Journal of Psychotherapy & Counselling, 27*(1–2). https://doi.org/10.1080/13642537.2025.2459375

Moodley, R. (1999). In *Challenges and transformations: Counselling in a multicultural context*.

Moodley, R., & Kinha, B. (2015). Therapy without borders: Bridging counseling and psychotherapy across cultures. In *International counseling case studies handbook*. https://doi.org/10.1002/9781119222781.ch35

Ratts, M. J., Singh, A. A., Nassar-Mcmillan, S., Butler, S. K., & McCullough, J. R. (2016). Multicultural and social justice counseling competencies: Guidelines for the counseling profession. *Journal of Multicultural Counseling and Development, 44*(1). https://doi.org/10.1002/jmcd.12035

Sodowsky, G. R., Taffe, R. C., Gutkin, T. B., & Wise, S. L. (1994). Development of the multicultural counseling inventory: A self-report measure of multicultural competencies. *Journal of Counseling Psychology, 41*(2). https://doi.org/10.1037/0022-0167.41.2.137

Stephen, M. C. (2017). In *Culture and values in intercultural communication*.

CHAPTER 10

Professional education and training in multicultural counselling and psychotherapy

Introduction

The increasing cultural, ethnic, linguistic, and religious diversity of contemporary societies has made multicultural competence a foundational requirement in counselling and psychotherapy. Practitioners are now expected not only to demonstrate technical proficiency, but also to possess the knowledge, awareness, and skills necessary to work ethically and effectively with clients from diverse cultural backgrounds. Consequently, professional education and training in multicultural counselling have become central to the preparation of counselors and psychotherapists across the globe. Professional training program play a critical role in shaping practitioners' attitudes toward cultural difference, power, and social justice. Effective multicultural education extends beyond theoretical knowledge to include self-reflection, experiential learning, supervision, and ongoing professional development. Training must address issues such as cultural identity, worldview, systemic oppression, bias, and the cultural limitations of dominant counselling models, while also equipping trainees to adapt interventions to the lived realities of diverse clients.

Leading accreditation and professional standards already underscore multicultural and social justice dimensions as core learning requirements. For example, CACREP's standards call for coverage of multicultural and pluralistic characteristics, theories of multicultural counselling and cultural identity development, multicultural counselling competencies, and the effects of power and privilege for counselors and clients (CACREP, 2016). These requirements signal that training program must ensure students develop not only knowledge but also reflective awareness, skills, and action orientations toward diversity, equity, and inclusion. Complementing such requirements, contemporary competency frameworks emphasize reflective knowledge of one's own positionality, critical awareness of privilege and oppression, and applied skills for working with clients' worldviews and lived experiences (Nassar-McMillan et al., 2015).

A Pragmatic Approach to Multicultural Counselling and Psychotherapy Skills Acquisition. https://doi.org/10.1016/B978-0-443-33939-4.00009-4

What is professional education and training in multicultural counselling and psychotherapy?

Professional Education and Training in Multicultural Counselling and Psychotherapy refers to the structured academic, clinical, and professional processes through which counselors and psychotherapists are prepared to work effectively, ethically, and sensitively with clients from diverse cultural, ethnic, linguistic, religious, and social backgrounds. It encompasses formal coursework, supervised clinical practice, experiential learning, and ongoing professional development aimed at developing multicultural competence as a core dimension of professional practice rather than a supplementary skill. At its core, this form of education integrates knowledge, self-awareness, and skills relevant to cultural diversity (Wilcox et al., 2022). Trainees are educated about cultural identity development, worldview differences, culturally bound expressions of distress, help-seeking behaviors, and the cultural assumptions embedded in dominant counselling theories. Equally important is the cultivation of self-reflective capacity, enabling practitioners to recognize their own cultural positioning, biases, and use of power within the therapeutic relationship. This reflective emphasis ensures that practitioners do not impose their values or culturally limited frameworks on clients.

Professional training in multicultural counselling and psychotherapy also emphasizes applied competence and ethical responsibility. Through supervised practicum experiences, case analysis, and culturally responsive interventions, trainees learn to adapt assessment, diagnosis, and treatment strategies to clients' sociocultural contexts. Training further addresses systemic and structural factors that influence mental health (Balva et al., 2023; Somerville et al., 2019). Ultimately, professional education in multicultural counselling is a continuous, developmental process designed to prepare practitioners to respond competently to diversity, promote equity and inclusion, and uphold ethical standards in an increasingly pluralistic world.

Characteristics/features of professional education and training in multicultural counselling and psychotherapy

Professional education and training in multicultural counselling and psychotherapy are distinguished by a set of core characteristics that respond to the realities of cultural diversity, social inequality, and globalization. Unlike traditional training models that often assume cultural neutrality, multicultural training explicitly recognizes culture as central to human development, help-seeking behavior, and therapeutic change (Ahmed et al., 2024). The following features outline the key elements that define effective professional preparation in this field.

Emphasis on cultural self-awareness and reflexivity

A fundamental feature of multicultural training is the systematic development of cultural self-awareness. Trainees are guided to examine their own cultural identities, socialization processes, values, beliefs, and implicit biases (Freetly Porter et al., 2025). This process of reflexivity enables counselors to recognize how their worldview, privilege, and positionality influence assessment, diagnosis, and therapeutic relationships. Rather than viewing culture as something that only clients possess, training frames culture as a dynamic factor shaping both the counselor and the counselling process.

Integration of culture across theory, assessment, and intervention

Multicultural education is characterized by the intentional integration of cultural considerations throughout all aspects of professional training. Culture is embedded within counselling theories, developmental models, assessment practices, and intervention strategies, rather than treated as a standalone course or topic (Kress et al., 2025). Trainees learn to critically evaluate dominant Foreign counselling models, identify their cultural assumptions, and adapt or modify interventions to align with clients' cultural contexts, belief systems, and explanatory models of distress (Lu, 2017).

Experiential, skills-based, and practice-oriented learning

Effective multicultural training places strong emphasis on experiential learning approaches that foster practical competence. These include role plays, analysis of culturally complex case studies, community engagement, cultural immersion experiences, supervised practicum placements, and reflective journaling (Duffey, 2024; Ramirez, 2021). Such methods allow trainees to practice culturally responsive communication, build relational sensitivity, and develop confidence in navigating cross-cultural therapeutic encounters. Learning is therefore not only cognitive, but also emotional, relational, and behavioral.

Focus on power, privilege, oppression, and social justice

Another defining characteristic is the explicit attention given to power dynamics and systemic influences on mental health. Training addresses issues such as racism, colonial legacies, discrimination, gender inequality, poverty, migration stress, and marginalization. Counselors are prepared to understand clients' difficulties within broader sociopolitical and structural contexts, rather than reducing them solely to individual pathology (Ang et al., 2024). This perspective supports advocacy, empowerment, and ethical responsibility as integral components of professional practice.

Development of ethical and culturally responsive practice

Multicultural training places strong emphasis on culturally informed ethical decision-making. Trainees are taught to consider cultural norms, values, and expectations when addressing issues such as confidentiality, informed consent, boundaries, family involvement, and help-seeking behaviors (Zhou, 2025). Ethical practice is framed as context-sensitive rather than rigidly universal, requiring ongoing reflection, consultation, and humility when working across cultural differences (Gallardo & Kaivan, 2013).

Commitment to lifelong learning and professional development

A key feature of professional education in multicultural counselling is the recognition that cultural competence is not a fixed endpoint but a continuous developmental process. Training programmes encourage ongoing learning through supervision, continuing professional education, research engagement, and self-reflection (Chang et al., 2017, 2024; Utley-Smith, 2017). Counselors are prepared to adapt to evolving cultural realities, emerging identities, and changing societal norms throughout their professional lives.

Contextual and global relevance

Finally, multicultural training is characterized by its responsiveness to local and global contexts. While drawing from international competency frameworks, effective programmes are grounded in the cultural realities, histories, and social structures of the communities they serve. This is especially critical in multicultural and non-foreign settings, where indigenous knowledge systems, spiritual beliefs, and communal values play a central role in wellbeing and healing (Branson et al., 2016; Dababneh et al., 2025; Srivastava et al., 2025).

Rationale for the chapter: Professional experience and research focus

The inclusion of this chapter is informed by my professional experiences in counselling education, training, supervision, and engagement with multicultural counselling contexts. Throughout my involvement in professional education and training in counselling and psychotherapy, I observed persistent gaps between the growing cultural diversity of client populations and the depth, structure, and consistency of multicultural content within training programmes. While multicultural counselling is often acknowledged as essential, it is frequently treated as a discrete module rather than an integrated and practice-oriented component of professional formation.

In working with both trainees and educators, I became increasingly aware of varied perceptions regarding the relevance, adequacy, and applicability of multicultural training.

Some trainees expressed uncertainty about translating theoretical knowledge into culturally responsive practice, while educators faced constraints related to curriculum design, institutional priorities, limited resources, and competing accreditation demands. These experiences highlighted tensions between policy expectations, pedagogical realities, and the lived demands of multicultural practice. Additionally, my engagement across diverse cultural and educational contexts revealed that many training models remain heavily influenced by Western theoretical frameworks, with limited adaptation to local cultural realities, indigenous knowledge systems, and sociohistorical contexts. This raised critical questions about the cultural validity, effectiveness, and ethical grounding of existing training approaches.

These cumulative experiences provided the impetus for a systematic examination of professional education and training in multicultural counselling and psychotherapy, leading to the development of the following research objectives:

Research objectives

1. To explore the current content and structure of professional education and training programmes in multicultural counselling and psychotherapy.
2. To investigate educators' and trainees' perceptions of the effectiveness and relevance of multicultural components within existing training curricula.
3. To identify the challenges and opportunities in implementing comprehensive multicultural training within professional counselling and psychotherapy education.

By grounding this chapter in both professional experience and empirical inquiry, it seeks to contribute to the ongoing dialog on how counselling education can better prepare practitioners for ethically responsive and culturally competent practice in increasingly diverse societies.

Research methodology

This study adopted a mixed-methods approach that integrated both quantitative and qualitative strategies to explore professional education and training in multicultural counselling and psychotherapy. Through this complimentary approach, the research aimed to capture both the breadth of patterns across a large sample and the depth of lived experiences, allowing for a richer and more nuanced understanding of the subject.

Situated within a pragmatic research paradigm, the study emphasized practical inquiry directed at solving real-world educational challenges. Pragmatism, as a guiding philosophy, supports methodological pluralism, recognizing that no single approach can fully address complex research questions in multicultural contexts. Ontologically, the study assumed that realities within professional education are multiple and constructed by stakeholders' experiences, shaped by institutional, cultural, and historical contexts. Epistemologically, it embraced the view that knowledge is co-created through interaction between the researcher and participants, valuing both empirical data and subjective meaning. The axiological stance acknowledged the researcher's responsibility to approach the topic with cultural humility, reflexivity, and respect for participants' diverse backgrounds and perspectives.

The sample size comprised of 450 participants across universities, hospitals, NGOs, and private training institutes in Nigeria. This provided a broad assessment of the scope, effectiveness, challenges, and opportunities present in current training program. Complementing this, the qualitative phase comprised semi-structured interviews with 12 purposively selected participants, including six postgraduate trainees and six educators with substantial experience in multicultural counselling education. This phase aimed to deepen the understanding of how multicultural content is perceived and enacted in practice. Sampling techniques reflected the mixed-methods design. The quantitative phase employed stratified random sampling to ensure representation across institutional types and participant demographics, while the qualitative phase relied on purposive sampling to select participants who could offer rich, contextually grounded insights based on their expertise and involvement.

Data collection for the survey was conducted using structured, self-administered questionnaires, while qualitative data were gathered through in-depth, audio-recorded interviews guided by a carefully developed interview protocol. These instruments were designed to complement each other, providing both quantitative and qualitative insights into professional education and training in multicultural counselling and psychotherapy.

The Questionnaire for Professional Education and Training in Multicultural Counselling and Psychotherapy (QPETMCP) comprised 26 items organized into four thematic sections. The first section focused on the main topics and approaches currently included in professional education and training program. The second section explored the perceived effectiveness and relevance of multicultural components within these program. The third section examined the challenges encountered in integrating inclusive multicultural training into counselling and psychotherapy education, while the fourth section identified opportunities available for enhancing multicultural education and practice. Respondents rated each item on a four-point Likert scale, ranging from Strongly Agree to Strongly Disagree, enabling the collection of structured data reflecting the diversity of participants' views.

In addition to the questionnaire, a semi-structured interview protocol was developed to guide in-depth qualitative interviews. The protocol contained open-ended questions designed to explore participants' experiences with multicultural training, perceptions of its practical relevance, observed challenges, and recommendations for improving program design and delivery. The flexible format of the interview protocol allowed for follow-up probes, encouraging participants to elaborate on significant points and thereby enriching the data with detailed narratives. To ensure the content validity and cultural appropriateness of these instruments, a multi-stage validation process was undertaken. Initial drafts of both the questionnaire and interview protocol were submitted to a panel of experts with recognized experience in counselling psychology, multicultural education, and educational measurement. These experts critically reviewed the instruments for clarity, relevance to the study's objectives, and cultural sensitivity within the African and broader multicultural contexts. Based on their feedback, revisions were made to refine item wording, remove ambiguity, and enhance the alignment of questions with the research objectives.

Subsequent to expert review, pilot testing was conducted to further assess the clarity and usability of the instruments. The questionnaire was administered to a small group of counselling educators and postgraduate trainees who were encouraged to provide feedback on item clarity, structure, and comprehensibility. Analysis of pilot data and feedback led to further adjustments aimed at improving precision and contextual relevance. To further establish the reliability of the questionnaire, internal consistency analysis was conducted following the pilot test. The Cronbach's alpha coefficients obtained for the four sections of the Questionnaire for Professional Education and Training in Multicultural Counselling and Psychotherapy (QPETMCP) were 0.82 for the section on main topics and approaches 0.85 for perceived effectiveness and relevance, 0.80 for challenges, and 0.83 for opportunities. The general Cronbach's alpha for the entire instrument was 0.84. These values exceed the commonly accepted threshold of 0.70, indicating a satisfactory level of internal consistency and suggesting that the questionnaire items reliably measured the intended constructs.

Similarly, the interview protocol was piloted through an interview with an experienced counselling educator, which provided an opportunity to evaluate the logical flow, timing, and ability of the questions to elicit comprehensive responses. Minor modifications followed, including rephrasing some items and incorporating additional prompts to facilitate deeper exploration. Through these combined efforts involving expert evaluation and empirical pilot testing, both instruments were refined to ensure their validity and reliability as tools for investigating professional education and training in multicultural counselling and psychotherapy. The integration of quantitative and qualitative approaches through these instruments positioned the study to offer a comprehensive understanding of the complexities, challenges, and prospects within the field. The quantitative data were analyzed using descriptive statistics, including means, standard deviations, and confidence intervals, to summarize participants' responses across key themes. Qualitative data underwent thematic analysis, allowing patterns and sub-themes to emerge inductively from participants' narratives, capturing shared experiences as well as divergent views.

Ethical considerations were central throughout the research process. Ethical approval was obtained from the University of Nigeria, Department of Counselling and Human Development Studies review board. All participants were informed of the study's purpose, their voluntary participation, and their right to withdraw at any stage without penalty. Informed consent was obtained before participation, and measures were taken to ensure confidentiality and anonymity in data handling and reporting. Reflexive awareness of cultural sensitivity and potential power dynamics between researchers and participants was maintained to uphold respect and integrity in representing participants' voices.

Results

Participants and ethical considerations

A total of 12 participants took part in the study, comprising six postgraduate trainees and six educators involved in professional education and training in multicultural counselling and psychotherapy. All participants provided informed consent prior to the interviews, including consent for audio recording and transcription. Confidentiality and anonymity were assured, and participant identifiers (T1–T6 for trainees; E1–E6 for educators) were used throughout the analysis.

Participant profiles

The trainee group represented a range of training stages and practice settings, including master's and doctoral programmes in counselling psychology, clinical psychology, and psychotherapy. Their professional engagements included supervised clinical placements, peer counselling roles, community mental health clinics, refugee support agencies, university wellness centers, and non-governmental organizations serving immigrant and marginalized populations. Duration of involvement in multicultural training ranged from under 1 year to approximately two and a half years. Educators included professors, senior lecturers, program directors, clinical supervisors, and curriculum developers with experience ranging from eight to 20 years. Their roles involved teaching multicultural counselling courses, supervising trainees, coordinating diversity initiatives, and designing or leading graduate-level counselling and psychotherapy programmes.

Core content of multicultural education and training

Across trainee and educator interviews, there was strong convergence regarding the core topics emphasized in multicultural counselling education. Participants consistently identified cultural identity, intersectionality, cultural humility, power and privilege, systemic oppression, and ethical practice as foundational areas of training. Additional themes included cross-cultural communication, culturally responsive assessment, trauma-informed care for diverse populations, and the impact of stigma and discrimination on mental health.

Educators emphasized the integration of culturally adapted evidence-based practices and the critique of dominant Western models, while trainees highlighted learning related to microaggressions, bias awareness, and practical strategies for engaging clients from diverse cultural backgrounds.

Teaching methods and pedagogical approaches

Participants described a range of teaching and learning methods used to deliver multicultural content. These included lectures, case studies, role-plays, reflective journals, experiential exercises, group discussions, and supervised clinical practice. Cultural self-assessment tools, cultural genograms, and analysis of therapy recordings were commonly used to promote self-reflection and applied learning.

Both trainees and educators reported that experiential and practice-oriented approaches—such as role-plays, community engagement, and reflective supervision—were perceived as more effective than didactic methods alone. Cultural immersion activities and guest speakers from diverse communities were viewed as valuable but inconsistently incorporated across programmes.

Inclusion of local cultural and indigenous perspectives

The integration of local cultural perspectives and indigenous counselling practices varied across programmes. Some trainees and educators reported intentional inclusion of indigenous and culturally grounded practices, such as storytelling, talking circles, land-based healing, and the use of proverbs or collective narratives in therapy. Others noted that exposure to indigenous approaches was limited, optional, or dependent on individual instructors rather than embedded within the core curriculum.

Educators generally reported greater efforts to incorporate local and indigenous perspectives, while trainees more frequently experienced these elements as peripheral rather than central to their training.

Alignment with realities of multicultural practice

Participants expressed mixed views regarding how well current training prepares trainees for real-world multicultural practice. While most acknowledged that programmes were effective in building awareness and foundational knowledge, both trainees and educators identified a gap between theory and applied competence. Common concerns included limited exposure to diverse client populations, insufficient opportunities to practise managing complex cultural dynamics, and a need for more context-specific training. Educators similarly recognized that although curricula address key multicultural issues, greater emphasis on community-based practice and hands-on learning is required to strengthen clinical readiness.

Perceived effectiveness of multicultural training

On the whole, participants described current multicultural training programmes as moderately effective. Trainees reported increased cultural awareness and sensitivity but varying levels of confidence in applying skills during therapy sessions. Educators echoed this assessment, noting that programmes are successful at introducing concepts but less consistent in developing advanced multicultural competencies.

Influence of training on practice

Both trainees and educators provided examples illustrating how multicultural training influenced clinical practice. These included the application of cultural humility to build therapeutic rapport, use of culturally adapted interventions, effective collaboration with interpreters, employment of cultural genograms, recognition and management of microaggressions, and implementation of trauma-informed approaches with clients from conflict-affected or marginalized backgrounds. Educators also shared examples of supervisees applying cultural formulation, narrative approaches, and intersectional frameworks to enhance therapeutic outcomes.

Most impactful elements of training

Participants identified cultural self-awareness, reflection on personal biases, experiential learning activities, and applied case work as the most impactful aspects of their training. Role-plays, case studies, and trauma-informed frameworks were frequently cited as particularly valuable in translating multicultural concepts into practice.

Summary of key qualitative findings

The findings indicate broad agreement between trainees and educators on the importance of multicultural education in counselling and psychotherapy. While core content areas and pedagogical intentions are well established, participants highlighted ongoing challenges related to practical application, consistent integration of indigenous perspectives, and alignment with the complexities of real-world multicultural practice.

Quantitative results

The demographic analysis presented in Table 10.1 offers a detailed view of the composition of the sample of 450 participants who completed the study questionnaire. The sample included slightly more female participants, accounting for approximately 54% of respondents, compared to around 46% male participants. The 95% confidence interval for the proportion of females ranges between 0.493 and 0.587, suggesting this proportion is reasonably stable in the population represented. The P-value of 0.099 indicates that this difference from an even distribution is not statistically significant, with the Vovk-Sellke Maximum p-Ratio (VS-MPR) of 1.608 reflecting modest odds favoring the alternative hypothesis over the null.

In terms of age distribution, the majority of participants were either in the 31–40 age group, comprising about 39% of the sample, or in the 20–30 age group, representing roughly 37%. Smaller proportions were found among those aged 41–50, accounting for around 17%, and those above 50, who made up about 6% of the sample. The consistently low P-values (all below 0.001) and very high VS-MPR values, for instance, 263,545.058 for the 20–30 age group—indicate statistically significant departures from an even distribution, suggesting a clear concentration of younger to mid-career professionals in the study. Regarding academic qualifications, more than half of the participants (about 56%) held a master's degree (M.Sc./M.A.), while approximately 26% had a bachelor's degree, 15% held a Ph.D., and only about 3% fell into the category of "Other" qualifications. The proportion of participants with master's degrees was statistically significant compared to an expected distribution ($P = .016$, VS-MPR = 5.530), confirming the dominance of this qualification level in the sample. The very small share of participants with other qualifications highlights a fairly homogeneous educational background oriented around formal postgraduate training.

In examining professional experience, most respondents reported between 1 and 5 years (about 41%) or 6–10 years (around 37%) of professional experience, with notably smaller shares for those with 11–15 years (approximately 16%) and over 15 years (around 6%). The low P-values (all $<.001$) and high VS-MPR figures, such as 263,545.058 for the 6–10 years category, highlight a significant tilt toward early- and mid-career professionals within the sample. The institutional affiliation of participants further illustrates the professional context of the study. More than half of the sample, about 53%, were affiliated with universities. Smaller proportions were drawn from private training institutes (around 19%), NGOs (approximately 15%), hospitals and clinics (around 10%), and other organizations (only about 2%). While the proportion of university-based participants did

Table 10.1: Ana ysis of demographic information.

Variable	Level	Counts	Total	Proportion	*P*	VS-MPR[a]	95% CI for proportion	
							Lower	Upper
Gender	Male	207	450	0.460	0.099	1.608	0.413	0.507
	Female	243	450	0.540	0.099	1.608	0.493	0.587
Age	20.3	168	450	0.373	<.001	263,545.058	0.328	0.420
	31.4	177	450	0.393	<.001	4441.330	0.348	0.440
	41.5	78	450	0.173	<.001	$6.074 \times 10^{+43}$	0.139	0.212
	Above 50	27	450	0.060	<.001	$1.319 \times 10^{+89}$	0.040	0.086
Academic qualification	B.Sc./B.A.	118	450	0.262	<.001	$5.281 \times 10^{+21}$	0.222	0.305
	M.Sc./M.A.	251	450	0.558	0.016	5.530	0.511	0.604
	Ph.D.	68	450	0.151	<.001	$7.040 \times 10^{+50}$	0.119	0.188
	Other	13	450	0.029	<.001	$4.875 \times 10^{+107}$	0.015	0.049
Years of professional experience	1.5	183	450	0.407	<.001	450.430	0.361	0.454
	6.1	168	450	0.373	<.001	263,545.058	0.328	0.420
	11.15	71	450	0.158	<.001	$4.503 \times 10^{+48}$	0.125	0.195
	Above 15	28	450	0.062	<.001	$8.818 \times 10^{+87}$	0.042	0.089
Institution/Organisation type	Hospital/Clinic	47	450	0.104	<.001	$1.797 \times 10^{+68}$	0.078	0.136
	Private training institute	86	450	0.191	<.001	$4.165 \times 10^{+38}$	0.156	0.231
	University	239	450	0.531	0.203	1.136	0.484	0.578
	NGO	69	450	0.153	<.001	$1.285 \times 10^{+50}$	0.121	0.190
	Other	9	450	0.020	<.001	$1.012 \times 10^{+114}$	0.009	0.038

Proportions tested against value: 0.5.
[a]Vovk-Sellke Maximum *P* -Ratio: Based on the *P* -value, the maximum possible odds in favor of H_1 over H_0 equals $1/(-e\,P\log(P))$ for $P \leq .37$.

not significantly deviate from an even distribution ($P = .203$), the smaller proportions of other institutional types were statistically significant, as reflected by their very low *P*-values and large VS-MPR values.

Results of research question one: What are the main topics and approaches included in current professional education and training program on multicultural counselling and psychotherapy?

The analysis addressing the first research question explored the main topics and approaches currently included in professional education and training program on multicultural counselling and psychotherapy. Table 10.2 presents the descriptive statistics for participants' responses to items assessing these program contents. On the whole, the mean scores for all items clustered around 3 on a 4-point scale, indicating generally positive perceptions about the extent to which these topics and approaches are integrated into current training. Specifically, the highest mean score was observed for the item addressing ethical issues in multicultural contexts (Mean = 3.029, SD = 0.911), suggesting that ethical considerations related to multicultural practice are relatively well embedded within existing curricula. Training covering cultural competence also showed a comparable mean (Mean = 3.022, SD = 0.955), highlighting that this aspect remains a central focus in professional preparation.

Table 10.2: Descriptive statistics showing content of professional education and training in multicultural counselling.

	Mean	Std. error of mean	95% Confidence interval mean		Std. deviation
			Upper	Lower	
Courses explicitly cover cultural awareness	3.004	0.045	3.094	2.915	0.963
Training covers cultural competence	3.022	0.045	3.111	2.934	0.955
Program include working with diverse ethnic & religious groups	2.989	0.045	3.078	2.900	0.961
Experiential learning methods used	3.002	0.044	3.089	2.916	0.933
Focus on systemic oppression and social justice	2.987	0.044	3.074	2.900	0.939
Addresses ethical issues in multicultural contexts	3.029	0.043	3.113	2.944	0.911
Integrates local cultural knowledge & indigenous practices	2.978	0.046	3.069	2.887	0.983

Courses explicitly covering cultural awareness (Mean = 3.004, SD = 0.963) and the inclusion of experiential learning methods such as role-plays and simulations (Mean = 3.002, SD = 0.933) were also rated positively by participants, pointing to the prominence of both conceptual knowledge and practice-based learning strategies. The inclusion of content on working with clients from diverse ethnic and religious backgrounds (Mean = 2.989, SD = 0.961) and the focus on systemic oppression and social justice issues (Mean = 2.987, SD = 0.939) received slightly lower, but still generally favorable, mean ratings. The item assessing integration of local cultural knowledge and indigenous practices had the lowest mean among the items (Mean = 2.978, SD = 0.983), suggesting this remains an area with relatively less emphasis within the current training landscape.

On the whole, these results suggest that while multicultural counselling and psychotherapy program broadly cover cultural competence, awareness, ethical considerations, and experiential approaches, there may still be opportunities to deepen content related to systemic oppression, social justice, and especially local cultural and indigenous perspectives.

Results of research question two: How do educators and trainees perceive the effectiveness and relevance of multicultural components in their training?

The findings addressing the second research question explored how educators and trainees perceive the effectiveness and relevance of multicultural components included in their professional training. Table 10.3 presents the descriptive statistics summarizing participants' views across several items measuring this perception. Generally, the mean scores clustered closely around 3 on a 4-point scale, indicating a broadly favorable assessment of these components' contribution to professional readiness. The item with the highest mean score was the perception that case studies used in training reflect diverse cultural scenarios (Mean = 3.047, SD = 0.908). This suggests participants see practical examples and case-based learning as especially relevant in connecting multicultural theory to practice. Similarly, the perception that training content aligns with real-world practice achieved a slightly lower, but still positive mean (Mean = 3.036, SD = 0.897), indicating participants generally believe their training corresponds well with the multicultural challenges they encounter or anticipate in professional contexts.

Participants also rated highly the perception that multicultural components are effectively assessed within their program (Mean = 3.031, SD = 0.971), and that training improved their competence to counsel clients from diverse backgrounds (Mean = 3.020, SD = 0.957). These findings point to a sense that multicultural modules contribute to building practical counselling skills and are evaluated in ways that reinforce learning. Slightly lower, though still generally positive, mean scores were found for trainers' demonstration of cultural sensitivity (Mean = 3.002, SD = 0.977) and the impact of

Table 10.3: Descriptive statistics showing perceived effectiveness and relevance of ....

	Mean	Std. error of mean	95% Confidence interval mean Upper	Lower	Std. deviation
Content aligns with real-world practice	3.036	0.042	3.119	2.952	0.897
Improved competence to counsel diverse clients	3.020	0.045	3.109	2.931	0.957
Case studies reflect diverse scenarios	3.047	0.043	3.131	2.963	0.908
Trainers demonstrate cultural sensitivity	3.002	0.046	3.093	2.912	0.977
Increased awareness of own cultural biases	2.998	0.045	3.086	2.910	0.950
Multicultural components assessed effectively	3.031	0.046	3.121	2.941	0.971
Knowledge gained enhanced confidence in multicultural counselling	2.998	0.045	3.086	2.910	0.947

training on raising awareness of one's own cultural biases (Mean = 2.998, SD = 0.950). The lowest mean, though still near 3, was for the perception that knowledge gained enhanced confidence in multicultural counselling (Mean = 2.998, SD = 0.947), suggesting there remains some space to deepen the sense of applied confidence among trainees.

On the whole, the results show that educators and trainees view the multicultural content in current training program as largely effective and relevant, particularly in terms of practical alignment with real-world counselling scenarios and improvement of multicultural competence. Nonetheless, slightly lower ratings for trainers' cultural sensitivity and the translation of knowledge into felt confidence highlight areas where program delivery could further strengthen experiential and reflective components, ensuring trainees not only understand multicultural concepts but also feel equipped and self-aware in applying them in diverse professional contexts.

Results for Research Question: What challenges and opportunities exist in integrating inclusive multicultural training into professional education and psychotherapy program?

The analysis for the third research question examined the challenges encountered in integrating inclusive multicultural training into professional education and psychotherapy program. As shown in Table 10.4, participants' responses indicate a general agreement that these challenges are significant, with mean scores clustering around 3 on a 4-point scale, reflecting consistent perceptions across the sample. The highest mean was found for the difficulty of balancing multicultural content with other core professional subjects

Table 10.4: Descriptive statistics showing challenges in integrating inclusive multicultural training into professional education and psychotherapy program.

	Mean	Std. error of mean	95% Confidence interval mean		Std. deviation
			Upper	Lower	
Limited qualified trainers with multicultural expertise	2.993	0.044	3.080	2.906	0.938
Inadequate time allocated to multicultural topics	2.971	0.047	3.063	2.880	0.988
Resistance from faculty or students toward multicultural content	3.071	0.043	3.156	2.986	0.915
Lack of updated teaching materials reflecting local contexts	3.058	0.044	3.143	2.972	0.923
Insufficient institutional funding and support	3.036	0.045	3.123	2.948	0.946
Difficulty balancing multicultural content with other subjects	3.080	0.042	3.162	2.998	0.887
Minimal opportunities for practical field experience	3.002	0.044	3.088	2.916	0.926

(Mean = 3.080, SD = 0.887). This suggests that educators and trainees perceive program schedules as already dense, making it challenging to give sufficient time to multicultural training without compromising other essential topics. Closely following this, resistance from faculty or students toward multicultural content had a mean of 3.071 (SD = 0.915), indicating that attitudinal barriers remain a notable obstacle to fully embedding multicultural perspectives within curricula.

A similarly high mean was observed for the lack of updated teaching materials reflecting local cultural contexts (Mean = 3.058, SD = 0.923). This underscores a perceived gap between the available resources and the realities of local cultural diversity, potentially limiting the depth and authenticity of multicultural education. Insufficient institutional funding and support also emerged as a significant challenge (Mean = 3.036, SD = 0.946), suggesting that resource limitations can restrict the ability of program to expand multicultural components meaningfully. Other challenges, including minimal opportunities for practical field experience in diverse cultural settings (Mean = 3.002, SD = 0.926) and the limited number of qualified trainers with multicultural expertise (Mean = 2.993, SD = 0.938), were also rated as substantial barriers. The lowest mean among these items, though still high, was inadequate time allocated to multicultural topics (Mean = 2.971, SD = 0.988), reflecting that although time constraints are acknowledged, they may be seen as slightly less pressing compared to structural and resource-related issues.

Collectively, these results point to a shared perception that while there is recognition of the importance of multicultural education, its integration is hindered by structural challenges such as overloaded curricula, limited institutional support, a shortage of qualified trainers, and the need for updated, locally relevant materials. This highlights the complexity of translating multicultural ideals into sustainable educational practice and points to the need for both institutional commitment and resource investment to address these persistent barriers.

The results related to the final research question explored the perceived opportunities for enhancing the integration of inclusive multicultural training into professional education and psychotherapy program. As shown in Table 10.5, the mean scores across these items were clustered just below or slightly above 3 on a 4-point scale, indicating generally positive perceptions of existing and emerging opportunities in this area. The highest mean score was reported for the availability of multicultural workshops and conferences for professional development (Mean = 3.036, SD = 0.919). This suggests participants recognize ongoing professional events as valuable platforms for expanding knowledge, exchanging practices, and strengthening multicultural competence beyond the classroom. Similarly, collaboration opportunities with international institutions (Mean = 3.020, SD = 0.966) were viewed as promising, highlighting the perceived benefit of drawing on global expertise and diverse perspectives to enrich local curricula.

The use of digital technologies to deliver multicultural content and facilitate global learning connections had a slightly lower mean (Mean = 2.951, SD = 0.931), though still indicating On the whole agreement that technology presents practical avenues to make multicultural training more accessible and dynamic. The rising interest among students

Table 10.5: Descriptive statistics showing opportunities in integrating inclusive multicultural training into professional education and psychotherapy program.

			95% Confidence interval mean		
	Mean	Std. error of mean	Upper	Lower	Std. deviation
Availability of multicultural workshops and conferences	3.036	0.043	3.121	2.950	0.919
Collaboration opportunities with international institutions	3.020	0.046	3.109	2.931	0.966
Use of digital technologies for multicultural content	2.951	0.044	3.037	2.865	0.931
Rising interest among students and practitioners	2.942	0.044	3.030	2.855	0.942
Growing demand from clients for culturally responsive services	2.971	0.046	3.061	2.881	0.972

and practitioners in specializing in multicultural counselling (Mean = 2.942, SD = 0.942) also emerged as a perceived opportunity, suggesting that evolving professional motivations may drive deeper integration of multicultural content into training programme. Finally, the growing demand from clients and communities for culturally responsive counselling services (Mean = 2.971, SD = 0.972) reflects how societal needs are increasingly shaping the direction and relevance of professional education. This demand appears to create both external pressure and justification for institutions to prioritize and expand multicultural training components.

Triangulation

Triangulation in this study served as an essential methodological strategy to strengthen the validity and richness of the findings by integrating data from multiple sources and perspectives. Quantitative data were collected through the structured questionnaire, which captured the breadth of views from a large sample of 450 participants, including trainees and educators from diverse institutional backgrounds. This phase provided numerical insights into the scope of multicultural content, perceived effectiveness, existing challenges, and emerging opportunities in professional education and training. Complementing this, qualitative data were gathered through in-depth interviews with a purposively selected group of 12 participants, comprising six postgraduate trainees and six experienced educators. The qualitative phase enabled a deeper exploration of personal experiences, contextual realities, and nuanced perspectives that could not be fully captured by closed-ended survey items alone. Through thematic analysis, these narratives illuminated how training program are experienced in practice, revealed tensions between theoretical coverage and applied competence, and highlighted both subtle and systemic barriers and opportunities that shape multicultural education.

The convergence of results such as consistent recognition of the importance of cultural competence and ethical training, alongside shared concerns over practical gaps and resource constraints reinforced the credibility of the study's conclusions. At the same time, the qualitative insights added depth to the numerical patterns, illustrating, for instance, how trainees value experiential learning yet still feel underprepared for complex cultural dynamics in real practice. On the whole, this triangulated approach not only enhanced the robustness of the study but also ensured that both the measurable scope of multicultural training and the lived experiences of those engaged in it were meaningfully represented, providing a richer foundation for recommendations aimed at improving professional education in multicultural counselling and psychotherapy.

Discussion of findings

Core topics and approaches in multicultural education and training

The study revealed that professional education and training programmes in multicultural counselling and psychotherapy consistently emphasize several interrelated core areas: ethical practice, cultural competence, cultural awareness, and experiential learning. Participants highlighted that these elements form the backbone of most curricula, reflecting a broad consensus on the necessity for trainees to acquire not only theoretical knowledge but also practical skills and ethical grounding (Xian & Hassan, 2022). This combination equips trainees to navigate the complex and diverse cultural landscapes encountered in clinical practice.

Ethical practice emerged as a particularly central focus, often framed within the context of multicultural engagement. Trainees and educators reported that ethical decision-making in counselling is inherently connected to cultural awareness. This includes respecting diverse cultural values, maintaining appropriate boundaries, ensuring culturally informed consent, and addressing potential conflicts between ethical standards and clients' cultural practices. Emphasizing ethics in multicultural training helps trainees develop sensitivity to dilemmas that may arise from cultural misunderstandings, fostering professional integrity while promoting culturally responsive interventions. Furthermore, cultural competence and awareness were consistently reported as integral to the curriculum. Trainees described learning frameworks that encompass knowledge about cultural identities, power dynamics, social determinants of mental health, and the impact of systemic inequities on client experiences. Awareness of one's own cultural assumptions and biases was highlighted as essential, with reflective exercises designed to enhance self-examination and humility. Educators stressed the importance of understanding intersectionality, acknowledging that clients often navigate overlapping social identities that influence mental health needs and therapeutic engagement.

Experiential learning approaches were described as particularly effective in translating theoretical knowledge into practice. Methods such as role-plays, simulations, reflective journaling, supervised clinical practice, and case-based discussions allow trainees to engage actively with culturally diverse scenarios. Both trainees and educators reported that these approaches promote self-awareness, empathy, and practical competence, preparing students to respond adaptively to real-world challenges. Experiential learning also facilitates the development of cultural humility, encouraging trainees to recognize the limitations of their knowledge and to approach clients with openness and curiosity.

Despite the strong integration of ethics, cultural competence, and experiential learning, participants noted that coverage of systemic oppression, social justice, and indigenous or local cultural practices was comparatively limited. While these areas are acknowledged as important, they often receive less emphasis or inconsistent integration across modules. This gap suggests a need for more intentional inclusion of structural and context-specific perspectives that prepare trainees to critically examine and address the broader societal factors impacting client well-being. Enhancing these components could foster a more holistic approach to multicultural training, bridging individual competence with systemic awareness.

Perceived effectiveness and relevance

Both educators and trainees consistently described the multicultural components of their training as highly relevant and meaningful to their professional development. Participants reported that engagement with these components increased their confidence in working with clients from diverse cultural backgrounds, enhanced their cultural awareness, and heightened their sensitivity to complex cultural dynamics within therapeutic settings (Chu et al., 2022). Trainees emphasized that exposure to diverse perspectives and structured guidance in understanding cultural differences helped them feel better equipped to navigate culturally nuanced clinical encounters. Reflective practice emerged as one of the most impactful elements of training. Trainees described how structured reflection on their own cultural assumptions, biases, and values fostered a mindset of cultural humility, encouraging ongoing self-examination and openness to learning from clients. Educators reported that reflective journaling, guided discussion, and supervision sessions allowed trainees to connect theory with personal experience, reinforcing both cognitive understanding and emotional insight into multicultural practice. Experiential learning activities such as case studies, role-plays, and simulated sessions were highlighted as instrumental in translating theoretical concepts into practical skills. Participants consistently noted that these exercises enabled them to rehearse culturally sensitive interventions, consider multiple perspectives, and develop strategies for addressing challenges in real-world therapeutic scenarios. Such hands-on learning was reported to strengthen trainees' ability to adapt interventions to meet the unique needs of clients from varied cultural backgrounds, while also promoting empathy and interpersonal flexibility.

Despite these strengths, participants identified limitations in terms of depth and practical integration. While the training was effective in establishing foundational knowledge and awareness of multicultural principles, opportunities for extended, supervised application with diverse client populations were sometimes limited. Some trainees reported that while they understood cultural frameworks conceptually, they felt less confident in applying these frameworks to complex or high-stakes clinical situations. Educators echoed this concern, noting that logistical constraints, limited access to culturally diverse client populations, and time restrictions within the curriculum can reduce the extent to which experiential learning fully prepares trainees for real-world practice.

Challenges in integrating multicultural training

The study revealed several significant challenges in embedding multicultural content expansively and effectively within professional education and training programmes. One of the most frequently cited obstacles was the limited availability of qualified educators and supervisors with expertise in multicultural counselling. Participants noted that instructors need not only theoretical knowledge but also practical experience in culturally responsive practice. A shortage of such qualified faculty can result in superficial coverage of multicultural topics, inconsistent instruction, or overreliance on outdated frameworks, limiting trainees' ability to develop advanced skills for addressing real-world cultural complexities. Time constraints within curricula were also highlighted as a critical challenge. Participants reported that multicultural training often competes with core clinical skills, assessment methods, and theoretical coursework. When multicultural content is confined to a few modules or single-semester courses, trainees may gain awareness but lack sufficient practice or reinforcement to achieve competence. Sustained and integrated exposure across multiple courses is therefore necessary to move beyond theoretical understanding toward applied proficiency.

Resistance from faculty or students emerged as another barrier. Some participants described discomfort with addressing issues of systemic inequity, cultural bias, or social justice, either due to perceived threats to existing norms or personal unease with self-examination. Such resistance can undermine engagement, reduce the perceived importance of multicultural content, and limit open dialogue in classrooms and supervision sessions. Finally, inadequate teaching resources reflecting local and indigenous cultural contexts posed a significant challenge. While programmes often included international or Western-based frameworks, resources tailored to local traditions, languages, and indigenous healing practices were reported as limited. Participants noted that this gap makes it difficult to provide contextually relevant training, potentially leaving trainees unprepared to meet the cultural realities of their clients. The combination of these challenges highlights the structural, institutional, and pedagogical barriers that can constrain the effectiveness of multicultural education, particularly in preparing trainees to address systemic inequities and complex cultural scenarios.

Opportunities for strengthening multicultural training

Despite the challenges identified, the study highlighted numerous promising opportunities for enhancing multicultural education within professional counselling and psychotherapy programmes. One key opportunity lies in professional development workshops and conferences focused specifically on multicultural competence. Participants indicated that these activities provide structured spaces for experiential learning, reflection, and networking, allowing trainees and educators to deepen their understanding of cultural diversity, learn innovative interventions, and exchange best practices across institutions. Such opportunities also reinforce the integration of theory with real-world application, enhancing the preparedness of trainees to navigate culturally complex scenarios.

International collaboration and cross-institutional partnerships were noted as valuable avenues for curriculum enrichment. Participants emphasized that collaboration with institutions in different cultural and national contexts broadens perspectives, promotes critical reflection on dominant therapeutic models, and facilitates the adaptation of global insights to local practice. These partnerships can support knowledge exchange, introduce culturally grounded methodologies, and provide exposure to a wider range of client populations, contributing to the development of more globally competent practitioners.

Digital learning platforms and technology-based approaches were consistently highlighted as innovative tools for advancing multicultural training. Online case discussions, virtual cultural immersion experiences, webinars, and interactive modules allow trainees to access diverse cultural perspectives and engage in reflective practice without the constraints of geographic location or limited local resources. Participants indicated that technology not only expands access to training materials but also supports ongoing dialog with peers and practitioners from diverse cultural backgrounds, fostering continuous learning and intercultural competence. The growing interest among students in multicultural issues represents another opportunity. Trainees increasingly recognize the importance of cultural competence for effective practice, which motivates engagement with training and promotes proactive learning. Similarly, societal and client demand for culturally responsive mental health services provides external impetus for programmes to strengthen multicultural content. Participants observed that these societal shifts create a supportive environment for institutional investment in curriculum development, faculty training, and experiential learning initiatives.

Curriculum for education and training in multicultural counselling and psychotherapy

Drawing directly from the empirical findings of this study, the following curriculum framework is proposed to guide education and training in multicultural counselling and psychotherapy. The curriculum is intended to function as a practical, adaptable framework for teaching and learning, rather than a prescriptive or context-bound syllabus. It responds to the core strengths, gaps, challenges, and opportunities identified by educators and trainees, and is designed to support the development of culturally responsive, ethically grounded, and practice-ready professionals.

Rationale for the curriculum

The study findings indicate that while existing programmes place strong emphasis on cultural competence, ethics, and experiential learning, there are limitations in depth, practical integration, attention to systemic issues, and inclusion of local and indigenous knowledge. This curriculum is therefore structured to strengthen these areas by embedding multicultural perspectives across all stages of professional education, rather than treating them as stand-alone or supplementary content. The curriculum conceptualizes multicultural competence as an ongoing developmental process that integrates knowledge, self-awareness, skills, and contextual engagement.

Curriculum goals

The central goal of the curriculum is to prepare counselors and psychotherapists who are capable of working ethically, reflexively, and effectively with culturally diverse individuals, families, and communities. Specifically, the curriculum aims to:

- Develop strong cultural self-awareness and cultural humility among trainees
- Build applied skills for culturally responsive assessment and intervention
- Strengthen ethical decision-making within multicultural contexts
- Enhance understanding of systemic, structural, and social determinants of mental health
- Integrate local, indigenous, and community-based knowledge into professional practice

Core curriculum domains

Foundational Knowledge in Multicultural Counselling: This domain introduces key concepts such as culture, identity, intersectionality, power, privilege, ethics, and cultural formulations in counselling and psychotherapy. Content focuses on how cultural contexts shape mental health experiences, help-seeking behaviors, and therapeutic relationships. The emphasis is on conceptual clarity while encouraging critical engagement with dominant models.

Self-Awareness, Reflexivity, and Cultural Humility: Informed by the study's findings on the value of reflective practice, this domain prioritizes ongoing self-examination. Trainees engage in structured reflective activities including journaling, cultural genograms, guided group dialog, and reflective supervision. The aim is to foster cultural humility, ethical sensitivity, and awareness of personal and professional positioning.

Applied Skills and Experiential Learning: Consistent with participants' emphasis on experiential learning, this domain focuses on translating theory into practice. Teaching and learning strategies include role-plays, simulations, case-based learning, and supervised clinical practice with diverse populations. Skills addressed include culturally informed assessment, communication across cultural differences, ethical boundary management, and adaptation of therapeutic approaches.

Systemic, Social Justice, and Contextual Perspectives: Responding to the identified gaps in existing training, this domain explicitly addresses systemic oppression, inequality, and social determinants of mental health. Trainees explore how structural factors influence client experiences and access to care, and how counselors can engage ethically with advocacy, referral, and community resources.

Local, Indigenous, and Community-Based Knowledge: This domain integrates local cultural perspectives and indigenous counselling practices relevant to the training context. Learning activities may include engagement with community leaders, guest facilitators, culturally grounded case studies, and community-based learning placements. The focus is on contextual relevance and respectful integration of indigenous knowledge systems into professional practice (Table 10.6).

Teaching and learning approaches

The curriculum for education and training in multicultural counselling and psychotherapy is designed around learner-centered and experiential pedagogical strategies that actively engage trainees in both theoretical and practical aspects of multicultural practice. Interactive seminars and workshops form a core part of this approach, providing opportunities for discussion, collaborative problem-solving, and hands-on exercises such as case analyses, role-plays, and skill demonstrations that simulate realistic counselling scenarios. These activities enable trainees to apply theoretical concepts in a supportive, experiential environment. Reflective practice is central to the curriculum, fostering cultural humility and self-awareness. Trainees engage in structured exercises, including journaling, creating cultural genograms, and participating in guided group discussions, which encourage critical examination of personal cultural assumptions, biases, and professional identity.

Supervised fieldwork provides practical experience in diverse clinical settings. Through mentorship and feedback, trainees learn to translate classroom knowledge into culturally competent counselling strategies, navigate ethical dilemmas, and develop practical skills that reflect the complexities of real-world practice. Furthermore, community engagement is integrated to enhance understanding of local and indigenous contexts. By participating in community programs, collaborating with local organizations, and observing traditional or indigenous healing practices, trainees gain insights into the cultural, social, and contextual factors that influence mental health and therapeutic approaches.

Table 10.6: Proposed module structure.

Module	Title	Core focus	Key learning activities	Expected outcomes
Module 1	Foundations of multicultural counselling and psychotherapy	Culture, identity, intersectionality, power, ethics, cultural formulations	Interactive seminars, guided readings, critical discussions	Conceptual understanding of multicultural foundations and ethical awareness
Module 2	Self-awareness, reflexivity, and cultural humility	Cultural self-exploration, bias awareness, professional identity	Reflective journaling, cultural genograms, facilitated group dialog, supervision	Development of cultural humility and reflective professional practice
Module 3	Applied skills and culturally responsive interventions	Culturally informed assessment, communication, and intervention	Role-plays, simulations, case analyses, skills laboratories	Practical competence in culturally responsive counselling and psychotherapy
Module 4	Ethics, power, and professional decision-making	Ethical dilemmas, boundaries, informed consent, power dynamics	Case-based ethical analysis, supervised discussions, reflective supervision	Strengthened ethical judgment in complex multicultural contexts
Module 5	Systemic, social justice, and community perspectives	Social determinants of mental health, systemic oppression, advocacy	Community-based learning, policy analysis, collaborative projects	Ability to situate counselling practice within social and structural realities
Module 6	Local, indigenous, and contextually grounded practices	Indigenous knowledge systems, local healing practices	Guest facilitators, community engagement, culturally specific case studies	Contextually relevant and culturally respectful professional practice
Module 7	Supervised practice and integration	Integration of knowledge, skills, and reflexivity	Supervised placements, integrative case presentations, reflective portfolios	Readiness for professional practice in diverse cultural contexts

In addition, technology-supported learning extends the reach of the curriculum by providing access to international perspectives, diverse case materials, and collaborative platforms. Online discussions, webinars, and virtual simulations allow trainees to engage in cross-cultural scenarios that might not be available locally, promoting reflective dialog and exposure to global practices. Collectively, these teaching and learning approaches are designed to be mutually reinforcing. They ensure that trainees develop a robust theoretical foundation, practical skills, and the reflective capacity necessary for culturally responsive, ethically grounded, and contextually informed counselling and psychotherapy practice.

Assessment and evaluation

Assessment within the curriculum is designed to move beyond traditional knowledge-based evaluation to capture the full range of competencies required for effective multicultural counselling and psychotherapy. Trainees are evaluated through a combination of reflective journals, practical skills demonstrations, case analyses, and supervisor feedback. Reflective journals provide insight into trainees' self-awareness, critical thinking, and evolving understanding of cultural humility and ethical practice. Skills demonstrations and case analyses allow instructors to assess the practical application of counselling techniques and culturally responsive interventions in simulated or real-world scenarios. Supervisor feedback during fieldwork and practicum placements ensures ongoing guidance, constructive critique, and reinforcement of best practices. This expanded approach aligns assessment with the developmental and iterative nature of multicultural competence, fostering continuous learning, reflective practice, and the integration of knowledge, skills, and ethical reasoning.

Implementation considerations

The curriculum for education and training in multicultural counselling and psychotherapy has been designed to be flexible and adaptable, allowing it to fit diverse cultural, institutional, and professional contexts. It can be delivered as a stand-alone program for postgraduate or professional trainees, fully integrated across existing courses within a degree program, or embedded within professional development and continuing education pathways. This flexibility ensures that institutions with varying resources, student populations, and program structures can implement the curriculum effectively. Considerations for successful implementation include ensuring access to qualified educators, allocating sufficient time for experiential and reflective components, integrating technology to support learning and community engagement, and adapting content to reflect local cultural knowledge, indigenous practices, and systemic contexts. Additionally, ongoing evaluation and feedback mechanisms are recommended to continuously refine the curriculum and ensure alignment with evolving professional and societal needs.

Requirements for participation and graduation

Participation in the curriculum for multicultural counselling and psychotherapy requires active engagement, commitment to experiential learning, and adherence to professional and ethical standards. Trainees are expected to attend all scheduled lectures, seminars, workshops, and supervised fieldwork sessions. They must actively participate in reflective exercises, case discussions, and community engagement activities, demonstrating openness to self-examination and willingness to explore personal biases and cultural assumptions.

Assessment of trainee performance encompasses multiple dimensions, including mastery of theoretical knowledge, practical application of counselling skills, reflective capacity, and ethical decision-making. Trainees must successfully complete assignments such as reflective journals, case analyses, skills demonstrations, and supervised practicum evaluations. Participation in technology-supported learning activities, such as online discussions and virtual simulations, is also required to ensure exposure to diverse perspectives and international practices.

Graduation from the program is contingent upon the successful completion of all curriculum requirements, demonstrating competence across cognitive, practical, and ethical domains. Trainees must show evidence of cultural awareness, cultural humility, and the ability to apply multicultural counselling principles in diverse clinical contexts. Only those who meet the established benchmarks in both formative and summative assessments, and who adhere to the ethical and professional standards of practice, are eligible for certification or degree conferral. These requirements ensure that graduates are well-prepared to provide competent, culturally responsive, and ethically grounded counselling and psychotherapy services.

Practicum exercise

The practicum exercise is a central component of the curriculum for multicultural counselling and psychotherapy, providing trainees with hands-on experience in real-world settings. The practicum is designed to integrate theoretical knowledge, practical skills, and reflective practice, enabling trainees to develop competence in culturally responsive counselling.

Trainees engage with diverse client populations under the supervision of experienced educators and clinical supervisors. Practicum activities may include conducting assessments, developing treatment plans, implementing culturally adapted interventions, and participating in multidisciplinary team meetings. Supervisors provide ongoing feedback, mentor reflective practice, and guide ethical decision-making in complex cultural contexts.

Reflective exercises are embedded within the practicum to encourage critical self-examination and cultural humility. Trainees maintain reflective journals, participate in debriefing sessions, and engage in peer discussions to analyze their experiences and evaluate their professional growth.

The practicum also emphasizes community engagement and exposure to local and indigenous cultural practices, allowing trainees to understand cultural contexts, social determinants of mental health, and culturally informed therapeutic approaches. Assessment of practicum performance includes evaluation of practical skills, ethical reasoning, cultural competence, and the ability to apply knowledge in diverse clinical situations.

By participating in the practicum exercise, trainees develop the applied skills, ethical awareness, and cultural responsiveness necessary for competent and effective multicultural counselling and psychotherapy practice.

Role of educators and supervisors

Educators and supervisors play a central role in implementing the curriculum for education and training in multicultural counselling and psychotherapy. Their responsibilities extend beyond knowledge transmission to include modeling cultural humility, facilitating reflective practice, and guiding the practical application of skills in diverse contexts. Educators are responsible for designing and delivering content that is both theoretically rigorous and contextually relevant. They provide interactive lectures, workshops, and seminars that encourage critical discussion, cultural self-exploration, and ethical reasoning. By incorporating case studies, role-plays, and experiential exercises, educators help trainees bridge the gap between theory and practice.

Supervisors provide direct mentorship and support during fieldwork and practicum experiences. They observe and provide feedback on trainees' clinical skills, ethical decision-making, and culturally responsive interventions. Supervisors also facilitate reflective discussions, helping trainees identify personal biases, assess their own cultural assumptions, and refine their professional identity.

Both educators and supervisors are instrumental in creating a learning environment that is safe, inclusive, and respectful of diverse perspectives. Their modeling of ethical, culturally competent practice directly influences trainees' development, reinforcing the values, knowledge, and skills required for effective multicultural counselling and psychotherapy. Continuous professional development for educators and supervisors is essential to maintain up-to-date knowledge of best practices, emerging cultural issues, and innovative pedagogical methods.

Supportive policy

Effective implementation of a curriculum in multicultural counselling and psychotherapy requires the presence of supportive institutional and professional policies. Such policies provide the structural framework, resources, and guidance necessary to sustain high-quality, culturally responsive education and training. Supportive policies may include clear institutional commitment to diversity, equity, and inclusion, ensuring that multicultural content is integrated throughout academic and professional programmes. They should outline standards for faculty qualifications, including expertise in multicultural counselling and competence in culturally responsive pedagogical methods.

Policies should also mandate adequate allocation of time, funding, and resources for experiential learning, reflective practice, and community engagement activities. Access to technology-supported learning platforms, culturally relevant teaching materials, and opportunities for international collaboration can be formalized through institutional policy to ensure consistency and sustainability. Assessment and evaluation frameworks should be supported by policy to ensure that multicultural competencies are systematically measured, including reflective, practical, and ethical dimensions. Policies that encourage ongoing professional development for educators and supervisors help maintain curriculum quality and ensure responsiveness to emerging societal and cultural needs. Finally, supportive policies should promote a safe and inclusive learning environment, addressing potential resistance or barriers, fostering collaboration, and ensuring that all trainees have equitable opportunities to develop competencies in multicultural counselling and psychotherapy.

Pedagogical principles guiding the curriculum

The curriculum for education and training in multicultural counselling and psychotherapy is guided by a set of pedagogical principles that reflect both the findings of the study and contemporary best practices in professional education. These principles ensure that teaching and learning processes are ethically grounded, learner-centered, and responsive to cultural complexity.

Learner-Centered and Developmental Approach: The curriculum adopts a learner-centered orientation that recognizes trainees as active participants in their professional development. Learning is viewed as a developmental process, acknowledging that multicultural competence evolves over time through repeated exposure, reflection, and practice rather than through the mastery of fixed content.

Experiential and Practice-Oriented Learning: Consistent with the study findings, experiential learning forms the backbone of the curriculum. Role-plays, simulations, supervised practice, and community engagement are prioritized to bridge the gap between theory and practice. These methods allow trainees to apply concepts in realistic contexts and to develop practical, transferable skills.

Reflective Practice and Cultural Humility: Reflection is embedded throughout the curriculum to promote cultural humility and ethical sensitivity. Structured reflective activities encourage trainees to critically examine their own cultural identities, assumptions, and power positions, fostering lifelong reflective practice rather than a static notion of competence.

Integration of Ethics Across Learning: Ethical practice is not treated as a separate or isolated topic but is integrated across all modules. Ethical reasoning is consistently linked to cultural awareness, power dynamics, informed consent, and professional responsibility, reflecting the inseparability of ethics and multicultural practice.

Contextual and Social Justice Orientation: The curriculum is grounded in an understanding of counselling and psychotherapy as practices shaped by social, historical, and structural contexts. Teaching and learning emphasize systemic factors, social justice, and advocacy, preparing trainees to respond ethically to inequities that affect clients and communities.

Respect for Local and Indigenous Knowledge: A key pedagogical principle is respect for local, indigenous, and community-based knowledge systems. The curriculum encourages culturally grounded learning by engaging with local contexts and valuing multiple ways of knowing alongside established psychological frameworks.

Institutional mechanisms

Institutional mechanisms play a critical role in ensuring the effective implementation and sustainability of a curriculum in multicultural counselling and psychotherapy. These mechanisms encompass the structures, processes, and support systems that facilitate integration of multicultural content and maintain high standards of education and training.

Governance structures are central, with dedicated committees or oversight bodies tasked with guiding curriculum development, implementation, and evaluation. These bodies ensure alignment with institutional priorities, professional standards, and regulatory requirements. Adequate allocation of resources, including financial support, technology, and skilled personnel, is essential to provide faculty development, culturally relevant teaching materials, digital learning platforms, and community engagement opportunities.

Ongoing professional development for educators and supervisors is a key mechanism, enabling them to maintain culturally responsive pedagogical skills, supervision techniques, and awareness of emerging multicultural issues. Curriculum integration processes and monitoring systems ensure that multicultural content is coherent, continuous, and consistently applied across all courses and programmes.

Collaborations and partnerships with local communities, indigenous groups, and international institutions further enrich the learning experience, offering trainees practical exposure and diverse perspectives. Finally, mechanisms for policy implementation and compliance oversight ensure that diversity, equity, and inclusion principles are actively applied, meeting ethical, accreditation, and legal standards.

Limitations and future directions

While the curriculum for education and training in multicultural counselling and psychotherapy is designed to be comprehensive and evidence-informed, several limitations must be acknowledged. First, the curriculum may be influenced by the specific cultural, institutional, and professional contexts in which it was developed, potentially limiting generalizability to other settings. Second, despite integrating local and indigenous practices, the depth and diversity of these elements may not fully capture all cultural nuances relevant to different client populations. Third, resource constraints, including availability of qualified educators, access to technology, and community partnerships, could affect implementation fidelity and the extent to which experiential learning can be realized.

Future directions include expanding research to evaluate the curriculum's effectiveness across diverse institutions and cultural settings, incorporating emerging issues in multicultural mental health, and exploring innovative teaching methods, such as virtual reality simulations or cross-cultural exchanges. Continuous feedback from trainees and educators should be used to refine modules, enhance integration of local and indigenous practices, and strengthen assessment methods that capture both reflective and applied competencies. Additionally, efforts should be made to build institutional capacity, ensuring sustainable implementation, equitable access, and ongoing professional development for educators and supervisors. By addressing these limitations and pursuing these future directions, the curriculum can evolve to better prepare culturally competent, ethically grounded, and responsive counselling professionals.

Career opportunities in multicultural counselling and psychotherapy

Graduates of education and training programmes in multicultural counselling and psychotherapy are well-prepared for a wide array of professional roles across various sectors. In clinical and community mental health centers, they provide culturally responsive therapy to individuals, families, and groups, addressing the unique mental health needs of diverse populations. Their expertise enables them to design and implement interventions that are sensitive to cultural values, traditions, and social determinants of mental health. In educational settings, including schools, colleges, and universities, professionals support students' emotional well-being, develop inclusive mental health programs, and train faculty in culturally competent counselling practices. They play a crucial role in fostering safe and supportive environments that respect diversity and promote equity.

Governmental and non-governmental organizations, social services, refugee and immigrant support agencies, and community-based programs offer opportunities for practitioners to design culturally informed policies, provide direct services, and engage in advocacy for marginalized populations. Graduates may also pursue roles in research, program evaluation, and policy development, contributing to evidence-based practices that enhance multicultural mental health services. Also, private practice presents avenues to specialize in culturally competent psychotherapy, providing tailored interventions that consider clients' cultural backgrounds, belief systems, and community contexts. Additionally, professionals may engage in training, supervision, and consultancy roles, supporting the development of multicultural competence among other practitioners. As societies become increasingly diverse and awareness of cultural factors in mental health grows, the demand for professionals with expertise in multicultural counselling continues to rise. This field offers dynamic, rewarding career paths where graduates can make meaningful contributions to individual, community, and societal well-being, bridging cultural gaps in mental health care and fostering inclusive therapeutic practices.

Chapter conclusion

This chapter has presented a comprehensive overview of professional education and training in multicultural counselling and psychotherapy. It has highlighted the core components of an effective curriculum, including ethical practice, cultural competence, cultural awareness, experiential learning, reflective practice, and the integration of local and indigenous cultural perspectives. Teaching and learning approaches, assessment strategies, implementation considerations, and institutional mechanisms were discussed to demonstrate how curricula can be structured to develop culturally responsive, ethically grounded, and competent counselling professionals.

The chapter also addressed the roles of educators and supervisors, the importance of supportive policies, and the significance of practicum exercises in providing hands-on learning opportunities. Challenges in integrating multicultural training, such as limited resources and resistance, were acknowledged, alongside opportunities for enhancement, including professional development, international collaboration, digital learning, and community engagement.

Finally, limitations of the curriculum and directions for future development were explored, emphasizing the need for ongoing research, iterative refinement, and sustainable implementation strategies. Overall, the chapter underscores that a well-designed, flexible, and contextually relevant curriculum is essential for preparing counselling professionals who can effectively meet the diverse needs of clients in multicultural contexts.

Insight and new dimension of research

This chapter offers several fresh insights and extends existing knowledge on multicultural counselling and psychotherapy training in meaningful ways. One of the most important insights lies in how educators and trainees collectively perceive multicultural competence not merely as a set of knowledge areas but as a dynamic process requiring constant critical reflection, adaptation, and lived experience. This perspective highlights a shift from viewing multicultural competence as an add-on module to recognizing it as an integral foundation of ethical professional identity and practice.

A notable new dimension highlighted by the research is the tension between global theoretical frameworks and local cultural realities. While previous studies have often focused on curriculum content in broad terms, this study draws attention to the underexplored challenge of contextual relevance, specifically, the scarcity of updated teaching materials and indigenous knowledge that reflect local cultural narratives. This finding suggests that training program must do more than teach cultural theories; they must actively collaborate with local communities to co-create culturally grounded resources and practices. Another important contribution of this study is the identification of external forces such as rising client demand, student motivation, and digital innovation as potential levers for change. Unlike much of the literature that focuses primarily on internal institutional reform, these findings suggest that broader social and technological shifts can act as catalysts for embedding multiculturalism more deeply into training. This perspective expands the discussion from curriculum design alone to include the wider sociocultural and digital ecosystems in which training occurs.

The chapter also surfaces the need to reconceptualize multicultural competence as an evolving, practice-based skill rather than a static set of knowledge areas assessed through traditional methods. This insight calls for more innovative approaches to teaching and evaluation, such as immersive community engagement, reflective supervision, and real-world scenario analysis, that extend beyond the classroom and into professional contexts. Finally, by combining quantitative data from a large sample with qualitative interviews from both educators and trainees, the research adds a layered understanding of how multicultural training is experienced on the ground. This methodological triangulation offers a fuller picture than many previous studies that focused narrowly on either student perceptions or curriculum content alone. Collectively, these insights highlight the need for future research to explore context-specific, practice-oriented, and digitally supported approaches to multicultural training. This new dimension invites scholars, educators, and policymakers to move beyond conventional frameworks and design culturally responsive training that is both ethically grounded and practically effective in an increasingly diverse world.

References

Ahmed, N., Liu, X., Al-Hazwani, I., & Huang, E. M. (2024). Cultural dimensions and mental health technology: A systematic review of Hofstede's dimensions in shaping mental health experiences. In *Conference on human factors in computing systems - Proceedings*. https://doi.org/10.1145/3613905.3650842

Ang, J. Y. Z., Prasai, A., & Wright, A. J. (2024). The use of the Wright–Constantine structured cultural interview (WCSCI) in culturally responsive clinical practice: A qualitative study of clinician experience. *Professional Psychology: Research and Practice, 56*(1). https://doi.org/10.1037/pro0000604

Balva, D., Mandas, P., & Sacco-Bene, C. (2023). Re-envisioning multiculturalism: Promoting and applying disability competencies within clinical supervision. In *Facilitating social justice, service delivery, and advocacy through multicultural counseling competencies*. https://doi.org/10.4018/978-1-6684-6155-6.ch001

Branson, A., Cardona, B., Ng, K. M., & Killian, T. (2016). Internationalized intersectional experiential learning environments that go beyond U.S. contexts: Malaysia as a case example. *The Family Journal, 24*(3). https://doi.org/10.1177/1066480716648675

CACREP. (2016). In *2016 CACREP standards*.

Chang, L. C., Guo, J. L., & Lin, H. L. (2017). Cultural competence education for health professionals from pre-graduation to licensure delivered using Facebook: Twelve-month follow-up on a randomized control trial. *Nurse Education Today, 59*. https://doi.org/10.1016/j.nedt.2017.09.005

Chang, L. C., Lin, H. L., Lin, T. Y., & Liao, L. L. (2024). Evaluation of a hybrid learning module on cultural competence for the postgraduate year of nursing programs in Taiwan: A quasi-experimental study. *Sage Open, 14*(2). https://doi.org/10.1177/21582440241256838

Chu, W., Wippold, G., & Becker, K. D. (2022). A systematic review of cultural competence trainings for mental health providers. *Professional Psychology: Research and Practice, 53*(4). https://doi.org/10.1037/pro0000469

Dababneh, N. E., Dababneh, S., Barakat, S., Cox, J., Chiskamish, W., Kelly, A. S. V., Pootoo, S., Ilisituk, P., Sala, M., Kitishimik, P., Weetaltuk, S., Kumarluk, A., Moorhouse, R., Inukpuk, M., Lefson, M., & Litvinov, I. V. (2025). Foundations of Canadian Indigenous Medicine (Part II): Traditional dermatologic first aid practices in first nations and inuit communities in Canada. *Journal of Cutaneous Medicine and Surgery, 29*(4). https://doi.org/10.1177/12034754251341847

Duffey, M. (2024). Using historical site visits and photography to develop ethnocultural empathy in a multicultural counseling course. *Journal of Creativity in Mental Health, 19*(1). https://doi.org/10.1080/15401383.2022.2115434

Freetly Porter, E., Owen, J., Rousmaniere, T., Kivlighan, D. M., Narvaez, R. C., & Heshmati, S. (2025). Multicultural orientation and deliberate practice coaching: An empirically supported case study. *Counselling and Psychotherapy Research, 25*(4). https://doi.org/10.1002/capr.70047

Gallardo, M. E., & Kaivan, N. (2013). Integrating ethical considerations in multicultural curriculum and training: Expanding the classroom to the community. In *Handbook of multicultural mental health: Assessment and treatment of diverse populations* (2nd ed.). https://doi.org/10.1016/B978-0-12-394420-7.00029-1

Kress, V. E., Caputo, L. G. D., & Forner, E. (2025). Relational-cultural theory as a framework for counselor leadership. *Journal of Counselor Leadership and Advocacy, 12*(1). https://doi.org/10.1080/2326716X.2024.2332183

Lu, J. (2017). Multicultural counseling knowledge and awareness scale: Re-exploration and refinement. *International Journal for the Advancement of Counselling, 39*(1), 14–27. https://doi.org/10.1007/s10447-016-9279-2

Nassar-McMillan, S., Kent Butler, S., Rafferty McCullough Georgia, J., & Hipolito-Delgado, C. (2015). In *Multicultural and social justice counseling competencies by Association for Multicultural Counseling and Development Executive Council A Division of the American Counseling Association by American Counseling Association Governing Council.*

Ramirez, S. (2021). Cultural exposure as a creative experiential learning intervention. *Journal of Creativity in Mental Health, 18*(1). https://doi.org/10.1080/15401383.2021.1949420

Somerville, W., Marcus, S., & Chang, D. F. (2019). Multicultural competence–focused peer supervision: A multiple case study of clinical and counseling psychology trainees. *Journal of Multicultural Counseling and Development, 47*(4). https://doi.org/10.1002/jmcd.12158

Srivastava, D., Srivastava, S., Kukreti, A., & Sharma, S. (2025). A role of evidence-based resource and training in the indigenous practices of healthcare. In *Integrated pathy: Re-envisioning healthcare and wellness using India as a case study*. https://doi.org/10.1016/B978-0-443-29040-4.00008-6

Utley-Smith, Q. E. (2017). Meeting a growing need: An online approach to cultural competence education for health professionals. *Nursing Education Perspectives, 38*(3). https://doi.org/10.1097/01.NEP.0000000000000120

Wilcox, M. M., Gale, M. M., McLaughlin, K. L., Squyres, E., Burish, E. C., & Khojasteh, J. (2022). Development and initial validation of the multicultural training and education questionnaire. *Training and Education in Professional Psychology, 16*(1). https://doi.org/10.1037/tep0000344

Xian, C. K., & Hassan, S. A. (2022). Interventions to improve multicultural counseling competence: A systematic review. *International Journal of Academic Research in Business and Social Sciences, 12*(11). https://doi.org/10.6007/ijarbss/v12-i11/15725

Zhou, Y. (2025). Ethical practice in the majority world: A framework for psychotherapists trained in the minority world. *American Psychologist*. https://doi.org/10.1037/amp0001511

Index

'*Note*: Page numbers followed by "f" indicate figures and "t" indicate tables.'

D

E

R

S

T

U

V

W

Y